POWER PRESSURE COOKER XL COOKBOOK

350 Irresistible Electric Pressure Cooker Recipes for Quick, Easy, and Healthy Meals

ISBN: 1974047423
ISBN-13: 978-1974047420

POWER PRESSURE COOKER XL COOKBOOK

150 Amazing Electric Pressure Cooker Recipes for Fast, Healthy, and Incredibly Tasty Meals

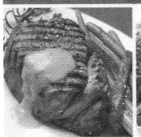

VANESSA OLSEN

Power Pressure Cooker XL Cookbook:

150 Amazing Electric Pressure Cooker Recipes for Fast, Healthy, and Incredibly Tasty Meals

Vanessa Olsen

TABLE OF CONTENTS

Introduction

Back before processed and packaged food, everyone ate better. Growing a garden was a necessity, not a hobby, and buying meat and other food locally was just part of normal life. Then, corporations began seriously getting into the food game, and used science to concoct all kinds of preservatives and fillers to make food bigger, longer-lasting, and more addicting. People stopped growing their own food and instead bought from stores, where stuff in a package was cheap and convenient. The effects on society's health could not be clearer - obesity, heart disease, allergies, and so on.

We can't go back to the way things were, but you can make better choices. Organic produce, wild-caught and grass-fed meats, and whole-grains are just a few of the options available to you. Another way to live more healthfully? Using a pressure cooker. It's the healthiest method for cooking food, retaining up to 90% of a food's nutritional value, and it's also the fastest. Even if your life is hectic, you can make delicious and healthy meals at home, and leave the packaged and artificial food behind.

This book tells you everything you need to know about the Power Pressure Cooker XL, a popular electric pressure cooker, including how to use it, how to keep it clean, and how to troubleshoot common problems. Once you've gotten a better understanding of the cooker, it's time to get into the recipes. There's breakfast, beef, lamb, chicken, pork, seafood, soups, rice, pasta, side dishes, sauces, desserts, and more. Every recipe includes nutritional info and easy-to-follow steps, so even if you've never used a pressure cooker before, you'll have no trouble following along.

Chapter 1

The History of the Pressure Cooker

When humans first began cooking their food, it didn't take long for them to figure out that putting a lid on a pot would make water boil faster, and as a result, faster cooking times. However, the first pressure cooker that we know of wasn't invented until the 17th century, when French mathematician Denis Papin began experimenting with what he called a "bone digester." He created a cooking vessel with an airtight seal, so no steam could escape. The pressure would build up, and temperatures in the pot would get so high that it could turn extremely tough meats into tender eats. Papin's invention was well-received by the king, but because the bone digester was so big and expensive, it never entered anyone's home as a viable cooking tool.

The next appearance of the pressure cooker was as the pressure *canner* in 1810. Napoleon needed a way for his men to carry food across long distances without it spoiling, so a confectioner adapted the pot-with-an-airtight-seal concept and created the first pressure canner. Nobody used this to prepare daily meals, but by 1939, the first stovetop pressure cooker was released at the World's Fair.

This model was popular during the Great Depression and WWII, and tons of companies began jumping into the cooker game. This resulted in a lot of bad cookers without enough safety features, so pressure cookers got the reputation of exploding and causing huge messes. This reputation endures to this day, but thankfully, most modern pressure cookers are extremely safe. Electric pressure cookers are especially kitchen-friendly and as safe as crockpots. From the bulky bone digester to the sleek, user-friendly Power Pressure Cooker XL, pressure cookers have come a long way.

Why you should get an electric pressure cooker

The one thing that hasn't changed about the pressure cooker is just how convenient and fast it is. In fact, the benefits have only increased with time as technology improves. Here are the main reasons why you should give in and get an electric pressure cooker:

Speed

The biggest selling point of pressure cookers is how fast they cook food. Usually slow-cooking foods like beans, rice, and oatmeal are done in significantly less time, with steel-cut oats taking 10 minutes and rice about 3 minutes. That time does not factor in the time it takes for the cooker to reach pressure or the pressure release (which we will get into more later), but cooking method comparisons have shown the pressure cooker wins on speed every time.

Health benefits

Pressure cooking is not only fast, it's the healthiest cooking method. That means that the food it produces has the most preserved nutrition compared to baking, frying, and even steaming. Up to 80-90% of the vitamins and minerals stay in the food, which is incredible. Why? It's because the longer foods take to cook, the more nutrients are lost. Some people are concerned about the high temperatures of pressure cookers and that more delicate foods like vegetables would lose their health value, but that's why pressure cookers discriminate between low and high pressure. That's another part of the pressure cooker that we'll cover more in depth.

Versatile

Pressure cookers can make just about any type of meal. If you glance at the Table of Contents, you'll get an idea of just how many dishes you can make with just one kitchen tool. Soups and stews make sense, but you can also make steaks, pasta, and cakes. That's because the pressure cooker basically acts like a pot or a steamer, so when you put an oven-safe container like a ramekin inside, it will cook whatever food you've put in the dish, like creme brulee. A steamer basket or trivet are must-have accessories if you want to enjoy all the possibilities a pressure cooker offers.

Very safe

The biggest distinction between stove top cookers and electric pressure cookers is safety.

While stove top cookers are way safer than they used to be, they are still riskier than electric ones. An electric pressure cooker is packed with features like anti-block shields, cool-touch construction, and more. They also don't reach as high of a pressure as stovetop cookers do, so they don't get as hot. This means slightly slower cooking times, but for most people, a few extra minutes is worth it when you don't have to babysit a hot burner and cooker.

Chapter 2

Meeting the Power Pressure Cooker XL

Steam Release Valve

Large Arm Handle

Safe Lock Lid

Stainless Steel Housing

Non-Stick Inner pot
6 Qt. Capacity
(Not Shown)

Digital Display Panel

One Touch Preset Buttons

cooking time
up to
70%
Faster
than conventional cooking

Take a look at the image above. That's the Power Pressure Cooker XL. As you can see, it looks a lot like a crockpot. It has a lid, body, and digital control panel. The PPCXL comes in four sizes: 6-quart, 8-quart, 8-quart deluxe, and 10-quart. The 8-quart deluxe comes with a steaming rack, a canning lid, and three color options. For most families, a 6-quart is a good size, though for recipes that make enough food for eight or more, an 8-quart allows you to make everything in one batch.

The most important technical spec on this model is that the PSI tops at 7.2. PSI stands for "pounds per square inch.".

Right now, let's walk through the display panel and what all the buttons mean. You will find the following on your cooker:

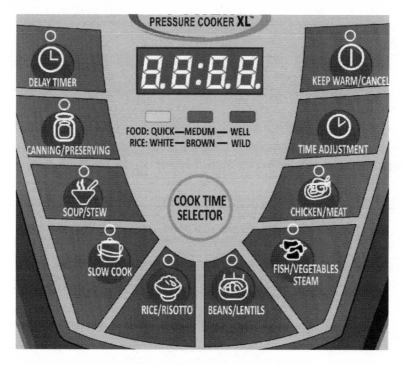

Delay Timer - This lets you delay cooking time. None of the recipes in this book use this button.

Canning/preserving - This goes to 12 PSI, and makes it possible to pressure can in the PPCXL.

Soup/Stew - The PSI is automatically 7.2, which is true for all the buttons except the canning. The only difference is the default time, which for soup/stew is 10 minutes.

Slow cook - The default time is 2 hours, and you can adjust up to 6 or 12 hours.

Rice/Risotto - Default time is 6 minutes.

Keep warm/Cancel - If you choose the wrong function, hit this button to reset. When the pressure cooker is finished for the time you chose, the cooker automatically switches to the Keep Warm function.

Time adjustment - After choosing a cooking program, you can change the default time by pressing this button.

Chicken/Meat - Default time is 15 minutes

Fish/Vegetables/Steam - Default time is 2 minutes

Cook Time Selector - When you have chosen a cooking program, you can push this button to adjust to "Medium" or "Well" for meat, or "White," "Brown," or "Wild," for different types of rice.

Before using your cooker

Before you start cooking up a storm with your new cooker, you should be sure to refer to the manual. It has important safety information, and walks you through how to clean your cooker before you use it for the first time. It shows you how to put the lid on, where the rubber gasket should be placed, and so on. The rubber gasket is what ensures an airtight seal, and it looks like a ring. The manual will also provide pictures on what it looks like when the cooker lid is on correctly, and how to open and close the steam valve. A closed steam valve is what keeps all the pressure inside.

Using the PPCXL

So, how do you actually use an electric pressure cooker? Let's walk through a recipe to find out. It's a simple roast chicken recipe, but it involves most of the steps you'll encounter in this cookbook. There are just a handful of ingredients:

- o Three, 2-lb whole chickens
- o 2 tablespoons olive oil
- o 1 tablespoon onion powder
- o 1 tablespoon garlic powder
- o 1 chopped sprig rosemary
- o 1 chopped sprig thyme
- o Salt and pepper

First, you mix all the spices in a bowl. Next, put the inner pot into your cooker and hit "Chicken/Meat." Since there is no "brown" or "sauté" setting on the PPCXL, you can use the Chicken/Meat button and just leave the lid off.

Pour oil into the pot and wait for it to get hot. Season the chicken in the meantime. When seasoned, you're going to brown the chicken in the oil. When golden all over, leave the chicken in the pot and put on the lid. Lock it, and turn the valve to "closed." Hit the "keep warm/cancel" button and select the "Soup/Stew." You're going to hit the "Cook Time Selector" button until the panel says "30," meaning 30 minutes. It will take anywhere from 10-20 minutes for the cooker to reach pressure, and then the timer starts.

A note on time: Cooking time changes if you are above sea level. For every 1,000 feet above a 2,000-feet elevation, increase time by 5%. The time it takes for the cooker to build to pressure will also take longer the further you're above sea level, so keep that in mind. In recipes, the time it takes for pressure build-up is usually not included.

When time is up, you're going to perform a quick-release. This means that you (carefully) open the steam valve to let the pressure out. The steam will be hot, and it will make a hissing noise. If the recipe had called for a "natural" release, that means you hit "cancel" or unplug the cooker, and just wait for the pressure to come down by itself. Certain recipes need that time to finish cooking.

Canning with the PPCXL

The most unique setting on the PPCXL is the pressure canning button. It reaches 12 PSI and can be adjusted to 45 or 120 minutes. However, we will not be using the canning setting in this book.

Chapter 3

Troubleshooting

The Power Pressure Cooker XL is convenient and sturdy, but there are still possible problems you should be aware of, so you can work through them. These are the most common issues you might come across:

- Cooker won't reach pressure
- Food is undercooked
- Food is overcooked
- Water/steam leaks out
- Lid is getting stuck
- Food is spraying out

Solution #1: Cooker won't reach pressure

If the cooker isn't coming to pressure, there are a few things to check out. The first one is to make sure that the gasket (silicone ring) is secure on the lid. Check for cracks or food that might have built up and is preventing the lid from sealing properly. Clean the gasket well. If there are cracks, you'll have to replace it.

Solution #2: Food is undercooked

If the food in the cooker isn't done in the time written in the recipe, you might have filled the cooker with too much water, used frozen food, there's a thick liquid or sauce in the recipe, or you've simply put too much food in the cooker. Double-check the amount of liquid you used and always measure, since it's easy to splash just a ½ cup more than necessary, which can make a big difference. If you're using frozen food, that's just fine, but it does take longer to cook and can add up to a half hour to the recipe's cooking time. Either plan on that longer time or be sure to thoroughly thaw the frozen items.

If there's a thickener in the recipe like cornstarch or flour, it can thicken the liquid and increase cooking time. Add the thickener later. Since thickeners are never raw, it's perfectly safe to add it after everything else has cooked. The last reason the food might not be cooking fast enough is that you've overfilled the cooker. Always be sure to fill it ⅔ of the way, and if you're making grains or other foamy foods, ½ of the way.

If the food is just *barely* undercooked, simply turn the heat on with the lid off, and finish it that way. Putting it under pressure again can tip it over the edge, so it ends up overcooked.

Solution #3: Food is overcooked

Pressure cookers are powerful, and it's common for beginners to find their meals overcooked or even burned. A lot of home cooks add a few minutes to cooking time "just to be sure," but with a pressure cooker, that can be the difference between perfectly-cooked food and overcooked food. Never add time to the recipe.

What if the food is burned? This doesn't necessarily mean the cooking time should be extended. Instead of adding time, try putting the food in a steamer basket or separating it from the bottom of the cooker with a trivet. Vegetables in particular are more prone to burning, so to be safe, a steamer basket is usually recommended. Burned food can also mean that you're not using enough water, so just be sure that you're pouring in the *minimum* required for your pressure cooker size.

Solution #4: Water/steam is leaking out

Water leaking from the cooker's valve is pretty common, and it usually means there is food building up in the vent pipe. Just make sure to clean out all valves and vent pipe every 2-3 times you use the cooker, and the problem should go away. Steam leakage can also mean the gasket isn't secure enough, so check on that. If it keeps happening, it's probably time for a new gasket.

Solution #5: The lid is stuck

Even after you've opened up the steam valve and let the pressure out from the cooker, the lid sometimes get stuck. This is because there's still pressure trapped in there. To get all of it out, take off the pressure valve and turn on the cooker again to heat up. This new heat will push the "old" leftover pressure out, and you should be able to open the lid again.

Solution #6: Cooker is spraying out food

When you turn the pressure valve, sometimes food or foam sprays out, which can hurt if it hits your skin. There are a few ways to avoid this. One is to use a natural pressure release instead. Really foamy foods like grains, fruit, oats, and beans almost always require a natural pressure release, so start doing that. Another reason might be because there's a thickener in the cooker, like flour. Add the thickener later after you've released the pressure. The most common reason spraying happens is that the cooker is simply too full. Stick to that ⅔ rule, and for those foamy foods, only fill it ½ way.

Cleaning solutions

Once you've used your cooker for a while, you might discover that it isn't as shiny and pretty as it used to be. There are ways you can tackle different types of stains and keep your pressure cooker in good shape. The most common blemishes are:

> Mineral stains
> Alkali stains
> Heat tint

Cleaning mineral stains

If your tap water has minerals, the aluminum of your pressure cooker can begin to stain. The best way to clean these off is with vinegar and lemon juice. Rub the stain with vinegar and let it sit on the stain for 4-5 hours. Rinse with water and then polish with real lemon juice. Rinse again in hot water and dry right away. Remember to use a soft cloth or sponge, so you don't scratch the surface.

Cleaning alkali stains

Alkali stains are caused by certain cleaning solutions that have baking soda or ammonia. If the pot just has some light stains, you can actually get rid of them by cooking foods with acid. For the heavier stains, boil a mixture of tartar cream (2-3 tablespoons), a few drops of vinegar, and a quart of water for a max of 10 minutes. Then, scrub well with a soapy sponge and rinse.

Heat tint

These stains appear when your pressure cooker gets too hot or runs without enough water. It causes blue-purple discoloration, and you can't get rid of it. However, you can be sure that the stain doesn't get worse, because dark stains indicate that your pressure cooker is wearing down. When you aren't worsening the heat tint, it can fade.

Chapter 4

Converting Slow Cooker Recipes

Electric slow cookers are similar to electric pressure cookers, but because they are designed to cook slowly while the pressure cooker is built for speed, it does change how you would prepare a recipe originally written for a slow cooker. There are four things you need to think about when you're converting a dish: amount of food, liquid, the types of ingredients, and time.

Step 1: Decide if you need to cook the meal in batches

Slow cookers can hold more food than pressure cookers, and since your Power Pressure Cooker XL can only be filled a max of ⅔ of the way for safety reasons, you might need to half a recipe or cook the meal in batches. Look at the ingredient list and amounts in the slow cooker recipe, and determine what to do.

Step 2: Reduce the amount of liquid you start with

Slow cookers lose liquid in the cooking process, unlike pressure cookers, so odds are you are going to start off using less liquid in your pressure cooker recipe than the slow cooker one. The best way to figure out how much liquid you need to put in is to decide how much liquid you want at the end. Always start with the minimum liquid requirement for your cooker, and then go up from there.

As a general rule, you'll need enough liquid to just cover whatever food you put directly in the cooker, like meats and pasta, while food that's in a steamer basket needs liquid to generate enough steam. This part is probably the trickiest conversion, so I find it helpful to just look up a similar recipe that's already been adapted for a pressure cooker. Unless the slow cooker recipe is really unique, there is probably an existing pressure cooker one out there that can help.

Step 3: Pick out the ingredients you want to sauté beforehand

Since pressure cooking on its own doesn't add much flavor to foods compared to roasting or grilling, it's all about prepping ingredients so they bring the most flavor possible to a dish. This will mean cooking "aromatics" before bringing the cooker to pressure. Aromatics include onions, garlic, herbs, ginger, celery, and carrots. Look at your slow cooker recipe and pick those out to sauté in the cooker with the lid off, usually with cooking oil.

Step 4: Reduce cooking time

The biggest change in converting slow cooker recipes to the pressure cooker will be time. As a general rule, cutting the cooking time by ⅔ is the way to go. Prep will be the same, of course, and since slow cookers don't have pressure to release, ones that include ingredients that require a natural pressure release will also take longer from start to finish. The time you end up with will not have automatically factored in the above sea-level rule, so remember to apply that.

Cooking charts

For charts on how long certain foods take to cook in the Power Pressure Cooker XL, we are not allowed to reproduce the charts, so refer to your manual on the "General Operating Instructions" page.

Chapter 5

Breakfasts

Vanilla Latte Oatmeal

<u>**Serves**</u>: 4

<u>**Time:**</u> 27 minutes (12 minutes cook time, 10 minutes natural pressure release, 5 minutes thickening time)

There's nothing quite like a smooth, creamy vanilla latte to start off your day. How about getting that experience in a bowl of steel-cut oats? With milk, dark chocolate, vanilla, and espresso, you can enjoy the flavors of a coffeehouse classic. The recipe makes enough for four servings.

<u>Ingredients:</u>

- 2 ½ cups water
- 1 cup steel-cut oats
- 1 cup milk
- 2 tablespoons white sugar
- 1 tablespoon finely-grated dark chocolate
- 2 teaspoons pure vanilla extract
- 1 teaspoon espresso powder
- ¼ teaspoon salt

<u>Directions:</u>

1. Pour the milk and water into your Power Pressure Cooker XL.
2. Add sugar, oats, espresso powder, and salt.
3. Stir until the espresso has completely dissolved.
4. Close and lock the lid.
5. Press "Soup/Stew" and then adjust time to 12 minutes.
6. When time is up, turn off the cooker by hitting "cancel."
7. Give the cooker 10 minutes to release most of its pressure naturally.
8. Turn the valve to release any leftover pressure before opening the lid.
9. Pour in the vanilla extract and put the lid back on, but don't bother sealing it.
10. Let the oats rest for 5 minutes so they thicken to the proper texture.
11. Stir in the grated chocolate before serving.

<u>Nutritional Info (¼ recipe)</u>

Total calories: 212

Protein: 6

Fat: 6

Carbs: 34

Fiber: 5

Coconut Milk Oats

Serves: 8
Time: 12 minutes

Coconut milk is one of my favorite ingredients, especially the full-fat kind. It makes steel-cut oats amazingly creamy and with just a hint of that coconut sweetness. I like to make a big batch on the weekends and have oats for breakfast the whole week.

Ingredients:

- 4 cups water
- 2 cups steel-cut oats
- 2 cups full-fat coconut milk

Directions:

1. Pour water and milk into your Power Pressure Cooker XL.
2. Stir in oats and then secure the lid.
3. Select "Soup/Stew," and adjust time to 12 minutes.
4. When the timer beeps, hit "cancel" and open up the steam valve for a quick-release.
5. Open the lid and stir the oats. They will be soupy until you stir, and they will continue to thicken as they cool.
6. Serve with toppings and spices, like fresh fruit, granola, cinnamon, brown sugar, or honey.

Nutritional Info (⅛ recipe):

Total calories: 189
Protein: 4
Carbs: 28
Fat: 6
Fiber: 5

Pear Oats with Walnuts

Serves: 4
Time: 12 minutes (5 minutes prep time, 7 minutes cook time)

Rolled oats cooked with almond milk is a perfect breakfast when you need healthy comfort food. You pressure cook pears, too, and they become almost like caramel with their natural sweetness coming through. To top off the breakfast, there are chopped walnuts and cinnamon.

Ingredients:

- ☐ 2 cups peeled and cut pears
- ☐ 2 cups almond milk
- ☐ 1 cup rolled oats
- ☐ ½ cup chopped walnuts
- ☐ ¼ cup white sugar
- ☐ 1 tablespoon melted coconut oil
- ☐ ¼ teaspoon salt
- ☐ Dash of cinnamon

Directions:

1. Put the trivet in your PPCXL and pour in 1 cup of water.
2. Mix all the ingredients (minus cinnamon + walnuts) in a bowl that's safe for your pressure cooker.
3. Put the bowl on top of the trivet and seal the lid.
4. Hit "Rice/Risotto" and cook for 7 minutes.
5. When the timer beeps, hit "cancel" and quick-release.
6. Serve with cinnamon, walnuts, and a little salt.

Nutritional Info (¼ recipe per serving):

Total calories: 288
Protein: 5
Carbs: 39
Fat: 13
Fiber: 4.5

Ricotta-Blackberry Breakfast Cake

Serves: 6
Time: 55 minutes (5 minutes prep time, 30 minutes cook time, 10 minutes natural pressure release, 10 minutes cook time)

Cake for breakfast isn't usually a healthy option, but this recipe is full of great ingredients like whole-wheat flour, Greek yogurt, and part-skim ricotta, which offers protein without all the fat. If you really want to cut calories, leave off the glaze.

Ingredients:

Cake

- [ ] 5 eggs
- [ ] 1 cup whole-wheat flour
- [ ] ¾ cup part-skim ricotta cheese
- [ ] ¾ cup Greek-style vanilla yogurt
- [ ] ½ cup blackberry compote
- [ ] ¼ cup sugar
- [ ] 2 tablespoons melted butter
- [ ] 2 teaspoons baking powder
- [ ] 2 teaspoons vanilla

Glaze

- [ ] ¼ cup Greek-style vanilla yogurt
- [ ] 1-2 tablespoons powdered sugar
- [ ] 1 teaspoon milk
- [ ] ½ teaspoon pure vanilla

Directions:

1. Prepare a 6-cup Bundt pan with cooking spray.
2. Mix the sugar and eggs in a large bowl.
3. Blend in the ricotta cheese, melted butter, vanilla, and yogurt.
4. In another bowl, mix the flour, baking powder, and salt.
5. Pour dry into the wet ingredients, and mix together.
6. Pour cake batter into the Bundt pan.
7. Swirl ½ cup of the compote on top of the batter using a tablespoon.
8. Pour 1 cup of water into your cooker and lay down a trivet.

9. Put the Bundt pan on the trivet and lock the lid.
10. Select "Chicken/Meat" and add 5 minutes, so you're cooking the cake for 30 minutes.
11. While the cake cooks, whisk together the milk, vanilla, yogurt, and powdered sugar.
12. When the timer goes off, hit "cancel" or unplug the cooker, and wait 10 minutes.
13. Open the valve to let out any leftover pressure.
14. Carefully remove the Bundt pan and let it set out for 10 minutes.
15. With a knife, cut around the edges before flipping upside down on a plate.
16. Drizzle on the glaze and serve!

Nutritional Info (⅙ recipe w/ glaze)
Total calories: 323
Protein: 13
Fat: 13
Carbs: 42
Fiber: 1

Steel-Cut Oats with Mushroom + Rosemary

Serves: 4

Time: 50 minutes (10 minutes prep time, 30 minutes cook time, 10 minutes natural pressure release)

Savory oatmeals are "in" right now, and this recipe makes it clear why. Earthy mushrooms bulk up the oats even more for a really satisfying meal, while rosemary adds a herbal brightness. The smoked gouda cheese is also a real showstopper, and elevates the whole dish into pure lip-smacking goodness.

Ingredients:

- ☐ 14-ounces of chicken broth
- ☐ 8 ounces of sliced crimini mushrooms
- ☐ 1 cup steel-cut oats
- ☐ ½ cup water
- ☐ ½ diced onion
- ☐ ½ cup finely-grated smoked gouda cheese
- ☐ 3 sprigs of rosemary
- ☐ 2 tablespoons butter
- ☐ 2 minced garlic cloves
- ☐ Salt and pepper to taste

Directions:

1. Melt the butter in your Power Pressure Cooker XL on the "Chicken/Meat" setting, with the lid off.
2. When the butter has melted, add the diced onion and mushrooms, and cook for 3 minutes.
3. Add garlic and stir for another minute or so.
4. Add oats and toast for just one minute.
5. Pour in the water, broth, thyme sprigs, and salt.
6. Lock the lid in place.
7. Hit "cancel" to reset the cooker and then select "Chicken/Meat" again. Adjust the time to 30 minutes.
8. When time is up, turn off the cooker and wait 10 minutes.
9. Turn to valve to quick-release any remaining pressure.
10. Open up the lid and stir in the cheese until melted.
11. Season to taste with salt and pepper before serving.

Nutritional Info (¼ recipe)

Total calories: 266
Protein: 9
Fat: 12
Carbs: 31
Fiber: 5

Tomato-Spinach Quiche

Serves: 6
Time: 39 minutes (5 minutes prep time, 24 minutes cook time, 10 minutes natural pressure release)

Quiche is a fancy word, but making it is actually very simple. There's only a handful of ingredients, like baby spinach, tomato, green onions, and cheese. This makes a quiche large enough for a crowd of six friends, so you're going to be using 12 eggs.

Ingredients:

- ☐ 12 fresh eggs
- ☐ 4 tomato slices
- ☐ 3 cups chopped baby spinach
- ☐ 3 sliced green onions
- ☐ 1 ½ cups water
- ☐ 1 cup diced tomato
- ☐ ½ cup milk
- ☐ ¼ cup shredded Parmesan cheese
- ☐ Salt and pepper to taste

Directions:

1. Put a trivet in the PPCXL and add 1 ½ cups of water.
2. Whisk together the eggs, milk, salt, and pepper in a bowl.
3. Mix the spinach, green onions, and diced tomato in an oven-safe 1 ½-quart baking dish.
4. Pour the egg mixture into the dish and mix everything.
5. Lay down the tomato slices evenly on top, followed by the cheese.
6. Lower the dish into the cooker so it sits on the trivet, and secure the lid.
7. Hit "Chicken/Meat" and adjust time to 24 minutes.
8. When the timer goes off, hit "cancel" to turn off the cooker.
9. Wait 10 minutes before quick-releasing the pressure.
10. Serve hot!

Nutritional Info (⅙ recipe)

Total calories: 177   Carbs: 3
Protein: 15   Fiber: 0
Fat: 11

Jalapeno Egg Poppers

Serves: 6

Time: 23 minutes (5 minutes prep time, 8 minutes cook time, 10 minutes natural pressure release)

These cheesy, spicy eggs are served in Mason jars, and pack in 18 grams of protein per serving! It's a great low-carb breakfast for days when you need a lot of energy for your morning. The best part is that you can make enough for a whole week's worth of breakfasts.

Ingredients:

- ☐ 12 beaten eggs
- ☐ 4 seeded and chopped jalapeno peppers
- ☐ 2 cups water
- ☐ 1 cup shredded cheese
- ☐ 1 teaspoon lemon pepper seasoning

Directions:

1. Mix eggs and lemon pepper seasoning together in a bowl.
2. Add in cheese and jalapenos.
3. Divide "batter" between six Mason jars.
4. Pour water into your pressure cooker and lower in trivet.
5. Put Mason jars on the trivet, with their lids set on top. If you can't fit all of them, you'll need to do a second batch.
6. Seal the pressure cooker lid.
7. Hit "chicken/meat" and adjust cook time to 8 minutes.
8. When the timer beeps, hit "cancel" and wait for the pressure to come down naturally. Remove jars and repeat cooking process for remaining poppers.
9. Eat poppers right away or store in the fridge for up to one week for breakfasts.

Nutritional Info (⅙ recipe per serving):

Total calories: 219
Protein: 18
Carbs: 2
Fat: 16
Fiber: .4

Ramekin Huevos Rancheros

<u>**Serves:**</u> 1
<u>**Time**</u>: 20 minutes

It's very simple, but there's something about a runny egg, fresh salsa, and crisp tortilla chips that's addicting. Make a single-serving of the classic huevos rancheros using a ramekin and Power Pressure Cooker XL cooker, and get in your protein for the morning.

<u>Ingredients</u>:

- ☐ 3 fresh eggs
- ☐ 1 cup cold water
- ☐ ½ cup of your favorite salsa
- ☐ Salt and pepper to taste
- ☐ Tortilla chips

<u>Directions</u>:

1. Get a ramekin and pour in salsa.
2. Crack the three eggs on top.
3. Wrap the ramekin tightly in aluminum foil.
4. Pour 1 cup of cold water into the Power Pressure Cooker XL.
5. Put the ramekin in the steamer basket and lower into cooker.
6. Seal the lid.
7. Push the "Chicken/Meat" button and adjust time to 20 minutes.
8. When the timer beeps, turn off the cooker and quick-release.
9. Serve the breakfast in the ramekin, with chips for dipping.

<u>Nutritional Info (½ recipe)</u>
Total calories: 195
Protein: 12
Fat: 10
Carbs: 14
Fiber: 0

Baked Eggs with Smoked Salmon

Serves: 4
Time: About 6 minutes (4 minutes cook time)

Melty, creamy eggs are perfectly complimented by salty smoked salmon in this easy ramekin breakfast. They only take 4 minutes on low pressure, and pack in 19 grams of protein.

Ingredients:

- ☐ 4 slices of smoked salmon
- ☐ 4 eggs
- ☐ 1 cup of water
- ☐ A splash of cream per ramekin
- ☐ Sprinkle of fresh chives
- ☐ Just enough olive oil to coat the pot

Directions:

1. Pour 1 cup of water into your cooker and lower in the trivet.
2. Grease ramekins with olive oil and lay down a piece of salmon.
3. Crack an egg on top and pour in a little cream.
4. Wrap the ramekins tightly in foil.
5. Put the ramekins on top of the trivet and seal the lid.
6. Click on "Rice/Risotto" and adjust time to 4 minutes.
7. When time is up, hit "cancel" and quick-release.
8. Serve!

Nutritional Info (1 ramekin per serving):
Calories: 240
Protein: 19
Carbs: 2
Fat: 17
Fiber: 0

Cheesy Sausage Frittata

Serves: 4
Time: 22 minutes (5 minutes prep time, 17 minutes cook time)

This easy egg dish is cheesy, meaty, and low-carb. You're going to be using the pressure cooker like an oven, and "bake" the frittata in a greased soufflé dish that sits in a steamer basket. The dish is also wrapped in foil, which helps speed up the cooking time.

Ingredients:

- ☐ 4 beaten eggs
- ☐ 1 ½ cups water
- ☐ ½ cup cooked ground breakfast sausage
- ☐ ¼ cup grated sharp cheddar cheese
- ☐ 2 tablespoons sour cream
- ☐ 1 tablespoon butter
- ☐ Salt and pepper to taste

Directions:

1. Grease a 6 or 7-inch soufflé dish with cooking spray.
2. Whisk the eggs and sour cream in a bowl.
3. Stir in sausage, cheese, salt, and pepper.
4. Pour into the soufflé dish and wrap tightly in foil.
5. Pour water into the cooker and lower in the steamer rack.
6. Put the dish into the rack and seal the lid.
7. Select the "Chicken/Meat" button and adjust time to 17 minutes.
8. When time is up, turn off the cooker and quick-release the pressure.
9. Serve right away with the butter melting on top.

Nutritional Info (¼ recipe):

Total calories: 282
Protein: 16
Carbs: 1
Fiber: 0
Fat: 12

Potato-Pepper Egg Bake

Serves: 2
Time: 27 minutes (10 minutes prep time, 17 minutes cook time)

For a meatless egg bake, potatoes and bell peppers are a good choice because they provide a lot of flavor and are satisfying. You layer the bake in a baking dish, and then use the pressure cooker instead of the oven. It cooks much faster that way, and preserves the nutrition in all the ingredients.

Ingredients:

- ☐ 4 beaten eggs
- ☐ 1 ½ cups water
- ☐ 1 big, sliced yellow potato
- ☐ ½ sliced onion
- ☐ ½ sliced red bell pepper
- ☐ ¼ cup cheddar cheese
- ☐ 2 tablespoons sour cream
- ☐ 1 ½ tablespoons olive oil
- ☐ Salt and pepper to taste

Directions:

1. Turn the Power Pressure Cooker XL to the "Chicken/Meat" setting and add oil.
2. When shiny and hot, add potatoes, so they don't overlap.
3. After 4 minutes, flip the potatoes.
4. After 2 minutes, add onion and cook for another 2 minutes.
5. Toss in the bell pepper and keep cooking until the onion turns clear.
6. Remove everything from the pot and plate for now.
7. Pour water into the pot and lower in the trivet.
8. Prepare a 6-inch baking dish with butter.
9. In a bowl, whisk eggs, sour cream, salt, and pepper.
10. Add ½ of the potatoes, onion, and bell pepper mixture - layering in that order - into the dish, seasoning with a sprinkle of salt and pepper.
11. Pour half of the eggs on top.
12. Top with half the cheese.
13. Repeat the potato/onion/pepper layering, finishing off with the rest of the eggs and cheese.

14. Wrap tightly in foil and put on top of the trivet.
15. Seal the lid.
16. Hit "Chicken/Meat" again and cook for 17 minutes.
17. When time is up, quick-release the pressure.
18. Serve!

Nutritional Info (½ recipe):

Total calories: 470
Protein: 19
Carbs: 38
Fiber: 5
Fat: 10

Chapter 6

Beef + Lamb

Seasoned Boiled Beef + Salsa Verde Sauce

<u>Serves:</u> 4

<u>Time:</u> 1 hour, 52 minutes (10 minutes prep time, 72 minutes cook time, 30 minutes natural pressure release)

This Italian-style beef seasoned with bold flavors like rosemary, thyme, and peppercorns proves that boiled meat doesn't equal tasteless meat. On top of the unbelievably-tender beef is a salsa verde sauce made with hard-boiled egg yolks, garlic, capers, and a few other pantry staples. It adds a gorgeous pop of green to the plate and bright flavors to go with the beef's more earthy profile.

<u>Ingredients:</u>

Beef

- ☐ 6 cups water
- ☐ 2 pounds of beef round
- ☐ 1 halved celery stalk
- ☐ 6 garlic cloves
- ☐ 1 halved carrot
- ☐ 1 halved onion
- ☐ 2 sprigs of thyme
- ☐ 1 sprig of rosemary
- ☐ 1 bay leaf
- ☐ 3 tablespoons salt
- ☐ 1 teaspoon peppercorns
- ☐ Splash of white wine vinegar

Salsa verde

- ☐ 3 hard-boiled egg yolks
- ☐ 2 peeled garlic cloves
- ☐ 2 bunches of parsley
- ☐ ½ cup white wine vinegar
- ☐ ¼ cup olive oil
- ☐ 1 teaspoon capers
- ☐ 1 teaspoon salt
- ☐ 1 teaspoon pepper

<u>Directions:</u>

1. Tie the herbs together with a piece of kitchen spring.
2. Pour water into the PPCXL and add carrot, onion, bay leaf, celery, herbs, vinegar, and salt.
3. Hit "Chicken/Meat" and bring liquid to a boil.
4. Add in your meat and bring to a boil again before sealing the lid.
5. Hit "cancel" and then "Chicken/Meat" again, adjusting time to 72 minutes.
6. When time is up, turn off the cooker and wait for a natural pressure release.

7. In the meanwhile, mix hard-boiled eggs with vinegar in a bowl.
8. Blend capers, parsley, oil, salt, pepper, and garlic in a food processor.
9. Add the yolk/vinegar and mix for another 30 seconds.
10. Gradually pour in more oil until the mixture is like a sauce.
11. When the cooker is safe to open, plate the meat.
12. Turn the cooker back to "Chicken/Meat" and simmer for 5 minutes to reduce.
13. If desired, strain the broth to get rid of extra fat.
14. Serve sliced meat with broth and salsa verde on top.

Nutritional Info (½ pound of beef w/ broth and sauce):

Total calories: 589
Protein: 53
Carbs: 12
Fat: 37
Fiber: 0

Beef Bourguignon

<u>Serves:</u> 6

<u>Time:</u> 45 minutes (5 minutes prep time, 18 minutes cook time, 15 minutes natural pressure release, 5 minutes simmer time)

One of the must-knows from French cuisine, this rich beef stew packed with mushrooms, carrots, and onion is surprisingly easy and involves just some simple chopping and throwing everything into the pressure cooker for 18 minutes. A combo of water and flour is mixed in at the very end to thicken the liquid, and that's it!

<u>Ingredients:</u>

- ☐ 1 ½ pounds boneless beef chuck roast cut into 1-inch cubes
- ☐ 2 ⅔ cups halved fresh mushrooms
- ☐ 1 bay leaf
- ☐ 4 peeled and chopped carrots
- ☐ 2 minced garlic cloves
- ☐ ¾ cup chopped onions
- ☐ ⅔ cup dry red wine
- ☐ ⅔ cup beef broth
- ☐ ¼ cup water
- ☐ 2 tablespoons tomato paste
- ☐ 2 tablespoons flour
- ☐ ¾ teaspoon sea salt
- ☐ ¼ teaspoon black pepper

<u>Directions:</u>

1. Minus the water and flour, put everything in your PPCXL and seal the lid.
2. Select "Chicken/Meat" and cook for 18 minutes.
3. When time is up, turn off the cooker and wait for a natural pressure release.
4. Pick out the bay leaf.
5. In a separate bowl, whisk (cold) water with flour.
6. Pour into the cooker and stir till smooth.
7. Turn the cooker back to "Chicken/Meat," but keep the lid off.
8. The stew will thicken.
9. When simmered for a few minutes, it's ready to serve!

Nutritional Info (⅙ recipe):

Total calories: 451
Protein: 33.7
Fat: 10.6
Carbs: 51.5
Fiber: 4.1

Garlic-Ginger Pot Roast

<u>Serves:</u> 8

<u>Time:</u> 1 hour, 4 minutes (10 minutes prep time, 54 minutes cook time)

Pot roasts are perfect for cold autumn or winter nights. They're typically cooked in a slow cooker for hours, but this faster version takes just 54 minutes. If you're a garlic lover, this recipe uses six whole cloves. Fresh ginger adds complexity, and the red potatoes and carrots make this a one-pot dinner.

<u>Ingredients:</u>

- ☐ 4 pounds boneless chuck roast
- ☐ 1 pound halved red potatoes
- ☐ 4 cups beef broth
- ☐ 6 minced garlic cloves
- ☐ 3 peeled and chopped carrots
- ☐ 3-inch piece of halved and smashed fresh ginger
- ☐ 2 tablespoons soy sauce
- ☐ 2 teaspoons olive oil
- ☐ Salt and pepper to taste

<u>Directions:</u>

1. Season roast well with salt and pepper.
2. Turn your PPCXL to "Chicken/Meat" and add olive oil.
3. When hot, brown the roast evenly before putting on a plate.
4. Pour broth into the cooker and stir, scraping up any stuck-on meat.
5. Add in soy sauce.
6. Return the roast to the cooker and add garlic, ginger, carrots, and potatoes.
7. Seal the lid and adjust time on "Chicken/Meat" setting to 54 minutes.
8. When time is up, turn off the cooker and quick-release.
9. Serve right away!

<u>Nutritional Info (⅛ recipe per serving):</u>

Total calories: 403
Protein: 38
Carbs: 12
Fat: 12
Fiber: 1.8

Flank Steak Tacos with Homemade Coleslaw

<u>Serves:</u> 4
<u>Time:</u> 55 minutes (5 minutes prep time, 45 minutes cook time, 5 minutes rest time)

Steak tacos are one of my favorite weeknight meals, especially when they're served with a crunchy, slightly spicy coleslaw. The flank steak cooks in the Power Pressure Cooker XL with two kinds of salsa and sautéed onion, while the cabbage is tossed with dressing made from mayo, hot sauce, and lime juice.

Ingredients:

Steak

- [ ] 2 pounds of flank steak
- [ ] 8 small flour or corn tortillas
- [ ] 1 ½ cups salsa verde
- [ ] ¾ cup tomato salsa
- [ ] 1 large chopped onion
- [ ] 2 tablespoons olive oil
- [ ] 1 teaspoon ground cumin
- [ ] 1 teaspoon chili powder

Coleslaw

- [ ] 4 cups sliced green cabbage
- [ ] 2 cups sliced red cabbage
- [ ] 2 sliced green onions
- [ ] ½ cup chopped cilantro
- [ ] 4 tablespoons mayonnaise
- [ ] 3 tablespoons lime juice
- [ ] ½ teaspoon hot sauce of choice
- [ ] Salt to taste

Directions:

1. Turn your Power Pressure Cooker XL to "Chicken/Meat" and heat the olive oil.
2. When hot and shimmering, add onions and cook until soft.
3. While that cooks, trim the steak and cut first lengthwise, and then crosswise.
4. Add ground cumin and chili powder to the pressure cooker.
5. Add steak and both salsas after 1 minute.

6. Close and seal the lid.
7. Select "Chicken/Meat" and adjust time to 45 minutes.
8. When the timer beeps, hit "cancel" and quick-release.
9. Remove the meat and put on a plate.
10. Let it rest for a few minutes before checking the temperature.
11. If not cooked all the way through, return to the pot and turn on "Chicken/Meat" again, but don't bring it to pressure.
12. When cooked, rest again before shredding.
13. To prepare coleslaw, mix hot sauce, mayo, and lime juice together.
14. Add cabbages, cilantro, and green onions.
15. Sprinkle on salt.
16. Serve tacos with shredded meat and coleslaw.

Nutritional Info (2 tacos per serving):

Total calories: 713
Protein: 54
Carbs: 40
Fat: 36
Fiber: 8

Stuffed Flank Steak

<u>Serves:</u> 2
<u>Time:</u> 37 minutes (5 minutes active time, 27 minutes cook time, 5 minutes rest time)

Steak goes on steak in this recipe, and in between is a stuffing of breadcrumbs, onion, celery, garlic, and onion. It's cooked in the pressure cooker with diced tomatoes, broth, and seasonings like thyme and marjoram.

Ingredients:

- ☐ 1 pound flank steak
- ☐ 6 tablespoons beef broth
- ☐ 1 cup breadcrumbs
- ☐ 1 cup diced tomatoes
- ☐ 1 minced garlic clove
- ☐ ½ cup chopped onion
- ☐ ½ cup chopped celery
- ☐ 1 tablespoon butter
- ☐ ½ teaspoon salt
- ☐ ¼ teaspoon marjoram
- ☐ ¼ teaspoon thyme
- ☐ ⅛ teaspoon pepper

Directions:

1. Turn your cooker to "Chicken/Meat" and melt the butter.
2. Sauté the celery, onion, and garlic.
3. When the onion is softened, add seasonings, breadcrumbs, and 2 tablespoons of broth.
4. Cut flank steak in two.
5. Take the mixture from the pot and lay on top of one piece of steak, and then lay the other steak piece on top.
6. Secure with a toothpick.
7. Pour 4 tablespoons of broth and the diced tomatoes into the cooker, and then add the stuffed steak.
8. Seal lid and adjust time on the "Chicken/Meat" for 27 minutes.
9. When the timer beeps, turn off the cooker and wait for a natural pressure release.
10. Let the steak rest for 5 minutes before serving.

Nutritional Info (½ recipe per serving)

Total calories: 776
Protein: 69
Fat: 35
Carbs: 42
Fiber: 1

Flank Steak with Sweet Potato Gravy

<u>Serves:</u> 4

<u>Time:</u> 2 hours, 2 minutes (10 minutes prep time, 1 hour 12 minutes cook time, 40 minutes natural pressure release)

A healthier take on steak and gravy, this dinner for four uses sweet potatoes mixed with spices like sweet paprika, cayenne, and cloves. It's a great weeknight dinner for when you're really craving steak, but don't want to pay through the nose for it.

Ingredients:

- ☐ 2 pounds flank steak cut into four pieces
- ☐ 1 pound peeled and grated sweet potatoes
- ☐ 1 cup beef broth
- ☐ 1 chopped yellow onion
- ☐ 3 tablespoons tomato paste
- ☐ 1 tablespoon olive oil
- ☐ 1 tablespoon butter
- ☐ 1 tablespoon sweet paprika
- ☐ 2 teaspoons fresh thyme
- ☐ ½ teaspoon salt
- ☐ ¼ teaspoon cayenne
- ☐ ¼ teaspoon ground cloves

Directions:

1. Turn your PPCXL to "Chicken/Meat" and add butter.
2. When melted, brown the beef.
3. When brown, move the meat to a bowl and add the onion.
4. Once the onion is softened, add sweet potato, salt, thyme, cloves, and cayenne.
5. After 1 minute, pour in the broth and tomato paste.
6. Stir to dissolve and bring to a simmer.
7. Return the meat to the pot and seal the lid.
8. Adjust cook time to 1 hour, 12 minutes.
9. When time is up, hit "cancel" and wait for a natural pressure release.
10. Serve!

Nutritional Info (¼ recipe per serving):

Total calories: 594
Protein: 67
Carbs: 28
Fat: 22
Fiber: 4

Tortilla Beef Casserole

<u>Serves:</u> 6

<u>Time:</u> 1 hour, 11 minutes (15 minutes prep time, 36 minutes cook time, 20 minutes natural pressure release)

Meaty and hearty, this casserole is like a beef taco in a baking dish. It's layered with a beef sauce with crushed tomatoes and onion, corn tortillas, and cheese. It makes enough for six people, so it's great for big families or leftovers.

<u>Ingredients:</u>

- ☐ 6 corn tortillas
- ☐ 1 ¼ pounds lean ground beef
- ☐ 14-ounces of crushed tomatoes
- ☐ 1 chopped yellow onion
- ☐ 2 cups shredded cheddar cheese
- ☐ ¼ cup chopped cilantro
- ☐ 4 ½-ounces of mild green chiles with liquid
- ☐ 2 tablespoons olive oil
- ☐ 1 ½ tablespoons chili powder
- ☐ 1 tablespoon minced garlic
- ☐ ½ teaspoon ground cumin

<u>Directions:</u>

1. Turn the Power Pressure Cooker XL to "Chicken/Meat" and add oil.
2. When hot, cook the onion for three minutes.
3. Add garlic and chiles.
4. After 1 minute, brown the beef.
5. After 4 minutes, throw in cumin and chili powder.
6. Stir tomatoes and cilantro for 2 minutes.
7. Pour out the pot's mixtures into a bowl.
8. Clean and dry cooker.
9. Pour in 2 cups of water and add trivet.
10. Layer ½ cup of beef sauce into a 2-quart baking dish, then add a corn tortilla, sauce, and ½ cup of cheese.
11. Layer until all the ingredients are used.
12. Wrap the dish in parchment paper and then foil.

13. Put into the pressure cooker and seal the lid.

14. Adjust time on the "Chicken/Meat" to 36 minutes.

15. Turn off cooker and wait for a natural pressure release.

16. Cool the dish before serving.

Nutritional Info (⅙ recipe per serving):

Total calories: 447
Protein: 27
Carbs: 27.9
Fiber: 4
Fat: 24.3

Brown Sugar-Sesame Short Ribs with Peanut Sauce

<u>Serves:</u> 8

<u>Time:</u> 1 hour, 45 minutes (15 minutes prep time, 1 hour cook time, 30 minutes natural pressure release)

The flavors in this beef ribs recipe are mouthwatering and will make you want to lick every bit of sauce from your plate. The ribs are cooked in beef broth with soy sauce, brown sugar, ginger, garlic, and peanut butter, which all together create a sweet, nutty, gingery sticky sauce. Some chopped scallions for garnish add a pop of acid.

Ingredients:

- ☐ 3 pounds boneless beef short ribs
- ☐ ½ cup beef broth
- ☐ ½ cup soy sauce
- ☐ ¼ cup packed dark brown sugar
- ☐ 1 large halved and sliced leek (white and pale green parts only)
- ☐ 3 sliced scallions (green parts only)
- ☐ 2 tablespoons smooth peanut butter
- ☐ 2 tablespoons toasted sesame oil
- ☐ 1 tablespoon fresh minced ginger
- ☐ 1 tablespoon white sesame seeds
- ☐ 1 tablespoon minced garlic
- ☐ ½ teaspoon red pepper flakes

Directions:

1. Turn your cooker to "Chicken/Meat" and heat up the sesame oil.
2. When hot and shiny, brown your short ribs in batches.
3. When the ribs are brown, put on a plate.
4. Put red pepper flakes, garlic, ginger, and leeks into the cooker.
5. Sauté for 3 minutes before adding brown sugar.
6. When melted, pour in soy sauce, broth, and peanut butter.
7. Scrape up any stuck-on food bits.
8. When the peanut butter has become liquidy and melted, return the ribs to the pressure cooker.
9. Close and seal the lid.

10. Hit "cancel" before selecting "Chicken/Meat" again and adjusting time to 1 hour.
11. When the timer beeps, hit "cancel" and wait for a natural pressure release.
12. When all the pressure is gone, plate the ribs and ladle over the sauce.
13. Top with scallions.

Nutritional Info (⅛ of recipe):

Total calories: 665
Protein: 58
Carbs: 24
Fat: 37
Fiber: 1

Maple Syrup + Balsamic Beef

<u>Serves</u>: 8
<u>Time</u>: About 1 hour (20 minutes active time, 42 minutes cook time)

The two star ingredients of this recipe are the maple syrup and rich balsamic vinegar. They balance and compliment each other in all the right ways, creating a unique marinade that sticks to the beef. A few extra spices like garlic and ginger help cut through the sweetness, so the flavors are layered and complex. Serve as is or with a salad side.

<u>Ingredients:</u>

- ☐ 3 pounds of trimmed, sliced boneless chuck steak
- ☐ 1 cup bone broth
- ☐ 1 cup maple syrup
- ☐ ½ cup balsamic vinegar
- ☐ 2 tablespoons olive oil
- ☐ 1 ½ teaspoons salt
- ☐ 1 teaspoon finely-chopped garlic
- ☐ 1 teaspoon ground ginger

<u>Directions:</u>

1. Season your sliced meat with the ginger and salt.
2. Turn PPCXL to "Chicken/Meat," and heat olive oil.
3. Brown the beef all over and plate for now.
4. Add garlic to the pot and cook for 1 minute.
5. Stir in maple syrup, vinegar, and broth.
6. Put the beef back into the pot and seal the lid.
7. Hit "cancel," and then "Chicken/Meat" and adjust time to 42 minutes.
8. When the timer beeps, turn off the cooker and quick-release the pressure.
9. Serve right away!

<u>Nutritional Info (⅛ recipe per serving)</u>
Total calories: 1112
Protein: 43
Carbs: 33
Fat: 29
Fiber: 0

Beef & Broccoli

<u>Serves:</u> 4

<u>Time:</u> 39 minutes (14 minutes prep time, 5 minutes cook time, 10 minutes natural pressure release, 10 minutes simmer time)

If you're ordering Chinese, beef and broccoli is a common choice. This homemade version is not only just as tasty, it's easy and healthier. You only need to marinate the beef for 10 minutes, and then brown it with some cooked onions before bringing the Power Pressure Cooker XL to pressure. You cook the broccoli towards the end and thicken the sauce with potato starch. Serve with rice!

Ingredients:

Beef

- ☐ 3 pounds trimmed flank steak, cut into strips
- ☐ 1 pound broccoli florets
- ☐ ½ cup beef broth
- ☐ 1 diced onion
- ☐ 2 tablespoons potato starch

Marinade

- ☐ 5 minced garlic cloves
- ☐ ½ cup soy sauce
- ☐ 2 tablespoons fish sauce
- ☐ 1 tablespoon sesame oil
- ☐ ½ teaspoon Chinese Five Spice

Directions:

1. Storing in the fridge, soak the beef in the marinade for at least 10 minutes.
2. Turn your pressure cooker to "Chicken/Meat" and add oil.
3. When hot and shiny, cook the onions for 4 minutes.
4. Add beef with its marinade, and brown just a little before adding broth.
5. Hit "cancel" and seal the lid.
6. Select "Rice/Risotto" and adjust time down to 5 minutes.
7. When the timer beeps, turn off the cooker and wait for a natural pressure release.
8. Hit "Chicken/Meat" again and add broccoli.
9. Ladle out ¼ cup of hot cooking liquid and whisk in the potato starch till smooth.

10. Pour back into the pot and simmer until broccoli is cooked and sauce thickens.

11. Serve!

Nutritional Info (¼ recipe per serving):

Calories: 243
Protein: 25
Carbs: 10
Fat: 11
Fiber: 1

Peach-Bourbon Glazed Meatloaf

<u>Serves:</u> 4

<u>Time:</u> 1 hour, 11 minutes (12 minutes prep time, 54 minutes cook time, 5 minutes cool time)

Meatloaf grows up in this recipe with a delicious peach-bourbon glaze. It's made from smooth peach jam (if you can only find chunky preserves, you can puree them if you want a really smooth glaze), a decent bourbon, your favorite BBQ sauce, honey, and hot sauce. The meatloaf itself is a simple recipe with the classic beef, onion, breadcrumbs, an egg white, ketchup, basil, and some garlic.

<u>Ingredients:</u>

- ☐ 1 cup water (for pressure cooker)

Meatloaf
- ☐ 1 pound lean ground beef
- ☐ ⅔ cup diced onion
- ☐ ⅔ cup bread crumbs
- ☐ 1 egg white
- ☐ 2 tablespoons ketchup
- ☐ 2 chopped basil leaves
- ☐ 1 teaspoon minced garlic
- ☐ Salt and pepper to taste

Glaze
- ☐ 1 cup smooth peach jam
- ☐ ½ cup BBQ sauce
- ☐ ½ cup bourbon
- ☐ ¼ cup water
- ☐ ¼ cup honey
- ☐ 1 tablespoon Frank's hot sauce

<u>Directions:</u>

1. Prepare a one-quart baking dish with cooking spray.
2. With your hands, mix everything in the "Meatloaf" ingredient list to form a loaf.
3. To make glaze, mix all the glaze ingredients in a pan and bring to a boil on the stove. Simmer for 10 minutes until thoroughly mixed together and thickened a little.

4. Using a kitchen brush, brush glaze on top of the meatloaf.
5. Wrap meatloaf dish in foil.
6. Pour one cup of water into your PPCXL and lower in trivet.
7. Put the wrapped dish in the cooker on the trivet and seal the lid.
8. Select "Chicken/Meat" and adjust time to 54 minutes.
9. When the timer goes off, hit "cancel" and quick-release.
10. Remove the dish and unwrap.
11. Holding the loaf in place, carefully pour out any liquid from the dish into the sink.
12. Cool before serving.

Nutritional Info (¼ recipe per serving):

Total calories: 570
Protein: 27
Carbs: 119
Fat: 5
Fiber: 0

Leg of Lamb with Pomegranate

<u>Serves:</u> 4

<u>Time:</u> 30 minutes (10 minutes prep time, 20 minutes cook time)

Lamb is not the most common ingredient for most home chefs, but it's not difficult to prepare, and great for something different on holidays. The "gamey" taste of the lamb is made mild and earthy with a cooking broth made of pomegranate, mint, and garlic. While that cooks, you make an easy sauce from chicken stock, wine, butter, and flour. The final result is rich, fruity, garlicky, and buttery.

<u>Ingredients:</u>

Lamb
- ☐ 1 boneless leg of lamb
- ☐ 1 cup pomegranate juice
- ☐ ½ cup pomegranate seeds
- ☐ 4 peeled and minced garlic cloves
- ☐ 4 mint leaves
- ☐ 3 tablespoons olive oil
- ☐ 1 teaspoon salt
- ☐ 1 teaspoon black pepper

Sauce
- ☐ 1 cup chicken stock
- ☐ 1 cup white wine
- ☐ 2 tablespoons flour
- ☐ 2 teaspoons butter

<u>Directions:</u>

1. Rub minced garlic on the lamb and sprinkle on salt and pepper.
2. Turn the cooker to "Chicken/Meat" and add oil.
3. When hot, put leg in the PPCXL and brown all over.
4. Pour in pomegranate juice, seeds, and mint leaves.
5. Seal the lid and adjust time to 20 minutes.
6. In the meantime, mix melted butter and flour.
7. Bring wine and chicken stock to a boil in a saucepan, and stir in butter/flour.
8. Simmer for 5 minutes.

9. When time is up on the pressure cooker, turn off the cooker and quick-release the pressure.
10. Serve lamb with sauce.

Nutritional Info (¼ recipe per serving):

Total calories: 643
Protein: 142
Carbs: 18
Fat: 40
Fiber: 1

Easy Lamb with Fresh Herbs

<u>Serves:</u> 6

<u>Time</u>: 34 minutes (10 minutes prep time, 24 minutes cook time)

Fresh herbs are the perfect seasoning for lamb. They bring out the lamb's best flavors, so if you've never cooked lamb before, this recipe is a great starter. Garlic, of course, is a must, along with carrots, another aromatic. You brown the lamb with salt, pepper, and garlic, and then cook it in veggie stock, carrots, and herbs for 24 minutes. It's quick, easy, and high in protein and low in carbs.

<u>Ingredients:</u>

- ☐ 4 pounds cubed boneless lamb
- ☐ 1 ½ cups veggie stock
- ☐ 4 minced garlic cloves
- ☐ 1 cup sliced carrots
- ☐ 3 thyme sprigs
- ☐ 3 rosemary sprigs
- ☐ 3 tablespoons flour
- ☐ 2 tablespoons olive oil
- ☐ Salt and pepper to taste

<u>Directions:</u>

1. Turn your cooker to "Chicken/Meat" and heat the oil.
2. Season lamb with salt and pepper before adding to cooker with garlic.
3. Brown all over.
4. Stir in flour and gradually pour in stock.
5. Add carrots, rosemary, and thyme.
6. Seal the lid.
7. Adjust time to 24 minutes on the "Chicken/Meat" setting.
8. When time is up, turn off the cooker and quick-release.
9. Pick out the herb sprigs.
10. Serve hot!

Nutritional Info (⅙ recipe per serving):

Total calories: 921
Protein: 72
Carbs: 5
Fat: 65
Fiber: 1

Lamb and Feta Meatballs

<u>Serves:</u> 6-8

<u>Time:</u> 14 minutes (5 minutes prep time, 9 minutes cook time)

You're familiar with meatballs made from turkey or beef, maybe even chicken, but what about lamb? They're rich, yet healthy, and in this recipe, full of delicious add-ins like feta cheese, onion, and crushed tomato.

Ingredients:

- ☐ 1 ½ pounds ground lamb
- ☐ 4 minced garlic cloves
- ☐ One 28-ounce can of crushed tomatoes
- ☐ 6-ounce can of tomato sauce
- ☐ 1 beaten egg
- ☐ 1 chopped onion
- ☐ 1 chopped green bell pepper
- ☐ ½ cup breadcrumbs
- ☐ ½ cup crumbled feta cheese
- ☐ 2 tablespoons olive oil
- ☐ 2 tablespoons chopped parsley
- ☐ 1 tablespoon water
- ☐ 1 tablespoon chopped mint
- ☐ 1 teaspoon dried oregano
- ☐ ½ teaspoon salt
- ☐ ¼ teaspoon black pepper

Directions:

1. Mix lamb, bread crumbs, meat, feta, water, parsley, half of the minced garlic, pepper, and salt.
2. Form into 1-inch meatballs.
3. Turn the PPCXL to "Chicken/Meat" and heat oil.
4. Add in onion and bell pepper.
5. Cook for 2 minutes and then add rest of the garlic.
6. After another minute, stir in tomato sauce, crushed tomatoes and liquid, and oregano.
7. Season with salt and pepper.
8. Nestle the meatballs in the cooker and spoon over the sauce.

9. Seal the lid.
10. Adjust the cooking time to 11 minutes.
11. When time is up, hit "cancel" and quick-release the pressure.
12. Serve meatballs with crumbled feta and parsley.

Nutritional Info (⅙ recipe per serving):

Total calories: 384
Protein: 38
Carbs: 17
Fat: 6
Fiber: 0

Chapter 7

Chicken

Chicken Cacciatore with Burst Tomatoes

<u>Serves:</u> 4-6

<u>Time</u>: 31 minutes (10 minutes prep time, 16 minutes cook time, 5 minutes simmer time)

A classic Italian dish, this low-calorie chicken dish embraces fresh and bold flavors. Burst tomatoes release their juices in the cooker with tart red wine, garlic, oregano, and salt. The chicken is cooked in this mixture for 16 minutes, and then finished off with fragrant basil and salty olives.

Ingredients:

- ☐ 1 ½ pounds skinless boneless chicken breasts
- ☐ 1 pound cherry tomatoes
- ☐ 1 cup water
- ☐ ½ cup pitted and rinsed green olives
- ☐ 2 crushed garlic cloves
- ☐ ¼ cup tart red wine
- ☐ 1 fresh basil leaf
- ☐ 1 teaspoon dried oregano
- ☐ 1 teaspoon olive oil
- ☐ 1 teaspoon salt

Directions:

1. Turn your cooker to "Chicken/Meat" and heat olive oil.
2. Brown chicken breasts on both sides and move to a plate.
3. Put the washed tomatoes in a plastic bag and tie a knot.
4. Smash tomatoes once so they burst, but aren't completely obliterated.
5. Pour contents of bag into the cooker.
6. Add wine, water, garlic cloves, salt, and oregano.
7. Stir and scrape up any burned-on chicken bits.
8. When the alcohol smell has burned off, return the chicken and stir to coat.
9. Close and seal the lid.
10. Hit "cancel" and select the "Chicken/Meat" again right away, adjusting time to 16 minutes.
11. When time is up, turn off cooker and quick-release the pressure.
12. Open the lid and stir for another 5 minutes, letting the flavors really meld together. Use a meat thermometer to make sure the chicken is cooked to 165-degrees.

13. Serve with olives and torn-up pieces of the basil.

Nutritional Info (⅙ recipe per serving):

Calories: 81.3
Protein: 4.3
Carbs: 6.6
Fat: 6.4
Fiber: 0

Chicken Thighs with Pears and Cranberries

<u>Serves:</u> 4-6

<u>Time:</u> 33 minutes (15 minutes prep time, 18 minutes cook time)

Fruit is often underused in savory dishes, which is a shame, since it adds a natural sweetness or in this recipe's case, sweet *and* sour. You get boneless chicken thighs, which are cheap, and cook them with fresh pears and dried cranberries. Balsamic vinegar, butter, and shallots form a wonderfully-rich sauce.

Ingredients:

- ☐ 2 pounds boneless skinless chicken thighs
- ☐ 2 large firm peeled and sliced Bosc pears
- ☐ ⅔ cup chicken stock
- ☐ ¼ cup dried cranberries
- ☐ 1 chopped shallot
- ☐ 2 tablespoons butter
- ☐ 2 tablespoons balsamic vinegar
- ☐ ½ teaspoon dried dill
- ☐ ½ teaspoon salt
- ☐ ½ teaspoon pepper

Directions:

1. Hit the "Chicken/Meat" setting on your cooker and add butter.
2. When hot and melted, add chicken thighs (that you've seasoned with salt and pepper).
3. Brown all over in batches and place on a plate for now.
4. Put shallot and pears in the cooker.
5. When the shallot has softened, pour in vinegar, along with cranberries and dill.
6. When the vinegar is bubbling, pour in broth.
7. Return the chicken to the pot, stirring, and seal the lid.
8. Hit "cancel" and then hit "Chicken/Meat" again, adjusting time to 18 minutes.
9. When the timer beeps, turn off cooker and quick-release.
10. Stir once before serving.

Nutritional Info (⅙ per serving):

Total calories: 265
Protein: 30
Carbs: 15
Fat: 10
Fiber: 1.5

Bacon-Wrapped Drumsticks

<u>Serves</u>: 4-6

<u>Time:</u> 1 hour, 24 minutes/two batches (10 minutes prep time, 18-34 minutes cook time, 20-40 minutes natural pressure release)

They say everything is better with bacon, and they are not wrong. The skin of a chicken drumstick is replaced by a slice of bacon, and the whole thing is cooked in the Power Pressure Cooker XL with chicken stock, balsamic vinegar, rosemary, and garlic. Depending on the size of your cooker, you might need to do two batches, which would double the time it takes to make this recipe.

<u>Ingredients:</u>

- ☐ 3 pounds of chicken drumsticks with skin removed
- ☐ 8 slices of bacon
- ☐ ½ cup chicken stock
- ☐ 1 tablespoon fresh rosemary leaves
- ☐ 1 tablespoon balsamic vinegar
- ☐ 2 teaspoons minced garlic
- ☐ ½ teaspoon black pepper
- ☐ ½ teaspoon salt

<u>Directions:</u>

1. Season the drumsticks generously with salt and pepper, and wrap a slice of bacon around each one.
2. Turn your cooker to "Chicken/Meat" and when hot, brown the drumsticks evenly all over in batches.
3. You may need to pressure cooker the chicken in two batches; if so, sprinkle in half of the rosemary and garlic, and pour in half of the broth and vinegar.
4. Put half of the drumsticks in the cooker.
5. Seal the lid.
6. Select "Chicken/Meat" and cook for 18 minutes.
7. When time is up, turn off the cooker and wait for a natural pressure release.
8. Take out the drumsticks with a pair of tongs, and put on a plate that you tent with foil.
9. Save the liquid contents of the pot in another bowl.
10. Put the rest of the ingredients in the cooker and cook the other batch.

11. When all the drumsticks are cooked, heat up all sauce (and first batch of meat if necessary) and ladle over the chicken.

Nutritional Info (¼ recipe):

Total calories: 396
Protein: 47
Carbs: 1
Fat: 21
Fiber: 0

Coq Au Vin

<u>Serves:</u> 6

<u>Time:</u> 47 minutes (30 minutes prep time, 12 minutes cook time, 5 minutes simmer time)

Julia Child introduced American society to coq au vin, which literally means "rooster with wine." The name sounds intimidating, but when you use the Power Pressure Cooker XL, it's not difficult, and much faster. This recipe has all the essentials of the dish - chicken, mushrooms, carrots, onion, garlic, bacon, and seasonings like thyme and parsley.

Ingredients:

- ☐ 3 pounds boneless skinless chicken thighs
- ☐ 12-ounces quartered white mushrooms
- ☐ 1 cup chicken broth
- ☐ ½ cup diced bacon
- ☐ 2 sliced carrots
- ☐ 1 chopped yellow onion
- ☐ 2 chopped garlic cloves
- ☐ 2 sprigs thyme
- ☐ 1 bay leaf
- ☐ 3 tablespoons cold water
- ☐ 2 tablespoons chopped parsley
- ☐ 2 tablespoons cornstarch
- ☐ 1 tablespoon tomato paste
- ☐ 1 tablespoon butter
- ☐ 1 tablespoon vegetable oil
- ☐ Salt and pepper to taste

Directions:

1. Turn your cooker to "Chicken/Meat" and cook bacon.
2. Season chicken with salt and pepper, and add to the pot.
3. Brown on both sides and then return to a plate.
4. Add onions and cook until they are beginning to caramelize.
5. Add garlic and cook for just one minute.
6. Pour in the wine and scrape up any stuck-on bits.
7. When the wine has almost evaporated, add in broth, thyme, carrots, bay leaf, and tomato paste.

8. Put the chicken back in the cooker and seal the lid.

9. Select "Soup/Stew" and adjust time to 12 minutes.

10. In the meantime, heat oil and butter in a pan on the stove.

11. Cook mushrooms until golden and season with salt and pepper.

12. By now, the pressure cooker should be done, so turn it off and quick-release.

13. Take out the chicken and plate.

14. In a small bowl, whisk cold water and cornstarch until smooth.

15. Turn the cooker back to "Chicken/Meat."

16. Pour the water/cornstarch into the pot's cooking liquid and stir until thickened and boiling

17. Stir in mushrooms.

18. Serve chicken with sauce and parsley on top!

Nutritional Info (⅙ recipe):

Total calories: 281
Protein: 23.9
Carbs: 15
Fat: 12.4
Fiber: 2.2

Chicken Pot Pie

<u>Serves:</u> 6

<u>Time:</u> 14 minutes (10 minutes active time, 4 minutes cook time)

A new take on a classic, this chicken pot pie has the "dough" on top in the form of a biscuit. Beneath the fluffy, buttery goodness is chicken with potatoes, onion, and mixed veggies, all cooked in a homemade cream of chicken soup. Making that cream of chicken from scratch is easy and makes a huge difference in terms of quality.

Ingredients:

- 2 pounds of cubed boneless skinless chicken breasts
- 16-ounces of frozen (thawed) mixed veggies
- 3 cups chicken stock
- 3 peeled and chopped potatoes
- 1 can of biscuit dough, divided into four pieces
- ¼ cup diced onion
- 1 tablespoon potato starch
- 1 teaspoon Herbes de Provence
- 1 teaspoon salt

Cream of chicken soup
- 1 ½ cups cold milk
- 2 tablespoons potato starch
- 2 tablespoons room temp butter
- 2 teaspoons salt
- 1 ½ teaspoons Herbes de Provence
- 1 ½ teaspoons chicken bouillon
- Black pepper

Directions:

1. Whisk the "Cream of chicken soup" ingredients together.
2. Tumble chicken into the PPCXL and pour over stock.
3. Add potatoes, frozen, veggies, and onion.
4. Pour in homemade cream of chicken soup.
5. Put the four pieces of biscuit dough on top.
6. Season with Herbes de Provence and salt.

7. Close and seal the lid.
8. Press "Rice/Risotto" and reduce time to 5 minutes.
9. When time is up, hit "cancel" and wait for a natural pressure release.
10. To thicken sauce, ladle out ¼ cup of cooking liquid and mix in 1 tablespoon of potato starch.
11. Add back to pot and hit "Chicken/Meat."
12. Simmer until sauce is thickened and chicken has reached 165-degrees.
13. Serve!

Nutritional Info (⅙ recipe per serving)

Total calories: 458
Protein: 55
Carbs: 32
Fat: 12
Fiber: 1

Moroccan Chicken

Servings: 4
Time: 30 minutes (15 minutes prep time, 15 minutes cook time)

Morocco is a melting pot of cultures, from Arabic to Mediterranean. That means lots of spices, like cumin, cardamom, and coriander. If you haven't stocked your spice rack in a while, now is the time, because just by adding a few of those big flavors to plain ol' chicken, tomatoes, and onion, you get a fantastic dinner in just a half-hour.

Ingredients:

- Four ½-pound chicken quarters
- 24-ounce can of diced tomatoes
- 3 sliced onions
- ½ cup chicken stock
- 1 tablespoon cumin
- 1 tablespoon cardamom
- 1 tablespoon coriander
- 1 tablespoon salt
- 1 tablespoon black pepper
- Splash of olive oil

Directions:

1. Pour a splash of olive oil in the cooker and turn to "Chicken/Meat."
2. When hot, sear the chicken quarters on both sides to a golden-brown color.
3. Plate chicken.
4. Add onions to pot and cook until they're beginning to brown.
5. Add diced tomatoes, stock, and the rest of the spices.
6. Return to the chicken and add to the pot, spooning over the onions and tomatoes.
7. Seal the lid.
8. Cook on the "Chicken/Meat" setting for 15 minutes.
9. When time is up, turn off the cooker and quick-release.
10. Serve!

Nutritional Info (¼ recipe per serving)

Total calories: 281
Protein: 20
Carbs: 15
Fat: 16
Fiber: 4.5

Chicken Marsala

<u>Serves:</u> 4

<u>Time:</u> 33 minutes (15 minutes prep time, 18 minutes cook time)

Named for the wine that's used in the recipe, chicken marsala is a classic Italian-American recipe that has a rich, creamy mushroom sauce with garlic and parsley. You may have seen it on the menu at places like the Olive Garden, but homemade is so much better and surprisingly easy!

<u>Ingredients:</u>

- ☐ 4 meal-sized chicken thighs
- ☐ 1 cup chicken stock
- ☐ 8-ounces quartered cremini mushrooms
- ☐ 4-ounces Marsala wine
- ☐ 2-ounces cornstarch "slurry"
- ☐ 2 tablespoons chopped parsley
- ☐ 1 tablespoon minced garlic
- ☐ Salt and pepper to taste

Cooking Tip: Cornstarch slurry is one part cornstarch and two parts cold water.

<u>Directions:</u>

1. Season chicken thighs with salt and pepper, and coat in cornstarch.
2. Turn your PPCXL to "Chicken/Meat" and heat some olive oil.
3. Sear the chicken on each side until golden, and plate.
4. Add onions, garlic, and mushrooms and cook for 3 minutes.
5. Put the chicken back in the pot and mix in wine, stock, slurry, and parsley.
6. Seal the lid.
7. Adjust cooking time to 18 minutes.
8. When time is up, hit "cancel" and quick-release.
9. Serve right away!

<u>Nutritional Info (¼ recipe per serving)</u>

Total calories: 170
Protein: 28
Carbs: 3

Fat: 6
Fiber: 1

Sticky Sesame Chicken

<u>Serves:</u> 4

<u>Time:</u> 38 minutes (5 minutes prep time, 18 minutes cook time, 15 minutes natural pressure release)

This lip-smacking recipe is perfect for when you need your Asian food fix. Cooked in sweet chili sauce, hoisin sauce, soy sauce, and rice vinegar, the chicken gets that addicting sweet-spicy flavor, which is brightened with fresh ginger and garlic.

<u>Ingredients:</u>

- ☐ 6 boneless chicken thigh fillets
- ☐ ½ cup chicken stock
- ☐ 4 peeled and crushed garlic cloves
- ☐ 5 tablespoons hoisin sauce
- ☐ 5 tablespoons sweet chili sauce
- ☐ 1 ½ tablespoons sesame seeds
- ☐ 1 tablespoon soy sauce
- ☐ 1 tablespoon rice vinegar
- ☐ 1 chunk of peeled, grated fresh ginger

<u>Directions:</u>

1. Put chicken thighs flat in your PPCXL.
2. In a bowl, mix chili sauce, garlic, ginger, vinegar, broth, soy sauce, and sesame seeds.
3. Pour over chicken.
4. Seal the lid.
5. Select "Chicken/Meat" and adjust time to 18 minutes.
6. When the timer beeps, hit "cancel" and allow the pressure to come down naturally.
7. Serve chicken with rice!

<u>Nutritional Info (¼ recipe per serving):</u>

Total calories: 428
Protein: 30
Carbs: 52.9
Fat: 9
Fiber: 1

Chicken Leg Quarters with Herbs

<u>Serves:</u> 4-6

<u>Time:</u> 51 minutes (15 minutes prep time, 21 minutes cook time, 15 minutes natural pressure release)

Fresh herbs are a cheap, easy way to really elevate your chicken dishes. This recipe uses three - thyme, sage, and oregano. Other ingredients include white wine, onion, garlic, and celery. The dish is very aromatic, rustic, and satisfying.

<u>Ingredients:</u>

- ☐ 3 ½ pounds of skin-on chicken leg-and-thigh quarters
- ☐ 4 chopped celery stalks
- ☐ ½ cup chicken broth
- ☐ ½ cup dry white wine
- ☐ 1 chopped yellow onion
- ☐ 2 tablespoons olive oil
- ☐ 2 teaspoons minced garlic
- ☐ 2 teaspoons minced fresh sage
- ☐ 2 teaspoons fresh thyme
- ☐ 2 teaspoons minced oregano
- ☐ ½ teaspoon salt

<u>Directions:</u>

1. Heat the oil on the "Chicken/Meat" setting of your cooker.
2. Season the chicken with salt and pepper.
3. Brown chicken evenly for 3 minutes per side and move to a plate.
4. Add onion and celery to cooker.
5. After 5 minutes, add garlic and herbs.
6. After a minute or so, pour in broth and wine, scraping up any stuck food bits.
7. Return the chicken to the cooker and seal the lid.
8. Adjust time to 21 minutes on the "Chicken/Meat" setting.
9. When the timer beeps, turn off cooker and wait for a natural pressure release.
10. Serve hot!

Nutritional Info (¼ recipe per serving):

Total calories: 335
Protein: 49
Carbs: 5
Fat: 12
Fiber: 1

Filipino-Style Chicken

<u>Serves:</u> 5-6
<u>Time:</u> 18 minutes

With only six ingredients and four steps, this might be the easiest chicken recipe you can throw together on a busy night. With 5 pounds of chicken thighs, it makes enough for a group of five to six people, and only takes 18 minutes under pressure. Bold seasonings like garlic, bay leaves, and peppercorns infuse the chicken with lots of flavor, so even though it's easy and fast, it's still big on taste.

<u>Ingredients:</u>

- ☐ 5 pounds of chicken thighs
- ☐ 4 crushed garlic cloves
- ☐ 3 bay leaves
- ☐ ½ cup white vinegar
- ☐ ½ cup soy sauce
- ☐ 1 teaspoon black peppercorns

<u>Directions:</u>

1. Put everything in the cooker and seal the lid.
2. Select "Chicken/Meat" and cook for 18 minutes.
3. When the timer beeps, turn off the cooker and quick-release the pressure.
4. Serve with rice!

<u>Nutritional Info (⅕ recipe per serving):</u>
Total calories: 526
Protein: 90
Carbs: 9
Fat: 14
Fiber: 0

Chicken Curry

<u>Serves:</u> 6

<u>Time:</u> 1 hour, 20 minutes (1 hour marinate time, 10 minutes prep time, 10 minutes cook time)

Everyone should know how to make a decent curry. They're tasty, versatile, and full of fantastic spices that might be new to your palate. This chicken curry is pretty simple, and involves marinating the meat in a mixture of lemon juice, ginger, chili powder, coriander, turmeric, and salt. The chicken is cooked with onion, tomato, and more spices, like garam masala, an Indian spice mix.

<u>Ingredients:</u>

Chicken
- [ ] 6 boneless chicken breasts
- [ ] 1 chopped tomato
- [ ] 1 yellow onion
- [ ] 2 tablespoons olive oil
- [ ] 2 teaspoons garam masala powder
- [ ] 1 teaspoon chili powder
- [ ] 1 teaspoon grated ginger
- [ ] Salt

Dry rub
- [ ] Juice of 1 lemon
- [ ] 2 teaspoons garlic powder
- [ ] 2 teaspoons ginger powder
- [ ] 2 teaspoons coriander powder
- [ ] 1 ¼ teaspoons chili powder
- [ ] ½ teaspoon turmeric
- [ ] Salt

<u>Directions:</u>

1. Mix the dry rub together and rub on chicken.
2. Chill in the fridge for at least one hour.
3. When it's time to make the chicken, turn your cooker to "Chicken/Meat."
4. Heat oil and add chopped onion.

5. When translucent, throw in chili powder, ginger, garlic, and garam masala.
6. After a minute or so, add tomatoes and cook until soft.
7. Add chicken and cook in the pot a little until turning golden.
8. Seal the lid.
9. Adjust time on the "Chicken/Meat" setting to 10 minutes.
10. When time is up, turn off the cooker and quick-release the pressure.
11. Serve right away!

Nutritional Info (⅙ recipe per serving):

Total calorie: 234
Protein: 19.9
Carbs: 9.7
Fat: 12.7
Fiber: 3

French Onion Chicken Thighs

<u>Serves:</u> 4-6

<u>Time:</u> 1 hour, 6 minutes (30 minutes prep time, 21 minutes cook time, 15 minutes natural pressure release)

This chicken is infused with the rich flavors of French onion soup, - the wine, the butter, the herbs, and of course, the Gruyere cheese. It's a great recipe idea for guests, when you want to make chicken a bit fancier. Serve with veggies to cut through the richness.

Ingredients:

- ☐ 8 bone-in chicken thighs
- ☐ 3 big, thinly-sliced yellow onions
- ☐ 1 cup grated Gruyere cheese
- ☐ ½ cup dry white wine
- ☐ ½ cup beef broth
- ☐ 1 tablespoon butter
- ☐ 1 tablespoon olive oil
- ☐ 2 teaspoons fresh thyme
- ☐ ½ teaspoon sugar
- ☐ ½ teaspoon black pepper
- ☐ ½ teaspoon salt

Directions:

1. Turn your PPCXL to "Chicken/Meat" and melt butter.
2. Brown the chicken all over, 3 minutes each side.
3. Plate chicken.
4. Add onions, sugar, and salt to the pressure cooker.
5. Cook for 20 minutes, with the lid off.
6. Pour in wine and scrape up any stuck-on bits.
7. Add broth, pepper, and thyme before returning the meat.
8. Stir before sealing the lid.
9. Adjust cooking time to 21 minutes.
10. When time is up, hit "Cancel" and wait for a natural pressure release.
11. Sprinkle on the cheese and close the lid to melt the cheese.
12. Serve with sauce!

Nutritional Info (¼ recipe per serving):

Total calories: 483
Protein: 57
Carbs: 8
Fat: 23
Fiber: 0

Easy Butter Chicken

<u>Serves:</u> 4
<u>Time:</u> 27 minutes (15 minutes prep time, 12 minutes cook time)

Butter chicken is one of the most popular Indian recipes for beginners. It uses plenty of familiar spices like ginger, garlic, and paprika, and also garam masala, which is a classic Indian spice mix. The sauce is super creamy and buttery thanks to the coconut milk, and there's a little bit of crunch with some sliced almonds for garnish. If you're new to Indian cooking, this is a great dish to start with.

<u>Ingredients:</u>

- ☐ 3 pounds boneless, skinless chicken thighs
- ☐ 2 cans coconut milk (store in fridge overnight and keep watery part and creamy part separated)
- ☐ Two 6-ounce cans of tomato paste
- ☐ 2 cups canned tomatoes with liquid
- ☐ 1 ½ large chopped onions
- ☐ ½ cup chopped cilantro
- ☐ ½ cup sliced almonds
- ☐ 1 tablespoon butter
- ☐ 2 ½ teaspoons salt
- ☐ 2 teaspoons paprika
- ☐ 2 teaspoons ginger powder
- ☐ 2 teaspoons turmeric
- ☐ 2 teaspoons garlic powder
- ☐ 2 teaspoons garam masala
- ☐ 1 ½ teaspoons cayenne powder

<u>Directions:</u>

1. Turn your PPCXL to "Chicken/Meat" and melt butter.
2. Toss in salt and add onions.
3. When softened, add all the ground spices except garam masala.
4. Mix until the spices become aromatic.
5. Pour in canned tomatoes and watery part of the coconut milk.
6. Stir and scrape up any stuck-on spices.
7. Add chicken and stir, so the meat becomes covered.

8. Close and seal the lid.
9. Adjust time to 12 minutes.
10. When time is up, turn off the cooker and quick-release.
11. Stir in garam masala, cilantro, tomato paste, and creamy part of coconut milk.
12. Serve with almonds on top.

Nutritional Info (¼ recipe per serving):

Calories: 689
Protein: 55
Carbs: 29
Fat: 36
Fiber: 4

Lemon-Garlic Chicken

<u>Serves:</u> 8

<u>Time:</u> 39 minutes (10 minutes prep time, 24 minutes cook time, 5 minutes simmer time)

Bright and slightly floral, this chicken flavored with lemon juice and lots of garlic is perfect for cool summer evenings with a big glass of iced tea. For prep, you just cook the onions until they're starting to brown, and then throw the chicken in the pressure cooker with white wine, lemon juice, garlic, salt, paprika, and some dried parsley. When the chicken is cooked, you thicken the sauce with cornstarch and serve!

Ingredients:

- ☐ 2 pounds boneless skinless chicken breasts
- ☐ 5 minced garlic cloves
- ☐ ½ cup chicken broth
- ☐ 1 diced onion
- ☐ ¼ cup white wine
- ☐ 1 tablespoon olive oil
- ☐ 3 teaspoons cornstarch
- ☐ 1 teaspoon sea salt
- ☐ 1 teaspoon dried parsley
- ☐ ¼ teaspoon paprika
- ☐ Juice from one lemon

Directions:

1. Turn your cooker to "Chicken/Meat" and add oil.
2. When shimmering and hot, cook onions until soft and starting to brown.
3. Stir in the rest of the ingredients (minus the cornstarch) and seal the lid.
4. Adjust time to 24 minutes.
5. When the timer beeps, turn off the cooker and quick-release the pressure.
6. Ladle out ¼ cup of the cooking liquid and mix in cornstarch one teaspoon at a time.
7. When smooth, pour back into the pot.
8. Stir until the sauce thickens.
9. Serve hot!

Nutritional Info (⅛ recipe per serving):

Calories: 211
Protein: 22
Carbs: 6
Fat: 4
Fiber: 1

Chicken Dinner

<u>Serves:</u> 8

<u>Time:</u> 1 hour, 1 minute (5 minutes prep time, 36 minutes cook time, 20 minutes natural pressure release)

One of the best uses of the Power Pressure Cooker XL is to cook a whole chicken. This recipe is for a very basic chicken with green onion, sugar, ginger, salt, and soy sauce. Be sure to save the bones for stock!

<u>Ingredients:</u>

- ☐ 1 medium-sized, whole chicken
- ☐ 1 minced green onion
- ☐ 2 tablespoons white sugar
- ☐ 1 tablespoon cooking wine
- ☐ 1 minced piece of ginger
- ☐ 2 teaspoons soy sauce
- ☐ 2 teaspoons salt
- ☐ Just enough oil to coat the bottom

<u>Directions:</u>

1. Season the chicken with sugar and salt.
2. Pour oil into the cooker and heat.
3. Add chicken, breast-side down, and brown till golden.
4. Flip.
5. Add 1 teaspoon of salt into the bottom of the cooker.
6. Pour in wine and soy sauce, and seal the lid.
7. Choose "Chicken/Meat" and adjust time to 36 minutes. .
8. When time is up, hit "cancel" and let the pressure come down naturally before opening the cooker.
9. Serve chicken pieces with green onion on top and any side dishes you'd like.

<u>Nutritional Info (⅛ recipe per serving):</u>
Total calories: 131
Protein: 18
Carbs: 4
Fat: 5
Fiber: 0

Chapter 8

Pork

Honey Pork Ribs with Ginger Beer Sauce

<u>Serves:</u> 6

<u>Time:</u> 1 hour, 11 minutes (15 minutes prep time, 36 minutes cook time, 20 minutes natural pressure release)

Carbonated drinks are great in sauces, adding sugar and flavor. In this recipe, ginger beer is used as the liquid base, along with honey, lots of garlic, and earthy rosemary. If you think the sauce is too sweet, taste it before adding the raw meat (and before sealing the lid) and add more red pepper flakes.

<u>Ingredients:</u>

- ☐ 3 pounds trimmed boneless country-style pork ribs
- ☐ 12-ounces bottled ginger beer
- ☐ 4 big garlic cloves
- ☐ 4 big halved shallots
- ☐ 2 tablespoons honey
- ☐ 1 tablespoon olive oil
- ☐ 1 tablespoon butter
- ☐ One 6-inch rosemary sprig
- ☐ ½ teaspoon salt
- ☐ ½ teaspoon black pepper
- ☐ ½ teaspoon red pepper flakes

<u>Directions:</u>

1. Mix oil and butter in your PPCXL and heat.
2. When melted, lay down the ribs and brown all over. It'll be about 4 minutes per side.
3. Plate the ribs for now.
4. Add shallots and stir for 5 minutes before adding garlic.
5. Cook for just a second or so and then add honey and rosemary sprig.
6. After 10 seconds of stirring, pour in the ginger beer and scrape up any stuck-on food bits.
7. Sprinkle in salt, pepper, and red pepper flakes.
8. Return the ribs to the pressure cooker and seal the lid.
9. Hit "Chicken/Meat" and adjust time to 36 minutes.
10. When time is up, hit "cancel" and wait for a natural pressure release.
11. Before serving, pick out the rosemary sprig.

<u>**Nutritional Info (⅙ recipe per serving):**</u>
Total calories: 237
Protein: 14
Carbs: 12
Fat: 14
Fiber: 0

Pork-and-Egg Fried Rice

<u>Serves:</u> 4

<u>Time:</u> 31 minutes (10 minutes prep time, 6 minutes cook time, 10 minutes natural pressure release, 5 minutes egg time)

Fried rice is one of the ultimate late night suppers and any leftovers become breakfast. This take on "ham and eggs" uses a pork loin chop that is cooked skillet-style in the cooker, before the cooker is used to prepare the white rice. You scramble the egg right at the end and mix everything together with some veggies and the sliced meat.

Ingredients:

- ☐ 3 cups + 2 tablespoons water
- ☐ 2 cups long-grain white rice
- ☐ 8-ounces sliced pork loin chop (½-inch pieces)
- ☐ ½ cup frozen peas
- ☐ 1 big egg
- ☐ 1 peeled and chopped carrot
- ☐ 1 chopped onion
- ☐ 3 tablespoons vegetable oil
- ☐ 3 tablespoons soy sauce
- ☐ Salt and pepper to taste

Directions:

1. Turn your cooker to "Chicken/Meat" and heat oil.
2. Sauté the carrot and onion for 2 minutes.
3. Season pork with salt and pepper, and add to cooker.
4. Cook until the meat is cooked through, which should take about 5 minutes.
5. Hit "cancel" and remove meat, onion, and carrot.
6. Pour water into the cooker and scrape up any stuck-on bits.
7. Add rice, salt, and pepper and secure the cooker lid.
8. Hit "Rice/Risotto" and cook for the default time of 6 minutes.
9. When the timer beeps, hit "cancel" and wait 10 minutes before quick-releasing any leftover pressure.
10. With a spoon, carve a hole in the rice to expose the cooker bottom.
11. Pour in a little oil and crack in an egg, whisking it to scramble.
12. When the egg is cooked, add onion, carrot, pork, and peas.

13. Stir until everything is mixed and the peas have warmed through.

14. Serve!

Nutritional Info (¼ recipe per serving):

Calories: 547
Protein: 22
Fat: 2
Carbs: 81
Fiber: 3

Pork Loin with Apples and Red Onion

<u>Serves:</u> 6-8

<u>Time:</u> 56 minutes (15 minutes prep time, 36 minutes cook time, 5 minutes rest time)

Tart green apples, juicy pork, and bright, acidic red onions cook together with sweet white wine and chicken broth for a layered, rustic meal that would be perfect for a dinner party. Serve with a nice bottle of wine!

Ingredients:

- One 3-pound boneless pork loin roast
- 2 medium-sized Granny Smith apples
- 1 big halved and sliced red onion
- 4 thyme sprigs
- 2 bay leaves
- ½ cup sweet white wine
- ¼ cup chicken broth
- 2 tablespoons butter
- ½ teaspoon salt
- ½ teaspoon black pepper

Directions:

1. Add butter to the cooker and turn to "Chicken/Meat" to melt.
2. Lay down pork and brown for 4 minutes per side.
3. Plate browned meat.
4. Add onion to cooker and stir for 3 minutes.
5. Toss in bay leaves, thyme, and apples.
6. Deglaze the pot (scraping up burnt-on food bits) with the wine.
7. Next, pour in broth and sprinkle in salt and pepper.
8. Put the pork back in the cooker and seal the lid.
9. Hit "cancel" before selecting "Chicken/Meat" again and adjusting time to 36 minutes.
10. When time is up, turn off the cooker and quick-release.
11. Remove the bay leaf and pork.
12. Let the pork rest for 5 minutes before slicing.
13. Spoon sauce on top of meat to serve.

Nutritional Info (⅙ of recipe per serving):

Total calories: 621
Protein: 62
Carbs: 6
Fat: 36
Fiber: 1.3

Pomegranate-Pineapple Pork Shoulder

<u>Serves:</u> 15

<u>Time:</u> 49 minutes (5 minutes prep time, 24 minutes cook time, 20 minutes natural pressure release)

This versatile pork recipe can be eaten with rice, tacos, or just with the relish, which has pineapple chunks and pomegranate. The pork is juicy, sweet, and spicy with three kinds of chili powder and cumin.

Ingredients:

Pork
- ☐ 3 pounds boneless pork shoulder, cut into 1-inch cubes
- ☐ 12 smashed garlic cloves
- ☐ 1 diced onion
- ☐ 2 cups chicken stock
- ☐ 1 cup pomegranate juice
- ☐ 1 cup pineapple juice
- ☐ 1 cup diced fresh pineapple
- ☐ 3 tablespoons ancho chile powder
- ☐ 2 tablespoons chile powder
- ☐ 2 tablespoons ground cumin
- ☐ 2 tablespoons salt
- ☐ 1 tablespoon arbol chile powder

Relish
- ☐ ¾ cup diced pineapple
- ☐ ¼ cup pomegranate seeds
- ☐ 2 tablespoons red onion
- ☐ Couple squirts of lime juice
- ☐ Salt and pepper

Directions:

1. Rub spices on the pork and put in your PPCXL.
2. Add onion, garlic, juices, 1 cup diced pineapple, and chicken stock.
3. Seal the lid.
4. Select "Chicken/Meat" and adjust time to 24 minutes.

5. While that cooks, prepare the relish by mixing and seasoning.
6. When time is up, hit "cancel" and quick-release the pressure.
7. Remove pork with a slotted spoon and tent with foil in a bowl.
8. Turn the cooker back to "Chicken/Meat" and reduce the sauce for 15-20 minutes until thickened.
9. Serve pork with the sauce and relish, with a side like Mexican rice.

Nutritional Info (1/15 of recipe):

Total calories: 282
Protein: 23
Carbs: 7
Fat: 17
Fiber: 0

Blackberry-BBQ Pork Roast

<u>Serves:</u> 8

<u>Time:</u> Overnight + 2 hours, 8 minutes (Overnight marinate time, 10 minutes prep time, 1 hour 18 minutes cook time, 40 minutes natural pressure release)

Pork goes well with just about any kind of fruit. The fruit of choice in this recipe is blackberry, which adds just a bit of sweetness along with the brown sugar and molasses. To add heat, there's chili powder, cayenne, and Dijon. This incredibly tender, spicy-sweet BBQ is ideal for parties.

<u>Ingredients:</u>

Pork

- ☐ 2 cups water
- ☐ 3 pounds of boneless rolled pork roast
- ☐ 1 sliced onion
- ☐ ⅛ cup brown sugar
- ☐ 2 tablespoons chili powder
- ☐ 2 teaspoons garlic powder
- ☐ 1 teaspoon cayenne pepper

BBQ sauce

- ☐ 4-ounces fresh blackberries
- ☐ ½ cup ketchup
- ☐ ¼ cup blackberry jam
- ☐ 1 tablespoon olive oil
- ☐ 1 tablespoon Dijon mustard
- ☐ 1 teaspoon molasses
- ☐ 1 teaspoon lemon juice
- ☐ ¼ teaspoon onion powder
- ☐ Pinch of red pepper flakes

<u>Directions:</u>

1. To marinate the pork overnight, mix meat with ingredients in the "BBQ sauce" list and store in fridge.
2. When you're ready to prepare pork, put meat in a hot Power Pressure Cooker XL and save marinade.

3. On the "Chicken/Meat" setting, brown pork evenly before plating.
4. Pour water into the cooker with half of the onion.
5. Lower in cooking rack with the pork and pile the other half of the onion on top.
6. Seal the lid and adjust cooking time to 1 hour, 18 minutes.
7. When the timer beeps, hit "cancel" and wait for a natural pressure release.
8. While the pressure goes down, take the marinade and bring to a boil in a saucepan.
9. Reduce heat and simmer until thick and syrupy.
10. Serve pork with onions and BBQ sauce.

Nutritional Info (⅛ recipe)

Total calories: 617
Protein: 51
Carbs: 60
Fat: 19.7
Fiber: .7

Easy Crispy Pork Belly

Serves: 4

Time: 1 hour, 18 minutes (10 minutes prep time, 48 minutes cook time, 20 minutes natural pressure release)

Pork belly is like bacon, but *more*. It's deliciously fatty and crispy in all the right ways in this recipe. With a simple seasoning of garlic, salt, and pepper, it's meant to be served with a salad, with rice, in a taco, or any other way you like. It's a great first introduction to this particular cut of meat.

Ingredients:

- ☐ 1 pound pork belly
- ☐ ½-1 cup white wine
- ☐ 1 whole garlic clove
- ☐ Salt and black pepper to taste
- ☐ Enough olive oil to coat the bottom

Directions:

1. Turn your PPCXL to the "Chicken/Meat" setting and heat oil.
2. Sear the pork for 2-3 minutes on each side, crisping up the belly.
3. Add about a quarter-inch of wine.
4. Sprinkle salt and pepper over the pork, and add whole garlic clove.
5. Let the liquid come to a boil before sealing the lid.
6. Adjust cooking time to 48 minutes.
7. When the timer beeps, turn off the cooker and wait for a natural pressure release.
8. Open the cooker and remove the pork.
9. Cool until room temperature, and then slice.

Nutritional Info (¼ recipe per serving):

Calories: 610
Protein: 31
Carbs: 0
Fat: 61
Fiber: 0

Asian-Style Pork Chops and Broccoli

<u>Serves</u>: 4
<u>Time</u>: 30 minutes (10 minutes prep time, 12 minutes cook time, 8 minutes heat time)

These one-pot pork chops are easy and fast at only a half hour. The recipe uses Asian-inspired flavors like soy sauce, toasted sesame oil, and rice vinegar. At the very end, you use the cooker's heat to warm up frozen broccoli, so you get a whole meal.

Ingredients:

- Four ½-inch thick pork chops
- 6 medium scallions
- 4 cups frozen broccoli
- ½ cup chicken broth
- ¼ cup soy sauce
- 2 tablespoons brown sugar
- 1 ½ tablespoons toasted sesame oil
- 1 tablespoon rice vinegar
- 1 teaspoon minced garlic

Directions:

1. Turn your PPCXL to "Chicken/Meat" and add oil.
2. When hot, brown pork chops to a golden color.
3. Add onion and garlic, and cook for one minute.
4. Pour in broth, vinegar, soy sauce, and brown sugar.
5. Mix until the sugar is dissolved.
6. Close and seal the lid.
7. Adjust cooking time to 12 minutes.
8. When time is up, hit "cancel" and quick-release the pressure.
9. Add frozen broccoli and close the lid, but don't bring back to pressure.
10. After 8-10 minutes, the broccoli should be tender, and you're ready to eat!

Nutritional Info (¼ recipe)

Total calories: 199
Protein: 17
Carbs: 9

Fat: 11
Fiber: 2.4

Seasoned Pork Chops with Apricot Sauce

<u>Serves:</u> 4-6

<u>Time:</u> 44 minutes (15 minutes prep time, 29 minutes cook time)

The highlight of this pork recipe is the fantastic spice rub made from ground cinnamon, ginger, coriander, and cardamom. You sear the pork so the rub doesn't burn, and then cook it with sweet pearl onions, white wine, and apricot jam, which create a plate-licking sauce.

Ingredients:

- Two bone-in and trimmed 1 ¼-2 inch thick pork loin chops
- 1 cup pearl onions
- ½ cup apricot jam
- ¼ cup white wine
- 2 tablespoons olive oil
- 1 tablespoon butter
- ½ teaspoon ground cinnamon
- ¼ teaspoon ground ginger
- ¼ teaspoon ground coriander
- ¼ teaspoon ground cardamom
- ¼ teaspoon salt

Directions:

1. Coat both sides of the pork chops in oil and then rub on the dry spices.
2. Turn your cooker to "Chicken/Meat" and melt butter.
3. Brown chops on both sides until light golden.
4. Plate before adding onions to the cooker.
5. Stir for 4 minutes until brown.
6. Add wine and jam to cooker, and scrape up any stuck on bits.
7. When the jam has fully dissolved, return the chops and coat in sauce.
8. Seal the lid.
9. Adjust time to 29 minutes and cook.
10. When time is up, hit "cancel" and quick-release.
11. Serve chops with sauce!

Nutritional Info (¼ recipe per serving):

Calories: 425
Protein: 47
Carbs: 22
Fat: 19
Fiber: 1

Classic Baby Back Ribs

<u>Serves:</u> 4-8

<u>Time:</u> 38 minutes (18 minutes cook time, 15 minutes natural pressure release, 4-5 minutes broil time)

You'll notice this recipe doesn't have set ingredient amounts. This is an eyeball recipe, but don't worry, we'll walk you through what to do. It just involves "steaming" the ribs with water, a little apple cider vinegar, and salt for 18 minutes. Slather on some BBQ sauce afterwards and broil. That's it!

Ingredients:

- ☐ 1-2 slabs of baby back ribs
- ☐ Enough water to cover ribs
- ☐ Splash of apple cider vinegar
- ☐ Your favorite BBQ sauce
- ☐ Dash of salt

Directions:

1. Stack ribs in the steamer basket.
2. Pour in 1 inch of water and a splash of vinegar into your cooker, making sure it has the minimum required amount of liquid.
3. Lower basket into cooker and sprinkle in salt.
4. Seal the lid.
5. Hit "Chicken/Meat" and adjust time to 18 minutes.
6. When time is up, hit "cancel" and wait 15 minutes.
7. Quick-release the remaining pressure.
8. Lay ribs on parchment-lined baking sheet and cover with BBQ sauce.
9. Broil for 4-5 minutes and serve!

Nutritional Info (¼ recipe)

Total calories: 540
Protein: 38
Carbs: 0
Fat: 44
Fiber: 0

Hawaiian-Style Shredded Pork

<u>Serves</u>: 8
<u>Time</u>: 1 hour, 48 minutes

This simple pork recipe uses one key ingredient that makes it Hawaiian-style: the salt. Red coarse salt is the traditional seasoning for Kalua pig, and is one of the healthiest salts you can get. It has lots of minerals, isn't processed, and gives the meat a pure, clean flavor complimented by garlic and onion. Serve the pork on sandwiches or salads.

Ingredients:

- ☐ 5 pounds bone-in pork roast
- ☐ 6 minced garlic cloves
- ☐ 1 quartered onion
- ☐ 1 cup water
- ☐ 1 ½ tablespoons red Hawaiian coarse salt
- ☐ Black pepper to taste

Directions:

1. Cut the pork into three equal pieces and put them in your cooker.
2. Add garlic, onion, salt, and black pepper.
3. Pour in the water on the side, so you don't wash the spices off.
4. Close and seal the lid.
5. Hit "Chicken/Meat" and adjust time to 108 minutes, or, 1 hour 48 minutes.
6. When time is up, hit "Cancel" and wait for a natural pressure release.
7. Shred the pork before serving.

Nutritional Info (⅛ recipe per serving):
Total calories: 536
Protein: 51
Carbs: 2
Fat: 13
Fiber: 0

Garlic-Orange Shredded Pork

<u>Serves:</u> 8

<u>Time:</u> 3 hours, 6 minutes (2 hours marinate time, 10 minutes prep time, 36 minutes cook time, 15 minutes natural pressure release, 5 minutes broil time)

Bright with orange and garlic, this shredded pork is perfect for tacos. Other spices include cumin and ground chipotle chili pepper, so if you like heat with your tacos,

You aren't missing out. The meat should marinate for at least 2 hours to get the full flavor, so be sure to plan accordingly.

Ingredients:

Beef

- ☐ 4 pounds boneless cubed pork shoulder roast
- ☐ 3 tablespoons olive oil
- ☐ 2 teaspoons salt
- ☐ 1 ½ teaspoons ground cumin
- ☐ 1 teaspoon ground chipotle chili pepper
- ☐ 1 teaspoon black pepper

Other

- ☐ 2 cups fresh orange juice
- ☐ ¾ cup fresh lime juice
- ☐ 2 quartered onions
- ☐ 5 minced garlic cloves
- ☐ 2 cinnamon sticks
- ☐ 2 teaspoons dried oregano

Directions:

1. Mix all the "beef" ingredients together in a bag and store in the fridge for 2 hours.
2. When you're ready to make the recipe, turn your cooker to "Chicken/Meat."
3. Brown the meat until golden.
4. Add the rest of the ingredients and cook until the onions soften.
5. Seal the lid.
6. Adjust cooking time to 36 minutes.
7. When the timer beeps, hit "cancel" and let the pressure decrease naturally.
8. To crisp up the pork, put on a cookie sheet prepared with parchment paper and broil

for 5 minutes.

9. Shred before stirring pork back into the cooking liquid.

10. Serve!

Nutritional Info (⅛ recipe per serving)

Total calories: 506

Protein: 40

Carbs: 10

Fat: 33

Fiber: 0

Honey-Soy Pork Belly

Serves: 6

Time: 55 minutes (15 minutes prep time, 30 minutes cook time, 10 minutes broil time)

Honey and soy are a great flavor combination. Soy is salty and savory, and honey is sweeter than sugar. Add in the delicious crispiness of pork belly, and you have a pork dish unlike anything you've tasted before. Cook the pork first in the pressure cooker, while the sauce simmers, and then slather it on the meat before broiling.

Ingredients:

Pork

- ☐ 2 pounds cubed fatty pork belly
- ☐ ⅓ cup water
- ☐ 3 tablespoons sherry
- ☐ 2 tablespoons soy sauce
- ☐ 4 tablespoons honey
- ☐ 1-inch piece of peeled and smashed ginger
- ☐ 1 teaspoon sea salt

Sauce

- ☐ ¼ cup soy sauce
- ☐ ¼ cup hoisin sauce
- ☐ 2 tablespoons mirin
- ☐ 2-4 teaspoons sriracha
- ☐ 2 teaspoons sesame oil

Directions:

1. Pour ⅓ cup water into cooker and bring to a boil on the "chicken/meat" setting.
2. When the water is boiling, submerge pork cubes and cook for 3 minutes.
3. Immediately drain pork and rinse under cool water.
4. Leave in a colander while you mix the cooking liquid.
5. Mix sherry, soy sauce, and honey in the PPCXL and turn on "chicken/meat" again.
6. When hot, add pork cubes and coat.
7. Cook for 10 minutes to brown the pork.
8. Add in ginger and salt, and bring to a boil.
9. Seal the lid and adjust cook time t0 30 minutes.
10. While that cooks, mix sauce ingredients in a pan on the stove, and bring to a simmer.

11. When the pressure cooker timer goes off, remove pork and spread on a foil-lined baking sheet.
12. Turn your oven's broiler on.
13. Brush on sauce on both sides of the pork cubes and stick in the oven for 5 minutes.
14. Flip, brush with more sauce, and cook for another 5 minutes.
15. The pork should be crispy and delicious!

Nutritional Info (⅙ recipe per serving):

Total calories: 880
Protein: 16
Carbs: 19
Fat: 82
Fiber: 0

Smothered Pork Chops

<u>Serves:</u> 4
<u>Time:</u> 30 minutes (15 minutes prep time, 15 minutes cook time)

Comfort food can make the worst day better, and this half-hour pork chop recipe is the ticket. It's cooked in a sauce made from milk, white wine, garlic, and julienned onions. After browning the meat, they only take 15 minutes in the cooker, and everyone gets their own chop!

<u>Ingredients:</u>

- ☐ 4 bone-in pork chops
- ☐ 1 pound julienned onions
- ☐ 1 minced garlic clove
- ☐ ½ cup milk
- ☐ ½ cup white wine
- ☐ 3 tablespoons chopped parsley
- ☐ 3 tablespoons water
- ☐ 2 tablespoons lime juice
- ☐ 2 tablespoons butter
- ☐ 2 tablespoons cornstarch
- ☐ 2 tablespoons olive oil
- ☐ 1 tablespoon flour
- ☐ 1 tablespoon salt
- ☐ ½ tablespoon black pepper

<u>Directions:</u>

1. Put oil in the cooker and heat on the "Chicken/Meat" setting.
2. Season meat with salt and pepper.
3. Brown pork chops on each side and then plate.
4. Add onions and garlic to the pot and cook until the onions are clear.
5. Pour in wine and lime juice.
6. Mix water and cornstarch, and then stir the slurry into the pot.
7. Pour in milk and stir until thickened and smooth.
8. Return the pork chops to the pot.
9. Seal the lid.
10. Cook for 15 minutes.

11. When time is up, hit "cancel" and quick-release.

12. Serve chops with onion sauce on top.

Nutritional Info (¼ recipe per serving):

Total calories: 334
Protein: 26
Carbs: 14
Fat: 18
Fiber: 2

Hasselback Pork with Apples and Prosciutto

<u>Serves:</u> 6-8

<u>Time:</u> 48 minutes (15 minutes prep time, 18 minutes cook time, 15 minutes natural pressure release)

An impressive-looking roast that's easy to put together, this Hasselback-style pork is tender with sweet and salty flavors from sliced apples and prosciutto slices. Fresh sage also adds a lot, especially when you cook it in oil to get it crispy. To keep the pork cuts from flying open in the cooker, you will need skewers and kitchen string, which you can find at any home goods or grocery store.

<u>Ingredients:</u>

- ☐ 2.5-pound pork loin roast
- ☐ 12 slices of prosciutto
- ☐ 1 large cored and sliced apple
- ☐ ¾ cup white wine
- ☐ ¼ cup water
- ☐ 1 tablespoon of olive oil
- ☐ 1 small bunch of fresh sage

<u>Directions:</u>

1. Put the roast on a cutting board, fat-side down.
2. Cut ¾ of the way down through the roast every ½-inch, so there are slits in the pork, but it's still connected at the bottom.
3. Stuff a slice of prosciutto and round slice of apple into each cut.
4. Stick skewers through the roast horizontally, so everything is held in place.
5. For extra security, tie a piece of string around the roast.
6. Turn your cooker to "Chicken/Meat" and heat the olive oil with sage leaves.
7. When the oil is hot, brown the roast on both sides.
8. Hit "cancel" and pour in the water and wine.
9. Seal the lid.
10. Select "Chicken/Meat" again and adjust to 18 minutes.
11. When time is up, hit "cancel" and wait for a natural pressure release.
12. Serve the roast in slices, so everyone gets meat, apple, and prosciutto. Pour the cooking liquid on top as the sauce.

Nutritional Info (1 ½ slices per serving):

Total calories: 432.8
Protein: 51.1
Carbs: 3.4
Fat: 21
Fiber: 0

Yucatan Pork with Salsa

<u>Serves:</u> 6

<u>Time:</u> 1 hour, 39 minutes (15 minutes prep time, 54 minutes cook time, 30 minutes natural pressure release)

Yucatan pork is usually prepared in a fire pit, but for practicality, a pressure cooker is faster and easier. Fire-roasted tomatoes and orange juice bring some acidic sweetness. To get a roasty, smoky flavor, we use achiote paste, which is made from annatto seeds. It can be found just about anywhere.

Ingredients:

- 3 pounds pork shoulder roast cut into 1 ½-inch strips
- 15-ounces fire-roasted diced tomatoes
- 1 peeled and sliced onion
- ½ cup water
- ¼ cup of fresh-squeezed orange juice
- ¼ cup apple cider vinegar
- ½ of a 3.5-ounce package of achiote paste
- 2 teaspoons salt
- 1 teaspoon vegetable oil

Directions:

1. Heat oil in a skillet on the stovetop and add onion with a pinch of salt.
2. Once beginning to soften, add tomatoes and bring to a boil.
3. Reduce the heat and simmer.
4. In a separate bowl, mix apple cider vinegar, orange juice, achiote paste, and 2 teaspoons of your onion/tomato mixture.
5. Next, return 1 tablespoon of this whole mixture to the skillet and mix.
6. Season pork with salt, and toss with the rest of the achiote marinade from the bowl.
7. Pour water into your PPCXL and lower in a steamer basket.
8. Put pork strips in the basket and top with all of the skillet salsa.
9. Seal the lid.
10. Select "Chicken/Meat" and cook for 54 minutes.
11. When time is up, hit "cancel" wait for a natural pressure release.
12. Serve pork with cooked salsa.

Nutritional Info (½ pound of meat per serving):

Total calories: 662
Protein: 54
Carbs: 10
Fat: 41
Fiber: 0

Chapter 9

Seafood

Salmon Steaks Moutarde

<u>Serves:</u> 4

<u>Time:</u> 21 minutes (10 minutes prep time, 6 minutes cook time, 5 minutes simmer time)

This French dish gets its name from the Dijon mustard, which cooks on the salmon and is also in the sauce. That bright, spicy flavor is married with onion, thyme, white wine, and a bay leaf.

<u>Ingredients:</u>

- ☐ Four 1-inch thick salmon steaks
- ☐ Four sprigs of thyme
- ☐ 4 tablespoons Dijon mustard + 2 tablespoons
- ☐ 1 cup dry white wine
- ☐ 1 chopped small onion
- ☐ 1 bay leaf
- ☐ 1 tablespoon olive oil
- ☐ 1 tablespoon cornstarch

<u>Directions:</u>

1. Turn your PPCXL to "Chicken/Meat" and add oil.
2. When hot, add garlic and onion.
3. When the onion has softened, turn off the cooker.
4. Apply 1 tablespoon of mustard to each piece of salmon and lay on thyme sprig.
5. Put the salmon in a steamer basket and lower into the cooker.
6. Pour 1 cup of wine into the cooker with a bay leaf before sealing the lid.
7. Hit "Chicken/Meat" again and adjust time to 6 minutes.
8. When time is up, hit "cancel" and quick-release the pressure.
9. Remove the steaks and pick out the bay leaf.
10. In a bowl, mix 2 tablespoons of mustard with cornstarch.
11. Put in the cooker and hit "Chicken/Meat" again to simmer the sauce.
12. When the sauce has thickened a bit, serve with the steaks!

Nutritional Info (1 steak w/ sauce per serving):

Total calories: 492
Protein: 64
Carbs: 4
Fat: 16
Fiber: 0

Poached Salmon with Seasoned Sour Cream

Serves: 6

Time: 13 minutes (4 minutes prep time, 1 minute cook time, 8 minutes natural pressure release)

Poaching salmon is one of the fastest ways to cook; in a pressure cooker, it just takes *one minute* with a natural pressure release. The real star of the dish is the seasoned sour cream, which has fresh cucumber, dill, lemon juice, and white wine vinegar. It's a high protein, low-calorie meal that's big on taste.

Ingredients:

- ☐ 6 cups vegetable broth
- ☐ 1 ½ pounds skin-on salmon fillet
- ☐ 1 cup fat-free sour cream
- ☐ ¼ cup white wine vinegar
- ☐ 1 peeled and diced cucumber
- ☐ 2 tablespoons chopped, fresh dill
- ☐ 1 tablespoon + ½ teaspoon salt
- ☐ 2 teaspoons lemon juice

Directions:

1. Pour vinegar, broth, and 1 tablespoon of salt into your PPCXL.
2. Turn your cooker to "Chicken/Meat" and bring the liquid to a boil, stirring so the salt dissolves.
3. Add salmon, skin-side down.
4. Seal the lid.
5. Adjust the time to just 1 minute.
6. When time is up, hit "cancel" and wait 8 minutes.
7. Quick-release any pressure that's left.
8. In a separate bowl, toss sugar, salt, and cucumber.
9. Take out the fillets and put them on top of paper towels.
10. Cut into wedges.
11. Mix cucumbers with sour cream, along with the lemon juice and dill.
12. Serve salmon with seasoned sour cream!

Nutritional Info (¼ pound of salmon w/ sour cream per serving):

Total calories: 153
Protein: 25
Carbs: 10
Fat: 2
Fiber: 0

Baked Spicy-Lemon Fish

<u>Serves:</u> 2

<u>Time:</u> 26 minutes (15 minutes prep time, 11 minutes cook time)

Lemon loves fish, especially white fish like this dish's cod fillets. Lemon slices sit right on top of the fish and get wrapped in foil along with cooked onion, garlic, brown sugar, and seasonings. It's like a beautifully-fragrant, spicy, sweet present.

Ingredients:

- [ ] Two 6-ounce cod fish fillets
- [ ] 4 chopped garlic cloves
- [ ] 2 cups water
- [ ] 1 cup diced yellow onion
- [ ] 1 thinly-sliced lemon
- [ ] 2 tablespoons peanut oil
- [ ] 1 tablespoon light brown sugar
- [ ] Dash of turmeric
- [ ] Dash of black pepper
- [ ] Dash of red pepper flakes
- [ ] Dash of soy sauce

Directions:

1. Heat peanut oil in your PPCXL on the "Chicken/Meat" setting.
2. Add onion and cook until almost soft.
3. Add garlic, brown sugar, and dry spices, stirring so the sugar melts and mixes with the garlic and onion.
4. After 3 minutes, turn off the cooker.
5. Cut foil into two, 15-inch squares and fold in half.
6. Put fish fillets on pieces of foil, and evenly top with the onion mixture.
7. Lay lemon slices on the fish, so they're blanketed.
8. Fold the foil over the fish and seal the edges tightly.
9. Pour 2 cups of water into your cooker and lower in the steamer basket.
10. Put the fish packages in the basket and seal the lid.
11. Hit "Chicken/Meat" again and adjust time to 11 minutes.
12. When time is up, hit "cancel" and quick-release the pressure.
13. Serve hot!

Nutritional Info (1 packet per serving):

Total calories: 403
Protein: 53
Carbs: 13
Fat: 15
Fiber: 1

Smoked Trout Salad with Farro

<u>Serves:</u> 4

<u>Time:</u> 25 minutes (20 minutes cook time, 5 minutes dressing time)

What do you do with precooked smoked trout? Make a salad! With farro! Farro, especially semi-pearled farro, is one of the healthiest grains you can eat. It's probably the earliest cultivated grain, so it's health benefits have been evident for centuries. The salad dressing is made from a combo of sour cream and mayo, and seasoned with shaved fennel, lemon juice, sugar, black pepper, and Dijon mustard. It's a cold salad, so some time is needed to cool the farro.

<u>Ingredients:</u>

- ☐ 12-ounces skinned and chopped cooked smoked trout
- ☐ 1 big shaved fennel bulb
- ☐ 1 cup semi-pearled farro
- ☐ ½ cup low-fat mayonnaise
- ☐ ¼ cup low-fat sour cream
- ☐ 3 tablespoons fresh lemon juice
- ☐ 2 tablespoons Dijon mustard
- ☐ 1 teaspoon sugar
- ☐ 1 teaspoon ground black pepper

<u>Directions:</u>

1. Pour farro into pressure cooker with enough water to cover grain by 2 inches.
2. Seal the lid.
3. Select "Chicken/Meat" and adjust time to 20 minutes.
4. When time is up, hit "cancel" and quick-release.
5. Shave the fennel in a colander and pour over pot contents, so the farro can drain.
6. In the meanwhile, mix the salad dressing together.
7. Mix in fennel and farro, and add fish.
8. Serve!

<u>Nutritional Info (¼ recipe per serving):</u>

Total calories: 366
Protein: 27
Carbs: 43

Fat: 7
Fiber: 10

Gingery-Orange Sole

Serves: 4

Time: 17 minutes (10 minutes active time, 7 minutes cook time)

Sole is a tender white fish with a lovely, mild taste that's complimented by fresh orange and ginger. It's a perfect light supper or lunch, especially when you serve it with a side like rice pilaf, greens, or other steamed vegetables.

Ingredients:

- [ ] 4 sole fillets
- [ ] 3 spring onions
- [ ] 1 cup white wine
- [ ] Juice + zest of one orange
- [ ] Enough olive oil to coat fish
- [ ] Salt and pepper to taste
- [ ] Thumb-sized piece of chopped, grated ginger

Directions:

1. Dry fish with a paper towel before rubbing on olive oil.
2. Season with salt and pepper.
3. Pour white wine and orange juice into cooker, and then add orange zest, onions, and ginger.
4. Add fish to steamer basket and lower into pressure cooker.
5. Seal the lid.
6. Hit "Fish/Vegetable/Steam" and adjust time to 7 minutes.
7. When time is up, hit "cancel" and quick-release.
8. Serve!

Nutritional Info (¼ recipe per serving):

Total calories: 167
Protein: 16
Carbs: 8
Fat: 5
Fiber: 0

Creole-Style Cod

<u>Serves:</u> 4

<u>Time</u>: About 10 minutes (5 minute active time, 4 minutes cook time)

The secret to great fish is great seasoning, especially a white fish like cod, which is very mild on its own. This recipe goes Creole with flavors from garlic, bay leaves, green peppers, cayenne, and paprika. Like most fish recipes in the pressure cooker, this is very fast.

<u>Ingredients:</u>

- ☐ 2 pounds of cod fillet
- ☐ 28-ounces of chopped tomatoes
- ☐ 2 bay leaves
- ☐ 2 cups chopped onion
- ☐ 1 cup chopped celery
- ☐ ¼ cup olive oil
- ☐ ¼ cup white wine
- ☐ 2 minced garlic cloves
- ☐ 1 chopped green bell pepper
- ☐ 1 tablespoon paprika
- ☐ 1 teaspoon salt
- ☐ ½ teaspoon cayenne pepper

<u>Directions:</u>

1. Turn your PPCXL to "Chicken/Meat" and heat the oil.
2. Cook celery, garlic, onion, and green pepper until the veggies soften.
3. When the onion is clear, scoop out and plate.
4. Pour tomato juice from the can into the cooker, not the tomatoes yet, along with wine.
5. Lower in steamer basket.
6. Divide fish into four parts and add to basket.
7. Close and seal the lid.
8. Adjust cook time to 4 minutes.
9. When the timer beeps, turn off cooker and quick-release.
10. Pour in tomatoes, veggies from earlier, bay leaves, and seasonings.
11. Seal the lid again and cook for just 1 minute on "Chicken/Meat."
12. Serve fish with rice!

Nutritional Info (¼ recipe per serving)

Total calories: 247
Protein: 14
Carbs: 14
Fat: 20
Fiber: 1

Cod with Pineapple Salsa

<u>Serves:</u> 2

<u>Time:</u> 42 minutes (30 minutes prep/marinade time, 12 minutes cook time)

Enjoy a taste of the tropics with this white fish served with a pineapple and jalapeno salsa. To flavor the fish, it has to marinate for 30 minutes in creamy coconut milk, curry paste, ginger, garlic, and fish sauce.

Ingredients:

Marinade

- ☐ Two ½-pound frozen cod fillets
- ☐ 1 cup coconut milk
- ☐ 1 tablespoon fresh minced ginger
- ☐ 1 tablespoon Thai green curry paste
- ☐ 1 tablespoon fish sauce
- ☐ 2 teaspoons brown sugar
- ☐ 1 teaspoon minced garlic
- ☐ Zest of one lime
- ☐ Juice of ½ lime

Salsa

- ☐ ¾ cup of diced pineapple
- ☐ 1 chopped scallion
- ☐ 1 minced jalapeno chile
- ☐ Juice of 1 lime

Directions:

1. Mix marinade and fish together and store in fridge for 30 minutes. You are going to be saving the marinade, so do not throw it out.
2. While that sits, make the salsa.
3. Prepare PPCXL with 2 cups of water and lower in the steamer basket.
4. Before putting in the basket, wrap the fish with lime slices tightly in foil.
5. Seal the lid.
6. Hit "Chicken/Meat" and adjust time to 12 minutes.
7. While that cooks, heat up the marinade in a saucepan until it's boiling, and then reduce to a simmer.

8. When the cooker timer goes off, turn off the cooker and quick-release the pressure.

9. Serve fish with salsa, scallions, and a spoonful of sauce.

Nutritional Info (½ recipe per serving)

Total calories: 329
Protein: 11
Carbs: 24
Fat: 26
Fiber: 1.5

Creamy Tomato Haddock with Potatoes, Carrots, + Kale

<u>Serves</u>: 2

<u>Time</u>: 27 minutes (10 minutes prep time, 7 minutes cook time, 10 minutes simmer time)

With potatoes, carrots, kale, and a creamy tomato broth, this dish is almost like stew. The fish of choice is haddock, which should be wild if possible, because that's where all the nutrition and good flavor will be. The whole recipe takes less than a half hour, so it would be a great meal for a date night after seeing a movie.

Ingredients:

- ☐ 1 pound frozen wild haddock fillets
- ☐ 2 cups whole and peeled tomatoes with their juice
- ☐ 2 cups chicken broth
- ☐ 2 cups kale
- ☐ ½ cup heavy cream
- ☐ 1 peeled and chopped carrot
- ☐ 1 peeled and cubed potato
- ☐ 1 chopped onion
- ☐ 1 minced garlic clove
- ☐ 2 tablespoons chopped parsley
- ☐ 2 tablespoons butter
- ☐ 1 tablespoon chopped basil
- ☐ 2 teaspoons salt
- ☐ 1 pinch of crushed red pepper flakes
- ☐ Black pepper to taste

Directions:

1. Turn your cooker to the "Chicken/Meat" setting and add butter.
2. When melted, cook garlic and onion for just 3 minutes.
3. Pour in the chicken broth, tomatoes with their juice, carrots, potatoes, and basil.
4. Once the liquid is simmering, lower in the steamer basket with the fish.
5. Season the fish with crushed red pepper, black pepper, and salt.
6. Seal the lid.
7. Adjust cook time to 7 minutes.

8. When the timer beeps, turn off the cooker and quick-release.
9. Remove the steamer basket before pureeing the broth with a hand blender.
10. Stir in kale, cream, and the fish.
11. Let the residual heat of the broth warm everything for 5-10 minutes.
12. Serve!

Nutritional Info (½ recipe per serving):

Total calories: 550
Protein: 44
Carbs: 15
Fat: 24
Fiber: 1

Cod with Peas and Sliced Almonds

<u>Serves:</u> 4

<u>Time:</u> 9 minutes (5 minutes prep time, 4 minutes cook time)

Incredibly fast and easy, this fragrant dinner makes enough for four people. The fish cooks in the steamer basket above a broth made from chicken stock, garlic, oregano, parsley, paprika, and almonds. You add the peas at the very end and then garnish the fish with toasted almonds.

Ingredients:

- ☐ 1 pound frozen + thawed cod fish fillet
- ☐ 10-ounces frozen peas
- ☐ 1 cup chicken broth
- ☐ ½ cup packed parsley
- ☐ 2 halved garlic cloves
- ☐ 2 tablespoons sliced almonds
- ☐ 2 tablespoons fresh oregano
- ☐ 1 tablespoon olive oil
- ☐ ½ teaspoon paprika

Directions:

1. Blend garlic, herbs, paprika, and 1 tablespoon of almonds in a food processor.
2. Set aside for now.
3. Turn your pressure cooker to "Chicken/Meat" and heat up the olive oil.
4. Stir in almonds and toast until they begin to turn golden.
5. Remove and place on a paper towel.
6. Add broth and pulsed herb mixture into the cooker.
7. Cut fish into 4 pieces and put in the steamer basket before lowering it into the cooker.
8. Seal the lid.
9. Adjust cook time to 3 minutes.
10. When time is up, hit "cancel" and quick-release.
11. The fish should be an opaque color, and not clear anywhere.
12. Stir in the peas and close the lid, but don't bring to pressure.
13. After a minute or so, check their tenderness.
14. Serve with toasted almonds on top!

Nutritional Info (¼ recipe)

Total calories: 210
Protein: 26
Carbs: 11.7
Fat: 6.3
Fiber: 3.9

Halibut with a Dijon-Mustard Sauce

<u>Serves:</u> 4

<u>Time:</u> 15 minutes (10 minutes prep time, 5 minutes cook time)

Fish loves Dijon mustard, and halibut is no exception. Halibut is a white fish, but is denser than some of its siblings, with a steak-like bite to it. In addition to the mustard, you've got bright and fresh flavors from white wine, garlic, a bay leaf, and thyme.

<u>Ingredients:</u>

Fish

- ☐ Four 1-inch thick halibut fillets
- ☐ 1 bay leaf
- ☐ 1 chopped onion
- ☐ 1 cup dry white wine
- ☐ 1 minced garlic clove
- ☐ 4 tablespoons Dijon mustard
- ☐ ½ teaspoon dried thyme

Sauce

- ☐ 2 tablespoons Dijon mustard
- ☐ 1 tablespoon cornstarch

<u>Directions:</u>

1. Season your fish with 1 tablespoon of mustard and thyme.
2. Turn your cooker to "Chicken/Meat" and pour in just enough oil to coat the bottom.
3. Add onion and garlic.
4. When softened, pour in wine and bay leaf.
5. Lower fish (in the steamer basket) into the cooker and seal the lid.
6. Adjust cook time to 5 minutes.
7. When the timer beeps, turn off the cooker and quick-release the pressure.
8. Remove the bay leaf and fish.
9. In a bowl, mix the mustard with cornstarch.
10. Stir into the cooking liquid and turn back to "Chicken/Meat."
11. Simmer until the sauce boils and thickens.
12. Serve!

Nutritional Info (¼ recipe)

Total calories: 178
Protein: 21
Carbs: 4
Fat: 2
Fiber: 0

Seafood Gumbo

<u>Serves:</u> 6-8

<u>Time:</u> 33 minutes (15 minutes prep time, 13 minutes cook time, 5 minutes thickening time)

Gumbo is known for having a ton of ingredients, so we've tried to keep this recipe relatively simple. It uses oysters, shrimp, crab, and sausages. For veggies, there's celery, bell peppers, onion, and green onion. You cook the veggies first, and then the sausage goes under pressure for just 12 minutes. The seafood gets added last, and is under pressure for only 1 minute.

<u>Ingredients:</u>

- ☐ 24 shucked oysters
- ☐ 1 pound peeled and cleaned shrimp
- ☐ 1 pound crab meat
- ☐ 6 cups fish stock
- ☐ 2 chopped smoked sausages
- ☐ 3 chopped celery stalks
- ☐ 2 chopped red bell peppers
- ☐ 1 chopped onion
- ☐ ½ cup vegetable oil
- ☐ ½ cup chopped green onions
- ☐ ½ cup flour
- ☐ ¼ cup chopped parsley
- ☐ 2 tablespoons minced garlic cloves
- ☐ 2 tablespoons dried thyme
- ☐ Salt and pepper to taste

<u>Directions:</u>

1. Turn your PPCXL to "Chicken/Meat" and add 2 tablespoons of oil.
2. When hot, brown the celery, onions, garlic, and red pepper.
3. Pour in the fish stock along with black pepper, thyme, and sausages.
4. Close and seal the lid.
5. Adjust cook time to 12 minutes.
6. When time is up, hit "cancel" and quick-release.

7. To make your roux, which is the thickening agent, heat the rest of your olive oil in a skillet.
8. Stir in the flour until it becomes golden and nutty.
9. Mix roux in a bowl with a splash of fish stock and then pour into the pressure cooker.
10. Stir until it begins to thicken.
11. Add oysters, crab, and shrimp.
12. Seal the lid again and cook for the lowest pressure time, which is 2 minutes.
13. When time is up, quick-release again.
14. Serve gumbo with green onions and parsley.

Nutritional Info (⅙ recipe per serving):

Total calories: 135
Protein: 13
Carbs: 5
Fat: 7
Fiber: 0

Steamed Crab Legs with Garlic Brown Butter

<u>Serves:</u> 4

<u>Time:</u> About 11 minutes (5 minutes cook time, 6 minutes brown butter time)

Brown butter is magical, and if you've never had it with seafood, you'll never want regular butter again. Crab legs cook very quickly in a pressure cooker, about 5 minutes for frozen and 4 for fresh, and the dipping sauce is just butter, garlic, and lemon juice.

Ingredients:

Crab

- ☐ 2 pounds crab legs, fresh or frozen
- ☐ 1 cup water

Garlic brown butter

- ☐ 4 tablespoons salted butter
- ☐ 1 large minced garlic clove
- ☐ 1 halved lemon

Directions:

1. Pour water into your PPCXL and lower in the steamer basket with crab legs inside.
2. Seal the lid.
3. Hit "Chicken/Meat" and adjust time to 5 minutes, if you're using frozen legs. Select 4 minutes for fresh ones.
4. While that cooks, make your sauce.
5. Melt butter in a saucepan and keep cooking, stirring occasionally, until it becomes a richer golden color and begins to smell nutty.
6. Add garlic and stir until the garlic becomes fragrant.
7. Turn off the heat and add lemon juice.
8. When the pressure cooker timer beeps, hit "cancel" and quick-release the pressure.
9. Serve!

Nutritional Info (¼ recipe per serving):

Total calories: 346
Protein: 44
Carbs: 2
Fat: 7
Fiber: 0

White Fish with Beer and Potatoes

<u>Serves:</u> 6
<u>Time:</u> 48 minutes

This one-pot meal of white fish, potatoes, and a hearty beer-based sauce represents the best of the pressure cooker. You just throw everything into the cooker, seal the lid, and cook. It even has a quick-release.

Ingredients:

- ☐ 1 pound white fish
- ☐ 4 peeled and diced potatoes
- ☐ 1 sliced red pepper
- ☐ 1 cup beer
- ☐ 1 tablespoon olive oil
- ☐ 1 tablespoon oyster sauce
- ☐ 1 tablespoon sugar
- ☐ 1 teaspoon salt

Directions:

1. Put all the ingredients in your PPCXL and stir.
2. Close and seal the lid.
3. Hit "Chicken/Meat" and adjust time to 48 minutes.
4. When the timer beeps, quick-release the pressure.
5. Serve hot!

Nutritional Info (⅙ recipe per serving):
Total calories: 172
Protein: 16
Carbs: 22
Fat: 2
Fiber: 2

Halibut Stew with Turmeric

<u>Serves:</u> 8

<u>Time:</u> 17 minutes (5 minutes prep time, 12 minutes cook time)

This stew would be fairly dull if it wasn't for the turmeric. The slightly-bitter, citrusy flavor of the spice is perfect for the tender halibut, white potatoes, and earthiness that the bay leaf renders. Each bite is interesting, and your guests will wonder what makes this stew so addicting. If you haven't worked with turmeric before, err on the side of less is more, because the spice is strong.

Ingredients:

- ☐ 1 pound firm halibut divided into 8 pieces
- ☐ One 14.5-ounce can of chicken broth
- ☐ 4 quartered white potatoes
- ☐ 3 carrots cut into ½-inch chunks
- ☐ 1 finely-chopped onion
- ☐ ¼ cup dry white wine
- ☐ ¼ cup chopped parsley
- ☐ 2 minced garlic cloves
- ☐ 1 small red pepper
- ☐ 1 bay leaf
- ☐ Sprinkle of turmeric

Directions:

1. Pour wine, broth, potatoes, carrots, garlic, parsley, onion, and a sprinkle of turmeric in your PPCXL and seal the lid.
2. Select "Chicken/Meat" and cook for 6 minutes.
3. When time is up, hit "cancel" and quick-release.
4. Add red pepper and halibut before sealing the lid again.
5. Cook for another 6 minutes on the "Chicken/Meat" setting.
6. When the timer beeps, turn off the cooker and quick-release.
7. Pick out the bay leaf.
8. Season to taste with salt and pepper.

Nutritional Info (⅛ recipe per serving):

Total calories: 127
Protein: 10
Carbs: 20
Fat: 1
Fiber: 5

Chapter 10

Soups + Stews

Chicken-Avocado Soup

<u>Serves:</u> 4

<u>Time:</u> 31 minutes (5 minutes prep time, 21 minutes cook time, 5 minutes rest time)

This guacamole-inspired soup includes chicken, onion, and a jalapeno chile for heat. Savory and spicy, the cubed avocados at the very end add a burst of freshness, while the lime juice pops.

<u>Ingredients:</u>

- ☐ 6 cups chicken broth
- ☐ Two 1-pound bone-in chicken breasts w/ skin
- ☐ 2 halved, pitted, peeled, and diced avocados
- ☐ 1 chopped yellow onion
- ☐ ½ cup fresh lime juice
- ☐ 1 medium-sized stemmed and minced jalapeno chile
- ☐ 2 tablespoons minced garlic
- ☐ 1 tablespoon minced oregano
- ☐ 1 tablespoon olive oil
- ☐ 1 teaspoon salt
- ☐ 1 teaspoon black pepper

<u>Directions:</u>

1. Turn your PPCXL to "Chicken/Meat" and add oil.
2. While that heats up, season the chicken with salt and pepper.
3. When shimmering and hot, add chicken and brown on each side for 2 minutes.
4. Move browned chicken to a bowl.
5. Add onion to the cooker and cook until translucent.
6. Stir in garlic, jalapeno, and oregano for 1 minute.
7. Pour in broth and scrape up any stuck-on food bits.
8. Return the chicken to the pot and seal the lid.
9. Hit "cancel" and then "Chicken/Meat," adjusting time to 21 minutes.
10. When the timer beeps, hit "cancel" and quick-release the pressure.
11. Take out the chicken and let it rest for a few minutes on a plate.
12. Carefully pull off the skin.
13. Debone and chop meat into small pieces.
14. Stir into the pot with avocados and lime juice.

15. Serve right away!

Nutritional Info (¼ of recipe per serving):

Total calories: 290
Protein: 31.5
Carbs: 10.5
Fat: 13.7
Fiber: 4.1

Ground Beef Soup with Green Beans and Tomato

<u>Serves:</u> 6

<u>Time:</u> 46 minutes (10 minutes prep time, 36 minutes cook time)

With only a handful of ingredients, this hamburger soup comes together in under an hour. Green beans and tomato are a fantastic combination, and provide essential vitamins and minerals and garden-fresh flavor.

Ingredients:

- ☐ Two, 14.5-ounce cans of tomatoes with juice
- ☐ Two, 14-ounce cans of beef broth
- ☐ 1 pound lean ground beef
- ☐ ½ pound cut green beans
- ☐ 1 chopped onion
- ☐ 1 tablespoon minced garlic
- ☐ 1 teaspoon olive oil
- ☐ 1 teaspoon dried oregano
- ☐ 1 teaspoon dried thyme
- ☐ Salt and pepper to taste

Directions:

1. Turn your cooker to "Chicken/Meat" and heat the oil.
2. When the pot is hot, brown the beef.
3. Add in oregano, thyme, garlic, and onion.
4. Stir for 3 minutes and then add in tomatoes with the juice and broth.
5. Stir for a minute or so and then add green beans.
6. Seal the lid.
7. Hit cancel, and then "Chicken/Meat," adding time so you cook for 36 minutes.
8. When the timer beeps, hit "cancel" and quick-release the pressure.
9. Season with salt and pepper before serving.

Nutritional Info (⅙ recipe per serving):

Calories: 227

Protein: 17

Carbs: 10

Fat: 13

Fiber: 5

Easy Chicken Stew

<u>Serves</u>: 4

<u>Time</u>: 30 minutes

With only eight ingredients and zero prep time besides chopping, this is probably the quickest and easiest chicken stew you could make. Buttery Yukon Gold potatoes, juicy beefsteak tomatoes, and tender chicken breasts will satisfy your hunger and warm your soul.

<u>Ingredients:</u>

- ☐ 4 pounds chicken breasts
- ☐ 4 large peeled and chopped Yukon Gold potatoes
- ☐ 3 cups chopped beefsteak tomatoes
- ☐ 2 bay leaves
- ☐ ½ cup chicken broth
- ☐ 1 sliced onion
- ☐ Salt and pepper to taste

<u>Directions:</u>

1. Put everything in your PPCXL and stir once.
2. Secure and seal the lid.
3. Select "Chicken/Meat," and cook for 30 minutes.
4. When time is up, turn off the pot and quick-release.
5. Season to taste before serving.

<u>Nutritional Info (¼ recipe per serving):</u>
Calories: 593
Protein: 72
Carbs: 29
Fat: 18
Fiber: 1

Three-Bean Chili

<u>Serves:</u> 6-8

<u>Time:</u> 27 minutes (10 minutes prep time, 7 minutes cook time, 10 minutes natural release)

Chili can take hours, but because this recipe uses precooked beans and no meat, this one takes less than a half hour! It uses three kinds of beans - pinto, black, and red - and plenty of spices like dried oregano, cumin, and smoked paprika.

Ingredients:

- ☐ 3 ½ cups veggie broth
- ☐ One 14.5-ounce can diced tomatoes
- ☐ One 14.5-ounce can tomato sauce
- ☐ One 15-ounce can black beans
- ☐ ½ 15-ounce can red beans
- ☐ ½ 15-ounce can pinto beans
- ☐ 1 chopped red bell pepper
- ☐ 2 cups chopped onion
- ☐ ¾ cup chopped carrots
- ☐ ¼ cup chopped celery
- ☐ 2 tablespoons mild chili powder
- ☐ 1 tablespoon minced garlic
- ☐ 1 ½ teaspoons dried oregano
- ☐ 1 ½ teaspoons ground cumin
- ☐ 1 teaspoon smoked paprika

Directions:

1. Rinse and drain all the beans.
2. Turn your cooker to "Chicken/Meat" and heat.
3. Once hot, add garlic and onion and cook for 5 minutes.
4. Add the rest of the ingredients, minus tomato sauce and tomatoes.
5. Stir before sealing the lid.
6. Hit "Rice/Risotto" and adjust time to 7 minutes.
7. When time is up, turn off the cooker and wait for a natural pressure release.
8. Stir in tomatoes and tomato sauce.
9. Serve with parsley.

<u>**Nutritional Info (⅛ recipe per serving):**</u>
Total calories: 167
Protein: 10
Carbs: 32
Fat: 1
Fiber: 11.5

Chipotle Chicken Chili

<u>Serves:</u> 6

<u>Time:</u> 22 minutes (10 minutes prep time, 12 minutes cook time)

This fast but full-flavored chili is packed with beans, crushed tomato, onion, red bell pepper, and tender ground chicken. The spices are a combination of spicy (chili powder, cumin, and chipotle chiles) and sweet (brown sugar). Right before serving, you even stir in 2 tablespoons of cocoa powder, giving the chili a hint of deep, bitter-chocolatey goodness.

Ingredients:

- 1 pound ground chicken
- Two 14.5-ounce cans of crushed tomatoes
- 15-ounces rinsed and drained dark red kidney beans
- 1 cup chicken broth
- 3 minced garlic cloves
- 1 chopped red bell pepper
- 1 chopped onion
- 2 minced canned chipotle chiles
- 2 tablespoons of adobo sauce (from the can of chipotle chiles)
- 2 tablespoons chili powder
- 2 tablespoons brown sugar
- 2 tablespoons unsweetened cocoa powder
- 2 teaspoons olive oil
- 1 teaspoon ground cumin
- 1 teaspoon apple cider vinegar
- ¼ teaspoon salt

Directions:

1. Turn your cooker to "Chicken/Meat" and add oil.
2. Once hot, add garlic, bell pepper, onion, and ground meat.
3. Stir to break up the meat to let it brown while the veggies soften.
4. Add rest of the ingredients (minus vinegar and cocoa) and stir.
5. Seal the lid.
6. Adjust time to 12 minutes.
7. When time is up, hit "cancel" and quick release.
8. Stir in vinegar and chocolate before serving.

<u>**Nutritional Info (⅙ recipe per serving):**</u>

Total calories: 436
Protein: 42
Carbs: 39
Fiber: 12
Fat: 14

French Lentil-Chicken Stew with Bacon

<u>Serves:</u> 4

<u>Time:</u> 39 minutes (10 minutes prep time, 24 minutes cook time, 5 minutes simmer time)

Lentils are one of the healthiest ingredients you can find, and they're perfect for soup. Salty and fatty slab bacon and chicken add layers of delicious meaty flavor, while tons of parsley ensures freshness. The whole recipe only takes 39 minutes, so it's great for weekdays.

Ingredients:

- ☐ 1 quart chicken stock
- ☐ 2 ½ pounds bone-in, skin-on chicken thighs and drumsticks
- ☐ 8-ounces chopped slab bacon
- ☐ 8-ounces dried French lentils
- ☐ 2 peeled and chopped carrots
- ☐ 12 parsley sprigs, tied together
- ☐ 1 cup diced onion
- ☐ 2 bay leaves
- ☐ 2 tablespoons olive oil
- ☐ 2 teaspoons sherry vinegar
- ☐ Salt and pepper to taste

Directions:

1. Turn your cooker to "Chicken/Meat" and heat up the oil.
2. Cook the bacon for 1 minute and then add onions.
3. When softened, add lentils, chicken, parsley, carrots, bay leaves, and stock.
4. Season with salt and pepper before sealing the lid.
5. Push "Chicken/Meat" and adjust time to 24 minutes.
6. When time is up, turn off the cooker and quick-release the pressure.
7. Take out the chicken and parsley.
8. Turn the cooker to "Chicken/Meat" again and stir for 5 minutes to finish cooking the lentils.
9. Remove the meat from the bones and return to the cooker with sherry vinegar, salt, and pepper.
10. Serve!

Nutritional Info (¼ recipe per serving):

Calories: 1162
Protein: 100
Carbs: 18
Fat: 75
Fiber: 3

Veggie-Quinoa Soup

<u>Serves:</u> 6

<u>Time:</u> 17 minutes (2 minutes cook time, 5 minutes natural release, 10 minutes rest time)

At just over 200 calories with 11 grams of protein, this soup is healthy and delicious. A take on traditional veggie-noodle soup, it replaces the pasta with quinoa and adds two kinds of beans for fiber and protein. Spices like garlic, oregano, basil, and hot sauce ensure that every spoonful is layered and interesting.

Ingredients:

- ☐ 3 cups boiling water
- ☐ 24-ounces thawed, frozen mixed veggies
- ☐ One 15-ounce can of white beans
- ☐ One 15-ounce can of fire-roasted diced tomatoes
- ☐ One 15-ounce can of pinto beans
- ☐ ¼ cup rinsed quinoa
- ☐ 1 tablespoon minced garlic
- ☐ 1 tablespoon dried basil
- ☐ 1 tablespoon hot sauce
- ☐ ½ tablespoon dried oregano
- ☐ Salt and pepper to taste

Directions:

1. Mix all the ingredients in the PPCXL.
2. Seal the lid.
3. Select "Rice/Risotto" and reduce time to 2 minutes.
4. When time is up, turn off the cooker and wait for the pressure to come down on its own.
5. Let the soup rest for 10 minutes after the pressure is reduced.
6. Season to taste before serving.

Nutritional Info (1 ½ cups serving):

Total calories: 201
Protein: 11
Carbs: 37
Fat: 1.1
Fiber: 11

Homemade Chicken Noodle Soup

Serves: 4-6
Time: 39 minutes (5 minutes prep time, 24 minutes cook time, 10 minutes simmer time)

One of the best uses of the Power Pressure Cooker XL is making homemade chicken noodle soup. This winter-time classic warms the bones and heals the sick. It's much healthier homemade, and it only takes 39 minutes to make enough for 4-6 people.

Ingredients:

- One 5-pound chicken with giblets removed
- 5 cups water
- 4-ounces wide egg noodles
- 5 peeled and cut carrots
- 3 minced garlic cloves
- 2 sliced celery stalks
- 1 diced onion
- ¼ cup parsley
- 2 tablespoons soy sauce
- 1 tablespoon of olive oil
- Salt and pepper to taste

Directions:

1. Turn your cooker to "Chicken/Meat" and heat olive oil.
2. Cook the onions for 2-3 minutes.
3. Add celery, carrots, and garlic.
4. After a minute or so, put the whole chicken in the cooker with water, soy sauce, salt, and pepper.
5. Seal the lid.
6. Hit "cancel" and then select "Chicken/Meat" again and adjust time to 20 minutes.
7. When the timer beeps, turn off the cooker and quick-release the pressure.
8. Remove chicken and put it on a plate.
9. Turn cooker back to "Chicken/Meat" and bring to a boil.
10. Put in the noodles and cook for 5 minutes.
11. Shred the chicken and add to the pot once the noodles are done, along with parsley.

Nutritional Info (¼ recipe per serving):

Calories: 556
Protein: 93
Carbs: 9
Fat: 14
Fiber: 6

Coconut-Milk Corn Chowder

<u>Serves:</u> 6

<u>Time:</u> 32 minutes (10 minutes prep time, 7 minutes cook time, 15 minutes natural pressure release)

Rich, creamy, and intensely-flavored corn chowder is a fantastic and somewhat unusual idea for a fall meal. It's like a silky corn casserole. Instead of cream, we're using coconut milk, so it's good for those with dietary restrictions.

Ingredients:

- ☐ 5 ears' worth of corn kernels
- ☐ 3 chopped Yukon Gold potatoes
- ☐ 4 cups vegetable broth
- ☐ 1 cup full-fat coconut milk
- ☐ 3 minced garlic cloves
- ☐ 3 chopped carrots
- ☐ 1 tablespoon potato starch
- ☐ 1 tablespoon coconut oil
- ☐ Juice of 1 lime
- ☐ 1 teaspoon smoked paprika
- ☐ Cumin to taste
- ☐ Salt and pepper to taste
- ☐ Dash of red pepper flakes

Directions:

1. Turn your PPCXL to "Chicken/Meat" and add corn, onions, carrots, and red pepper flakes.
2. Once the onions are becoming translucent, add garlic.
3. After a minute, pour in the broth, corn cobs, potatoes, cumin, salt, and pepper.
4. Seal the lid and adjust cooking time to 7 minutes.
5. When the timer beeps, hit "cancel" and wait 15 minutes.
6. Remove the cobs.
7. In a bowl, mix potato starch and coconut milk.
8. Whisk in lime juice.
9. Pour into the cooker.
10. Turn on the "Chicken/Meat" setting again (lid 0ff) and let the flavors blend for a few

minutes.

11. Puree until smooth and season to taste.

Nutritional Info (⅙ recipe per serving)

Total calories: 217
Protein: 5
Carbs: 41
Fat: 6
Fiber: 3

White Winter Vegetable Stew

<u>Serves:</u> 4-6

<u>Time:</u> 24 minutes (5 minutes prep time, 7 minutes cook time, 10 minutes natural pressure release, 2 minutes simmer time)

Brimming with nutritious root veggies like carrots, parsnip, and celery root (which is *not* the same as celery), this wintery stew is light and fresh. It's perfect for lunches or as a small dinner with some crusty bread. Remember to add the peas last, and to just let the heat from the rest of the soup warm them through for a few minutes.

Ingredients:

- [ ] 1 ½ cups broth
- [ ] 3 cups diced celery root
- [ ] 2 bay leaves
- [ ] 1 cup diced parsnip
- [ ] 1 cup diced carrot
- [ ] 1 cup sliced leek
- [ ] ½ cup frozen peas
- [ ] ½ cup green lentils
- [ ] 1 sprig rosemary
- [ ] 1 sprig thyme
- [ ] Squirt of lemon juice
- [ ] Salt and pepper to taste

Directions:

1. Turn your cooker to "Chicken/Meat" and add leek.
2. Cook for just one minute before adding garlic.
3. After another minute, hit "cancel" and pour in broth along with carrots, lentils, parsnips, celery root, and herbs.
4. Seal the lid.
5. Select "Soup/Stew" and reduce time to 7 minutes.
6. When the timer beeps, hit "cancel" and allow for a natural pressure release.
7. Add peas, stir, and close the lid again, but don't bring to pressure.
8. After two minutes, season the soup with salt, pepper, and lemon juice.
9. Serve hot!

Nutritional Info (¼ recipe per serving)

Total calories: 103
Protein: 4
Carbs: 23
Fat: 0
Fiber: 5

Split Asparagus Soup

<u>Serves:</u> 4-6

<u>Time:</u> 1 hour, 4 minutes (10 minutes prep time, 54 minutes cook time)

Smooth and perfect for spring, this soup will even impress people who aren't crazy about asparagus. The natural brightness of the veggie is balanced by browned onions, garlic, salty ham, and just a bit of thyme. Serve with a side like garlic toast.

Ingredients:

- ☐ 2 pounds split asparagus
- ☐ 4 cups chicken broth
- ☐ 5 pressed garlic cloves
- ☐ 1 cup diced ham
- ☐ 1 diced onion
- ☐ ½ teaspoon dried thyme
- ☐ Salt to taste

Directions:

1. Pour just enough olive oil in your cooker to coat the bottom, and heat on the "Chicken/Meat" setting.
2. Add onions and cook for 5 minutes until beginning to brown.
3. Toss in garlic, ham, and pour in broth.
4. Simmer for a few minutes.
5. Add thyme and asparagus before sealing the lid.
6. Adjust cook time to 54 minutes.
7. When the timer beeps, hit "cancel" and quick-release.
8. Puree until smooth.
9. Season with salt and pepper before serving.

Nutritional Info (1 cup):

Total calories: 285
Protein: 14
Carbs: 18
Fat: 17
Fiber: 3

Cream of Mushroom Soup

<u>Serves:</u> 6
<u>Time:</u> 18 minutes (10 minutes prep time, 8 minutes cook time)

Love mushrooms? This is the soup after your own heart. It uses both fresh and dried mushrooms for really full flavor, and fragrant aromatics like celery and red onion. Potatoes add a buttery heartiness, while tart dry red wine provides a beautiful, fruity pop of acid.

Ingredients:

- [ ] 4 cups vegetable stock
- [ ] 1 ½ pounds fresh crimini mushrooms
- [ ] 1 ounce dried, rinsed oyster mushrooms
- [ ] 2 large peeled and chopped potatoes
- [ ] 1 cup fresh cream
- [ ] 1 medium-sized roughly-chopped red onion
- [ ] 1 roughly-chopped celery stalk
- [ ] 2 tablespoons tart dry red wine
- [ ] 1 tablespoon olive oil
- [ ] 1 teaspoon black pepper

Directions:

1. Slice a handful of the fresh mushrooms and then chop the rest.
2. Turn your cooker to "Chicken/Meat" and heat the olive oil.
3. Cook the sliced mushrooms until both sides are golden.
4. Plate them (these are a garnish) before cooking the celery and onion in the pot.
5. Once those are soft, move them to the side and add just enough chopped mushrooms to cover the bottom.
6. Stir until brown, which should be about 5 minutes.
7. Pour in the wine and scrape up any stuck-on bits, letting the wine evaporate.
8. When the wine is gone, stir in the rest of the fresh mushrooms, dried mushrooms, potatoes, stock, and salt.
9. Close and seal the lid.
10. Adjust cooking time to 8 minutes.
11. When the timer beeps, hit "cancel" and quick-release the pressure.
12. Stir in cream and black pepper before pureeing the soup with a hand blender.
13. Serve with browned, sliced mushrooms on top!

<u>**Nutritional Info (1 cup of soup per serving):**</u>
Calories: 255.8
Protein: 3.5
Carbs: 22.1
Fat: 17.5
Fiber: 3.0

Cheeseburger Soup

<u>Serves:</u> 4-6

<u>Time:</u> 23 minutes (10 minutes prep time, 8 minutes cook time, 5 minutes simmer time)

Full of the flavors of a really good cheeseburger, this recipe is proof that soup can be a meal. You use lean ground beef, onion, a yellow bell pepper, and cheese. To make the soup creamy, there's heavy cream and butter. Add this to your list of what to do with some pantry staples and enjoy!

Ingredients:

- ☐ 1 pound lean crumbled ground beef
- ☐ 3 cups chicken broth
- ☐ 2 cups shredded cheddar cheese
- ☐ ½ cup heavy cream
- ☐ ¼ cup dry white wine
- ☐ 1 large diced onion
- ☐ 1 chopped yellow bell pepper
- ☐ 3 tablespoons butter
- ☐ 2 tablespoons flour
- ☐ 1 teaspoon dried thyme
- ☐ ½ teaspoon black pepper
- ☐ ½ teaspoon salt
- ☐ ½ teaspoon dried marjoram

Directions:

1. Turn your cooker to "Chicken/Meat" and melt the butter.
2. Sauté the onion and bell pepper for 4 minutes.
3. Whisk in the flour, coating the veggies.
4. Slowly pour in the broth to dissolve the flour.
5. Whisk in the wine for 2 minutes.
6. Add beef and seasonings before sealing the lid.
7. Adjust the cooking time to 9 minutes.
8. When time is up, hit "cancel" and quick-release the pressure.
9. Check the meat with a thermometer and turn to "Chicken/Meat" again, even if it is cooked through.
10. If not cooked through, simmer until it is.

11. Stir in cream and cheese.

12. Once the cheese melts, serve!

Nutritional Info (¼ recipe per serving):

Calories: 448
Protein: 31
Carbs: 6
Fat: 6
Fiber: 1

Chapter 11

Rice and Pasta

Cheesy-Lemon Risotto

<u>Serves:</u> 6-8

<u>Time:</u> 18 minutes (10 minutes prep time, 6 minutes cook time, 2 minutes simmer time)

Fragrant from lemon zest and cheesy with Parmesan, this might be the perfect risotto. It's also got baby peas and parsley for a touch of freshness. Whether you're serving chicken, beef, pork, or fish, this under-20 minutes side dish will be a stand out.

Ingredients:

- ☐ 3 ½ cups vegetable broth
- ☐ 1 ½ cups Arborio rice
- ☐ 1 ½ cups frozen baby peas
- ☐ 1 chopped onion
- ☐ 2 tablespoons butter
- ☐ 2 tablespoons lemon juice
- ☐ 2 tablespoons chopped parsley
- ☐ 2 tablespoons Parmesan cheese
- ☐ 1 tablespoon olive oil
- ☐ 1 teaspoon lemon zest
- ☐ Salt and pepper to taste

Directions:

1. Turn your cooker to "Chicken/Meat" and heat up the olive oil and butter.
2. When the butter has melted and the oil is hot, sauté the onion until soft.
3. Stir rice in the pot for 2-3 minutes until toasty.
4. Add in broth and lemon juice.
5. Close and seal the lid.
6. Push "Rice/Risotto" and cook for the default time, which is 6 minutes.
7. When the timer beeps, hit "cancel" and quick-release the pressure.
8. Open the lid and turn the cooker back to the "Chicken/Meat" setting.
9. Pour in the rest of the broth and peas.
10. Stir everything until the peas have warmed through.
11. Add in 1 tablespoon of butter, lemon zest, and the parsley.
12. Season with salt and pepper before serving!

Nutritional Info (⅙ recipe):

Calories: 256
Protein: 6
Carbs: 46
Fat: 7
Fiber: 1

Sweet Thai Coconut Rice

<u>Serves:</u> 4

<u>Time:</u> 23 minutes (3 minutes cook time, 10 minutes natural release, 5-10 minutes rest time)

Creamy with coconut milk and sweet thanks to the natural flavor of Thai rice and sugar, this side dish is almost like a rice pudding. It would go very well with a contrasting flavor like salty pork belly or citrusy white fish. Make sure to get the full-fat coconut milk.

<u>Ingredients:</u>

- ☐ 1 ½ cups water
- ☐ 1 cup Thai sweet rice
- ☐ ½ can full-fat coconut milk
- ☐ 2 tablespoons sugar
- ☐ Sprinkle of salt

<u>Directions:</u>

1. Pour water and rice in your PPCXL.
2. Close and seal the lid.
3. Select "Rice/Risotto" and reduce time to 3 minutes.
4. When time is up, turn off the cooker and wait 10 minutes for the pressure to come down.
5. While that cooks, heat up the coconut milk, salt, and sugar in a pan.
6. When the sugar has melted, turn off the stovetop.
7. When the cooker is safe to open, mix the hot coconut milk mixture into your rice.
8. Put the lid back and let it sit for 5-10 minutes, without returning it to pressure.
9. Serve!

<u>Nutritional Info (¼ recipe):</u>
Total calories: 269
Protein: 4
Carbs: 47
Fat: 8
Fiber: 0

Three-Cheese Risotto with Peas

<u>Serves</u>: 6
<u>Time:</u> 22 minutes (10 minutes prep time, 12 minutes cook time)

This risotto is perfect for when you just can't pick one cheese, so you gotta go with three. Creamy mozzarella, umami Parmesan, and nutty Fontina all melt together into a trio of cheesiness with Arborio rice that's been cooked in chicken broth. Baby peas provide a pop of green.

Ingredients:

- ☐ 4 cups chicken broth
- ☐ 1 ½ cups white Arborio rice
- ☐ 1 cup frozen peas
- ☐ 1 chopped yellow onion
- ☐ ½ cup shredded mozzarella cheese
- ☐ ½ cup shredded Parmesan cheese
- ☐ ¼ cup shredded fontina cheese
- ☐ ¼ cup apple cider
- ☐ 3 tablespoons butter
- ☐ 1 tablespoon minced rosemary leaves
- ☐ 1 tablespoon apple cider vinegar
- ☐ ¼ teaspoon grated nutmeg

Directions:

1. Turn the PPCXL to "Chicken/Meat" and add butter.
2. When melted and hot, add onion and cook until softened.
3. Stir the rice in and coat in the butter.
4. Pour in vinegar and apple cider.
5. Keep stirring until the liquid is totally absorbed.
6. Pour in broth, nutmeg, and rosemary leaves.
7. Close and seal the lid.
8. Press "Soup/Stew" and adjust to 12 minutes.
9. When the timer beeps, turn off the cooker and quick-release the pressure.
10. Stir in the cheese and peas.
11. Put the lid on top without sealing so the trapped heat melts the cheese and warms up the peas.

12. Stir and serve!

Nutritional Info (⅙ recipe):

Total calories: 298
Protein: 9
Carbs: 44
Fat: 11
Fiber: 3

Shrimp and Spinach Risotto

Serves: 4

Time: 19 minutes (6 minutes prep time, 8 minutes cook time, 5 minutes simmer time)

Full of protein and iron, this dinner risotto looks and tastes fancy, but it's very easy to put together. Use precooked, frozen shrimp for convenience, and a good quality Parmesan cheese. Arborio rice is an Italian-style rice, and perfect for tender, rich risotto. I don't like to use anything else.

Ingredients:

- ☐ 16 medium-sized frozen + thawed shrimp
- ☐ 2 ¼ cups chicken broth
- ☐ 2 cups chopped fresh spinach
- ☐ 1 cup Arborio rice
- ☐ ½ cup finely-grated Parmesan cheese
- ☐ ¼ cup dry white wine
- ☐ 2 bay leaves
- ☐ 1 garlic clove
- ☐ 1 chopped celery stalk
- ☐ 1 chopped onion
- ☐ 1 tablespoon olive oil
- ☐ 1 tablespoon butter
- ☐ 2 teaspoons ground oregano
- ☐ ¼ teaspoon ground white pepper

Directions:

1. Turn the cooker to "Chicken/Meat" and let the butter and olive oil mix together.
2. When hot, stir in the garlic, celery, and onions.
3. When the onion has become clear and softened, stir in the rice to coat it in oil.
4. After a minute, pour in the wine, broth, bay leaves, white pepper, and oregano.
5. Once simmering, seal the lid.
6. Adjust cooking time to 8 minutes.
7. When time is up, hit "cancel" and quick-release.
8. Remove the bay leaves before adding shrimp and spinach.
9. Stir until the shrimp is warmed through and the spinach has wilted.
10. Before serving, stir in cheese.

Nutritional Information (¼ risotto recipe per serving):

Total calories: 224.6

Protein: 13.1

Carbs: 20.2

Fat: 9.3

Fiber: 1.9

Butter-Lemon Risotto

<u>Serves:</u> 6-8
<u>Time:</u> 21 minutes (10 minutes prep time, 6 minutes cook time, 5 minutes simmer time)

Simple and full of fresh, bright flavors, this recipe is a great introduction to using the pressure cooker for risotto. You cook onions in a hot mixture of butter and onion, and then toast the rice for just a minute or so. Cook the rice in broth and lemon juice for just six minutes, and then stir in peas, butter, parsley, and cheese! So easy and so tasty.

Ingredients:

- ☐ 3 ½ cups chicken broth
- ☐ 1 ½ cups Arborio rice
- ☐ 1 ½ cups frozen peas
- ☐ 1 chopped onion
- ☐ 2 tablespoons grated Parmesan
- ☐ 2 tablespoons butter
- ☐ 2 tablespoons lemon juice
- ☐ 2 tablespoons chopped fresh parsley
- ☐ 1 tablespoon olive oil
- ☐ Salt and pepper to taste

Directions:

1. Turn your cooker to the "Chicken/Meat" setting and melt the oil and 1 tablespoon of butter together.
2. When shimmering and hot, cook onion for 5 minutes.
3. Stir in the rice to coat it in oil.
4. After 3 minutes, pour in 3 cups of broth and lemon juice.
5. Seal the lid.
6. Adjust cooking time to 6 minutes.
7. When the timer beeps, hit "cancel" and quick-release.
8. Hit "Chicken/Meat" again and pour in rest of the broth and peas.
9. Let the peas warm through.
10. Stir in cheese, 1 tablespoon of butter, and parsley.
11. Season with salt and pepper before serving!

<u>**Nutritional Info (⅙ recipe per serving):**</u>
Total calories: 252
Protein: 6
Carbs: 44
Fat: 7
Fiber: 2

Cranberry-Walnut Quinoa

<u>Serves</u>: 4
<u>Time</u>: 12 minutes

Quinoa is naturally nutty, which compliments the walnuts in this recipe. To sweeten things up a bit, we add dried cranberries. For extra crunch, there are sunflower seeds. This would be a great side dish for pork, which goes very well with fruity and nutty flavors.

Ingredients:

- ☐ 2 cups water
- ☐ 2 cups dried cranberries
- ☐ 1 cup quinoa
- ☐ 1 cup chopped walnuts
- ☐ 1 cup sunflower seeds
- ☐ Salt to taste

Directions:

1. Rinse the quinoa and add to the PPCXL along with water and salt. .
2. Seal the lid.
3. Select "Chicken/Meat," and cook for 12 minutes.
4. When time is up, hit "cancel" and quick-release the pressure.
5. Add in dried cranberries, nuts, and sunflower seeds.

<u>Nutritional Info (¼ recipe per serving):</u>
Total calories: 584
Protein: 16
Carbs: 62
Fat: 34
Fiber: 5

One Pot Chili-Chicken Ziti

<u>Serves:</u> 4

<u>Time:</u> 14 minutes (5 minutes prep time, 9 minutes cook time)

Pasta dishes are big and easy to throw together, and in the pressure cooker, it's all a one-pot process. You literally just put everything in the cooker and cook for 9 minutes to get a chicken and whole-wheat pasta with green chilies, beans, tomatoes, and chili powder. Serve with cheese!

Ingredients:

- ☐ 1 pound cubed boneless skinless chicken breasts
- ☐ One 14-ounce can of diced tomatoes
- ☐ 1 ½ cups chicken broth
- ☐ 1 cup drained and rinsed pinto beans
- ☐ 8-ounces dried whole-wheat ziti
- ☐ One 4.5-ounce can chopped mild green chilies
- ☐ ⅓ cup chopped cilantro leaves
- ☐ 1 tablespoon chili powder
- ☐ 1 teaspoon ground cumin
- ☐ ½ teaspoon salt
- ☐ ½ teaspoon black pepper

Directions:

1. Stir everything in your Power Pressure Cooker XL and seal the lid.
2. Select "Soup/Stew" and adjust time to 9 minutes.
3. When the timer beeps, hit "cancel" and carefully quick-release the pressure.
4. Stir and serve!

Nutritional Info (¼ of recipe):
Total calories: 222
Protein: 17
Carbs: 29
Fat: 4
Fiber: 10.7

Chicken Lo Mein

<u>Serves:</u> 6
<u>Time:</u> 29 minutes (15 minutes prep time, 14 minutes cook time)

A staple of Chinese-American restaurants, Lo Mein is a noodle dish flavored with aromatics like garlic, carrots, onion, and bell pepper. This recipe uses diced chicken, but you can replace it with just about any protein, like beef or shrimp.

Ingredients:

- One 16 ounce box of linguini pasta
- ½ pound boneless + skinless diced chicken breasts
- 4 cups chicken broth
- 4 peeled medium-sized carrots, cut into strips
- 4 minced garlic cloves
- 1 bunch of green onions, cut into strips
- 1 medium-sized red bell pepper, cut into strips
- ¼ cup soy sauce
- 1 tablespoon sugar
- 2 teaspoons extra-virgin olive oil
- 1 teaspoon garlic powder
- ½ teaspoon red pepper flakes

Directions:

1. Snap the pasta in half, so it will fit in the cooker, but keep it in a bowl for now.
2. Turn your cooker to "Chicken/Meat" and heat the olive oil.
3. Brown the chicken on both sides and move to a plate.
4. In a separate bowl, mix soy sauce, broth, garlic powder, red pepper, and sugar.
5. Toss garlic in the pressure cooker and pour the liquid over.
6. Put the noodles in the cooker with the chicken and vegetables (except the green onion) and seal the lid.
7. Adjust the cooking time to 14 minutes.
8. When the timer beeps, hit "cancel" and quick-release.
9. Stir in green onion.
10. Season to taste before serving.

Nutritional Info (⅙ recipe per serving):

Total calories: 332
Protein: 17.6
Carbs: 53.9
Fat: .3
Fiber: 7.2

Spaghetti + Meatballs

<u>Serves</u>: 4
<u>Time</u>: 32 minutes (10 minutes prep time, 14 minutes cook time, 8 minutes rest time)

A one-pot meal, spaghetti and meatballs has never been easier than with the pressure cooker. It's just a box of noodles, a jar of sauce, and meatballs made from beef. The seasoning is easy, and you can add any herbs or spices if you have a favorite recipe. Remember to let the food rest in the warm cooker for 8 minutes after releasing the pressure.

Ingredients:

- ☐ 10 ounces of noodles
- ☐ 1 pound of ground beef
- ☐ 1 jar of spaghetti sauce
- ☐ 2 eggs
- ☐ ¼ cup breadcrumbs
- ☐ ¼ cup milk
- ☐ ½ minced garlic clove
- ☐ Salt and pepper to taste

Directions:

1. Mix beef, bread crumbs, egg, garlic, and seasonings in a bowl.
2. Mix spaghetti sauce and noodles in your PPCXL.
3. Fill the jar with water and pour into the cooker.
4. Turn your cooker to "Chicken/Meat."
5. While the liquid gets to a boil, roll golf ball-sized meatballs and put on top of the noodles.
6. Seal the lid.
7. Adjust cooking time to 14 minutes.
8. When time is up, hit "cancel" and quick-release.
9. Take off the lid and let the meal rest for 8 minutes.
10. Serve!

Nutritional Info (¼ recipe per serving):

Total calories: 703   Fat: 29
Protein: 32   Fiber: 0
Carbs: 71

Beefy Lasagna

<u>Serves:</u> 6

<u>Time:</u> 18 minutes (10 minutes prep time, 8 minutes cook time)

The best lasagna is beefy and cheesy, and this recipe is that and more. You brown the beef filling with onion and seasonings in the pot, and then layer it in the pressure cooker with no-boil noodles and a rich ricotta filling with parmesan cheese. It only takes 8 minutes to cook, and then you blanket the whole thing with mozzarella. The recipe makes enough for six hungry people.

<u>Ingredients:</u>

- ☐ 2 pounds ricotta cheese
- ☐ 24-ounces pasta sauce
- ☐ 1 pound of ground beef
- ☐ 8-ounces of no-boil lasagna noodles
- ☐ 1 package shredded mozzarella cheese
- ☐ 2 large eggs
- ☐ ⅓ cup grated Parmesan cheese
- ☐ ¼ cup water
- ☐ 1 diced onion
- ☐ 1 tablespoon olive oil
- ☐ 2 teaspoons minced garlic
- ☐ 1 teaspoon Italian seasoning
- ☐ Salt and pepper to taste

<u>Directions:</u>

1. Heat oil in the PPCXL on "Chicken/Meat" until it begins to smoke.
2. Add beef, onions, salt, and pepper.
3. Cook until the meat has browned and onions are translucent.
4. Add water and pasta sauce.
5. Stir and then pour into a bowl. Hit "cancel" on the cooker.
6. In a separate bowl, mix garlic, eggs, Italian seasoning, parmesan, salt, pepper, and ricotta cheese.
7. Pour ¼-inch of water into the cooker and layer in ⅕ of the beef filling into the cooker.
8. Lay a few noodles on top and then add 1/3 of the ricotta filling, followed by more

beef, and then noodles.

9. Keep layering until all the ingredients are used up. The final layer will be beef.
10. Seal the lid.
11. Hit "Chicken/Meat" and adjust the cooking time to 8 minutes.
12. When time is up, turn off the cooker and quick-release.
13. Sprinkle on mozzarella cheese and cool before serving.

Nutritional Info (⅙ recipe per serving):

Total calories: 408
Protein: 25.1
Carbs: 27.4
Fat: 22.1
Fiber: 2.6

Chicken Enchilada Pasta

<u>Serves:</u> 6
<u>Time:</u> 20 minutes (10 minutes prep time, 5 minutes cook time, 5 minutes broil time)

This fast and cheesy pasta bake is perfect for when you're so busy, you're considering takeout. You just cook the onions beforehand, and then all the ingredients go in the cooker for just 5 minutes. To finish it all off, it goes under the broiler, so the shredded Mexican cheese melts and browns into a delicious golden topping.

Ingredients:

- 2 large boneless skinless chicken breasts
- 3 cups dried rotini pasta
- One 19-ounce can enchilada sauce
- One 10-ounce can of tomatoes
- 2 cups shredded Mexican cheese
- 1 ¼ cups water
- 2 diced garlic cloves
- 1 cup diced onion
- 1 tablespoon vegetable oil
- 1 package taco seasoning

Directions:

1. Turn your cooker to "Chicken/Meat" and heat the oil.
2. Add onion and cook until it softens.
3. Throw everything else in the cooker, minus the cheese, and seal the lid.
4. Adjust the cooking time to 5 minutes.
5. When time is up, hit "cancel" and quick-release.
6. Open the lid and hit "Chicken/Meat" again to let the food cook for another minute.
7. Turn off cooker and pour pasta into a baking dish.
8. Sprinkle on cheese and stick under the broiler until the cheese melts.
9. Serve!

Nutritional Info (about ⅙ recipe per serving):
Total calories: 663   Carbs: 100
Protein: 31   Fiber: 4
Fat: 15

Pasta with Sausage + Bacon

<u>Serves:</u> 6

<u>Time:</u> About 2o minutes (15 minutes prep time, 5 minutes cook time)

Packed with two kinds of meat, this pasta dish is oh-so satisfying and comforting. You cook the bacon first, and then the sausage, which then finishes up in the cooker with the pasta, tomato puree, onion, and garlic. When time is up, you mix in cheese and basil, and top with the bacon!

Ingredients:

- ☐ 18-ounces of penne pasta
- ☐ 17-ounces of pork sausage
- ☐ 3.4-ounces bacon
- ☐ 2 cups tomato puree
- ☐ ¼ cup Parmesan cheese
- ☐ 2 minced garlic cloves
- ☐ 1 tablespoon olive oil
- ☐ A handful of chopped basil
- ☐ Salt to taste

Directions:

1. Turn the PPCXL to "Chicken/Meat" and when warm, add oil and bacon.
2. When the bacon has crisped up, move to a plate with a paper towel.
3. Add sausage to the cooker and cook through, stirring every few minutes so it doesn't stick.
4. Add garlic and onion.
5. After a few minutes, turn off the cooker.
6. Stir in pasta and a dash of salt.
7. Stir in pasta and pour in just enough water to cover.
8. Hit "Chicken/Meat" and adjust cook time to half of whatever time the pasta box suggests.
9. When time is up, carefully quick-release the pressure.
10. Stir in cooked bacon, cheese, and basil before serving!

Nutritional Info (⅙ recipe per serving)

Total calories: 716
Protein: 32
Carbs: 72
Fat: 32
Fiber: 0

Ranch Pasta Salad

Serves: 8

Time: 15 minutes (5 minutes prep time, 4 minutes cook time, 6 minutes cool/dressing time)

Using the pressure cooker to cook pasta is very efficient since it's so fast. When you need to make a dish for a summer gathering, try out this ranch pasta salad with homemade dressing. The pasta cooks in white wine, water, and seasonings for just 4 minutes before you mix it with the ranch dressing, peas, sweet onion, celery, and cucumber.

Ingredients:

Pasta

- 16 ounces/1 lb. of dry whole-wheat penne pasta
- 1 cup diced sweet onion
- 1 cup diced celery
- 1 cup fresh peas
- 1 cup diced cucumber
- ¼ cup cooked, crumbled bacon
- 2 tablespoons olive oil
- 2 tablespoons white wine
- 1 teaspoon coarse sea salt
- Black pepper

Ranch

- ½ cup plain Greek-style yogurt
- ½ cup buttermilk
- ½ cup sour cream
- 2 minced garlic cloves
- ¾ teaspoon dried chives
- ¾ teaspoon dried parsley
- ½ teaspoon salt
- ½ teaspoon black pepper
- ½ teaspoon dried dill

Directions:

1. Rinse pasta thoroughly.

2. Pour 2 tablespoons of oil into the cooker and stir in the pasta.
3. Pour in 3 ½ cups water, white wine, and coarse salt.
4. Seal the lid.
5. Hit "Rice/Risotto" and lower time to 4 minutes.
6. When the timer beeps, hit "Cancel" and quick-release.
7. In a small bowl, mix herb.
8. In another bowl, mix yogurt, buttermilk, and sour cream.
9. Mix in the herbs.
10. Store in the fridge.
11. To cool the pasta, pour into a colander and run under cold water.
12. Add in onion, celery, cucumber, and peas.
13. Stir half of the dressing into the pasta, and add more if desired.
14. Season well with salt and pepper.
15. Top with crumbled bacon before serving!

Nutritional Info (⅛ recipe per serving):
Total calories: 381
Protein: 17
Carbs: 22
Fat: 25
Fiber: 5.8

Tuna Noodles

<u>Serves:</u> 2
<u>Time:</u> 21 minutes (5 minutes prep time, 12 minutes cook time, 4 minutes simmer time)

Ingredients:

- ☐ 1 ¼ cups water
- ☐ 8-ounces of uncooked wide egg noodles
- ☐ 1 jar drained marinated, chopped artichoke hearts (save the liquid)
- ☐ 1 can diced tomatoes
- ☐ 1 can drained tuna
- ☐ ½ cup chopped red onion
- ☐ 1 tablespoon olive oil
- ☐ Handful of feta cheese
- ☐ Dried parsley for serving
- ☐ Pinch of dried basil
- ☐ Salt and pepper to taste

Directions:

1. Turn your PPCXL to "Chicken/Meat" and heat the oil.
2. Once shimmering and hot, cook the red onion for 2 minutes, stirring so it doesn't stick.
3. Add in the tomatoes, noodles, water, salt, pepper, and basil.
4. Seal the lid.
5. Adjust cooking time to 12 minutes.
6. When the timer beeps, hit "cancel" and quick-release the pressure.
7. Add in artichokes, artichoke liquid, and tuna.
8. Turn the cooker back to "Chicken/Meat" and simmer for 4 minutes, stirring everything together.
9. Top with parsley and feta cheese.

Nutritional Info (½ recipe per serving):

Total calories: 547
Protein: 8
Carbs: 18

Fat: 3
Fiber: 2

Pasta Fagioli with Cranberry Beans + Kale

<u>Serves:</u> 8

<u>Time:</u> 1 hour, 57 minutes (1 hour soak time, 10 minutes prep time, 12 minutes cook time, 15 minutes natural pressure release, 20 minutes simmer time)

High in fiber and protein, this pasta dish is full of juicy tomatoes, kale, aromatics like celery and garlic, and beautifully-colored cranberry beans. You're going to be quick-soaking the beans, which means boiling them for just one 1 minute, and then letting them soak for one hour. For extra vitamins, we use nutritional yeast, which adds a subtle cheesy flavor in addition to its nutritional value.

<u>Ingredients:</u>

- ☐ 26-ounces of canned, chopped tomatoes
- ☐ 10-ounces of chopped kale
- ☐ 2 cups small, whole-grain pasta
- ☐ 2 cups dried cranberry beans
- ☐ 7 minced garlic cloves
- ☐ 2 chopped celery stalks
- ☐ 1 chopped onion
- ☐ 3 tablespoons nutritional yeast
- ☐ 3 teaspoons dried basil leaves
- ☐ 2 teaspoons dried oregano
- ☐ 2 teaspoons salt
- ☐ 1 teaspoon minced fresh rosemary
- ☐ ¼ teaspoon red pepper flakes
- ☐ Black pepper to taste

<u>Directions:</u>

1. An hour before you plan on making the dish, pick out any rocks from the beans, rinse, and boil them in 2-inches of water for 1 minute.
2. Let them soak in water for 1 hour before draining and rinsing one more time.
3. When you're ready to make the recipe, turn your cooker to "Chicken/Meat."
4. Add onion and cook until it begins to soften.
5. Add in half of the garlic, along with all the celery, pepper flakes, and rosemary.
6. After 2 minutes of cooking, stir in tomatoes, 1 teaspoon oregano, 2 teaspoons basil, and the smoked paprika.

7. Once hot and simmering, pour in beans, 6 cups of water, and a dash of salt.
8. Seal the lid.
9. Adjust cooking time to 12 minutes.
10. When time is up, hit "cancel" and wait 15 minutes for a natural pressure release.
11. Add the rest of oregano, basil, and garlic.
12. Pour in the pasta and cook on "Chicken/Meat" until al dente.
13. Add in kale and turn off the cooker, but close - don't seal - the lid.
14. After 5 minutes, open the lid again and season with nutritional yeast and black pepper.
15. Serve!

Nutritional Info (⅛ recipe per serving):

Calories: 329
Protein: 19
Carbs: 61.7
Fat: 1.6
Fiber: 15

Chapter 12

Vegan

Tapioca Breakfast Parfait w/ Raspberries

<u>Serves:</u> 4

<u>Time:</u> 16 minutes (6 minutes cook time, 10 minutes natural pressure release)

A take on yogurt parfaits, this tasty breakfast replaces the dairy with pearl tapioca. Layered with the tapioca, which is cooked in almond milk and lightly flavored with lemon zest and vanilla, are fresh raspberries. You can replace the fruit with anything in season.

Ingredients:

- ☐ 2 cups fresh raspberries
- ☐ 2 cups unsweetened almond milk
- ☐ ½ cup small pearl tapioca
- ☐ ¼ cup organic sugar
- ☐ 1 teaspoon vanilla extract
- ☐ ½ teaspoon lemon zest
- ☐ Pinch of salt

Directions:

1. Rinse the tapioca in a fine-mesh strainer with cool water.
2. Pour milk into your PPCXL before adding salt and tapioca.
3. Close and seal the lid.
4. Select "Rice/Risotto" setting and cook on the default time of 6 minutes.
5. When the beeper goes off, wait for a natural pressure release.
6. Turn the valve to release any leftover pressure.
7. Mix in vanilla, sugar, and lemon zest.
8. Serve with alternating layers of pudding and raspberries.

Nutritional Info (¼ recipe)

Total calories: 180
Protein: 2
Fat: 2
Carbs: 39
Fiber: 1

Banana-Buckwheat Porridge

<u>Serves:</u> 4

<u>Time:</u> 17 minutes (7 minutes cook time, 10 minutes natural pressure release)

Buckwheat groats are an extremely healthy seed (not a grain) rich in fiber and protein. Pressure-cooking the buckwheat makes it easier to digest. To flavor the porridge, you've got naturally-sweet banana, raisins, vanilla, and cinnamon.

Ingredients:

- ☐ 3 cups almond milk
- ☐ 1 sliced banana
- ☐ 1 cup buckwheat groats
- ☐ ¼ cup raisins
- ☐ 1 teaspoon cinnamon
- ☐ ½ teaspoon vanilla extract

Directions:

1. Rinse off the buckwheat in a fine-mesh strainer before putting in the Power Pressure Cooker XL.
2. Add the rest of the ingredients (except the banana) and stir.
3. Lock and seal the lid.
4. Select "Rice/Risotto," and then adjust time to 7 minutes.
5. When time is up, hit "cancel" and wait for the pressure to come down naturally.
6. Open the lid and stir, adding more milk if the porridge is too thick.
7. Serve with the sliced banana.

Nutritional Info (¼ recipe):

Total calories: 240
Protein: 6
Carbs: 46
Fat: 4
Fiber: 5

Spiced Pear and Squash Soup

Serves: 4-6

Time: 28 minutes (5 minutes prep time, 8 minutes cook time, 15 minutes natural pressure release)

Delicata squash, often called sweet potato squash because of its flavor, is underused in favor of butternut. It's easier to prep and doesn't even need to be peeled in order to be edible. It's a perfect compliment to a fresh Comice pear. To keep the soup from being too sweet, there are plenty of Indian-inspired spices like ginger, turmeric, cayenne, and of course, curry.

Ingredients

4 cups vegetable broth
3 small delicata squash
1 small diced onion
1 peeled and cut Comice pear
2 tablespoons fresh, chopped parsley
1 tablespoon fresh lemon juice
3 teaspoons curry powder
1 teaspoon fresh grated ginger (or ½ teaspoon ground ginger)
½ teaspoon ground turmeric
½ teaspoon salt
Pinch of cayenne pepper
Black pepper to taste

Directions:

1. Turn your PPCXL to "Chicken/Meat."
2. When the pot is hot, cook the onion until softened.
3. Add the peeled and cut pear, turmeric, ginger, and curry.
4. Stir for 2 minutes, and then add in the broth and squash.
5. Seal the lid.
6. Press "Rice/Risotto" and adjust time to 8 minutes.
7. When the timer beeps, hit "cancel" and let the pressure come down naturally.
8. When the pressure is all gone, puree the soup until smooth.
9. Season generously with salt, pepper, cayenne, lemon juice, and chopped parsley.

Nutritional Info (⅙ recipe)

Total calories: 167
Protein: 3
Carbs: 27.5
Fat: 6.6
Fiber: 6.6

Mexican Baked Potato Soup

<u>Serves:</u> 4

<u>Time:</u> 37 minutes (10 minutes prep time, 12 minutes cook time, 15 minutes natural pressure release)

This soup is like a stuffed baked potato in a bowl. There's salsa, garlic, onion, and jalapeno for heat. You're also going to add ½ cup of nutritional yeast to mimic that cheesy goodness.

<u>Ingredients:</u>

- ☐ 4 cups diced potatoes
- ☐ 4 cups veggie broth
- ☐ 4 diced garlic cloves
- ☐ 1 diced onion
- ☐ ½ cup nutritional yeast
- ☐ ½ cup of your favorite salsa
- ☐ ⅛ cup seeded jalapeno peppers
- ☐ 1 teaspoon cumin
- ☐ ¼ teaspoon oregano
- ☐ Black pepper to taste

<u>Directions:</u>

1. Turn your pressure cooker to the "Chicken/Meat" setting.
2. When the pot is hot, add the garlic, jalapeno, and onion.
3. Stir and cook until the onion begins to brown.
4. Turn off the cooker before adding the salsa, potatoes, cumin, and oregano, and pouring in the broth.
5. Stir well before sealing the lid.
6. Select the "Soup/Stew" setting and adjust time to 12 minutes.
7. When time is up, turn off the PPCXL and wait for a natural pressure release.
8. For a creamy soup, puree with a blender.
9. Mix in the nutritional yeast and pepper before serving.

<u>Nutritional Info (¼ recipe):</u>

Total calories: 196
Protein: 10
Carbs: 30

Fat: 0
Fiber: 4

Sun-Dried Tomato Pesto Pasta w/ Chard

<u>Serves:</u> 4

<u>Time:</u> 23 minutes (10 minutes prep time, 3 minutes cook time, 10 minutes natural pressure release)

Simple and satisfying, this whole-wheat pasta is bright with pesto made with sun-dried tomatoes, walnuts, dill, and olive oil. Add wilted chard, and you've got a meal for a family of four.

Ingredients:

- ☐ 1 pound whole-wheat elbow macaroni
- ☐ 8 sun-dried tomatoes
- ☐ 6 thinly-sliced Swiss chard leaves
- ☐ 4 sliced garlic cloves
- ☐ 3 minced garlic cloves
- ☐ ¼ cup dill
- ☐ ¼ cup walnuts
- ☐ ¼ cup + 1 teaspoon olive oil
- ☐ 1 teaspoon red pepper flakes
- ☐ ½ lemon, juiced
- ☐ Salt to taste

Directions:

1. Process dill, walnuts, minced garlic, tomatoes, ¼ cup of olive oil, lemon juice, salt, and red pepper in a blender or food processor until you get a paste.
2. Pour 1 teaspoon of oil in your PPCXL and heat on the "Chicken/Meat" setting.
3. Add the sliced garlic and cook until golden-colored.
4. Add and cook chard until wilted and the liquid has evaporated.
5. Stir in the pasta with just enough water to cover everything.
6. Sprinkle in salt.
7. Close the pressure cooker lid.
8. Hit the "Fish/Vegetables/Steam" setting and add one minute, so you're cooking for a total of 3 minutes.
9. When finished cooking, turn off the cooker and wait for the pressure to reduce on its own.
10. Add your sundried pesto and stir.

11. Season with more salt before serving.

Nutritional Info (¼ recipe):

Total calories: 334
Protein: 9
Carbs: 37
Fat: 19
Fiber: 6

Black-Eyed Pea Masala

<u>Serves:</u> 8

<u>Time:</u> 28 minutes (10 minutes prep time, 8 minutes cook time, 10 minutes natural pressure release)

Replacing the traditional chicken with black-eyed peas, this spoonable hot dish is perfect for chilly evenings and as leftovers for lunch. To speed things up, you quick-soak the peas, which involves boiling them for 1 minute and then soaking them for 1 hour.

Ingredients:

- ☐ 2 cups dried black-eyed peas
- ☐ 2 cups water
- ☐ Two, 15-ounce cans of diced tomato
- ☐ 1 diced onion
- ☐ 1 tablespoon ginger paste
- ☐ 1 tablespoon minced garlic
- ☐ 2 teaspoons cumin seeds
- ☐ 2 teaspoons garam masala
- ☐ 1 teaspoon turmeric
- ☐ 1 teaspoon sugar
- ☐ 1 teaspoon salt
- ☐ ½ teaspoon cayenne

Directions:

1. Boil dried black-eyed peas for 1 minute and then let them sit in the water for at least 1 hour.
2. Turn the Power Pressure Cooker XL to "Chicken/Meat" and just coat the bottom with olive oil.
3. Cook diced onion until softened.
4. Toss in cumin seeds and cook for 1 minute, then add garlic and ginger.
5. Drain peas and add them and the rest of the ingredients into the cooker.
6. Seal the lid.
7. Select "Rice/Risotto," and add time so it reads 8 minutes.
8. When the timer beeps, hit "cancel" and let the pressure reduce naturally.
9. Season well and serve!

Nutritional Info (⅛ recipe):

Total calories: 178
Protein: 11
Carbs: 32.8
Fat: 0
Fiber: 5.8

Maple Syrup Cornbread

Makes: 12-16 squares

Time: 1 hour, 1 minute (5 minutes prep time, 26 minutes cook time, 30 minutes natural release/cool time)

With only 8 ingredients, this cornbread is surprisingly easy. In addition to the cornmeal, there's just flour, milk, oil, apple cider vinegar, baking powder, salt, and maple syrup, which gives the bread a beautiful rich sweetness. You'll never buy a mix again!

Ingredients:

- ☐ 2 cups milk
- ☐ 2 cups cornmeal
- ☐ 1 cup flour
- ☐ ⅓ cup vegetable oil
- ☐ 2 tablespoons maple syrup
- ☐ 2 teaspoons apple cider vinegar
- ☐ 2 teaspoons baking powder
- ☐ ½ teaspoon salt

Directions:

1. Mix milk and apple cider vinegar together in a small bowl.
2. In a separate bowl, mix the dry ingredients.
3. Add the oil and maple syrup to the vinegar/milk bowl.
4. Whisk until foaming.
5. Pour this bowl into the dry ingredients, and mix.
6. Grease a Bundt pan before pouring batter into it.
7. Pour ⅔ cup of water into the PPCXL and lower in a trivet.
8. Put the Bundt pan in the cooker and seal the lid.
9. Hit "Chicken/Meat" and adjust time to 26 minutes.
10. When the timer beeps, turn off the cooker and wait for the pressure to go down on its own.
11. Cool the pan before serving.

Nutritional Info (1 square per serving):

Total calories: 212
Protein: 5
Carbs: 33
Fat: 7
Fiber: 2.7

Refried Beans

<u>Serves:</u> 4

<u>Time:</u> 32 minutes + overnight bean soak (10 minutes prep time, 12 minutes cook time, 10 minutes natural pressure release)

Ingredients:

- [ ] 2 cups water
- [ ] 2 cups dried + soaked pinto beans
- [ ] 1 chopped onion
- [ ] 1 bunch chopped parsley leaves
- [ ] 1 tablespoon olive oil
- [ ] 1 teaspoon salt
- [ ] ½ teaspoon cumin
- [ ] ¼ teaspoon chipotle powder

Cooking Tip: To soak the dried beans the night before, cover with water and leave on the counter overnight, covered by a clean dish towel.

Directions:

1. Turn your cooker on to "Chicken/Meat" and heat the olive oil.
2. Sauté the onion, cumin, and chipotle powder.
3. When the onions are softening, pour in water and soaked beans.
4. Close and seal the lid.
5. Press "Soup/Stew" and adjust time to 12 minutes.
6. When time is up, turn off the cooker and wait 10 minutes.
7. Quick-release any leftover pressure.
8. Mash the beans to your desired texture.
9. Before serving, add salt and top with parsley.

Nutritional Info (¼ recipe):

Calories: 241
Protein: 15.8
Carbs:44.1
Fat: .7
Fiber: 10.8

Miso Soup

<u>Serves:</u> 4

<u>Time:</u> 12 minutes (5 minutes prep time, 7 minutes cook time)

This classic Japanese soup is the vegan version of chicken noodle in that it's perfect for when you're feeling sick. It has silken tofu, celery, onion, carrots, and of course, miso paste. Miso is made from soybeans, and has a mostly salty taste with just a hint of sweetness. It accentuates and deepens every other flavor around it.

Ingredients:

- 4 cups water
- 1 cup cubed silken tofu
- 2 chopped celery stalks
- 2 chopped carrots
- 1 sliced onion
- 2 tablespoons miso paste
- Dash of vegan-friendly soy sauce

Directions:

1. Pour water into the pressure cooker.
2. Add carrots, celery, tofu, and onion.
3. Secure the lid.
4. Press "Rice/Risotto" and add time, so you're cooking for 7 minutes.
5. When the timer beeps, turn off the cooker and release the pressure manually by turning the valve.
6. Spoon out one cup of broth.
7. Mix the miso paste in a bowl with this broth until the paste dissolves.
8. Pour back into the pressure cooker and stir.
9. Finish off with a dash of soy sauce before serving.

Nutritional Info (¼ recipe):

Total calories: 74
Protein: 4
Carbs: 9
Fat: 2
Fiber: 1

Wild Rice with Dried Fruit

<u>Serves:</u> 6-8

<u>Time:</u> 1 hour, 6 minutes (36 minutes cook time, 20 minutes natural pressure release, 10 minutes simmer time)

Looking for a vegan side to a holiday dinner? Wild rice is probably the healthiest rice variation out there, and when you add a mix of dried and fresh fruit, crunchy almonds, and spices like cinnamon and nutmeg, you have a delicious accompaniment anyone at your table can enjoy.

Ingredients:

- ☐ 3 ½ cups water
- ☐ 1 ½ cups wild rice
- ☐ 1 cup mixed dried fruit (apricots, raisins, cranberries, etc.)
- ☐ 1 chopped pear
- ☐ 2 peeled and chopped small apples
- ☐ ½ cup slivered almonds
- ☐ 2 tablespoons apple juice
- ☐ 1 tablespoon maple syrup
- ☐ 1 teaspoon cinnamon
- ☐ 1 teaspoon veggie oil
- ☐ ½ teaspoon ground nutmeg
- ☐ Salt and pepper to taste

Directions:

1. Pour water and rice into your PPCXL.
2. Seal the lid.
3. Select "Chicken/Meat," and adjust time to 36 minutes.
4. In the meantime, soak the dried fruit in apple juice.
5. After half an hour, drain the fruit.
6. When the timer beeps, hit "cancel" and wait for a natural pressure release.
7. Drain the rice.
8. Turn your pressure cooker to "Chicken/Meat" with the lid off, and heat the veggie oil.
9. Cook and stir apples, pears, and almonds for 2 minutes.
10. Add in two tablespoons of apple juice and cool for another 2-3 minutes.

11. Lastly, add in syrup, cooked rice, soaked fruit, and seasonings.

12. Continue cooking and stirring for 2-3 minutes to evaporate the liquid and blend flavors.

13. Serve!

Nutritional Info (⅛ recipe):

Total calories: 226
Protein: 6
Carbs: 43
Fat: 3
Fiber: 5.6

Simple Seitan Roast

<u>Serves:</u> 4

<u>Time:</u> 50 minutes (10 minutes prep time, 30 minutes cook time, 10 minutes natural pressure release)

Seitan is a popular meat substitute made from vital wheat gluten. For this simple roast, you're using ingredients like Worcestershire sauce, nutritional yeast, rosemary, garlic, thyme, and other spices common with meats like pork and chicken. When cooked, it should have a meaty texture that's not too soft and not too chewy when you slice into it.

Ingredients:

Seitan

- ☐ 1 ½ cups vital wheat gluten
- ☐ 1 cup vegetable broth
- ☐ ⅓ cup tapioca flour
- ☐ 3 tablespoons nutritional yeast
- ☐ 2 tablespoons coconut aminos
- ☐ 1 tablespoon vegan-friendly Worcestershire sauce
- ☐ 1 tablespoon olive oil
- ☐ 1 teaspoon garlic powder
- ☐ ½ teaspoon dried rosemary
- ☐ ½ teaspoon dried thyme
- ☐ ¼ teaspoon black pepper
- ☐ ¼ teaspoon sea salt

Cooking broth

- ☐ 3 cups veggie broth
- ☐ 2 cups water
- ☐ ¼ cup coconut aminos
- ☐ 2 tablespoons vegan-friendly Worcestershire sauce
- ☐ 1 teaspoon onion powder

Directions:

1. Look to the "Seitan" ingredient list and whisk together the dry ingredients.
2. In another bowl, mix the wet ingredients.
3. Gradually pour wet into dry.

4. Fold over the ingredients with a spatula, and then knead with your hands for a few minutes.
5. Mold into a round loaf.
6. Pull at the top, and then roll the loaf under itself so it's smooth.
7. Adjust the loaf's shape so it's more oblong.
8. Roll tightly in cheesecloth and tie off the ends.
9. Put the roast in the pressure cooker.
10. Pour in all the ingredients from the second ingredient list.
11. Secure and seal the lid.
12. Select "Chicken/Meat," and adjust time to 30 minutes.
13. When the timer beeps, hit "cancel" and wait 10 minutes before releasing the pressure.
14. Slice up and serve!

Nutritional Info (¼ recipe):

Total calories: 451
Protein: 42
Carbs: 51
Fat: 4
Fiber: 0

Jackfruit Lettuce Wraps

<u>Serves:</u> 4

<u>Time:</u> 23 minutes (10 minutes prep time, 3 minutes cook time, 10 minutes natural pressure release)

Jackfruit is one of the most exciting new vegan meat substitutes out there. When it's packed in water, it has a mild-enough flavor that is a great blank slate for "meaty" spices like this recipe's garlic, soy sauce, and hoisin. Less than 100 calories when you use the jackfruit as filling for a lettuce wrap, this is a perfect summer BBQ option for vegans.

Ingredients:

- [ ] 20-ounces of rinsed and drained jackfruit packed in water
- [ ] 2 cups shredded cabbage
- [ ] 4 sliced green onions
- [ ] 3-4 minced garlic cloves
- [ ] 1 small diced onion
- [ ] ½ cup vegetable broth
- [ ] ½ cup sliced baby carrots
- [ ] 5-ounces mushrooms
- [ ] 2 tablespoons soy sauce
- [ ] 1 tablespoon hoisin sauce
- [ ] 1 tablespoon olive oil
- [ ] 1 teaspoon minced ginger root

Directions:

1. Turn your PPCXL to "Chicken/Meat" and pour in olive oil.
2. When hot, add the diced onion, mushrooms, ginger, and garlic.
3. Cook until the onion is soft.
4. Add hoisin sauce, soy sauce, and broth and simmer for a minute or so.
5. Add the rest of the ingredients except green onions and cabbage.
6. Seal the lid.
7. Select "Fish/Vegetable/Steam" and add one minute.
8. When the timer beeps, hit "cancel" and wait for a natural pressure release.
9. Stir before shredding and serving with big lettuce leaves, cabbage, and green onions for garnish.

Nutritional Info (¼ recipe):

Total calories: 97
Protein: 4.2
Carbs: 12.7
Fat: 3
Fiber: 3.1

Sweet Potato + Black-Eyed Pea Bowl

<u>Serves:</u> 4
<u>Time:</u> 29 minutes (15 minutes prep time, 14 minutes cook time)

Packed with protein and fiber, this vegan lunch bowl has lots of satisfying flavors. There are sweet potatoes, which are very filling, black-eyed peas, and spinach. These are spiced with garlic, cumin, and coriander. Mix everything together with a little salt if necessary, and enjoy!

Ingredients:

- ☐ 3-4 halved sweet potatoes
- ☐ 4 smashed garlic cloves
- ☐ 2 cups spinach
- ☐ 1 ½ cups water
- ☐ 1 cup rinsed black-eyed peas
- ☐ 1 chopped onion
- ☐ 1 tablespoon tomato paste
- ☐ 1 tablespoon olive oil
- ☐ 1 teaspoon cumin seeds
- ☐ ½ teaspoon coriander seeds
- ☐ Dash of salt

Directions:

1. Turn your cooker to "Chicken/Meat" and heat oil.
2. Cook the onion until soft and then add garlic and cumin and coriander seeds.
3. After a minute, add water, tomato paste, and black-eyed peas.
4. Stir so the tomato paste dissolves.
5. Put the potatoes in the steamer basket, so the cut side is facing up, and lower into cooker.
6. Seal the lid and adjust time to 14 minutes.
7. When time is up, hit "cancel" and quick-release.
8. Remove the potatoes before adding spinach.
9. Throw in a dash of salt and wait until the spinach wilts.
10. Serve everything in a bowl.

Nutritional Info (¼ recipe per serving):

Total calories: 273.6
Protein: 8.2
Carbs: 48.5
Fat: 6.3
Fiber: 9.8

Chapter 13

Sides + Snacks

Steamed Edamame with Garlic

<u>Serves:</u> 4-6
<u>Time:</u> 3 minutes

Need a really fast vegetable side? This edamame takes advantage of the "Steam" setting for lightning-quick cooking. You take that time to mix up a garlic-soy sauce dressing on the stove, which you just toss with the pods when they're done.

Ingredients:

- ☐ 1 cup water
- ☐ 2 cups edamame in pods, fresh or frozen
- ☐ 3 minced garlic cloves
- ☐ 1 tablespoon soy sauce
- ☐ 1 teaspoon olive oil
- ☐ Pinch of sea salt

Directions:

1. Pour water into the PPCXL and put in the steamer basket.
2. Tumble edamame in the basket and seal the lid.
3. Select "Fish/Steam/Vegetables" and cook for 3 minutes.
4. While that steams, heat oil in a small pan on the stove.
5. Cook the garlic until fragrant, but not brown yet.
6. Pour in soy sauce and remove from heat.
7. When the pressure cooker beeps, carefully quick-release after turning it off.
8. Put the edamame in a bowl and toss with oil dressing.
9. Sprinkle on salt.

Nutritional Info (¼ recipe):

Total calories: 105
Protein: 8
Carbs: 8
Fat: 1
Fiber: 2

Stewed Tomatoes + Green Beans

<u>Serves</u>: 4-6

<u>Time</u>: 11 minutes (5 minutes prep time, 6 minutes cook time)

Green beans and tomatoes are beautiful together; both are fresh, with the tomatoes bringing more acid, and the green beans a more muted, nutty flavor. Garlic and olive oil blend everything together, and a finishing sprinkle of pink Himalayan salt - one of the purest salts you can buy - makes the whole dish pop and sparkle.

Ingredients:

- ☐ 1 pound green beans
- ☐ 2 cups chopped tomatoes
- ☐ 1 crushed garlic clove
- ☐ 1 tablespoon olive oil + 1 teaspoon
- ☐ Sprinkle of pink Himalayan salt

Directions:

1. Trim the ends off the green beans and prepare tomatoes.
2. Turn your cooker on to the "Chicken/Meat" setting and heat 1 teaspoon of oil.
3. Add garlic and cook until fragrant and slightly golden.
4. Stir in tomatoes, adding ½ cup of water if they start to stick to the bottom.
5. Put in the steamer basket, right on top of the tomatoes, and pour in the beans.
6. Sprinkle in some salt.
7. Close and seal the lid.
8. Push the "Rice/Risotto" button and cook for the 6 minutes.
9. When the timer beeps, turn off the cooker and quick-release the pressure.
10. Take out the steamer basket and mix cooked beans with the tomatoes.
11. Serve right away!

Nutritional Info (⅙ recipe per serving):

Total calories: 55.3

Protein: 1.6

Carbs: 6.3

Fat: 3.2

Fiber: 2.6

Collard Greens and Bacon

<u>Serves:</u> 4

<u>Time:</u> 12 minutes (5 minutes prep time, 7 minutes cook time)

Whether you live in the South or not, a good collard greens recipe is a must-know for home cooks. This one is very easy, but big with flavors from slab bacon, sweet onion, garlic, and balsamic vinegar.

Ingredients:

- ☐ 1 ½ pounds chopped collard greens, stems trimmed off
- ☐ ½ cup chicken broth
- ☐ 4-ounces diced slab bacon
- ☐ 1 chopped sweet onion
- ☐ 3 tablespoons balsamic vinegar
- ☐ 2 tablespoons tomato paste
- ☐ 1 tablespoon packed dark brown sugar
- ☐ 2 teaspoons minced garlic

Directions:

1. Turn cooker to "Chicken/Meat" and sauté bacon until nice and crispy.
2. Add in the onion and keep cooking until translucent.
3. Add in garlic and collard greens.
4. Stir for a few minutes to blend flavors.
5. Add vinegar, broth, tomato paste, and brown sugar.
6. Stir until the tomato paste and sugar have dissolved.
7. Secure and seal the cooker lid.
8. Select "Rice/Risotto" and adjust time to 7 minutes.
9. When the timer beeps, turn off the cooker and quick-release the pressure.
10. Stir well and serve!

Nutritional Info (¼ recipe per serving):

Calories: 241
Protein: 15
Carbs: 15
Fat: 12
Fiber: 6.5

Roasted Potatoes with Garlic

<u>Serves:</u> 4

<u>Time:</u> 28 minutes (10 minutes prep time, 8 minutes cook time, 10 minutes natural release)

Get the roasted flavor of potatoes without the long oven time with this simple recipe. The roasty, toastiness comes from browning the potatoes in oil, garlic, and rosemary before bringing the cooker to pressure. That time enriches the flavors and ensures a crisp outside to the potatoes.

Ingredients:

- ☐ 2 pounds baby potatoes
- ☐ 3 garlic cloves
- ☐ 4 tablespoons veggie oil
- ☐ ½ cup vegetable stock
- ☐ 1 fresh rosemary sprig
- ☐ Salt and pepper to taste

Directions:

1. Turn the cooker to "Chicken/Meat."
2. When the bottom is hot, add the oil and heat.
3. Stir in potatoes, garlic, and rosemary to brown the potatoes.
4. After 8-10 minutes of browning, poke each potato in the middle with a fork a few times.
5. Add in veggie stock and seal the cooker lid.
6. Select "Rice/Risotto" and add 2 minutes, so you are cooking for 8 minutes.
7. When the timer beeps, turn off the cooker and wait 10 minutes.
8. Quick-release any remaining pressure.
9. Season potatoes with salt and pepper before serving.

Nutritional Info (¼ recipe per serving):

Total calories: 336
Protein: 5
Carbs: 49
Fat: 14
Fiber: 7

Buttery Brussels Sprouts with Citrus Sauce

<u>Serves:</u> 8
<u>Time:</u> 5 minutes cook time

Brussels sprouts aren't the most popular side dish in the world, but that's probably because people haven't been making them this way. The pressure cooker ensures all the nutrition is preserved, and that the sprouts are totally tender. Their cabbage-like flavor is sweetened with maple syrup and butter, and brightened with a mixture of fresh orange, orange zest, and lemon juice.

Ingredients:

- 2 pounds Brussels sprouts
- 2 tablespoons maple syrup
- 2 tablespoons fresh orange juice
- 2 tablespoons lemon juice
- 1 tablespoon butter
- 1 teaspoon fresh grated orange zest
- ½ teaspoon salt
- ¼ teaspoon black pepper

Directions:

1. Cut off ¼-inch off the bottom of the sprouts and rinse under cool water.
2. Tumble into your cooker and pour in about ¾ cup of water, or however much it takes to cover the sprouts.
3. Seal the lid.
4. Hit "Rice/Risotto" and reduce time to 5 minutes.
5. While the sprouts cook, mix the rest of the ingredients in a saucepan over low heat.
6. When butter is melted and everything has mixed in evenly, remove from heat.
7. When time is up on the cooker, hit "cancel" and quick-release the pressure.
8. Pour sprouts into a bowl and roll in the sauce.

Nutritional Info (⅛ recipe per serving):

Total calories: 65
Protein: 3
Carbs: 12
Fat: 2
Fiber: 3

Quick Baked Potatoes

<u>Serves:</u> 4
<u>Time:</u> 32 minutes (12 minutes cook time, 20 minutes natural pressure release)

Have hot and ready baked potatoes in just 32 minutes with this recipe. You can cook up to 5 pounds with just 1 cup of water in the pressure cooker, and serve any way you want, whether you're making them for mashing, stuffing, or just eating with some butter and seasonings.

Ingredients:

- ☐ Up to 5 pounds of potatoes (4 potatoes for 4 servings)
- ☐ 1 cup of water
- ☐ Seasonings

Directions:

1. Pour water into your cooker and add steamer rack.
2. Put the potatoes in the rack and seal the lid.
3. Click "Chicken/Meat" and adjust time to 12 minutes.
4. When the timer beeps, hit "cancel" and wait 20 minutes for a natural pressure release.

Nutritional Info (1 potato per serving):

Total calories: 110
Protein: 4
Carbs: 26
Fat: 0
Fiber: 2

Corn Pudding

<u>Serves:</u> 4

<u>Time:</u> 40 minutes (10 minutes prep time, 30 minutes cook time)

Corn is popular during the autumn when the vegetable is in season, and warm, comforting pudding is an excellent way to use it. With a base of milk, cornmeal, eggs, and sour cream, the pudding is soft, creamy, and sweetened with only 1 tablespoon of sugar and the corn's natural flavor. It would be a great addition to any holiday meal.

Ingredients:

- ☐ 1 ½ cups water
- ☐ 2 beaten eggs
- ☐ 2 chopped shallots
- ☐ 1 cup fresh corn kernels
- ☐ ¾ cup whole milk
- ☐ ¼ cup sour cream
- ☐ 3 tablespoons cornmeal
- ☐ 1 tablespoon sugar
- ☐ Salt and pepper to taste

Directions:

1. Turn your cooker to "Chicken/Meat" and add butter.
2. When butter is melted, add shallots.
3. Hit "cancel" and let the heat from the butter cook the shallots.
4. In the meantime, mix milk, sour cream, cornmeal, eggs, pepper, and salt in a bowl.
5. Add the melted butter and shallots into the bowl.
6. Pour water into the cooker and lower in trivet.
7. Spray a 6 or 7-inch round baking dish and pour in pudding batter.
8. Wrap the whole thing in foil and put in the steamer rack.
9. Close and seal the lid.
10. Push "Chicken/Meat" again and adjust time to 30 minutes.
11. When the timer beeps, hit "cancel" and quick-release.
12. Cool the pudding before serving.

Nutritional Info (¼ recipe per serving):

Total calories: 207
Protein: 6
Carbs: 19
Fat: 7
Fiber: 1

Marsala Potatoes

<u>**Serves:**</u> 3-4
<u>**Time:**</u> 18 minutes (10 minutes prep time, 8 minutes cook time)

Sweet and dry, Marsala wine adds a richness to this otherwise simple potato dish with olive oil, salt, pepper, and rosemary. The diced potatoes only take about 8 minutes to cook and become infused with the Marsala, so you can have your side dish ready in less than 20 minutes, start to finish.

<u>Ingredients:</u>

- ☐ 4-5 medium diced washed and scrubbed potatoes
- ☐ 1 cup of Marsala wine
- ☐ 1 sprig fresh rosemary
- ☐ 1 tablespoon olive oil
- ☐ Salt and pepper to taste

<u>Directions:</u>

1. Pour oil in the PPCXL.
2. When hot, add potatoes, rosemary, salt, and pepper.
3. Stir to coat the potatoes for 5 minutes.
4. Pour in the wine and stir, so any stuck-on pieces of food come loose.
5. Close and seal the lid.
6. Select "Risotto" and adjust time to 8 minutes.
7. When time is up, hit "cancel" and quick-release.
8. You'll know the potatoes are done if they are easily pierced with a fork.

<u>Nutritional Info (¼ recipe per serving):</u>
Calories: 279
Protein: 13
Carbs: 45
Fat: 6
Fiber: 4.5

Fresh Beet Salad

<u>Serves:</u> 4-6

<u>Time:</u> 45 minutes (5 minutes prep time, 30 minutes cook time, 10 minutes cool time)

Beets are underrated as a veggie because they're rough and tough. In the pressure cooker, however, they become tender very quickly, and their skins rub right off after you run them under cold water. A dressing of minced garlic, parsley, olive oil, capers, salt, and pepper, and beautiful white balsamic vinegar balance out the natural earthiness of the beets.

Ingredients:

- 4 whole scrubbed beets
- 2 tablespoons capers
- 2 tablespoons white balsamic vinegar
- 1 minced garlic clove
- 1 tablespoon olive oil
- 1 tablespoon chopped parsley
- Salt and pepper to taste

Directions:

1. Pour 1 cup of water into the Power Pressure Cooker XL and lower in steamer basket.
2. Snip the tops of the beets.
3. Put the beets in the pressure cooker and seal the lid.
4. Select "Chicken/Meat" and adjust time to 30 minutes.
5. While the beets cook, prepare the dressing.
6. Mix garlic, parsley, capers, olive oil, salt, and pepper in a mason jar and shake.
7. When time is up on the cooker, hit "cancel" and quick-release.
8. The beets should be easily pierced by a fork.
9. Run under cold water and when you can handle them, use your fingers to rub off the skins.
10. Slice beets into discs and toss with the dressing.
11. Serve right away!

Nutritional Info (⅙ recipe per serving):

Calories: 43.1   Fat: 2.4
Protein: 0.7   Fiber: .8
Carbs: 5.4

Spaghetti Squash w/ Honey-Ginger Glaze

<u>Serves:</u> 4-6

<u>Time:</u> 39 minutes (24 minutes cook time, 10 minutes cool time, 5 minutes simmering time)

Spaghetti squash is one of the most versatile veggies out there. It gets done very quickly in a pressure cooker, and has a lovely nutty, lightly-sweet flavor. A honey-ginger glaze brings out that sweetness. You'll notice chicken base as an ingredient, which is a concentrated form of chicken broth. It has a stronger flavor than just stock.

<u>Ingredients:</u>

- [ ] One 3-lb spaghetti squash
- [ ] 1 cup water
- [ ] 1 cup honey
- [ ] ½ cup brown sugar
- [ ] 2 tablespoons butter
- [ ] 2 tablespoons cornstarch
- [ ] 2 tablespoons grated ginger
- [ ] 1 tablespoon chicken base
- [ ] Salt and pepper to taste

<u>Directions:</u>

1. Pour 1 cup of water into the pressure cooker and lower in steamer basket.
2. Put the spaghetti squash in the basket.
3. Close and seal the lid.
4. Press "Chicken/Meat" and adjust time to 24 minutes.
5. When the timer beeps, turn off cooker and quick-release.
6. Cut the squash in half once it's cooled a little.
7. While that continues to cool, pour out the water in the pressure cooker.
8. To make the glaze, melt butter in a skillet and add ginger.
9. Cook until ginger becomes fragrant.
10. Add chicken base, sugar, and honey.
11. In a bowl, mix cold water and cornstarch until smooth.
12. Pour into glaze and simmer for 5 minutes to thicken.
13. When the consistency is the way you want it, scrape out noodles of squash and toss in the glaze.

Nutritional Info (¼ recipe):

Total calories: 580
Protein: 3
Carbs: 128
Fat: 8
Fiber: 6

Hummus

<u>Serves:</u> 8-10

<u>Time:</u> 1 hour, 32 minutes (52 minutes cook time, 40 minutes natural pressure release)

Hummus is a delicious dip made from chickpeas, garlic, tahini, and seasonings. It's great with crackers, as a substitute for mayo, with cut veggies, and so on. You just throw chickpeas in the pressure cooker with water and some olive oil, and cook for 52 minutes. Then you blend everything till smooth, chill, and enjoy!

Ingredients:

- ☐ 4 cups water
- ☐ 6 tablespoons olive oil
- ☐ 8-ounces rinsed and dried chickpeas
- ☐ 3 minced garlic cloves
- ☐ ⅓ cup tahini
- ☐ ¼ cup fresh lemon juice
- ☐ 1 ½ teaspoons salt
- ☐ ½ teaspoon smoked paprika

Directions:

1. Pour 2 tablespoons oil, chickpeas, and water into the cooker.
2. Seal the lid.
3. Select "Chicken/Meat" and adjust time to 52 minutes.
4. When the timer beeps, turn off cooker and wait for a natural pressure release.
5. Drain the chickpeas and save one cup of the liquid.
6. Put chickpeas in food processor and blend with 4 tablespoons olive oil, garlic, lemon juice, salt, paprika, and ¼ cup of the cooking liquid.
7. Continue adding liquid to get the right texture.
8. Store in the fridge for up to 5 days.

Nutritional Info (⅛ recipe per serving):
Total calories: 264
Protein: 8
Carbs: 20
Fat: 3
Fiber: 6

Jalapeno Cheese Dip

<u>Serves</u>: 12

<u>Time:</u> 13 minutes (5 minutes prep time, 3 minutes cook time, 5 minutes natural pressure release)

This homemade cheese dip with the heat of jalapenos is a tasty treat for special occasions like big sports games. It uses both Colby and cheddar cheese, and tomatoes and jalapenos to cut through the fat with some heat and acid.

Ingredients:

- ☐ 8-ounces shredded cheddar cheese
- ☐ 8-ounces shredded Colby cheese
- ☐ 1 cup milk
- ☐ ½ cup canned tomatoes
- ☐ ½ cup pickled jalapenos
- ☐ 2 tablespoons butter
- ☐ 2 tablespoons flour
- ☐ 2 tablespoons lemon juice
- ☐ Salt and pepper to taste

Directions:

1. Melt the butter in your PPCXL on the "Chicken/Meat" setting.
2. Gradually whisk in flour until you get a paste.
3. Pour in milk and stir until smooth.
4. Let the mixture start to boil.
5. Stir in cheeses until melted.
6. Add tomatoes and jalapenos.
7. Seal the lid.
8. Adjust cooking time to just 3 minutes.
9. When the timer beeps, hit "cancel" and let the pressure decrease on its own.
10. Stir in lemon juice, salt, and pepper before serving.

Nutritional Information (1/12 recipe per serving):

Calories: 438   Fat: 28

Protein: 12   Fiber: 1

Carbs: 34

Crunchy Corn Niblets

<u>Serves:</u> 6

<u>Time:</u> 46 minutes + overnight soak time (36 minutes cook time, 10 minutes saucepan time)

Love snacking on something crunchy while you're watching a movie or TV show, but worry about how many calories are in potato chips? Try this homemade corn niblets, with less than 100 calories per serving, no carbs, and only 5 grams of fat! This recipe uses salt and chili powder for seasoning, but feel free to experiment. Also, remember you need to soak the dry corn overnight before preparing the recipe.

<u>Ingredients:</u>

- ☐ 2 cups dried corn
- ☐ 2 tablespoons olive oil
- ☐ 1 tablespoon chili powder
- ☐ 1 teaspoon salt

<u>Directions:</u>

1. Soak dry corn overnight in water.
2. When you're ready to make the recipe, pour into the PPCXL with the minimum requirement of water for the cooker.
3. Seal the lid and hit "Chicken/Meat," and adjust time to 36 minutes.
4. When time is up, turn off the cooker and quick-release the pressure.
5. Drain the corn and dry well with paper towels.
6. Heat olive oil in a saucepan and add corn, salt, and chili powder.
7. Roast over the stove until crunchy.

<u>Nutritional Info (⅙ recipe per serving):</u>
Total calories: 74
Protein: 0
Carbs: 0
Fat: 5
Fiber: 0

Loaded Potato Skins

<u>Serves:</u> 6

<u>Time:</u> 43 minutes (6 minutes prep time, 14 minutes cook time, 20 minutes cool time, 3 minutes broil time)

Stuffed with bacon, cheese, and sour cream, these game-day potato skins are not fooling around. They're not a health food, so to make the recipe lower-calorie, switch out the sour cream for Greek-style plain yogurt and the butter with coconut oil, and choose smaller potatoes.

Ingredients:

- ☐ 1 lb. chopped bacon
- ☐ 6 russet potatoes
- ☐ 12-ounces shredded cheddar
- ☐ 1 cup sour cream
- ☐ 1 cup water
- ☐ 2 tablespoons melted butter

Directions:

1. Turn your cooker to the "Chicken/Meat" setting and add bacon.
2. When crisp, turn off the cooker and plate, blotting with a paper towel to remove grease.
3. Clean the pressure cooker and pour in 1 cup of water.
4. Put the potatoes in the steamer basket and lower into cooker.
5. Seal the lid.
6. Select "Chicken/Meat" again and adjust time to 14 minutes.
7. When the timer beeps, turn off cooker and quick-release.
8. Take out the potatoes and let them cool.
9. Cut them in half and spoon out center.
10. Brush the skin with butter and lay on a baking sheet.
11. Fill scooped-out center with bacon and cheese.
12. Broil and then serve with sour cream.

Nutritional Info (2 potato halves each):

Total calories: 803
Protein: 38
Carbs: 33
Fat: 58
Fiber: 4

Spinach + Artichoke Dip

<u>Serves</u>: 4-6

<u>Time</u>: 17 minutes (5 minutes prep time, 12 minutes cook time)

One of the healthier of the snack dips, this creamy spinach + artichoke dip uses light mayo, sour cream, Parmesan cheese, and mozzarella cheese for its dressing. Seasonings are just simple garlic salt, black pepper, and a little cayenne pepper for spice. Serve with veggies, tortilla chips, Pita bread, or any other favorites.

Ingredients:

- ☐ 14-ounce can of drained and chopped artichoke hearts
- ☐ 10-ounces thawed and drained frozen chopped spinach
- ☐ 1 cup light mayo
- ☐ 1 cup grated Parmesan cheese
- ☐ 1 cup shredded mozzarella cheese
- ☐ ½ cup sour cream
- ☐ ¼ teaspoon garlic salt
- ☐ ¼ teaspoon black pepper
- ☐ Dash of cayenne pepper

Directions:

1. Mix everything in a sprayed 1-quart baking dish.
2. Wrap tightly in foil.
3. Pour 2 cups of water into the PPCXL and put in trivet.
4. Put the baking dish on the trivet and seal the cooker lid.
5. Hit "Chicken/Meat" and adjust time to 12 minutes.
6. When time is up, hit "cancel" and quick-release.
7. Stir and serve!

Nutritional Info (⅙ recipe per serving):

Total calories: 256
Protein: 4
Carbs: 12
Fat: 19
Fiber: 0

Chapter 14

Stocks, Sauces, and Sips

Everyday Chicken Stock

Makes: 2.5-3 quarts

Time: 1 hour, 54 minutes (1 hour, 24 minutes cook time, 30 minutes natural pressure release)

As a pantry essential, it can get expensive to keep buying chicken stock. In your pressure cooker, you can make up to 3 quarts for very little money using chicken bones and scraps, celery, onions, and bay leaves. Broth stored in the fridge lasts for about 4 days, while you can freeze it for up to 1 year.

Ingredients:

- ☐ 3 pounds of chicken bones/scraps
- ☐ 3 chopped celery stalks
- ☐ 2 bay leaves
- ☐ 2 chopped onions
- ☐ 1 tablespoon apple cider vinegar
- ☐ Enough water to cover bones

Directions:

1. Put chicken bones/scraps in your cooker, and then lay the veggies and bay leaves on top.
2. Pour in just enough water to cover the bones.
3. Stir in apple cider vinegar before sealing the lid.
4. Hit "Chicken/Meat" and adjust time to 1 hour and 24 minutes.
5. When the timer beeps, hit "cancel" and wait for a natural pressure release.
6. Before storing in the fridge, strain the broth and throw out the solids, and let it cool to room temperature.

Nutritional Info (1 cup per serving):

Total calories: 86
Protein: 6
Carbs: 8
Fat: 3
Fiber: 0

Tomato Vodka Sauce

<u>Makes:</u> 4 cups
<u>Time:</u> 23 minutes (8 minutes prep time, 15 minutes cook time)

If you've never tried vodka in tomato sauce, you've been missing out. The alcohol intensifies the flavors and aroma. People say that the vodka "unlocks" the potential in the ingredients, especially the tomatoes. Serve with a good pasta for a special spaghetti night!

Ingredients:

One 28-ounce can of peeled tomatoes
2 cups diced yellow onion
1 cup diced carrot
1 cup heavy cream
¼ cup vodka
2 tablespoons Parmesan cheese
1 tablespoon olive oil
¼ teaspoon crushed red pepper flakes
Salt and pepper to taste

Directions:

1. Heat oil on "chicken/meat" in your pressure cooker and add onion.
2. Cook for 8 minutes until clear.
3. Add in the carrots and tomatoes.
4. Seal the lid and adjust cook time for 15 minutes.
5. When time is up, hit "cancel" and quick-release.
6. Mix in vodka, cream, crushed red pepper flakes, and cheese. .
7. Turn back to "chicken/meat" and simmer to reduce the alcohol.
8. Puree in a blender and season to taste with salt and pepper before serving!

Nutritional Info (¼ recipe per serving):
Total calories: 404
Protein: 4
Carbs: 14
Fat: 33
Fiber: 3.5

Root Vegetable Sauce

<u>Serves:</u> 4

<u>Time:</u> 5 minutes (3 minutes prep time, 2 minutes cook time)

Did you know you can make a sauce out of any vegetable? It's true! If you're looking for a way to get more veggies in your diet, try out this delicious root vegetable sauce with turnips and baby carrots. Butter helps make the sauce smooth, while a bit of Parmesan cheese and ginger add layers of flavor.

Ingredients:

- ☐ 1 cup chicken broth
- ☐ 2 large chopped turnips
- ☐ 8-ounces baby carrots
- ☐ 2 tablespoons white sugar
- ☐ 2 tablespoons butter
- ☐ 2 tablespoons Parmesan cheese
- ☐ 2 teaspoons ground ginger

Directions:

1. Heat butter in your PPCXL on "chicken/meat."
2. Add turnips and carrots, and cook for 3 minutes.
3. Add the rest of the ingredients.
4. Seal the lid and adjust time to 2 minutes.
5. When time is up, hit "cancel" and quick-release.
6. Puree well before using!

Nutritional Info (¼ recipe per serving):

Total calories: 135
Protein: 2
Carbs: 18
Fat: 7
Fiber: 2.75

Broccoli Pesto

<u>Serves:</u> 4

<u>Time:</u> 10 minutes (7 minutes prep time, 3 minutes cook time)

Pesto is typically made with just basil, but when you need a fresh green sauce, broccoli works just as well. Flavors from onion, garlic, pine nuts, and of course, basil, get you that classic pesto taste, while a pinch of red pepper flakes adds just a bit of heat.

Ingredients:

- ☐ 1 ½ cups chopped broccoli florets
- ☐ 1 chopped onion
- ☐ 1 smashed garlic clove
- ☐ ½ cup fresh basil
- ☐ ⅓ cup toasted pine nuts
- ☐ ¼ cup vegetable broth
- ☐ 1 tablespoon olive oil
- ☐ 1 tablespoon lemon juice
- ☐ ¼ teaspoon red pepper flakes
- ☐ Salt to taste

Directions:

1. Turn your PPCXL to the "chicken/meat" setting and add olive oil.
2. When it's hot, add the onion and cook until soft.
3. Pour in vegetable broth, and add broccoli and a pinch of salt.
4. Seal the lid and adjust time to 3 minutes.
5. Quick-release the pressure when time is up.
6. Add the contents of cooker to a blender, with the rest of the ingredients.
7. Puree until smooth, and you have pesto!

Nutritional Info (¼ recipe per serving):

Total calories: 105
Protein: 3
Carbs: 6
Fat: 8
Fiber: 1

Italian-Style Meat Sauce

<u>Serves:</u> 6-8

<u>Time:</u> 54 minutes (20 minutes prep time, 24 minutes cook time, 10 minutes natural pressure release)

The key to a great meat sauce is flavor-layering. Since the pressure cooker isn't designed for slow simmering, cooking aromatics like garlic, carrot, celery, and onion beforehand is necessary to build those rich tastes. Once those are cooked, the sauce itself is made from two kinds of sausage, wine, crushed tomatoes, and herbs. The final result: amazing, hearty, flavor.

Ingredients:

Aromatics

- ☐ 3 crushed garlic cloves
- ☐ 1 diced onion
- ☐ 1 peeled and diced carrot
- ☐ 1 diced celery stalk
- ☐ 1 tablespoon olive oil
- ☐ ½ teaspoon salt
- ☐ ¼ teaspoon crushed red pepper flakes

Sauce

- ☐ 1 ¼ pounds hot Italian sausage
- ☐ 1 ¼ pounds sweet Italian sausage
- ☐ 28-ounce can crushed tomatoes
- ☐ 1 cup chicken broth
- ☐ ½ cup red wine
- ☐ 2-3 sprigs fresh thyme
- ☐ 1 sprig rosemary
- ☐ 1 sprig fresh basil
- ☐ 1 teaspoon black pepper

Directions:

1. Heat olive oil in your pressure cooker (on the "Chicken/Meat" setting) and add garlic, carrot, celery, and onion.
2. Toss in red pepper flakes and salt right away, and stir for 8 minutes.
3. Once the onion has softened, pour in the wine and scrape up any stuck bits.

4. Simmer for one minute before adding both sausages.
5. After 5 minutes of browning, pour in broth and tomatoes.
6. Tie the herbs together and add to pot.
7. Seal the lid.
8. Adjust the cook time to 24 minutes.
9. When time is up, hit "cancel" and wait 10 minutes before quick-releasing.
10. Season with pepper before serving.

Nutritional Info (1 cup per serving):

Total calories: 302
Protein: 20
Carbs: 6
Fat: 21
Fiber: 1

Cauliflower Alfredo Sauce

<u>Serves:</u> 2-4

<u>Time:</u> 14 minutes (5 minutes prep time, 4 minutes cook time, 5 minutes natural pressure release)

Cauliflower in place of cream might seem odd for an Alfredo sauce, but once you puree it, it makes a lot of sense. It cuts a *ton* of calories and fat, and adds valuable vitamins and minerals. Other than the cauliflower, there's only six ingredients - water, cheese, garlic, olive oil, salt, and pepper. It's the easiest sauce ever!

Ingredients:

- 12-ounces cauliflower florets
- 1 cup Parmesan cheese
- ½ cup water
- 2 minced garlic cloves
- 1 teaspoon olive oil
- Salt and pepper to taste

Directions:

1. Turn your Power Pressure Cooker XL to "Chicken/Meat" and heat oil.
2. Stir in the garlic for about 1 minute, and then pour in the water.
3. Put cauliflower in the steamer basket and lower into the cooker.
4. Seal the lid.
5. Adjust cook time to 4 minutes.
6. When the timer beeps, turn off the cooker and wait for the pressure to come down on its own.
7. When safe, open the lid and stir in cheese.
8. Let the sauce cool a little before pureeing.
9. Season before serving.

Nutritional Info (¼ recipe per serving):

Total calories: 101
Protein: 8
Carbs: 2
Fat: 7
Fiber: 2

Chai Tea

Makes: 1 ½ cups
Time: 3 minutes

The Power Pressure Cooker XL is a great cooker for chai tea, because it has a lower pressure than most cookers, which would cause the tea to burn and become bitter. This recipe makes 1 ½ cups, but you can make as many cups as you can safely fit in the cooker. It uses real masala spices like cardamom, cloves, and ginger for an authentic-tasting milky chai.

Ingredients:

- 1 cup water + ½ cup water
- 1 cup almond milk
- 2 crushed cardamom pods
- 2 crushed cloves
- 2 teaspoons sugar
- 1 ½ teaspoons black loose-leaf tea powder
- 1 teaspoon crushed ginger

Directions:

1. Pour 1 cup of water into the Power Pressure Cooker XL.
2. Add all the other ingredients (including ½ cup of water) into a bowl, and put it on top of the trivet inside the cooker.
3. Seal cooker.
4. Hit "Fish/Steam/Vegetable" and adjust time to 3 minutes.
5. When time is up, turn off the cooker and quick-release the pressure.
6. Strain the tea and serve!

Nutritional Info (1 ½ cups per serving):

Total calories: 93
Protein: 1
Carbs: 10
Fat: 4
Fiber: 0

Strawberry Soda Syrup

Makes: About 1 cup

Time: 33 minutes (18 minutes cook time, 10 minutes natural release, 5 minutes stovetop time)

The base of a great Italian soda is a good syrup. You can buy them, but making your own is easy and so much better-tasting. This recipe is for strawberry soda syrup, but you can sub in any fruit of your choice, like blackberries or blueberries.

Ingredients:

- ☐ 14-ounces washed and dried strawberries
- ☐ 2 cups white sugar
- ☐ 1 cup water

Directions:

1. Pour water into your PPCXL.
2. Put berries into your steamer basket and lower into the cooker.
3. Seal the lid.
4. Select "Chicken/Meat" and adjust time to 18 minutes.
5. When the timer beeps, hit "cancel" and wait for a natural pressure release.
6. Remove the steamer basket, and eat or throw out the berries.
7. Pour strawberry-infused cooking liquid into a measuring cup and remember what the amount is.
8. Pour into a saucepan and add twice the amount of sugar, so the ratio of water to sugar is 1:2.
9. Turn the stove on to medium-high, and stir until the sugar has dissolved and the liquid has become a syrup.
10. Store in the fridge for up to 2 months.

Nutritional Info (1 tablespoon per serving):

Total calories: 167
Protein: 0
Carbs: 46
Fat: 0
Fiber: 0

Peach Simple Syrup

Makes: About 1 cup

Time: 56 minutes (6 minutes cook time, 10 minutes natural release time, 30-4o minutes boil time)

Is it peach season and you have a whole bunch on hand you don't know what to do with? Make simple syrup! It's perfect for boozy summery drinks like daiquiris, brambles, and more. You can use it for non-alcoholic drinks too, and give iced tea a peachy upgrade. Simple syrup will last in the fridge for up to 2 weeks.

Ingredients:

- ☐ 4 cups fresh, chopped peaches
- ☐ 2 cups sugar
- ☐ 2 cups water

Directions:

1. Put the peaches and water into your cooker, and seal the lid.
2. Hit "Chicken/Meat" and adjust time to 6 minutes.
3. When the timer beeps, turn off the cooker and wait for a natural pressure release.
4. Take out the peaches and mash.
5. Strain back into the pressure cooker, squeezing out all the peach juice, and turn on to the "Chicken/Meat" setting again.
6. Bring to a boil before adding sugar.
7. Keep boiling until the liquid has reduced by half.
8. Turn off the cooker.
9. Let the syrup cool before pouring into clean glass jars.

Nutritional Info (1 tablespoon per serving):

Total calories: 97
Protein: 0
Carbs: 28
Fat: 0
Fiber: 0

Hot Mulled Cider

Makes: 12 cups

Time: 22 minutes (12 minutes cook time, 10 minutes natural release)

Also known as wassail, hot mulled cider is the winter beverage you've been missing out on. It has a gorgeous fragrance and flavors like vanilla, cinnamon, ginger, citrus, and nutmeg. Regular ol' apple cider won't cut it anymore.

Ingredients:

- ☐ 8 cups apple cider
- ☐ 4 cups orange juice
- ☐ 10 cloves
- ☐ 5 cinnamon sticks
- ☐ 2 split vanilla beans
- ☐ 1-inch piece of peeled ginger
- ☐ ½ teaspoon nutmeg
- ☐ Juice and zest of two lemons

Directions:

1. Pour juice and cider into the Power Pressure Cooker XL.
2. Add cinnamon, lemon, nutmeg, cloves, ginger, and vanilla beans in the steamer basket, and lower into cooker.
3. Seal the lid.
4. Hit "Chicken/Meat," and adjust time to 12 minutes.
5. When the timer beeps, hit "cancel" and wait for a natural pressure release.
6. Remove the steamer basket and throw away solids.
7. To keep the drink hot in the pressure cooker, hold on the "keep warm" setting.
8. Serve!

Nutritional Info (1 cup per serving):
Total calories: 83
Protein: 1
Carbs: 9
Fat: 0
Fiber: 0

Peppermint Crio Bru

<u>Serves:</u> 8

<u>Time:</u> 15 minutes (5 minutes cook time, 10 minutes natural release)

Ever heard of Crio Bru, the Whole-30 approved brand that sells 100% cacao beans that are roasted? You brew the beans like coffee, and it provides slow-burning energy that doesn't give you the jitters or headaches. They have a pumpkin spice and peppermint flavor, as well as different roasts.

<u>Ingredients:</u>

- ☐ 6 cups water
- ☐ 2 cups unsweetened vanilla almond milk
- ☐ ½ cup Crio Bru ground peppermint-flavored cocoa beans
- ☐ ⅓ cup agave syrup
- ☐ 1 teaspoon peppermint extract
- ☐ 1 teaspoon pure vanilla

<u>Directions:</u>

1. Mix beans, milk, water, peppermint extract, vanilla, and agave in the PPCXL.
2. Seal the lid.
3. Hit "Rice/Risotto" and adjust time to 6 minutes.
4. When the timer beeps, turn off the cooker and wait 10 minutes.
5. Quick-release any remaining pressure.
6. Strain liquid through a fine-mesh strainer and throw out the grounds.
7. Serve hot or cold!

<u>Nutritional Info (⅛ recipe per serving):</u>

Total calories: 59
Protein: 3
Carbs: 14
Fat: 3
Fiber: 0

Chapter 15

Desserts

Chocolate-Peppermint Steam Pudding

<u>Serves:</u> 4

<u>Time:</u> 3 hours, 17 minutes (5 minutes prep time, 12 minutes cook time, 3 hours cool time)

A classic Christmas flavor combination, dark chocolate and candy canes make up the heart and soul of this pudding. As a "steam pudding," which is British, it's not like the pudding we know. It's more like a light sponge cake. The glaze is made from just heavy cream and chocolate, complete with a sprinkling of candy cane dust. Serve with a good espresso or tall glass of cold milk.

Ingredients:

Pudding
- ☐ 1 cup flour
- ☐ 2 eggs
- ☐ ¾ cup brown sugar
- ☐ ½ cup heavy cream
- ☐ ½ cup room temperature butter
- ☐ 6-ounces melted dark chocolate
- ☐ 4 tablespoons cocoa powder
- ☐ 1 teaspoon pure vanilla
- ☐ 1 teaspoon baking powder
- ☐ 1 teaspoon crushed candy cane dust
- ☐ Pinch of salt

Glaze
- ☐ ½ cup heavy cream
- ☐ 1 cup semi-sweet chocolate chips

Directions:

1. In a bowl, mix sugar and butter.
2. Add eggs one at a time with flour, and mix.
3. Add melted chocolate and the rest of the ingredients in the "Pudding" list until just incorporated.
4. Grease a Bundt pan with cooking spray and spoon in pudding.
5. Put a pot lid on top of the pan.
6. Pour 2 cups of WARM water into the PPCXL and lower in the trivet or steamer

basket.

7. Put the covered Bundt pan in the cooker.

8. Secure and seal the cooker lid.

9. Hit the "Soup/Stew" button, and adjust time to 12 minutes.

10. When time is up, hit "Cancel" and carefully quick-release the pressure.

11. Cool the pudding for 2-3 hours. To remove from the pan, turn the pan over on a plate.

12. To make the glaze, bring cream to a boil and then stir in chocolate chips.

13. Glaze once the pudding is cooled, and finish off with a dusting of crushed candy cane pieces.

Nutritional Info (¼ recipe per serving):

Total calories: 1126

Protein: 15

Carbs: 100

Fat: 80

Fiber: 0

Blueberry-Nectarine Cobbler

<u>Serves</u>: 4-6

<u>Time:</u> 42 minutes (15 minutes prep time, 12 minutes cook time, 15 minutes natural pressure release)

Fruit cobblers are a fantastic summertime dessert that are great consumed warm after dinner or cold for breakfast. Because the fruit is frozen, you can also make it anytime. This cobbler uses nectarines and blueberries. The topping is simple, and basically consists of making a dough that you "drop" on the fruit.

Ingredients:

- ☐ 2 cups peeled, sliced frozen nectarines
- ☐ 2 cups frozen blueberries
- ☐ 1 cup flour
- ☐ ⅓ cup water
- ☐ ⅓ cup buttermilk
- ☐ ⅓ cup sugar + 1 tablespoon
- ☐ 2 tablespoons cubed cold butter
- ☐ 1 tablespoon cornstarch
- ☐ 1 ½ teaspoons baking powder
- ☐ 1 teaspoon lime juice
- ☐ ½ teaspoon salt
- ☐ ¼ teaspoon baking soda
- ☐ Pinch of cinnamon

Directions:

1. Mix flour, 1 tablespoon of sugar, baking powder, baking soda, and salt in a bowl.
2. Work in the butter with your hands until you get a mixture that feels like cornmeal.
3. Pour in buttermilk and mix until just moistened, being careful not to overmix.
4. Form the batter into a ball.
5. Hit "Chicken/Meat" on the cooker.
6. Add blueberries, nectarines, ⅓ cup sugar, lemon juice, water, cornstarch, and nutmeg.
7. Cook (without the lid) for about 2-3 minutes until the frozen fruit has softened and begun to lose their juice.
8. Hit "Cancel."
9. Rip off 1-inch pieces out of the big dough ball and lay on top of the fruit in the Power

Pressure Cooker XL like biscuits. You'll get about eight balls.

10. Secure and seal the lid.

11. Hit "Soup/Stew" and add 2 minutes, so you're cooking for 12 minutes total.

12. When the timer beeps, turn off the cooker and let the pressure decrease naturally.

13. Take off the lid and wait a few minutes for the liquid to thicken into more of a syrup.

14. Serve right away!

Nutritional Info (¼ recipe):

Total calories: 330
Protein: 5
Carbs: 66
Fat: 4
Fiber: 3

Classic Crème Brûlée

<u>Serves:</u> 6

<u>Time:</u> 2 hours, 22 minutes (5 minutes prep time, 7 minutes cook time, 10 minutes natural pressure release, 2 hours chill time)

The one dessert everyone needs to know how to make in a pressure cooker is crème brûlée. This custard is simple and elegant, with a gorgeous caramelized sugar topping. The actual cooking time is 7 minutes, while most of the overall time is chilling the dessert in the fridge. Make during the afternoon if you can, and serve after dinner.

<u>Ingredients:</u>

- 8 egg yolks
- 2 cups heavy cream
- 6 tablespoons very fine sugar
- ⅓ cup granulated sugar
- 1 ½ teaspoons vanilla
- Pinch of salt

<u>Directions:</u>

1. Pour 1 ½ cups of water into the cooker and lower in the trivet.
2. Whisk yolks, ⅓ cup of sugar, and salt in a bowl.
3. Whisk in the vanilla and cream until just blended.
4. Strain this mixture into a clean bowl and then into six ramekins.
5. Wrap ramekins tightly in foil and lower into cooker, so it's on top of the trivet.
6. Close and seal the lid.
7. Select "Rice/Risotto" and cook for 7 minutes.
8. When time is up, hit "cancel" and wait 10 minutes before quick-releasing.
9. Remove the ramekins, unwrap the foil, and let them cool.
10. When cool, cover in saran plastic and store in the fridge for at least 2 hours to chill completely.
11. Before serving, sprinkle 1 tablespoon of the very fine sugar on top of each custard and put under the broiler for 5 minutes. Watch the process carefully, and rotate the ramekins so it caramelizes evenly.

Nutritional Info (⅙ recipe):

Total calories: 210
Protein: 13
Carbs: 18
Fat: 10
Fiber: 3

Vanilla Sponge Cake

<u>Serves:</u> 6-8

<u>Time:</u> 1 hour, 5 minutes (15 minutes prep time, 40 minutes bake time, 10 minutes cool time)

This is the only pressure cooker recipe in this book that doesn't actually have you bring the cooker to pressure. You use it like a mini oven, where the heat accumulated from the "Chicken/Meat" setting does the baking. The cake is sweet and simple - powdered sugar, flour, milk, canola oil, eggs, baking powder, and vanilla. It's a great cake for serving with fruit, whipped cream, or ice cream.

Ingredients:

- ☐ 1 ½ cups powdered sugar
- ☐ 1 ¼ cups flour
- ☐ ½ cup milk
- ☐ ½ cup canola oil
- ☐ 2 room temperature eggs
- ☐ 1 ½ teaspoons baking powder
- ☐ ¾ teaspoon vanilla extract

Directions:

1. Prepare a 6-inch square pan with a little butter and flour.
2. Beat eggs and sugar together in a bowl.
3. Sift in the flour before adding milk and oil.
4. Mix in the vanilla and baking powder.
5. Turn your cooker to "Chicken/Meat" and heat the cooker.
6. Pour batter into the pan so it's ½-way full and has enough room to rise.
7. Put the pan into the cooker.
8. Remove the gasket from the pot lid before putting it on the cooker and sealing it.
9. The heat from the cooker will bake the cake. Bake for 40 minutes.
10. The cake should be cooked through, so only a few crumbs stick to a toothpick when you poke it into the cake's center.
11. Let the cake cool in the pan for 10 minutes before you invert it and serve!

Nutritional Information (⅙ recipe):

Total calories: 405
Protein: 6
Carbs: 49
Fat: 22
Fiber: 0

Chocolate Chip Cheesecake

<u>Serves:</u> 6

<u>Time:</u> 7 hours, 10 minutes (10 minutes prep time, 1 hour cook time, 6 hours water bath)

This might be the perfect cheesecake. It has a fudgy brownie crust and decadent filling made with cream cheese, sweetened condensed milk, and chocolate chips. You pressure-cook the brownie part first, and then cook it again with the filling. This cake needs to have a 6-hour water bath where it sits in the cooker undisturbed, so plan accordingly. The wait time is totally worth it.

<u>Ingredients:</u>

Crust

- ☐ 2 eggs
- ☐ ¾ cup white flour
- ☐ ½ cup sugar
- ☐ ½ cup butter
- ☐ ¼ cup cocoa powder
- ☐ 2 tablespoons honey
- ☐ ¾ teaspoon baking powder
- ☐ ¼ teaspoon salt

Filling

- ☐ 24-ounces of softened cream cheese
- ☐ 14-ounces of sweetened condensed milk
- ☐ 3 eggs
- ☐ ½ cup semi-sweet chocolate chips
- ☐ 2 teaspoons pure vanilla

<u>Directions:</u>

1. Melt butter and mix in the cocoa powder.
2. While that cools, mix the flour, sugar, baking powder, and salt together in a separate bowl.
3. In a third bowl, whisk the eggs until just blended.
4. Add eggs and cooled butter/cocoa mixture into the sugar/flour.
5. Make sure it's mixed well.
6. Prepare an 8-inch springform pan with cooking spray.

7. Pour in the brownie batter and wrap in foil.
8. Pour 2 cups of water into the PPCXL and lower in a trivet.
9. Put the wrapped batter pan in the cooker.
10. Secure and seal the lid.
11. Select "Chicken/Meat" and adjust time to 42 minutes.
12. In the meantime, prepare the filling.
13. In a mixer, beat the cream cheese until it becomes fluffy.
14. Slowly add in the condensed milk until just blended.
15. Mix in vanilla and eggs, being careful not to overmix.
16. Fold in chocolate chips.
17. Store in the fridge until the brownie is cooked.
18. When the pressure cooker timer goes off, hit "cancel" and quick-release the pressure.
19. Unwrap the foil and pour filling on top of the brownie crust.
20. Put back in the cooker, without foil this time, and seal the lid.
21. Hit "Chicken/Meat" and adjust time to 18 minutes.
22. Make sure that the cooker goes to "Keep Warm" when time is up. You're going to be giving the cake a water bath for 6 hours.
23. When that time is over, remove the cake and let it cool completely.
24. Serve right away or keep in the fridge before eating.

Nutritional Info (⅙ recipe):
Total calories: 184
Protein: 3.2
Carbs: 18
Fat: 11.2
Fiber: 0

Greek Yogurt Blueberry Cheesecake w/ Shortbread Crust

<u>Serves:</u> 8

<u>Time:</u> 1 hour, 21 minutes + 4 hours chill time (25 minutes prep time, 36 minutes cook time, 20 minutes natural pressure release)

Summer is a great time to make this simple cheesecake flavored with blueberry cream cheese and whole-milk Greek yogurt. The crust is made from a quick shortbread, and might be my favorite part of the whole cake. Don't forget fresh blueberries to serve on top after a four-hour chill time!

Ingredients:

- ☐ 1 cup water

Crust:
- ☐ 1 cup whole-wheat all-purpose flour
- ☐ ½ cup softened butter
- ☐ ¼ cup white sugar

Filling:
- ☐ 1 ½ cups whole-milk Greek yogurt
- ☐ 2 large eggs
- ☐ 4-ounces softened, blueberry-flavored cream cheese
- ☐ ¼ cup sugar
- ☐ 1 teaspoon vanilla
- ☐ Handful of blueberries

Directions:

1. Melt the butter and mix with flour and sugar.
2. With clean fingers, press down crust into the bottom and halfway up the sides of a 7-inch springform pan. Store in the fridge for 10 minutes, then bake in a 400-degree oven for 15 minutes.
3. In another bowl, begin to mix filling - sugar, yogurt, vanilla, and blueberry cream cheese - until smooth.
4. Add eggs in one at a time.
5. Pour batter into the pan with the crust.
6. Pour 1 cup water into the pressure cooker and lower in the trivet.

7. Put the cheesecake pan on top of the trivet and seal the lid.
8. Select "Chicken/Meat" and adjust time to 36 minutes.
9. When the timer beeps, hit "Cancel" and wait for a natural pressure release.
10. When the pressure is gone, open up the cooker and take out the cake.
11. If there's excess water on top, blot away with a paper towel.
12. Cool for 1-2 hours on the counter before storing in fridge for at least 4 hours.
13. To serve, top with a handful of fresh blueberries!

Nutritional Info (⅛ recipe per serving):

Total calories: 271
Protein: 8
Carbs: 23
Fat: 17
Fiber: 2

Personal Brownie Cakes

Serves: 4
Time: 36 minutes (10 minutes prep time, 21 minutes cook time, 5 minutes cool time)

There are few things better than the smell of baking brownies. This easy recipe takes only 21 minutes in the cooker, and four people get their own individual serving in a ramekin, you don't have to worry about cutting them. Serve hot with cold milk or vanilla ice cream for the perfect dessert.

Ingredients:

- ☐ 2 eggs
- ☐ ⅔ cup sugar
- ☐ ½ cup flour
- ☐ 4 tablespoons unsalted butter
- ☐ 4 tablespoons cocoa powder
- ☐ 2 tablespoons powdered sugar
- ☐ 2 tablespoons semi-sweet chocolate chips
- ☐ ¼ teaspoon vanilla extract

Directions:

1. Melt the butter and chocolate chips in a bowl.
2. Beat in the sugar.
3. Add in the eggs and vanilla.
4. Sift in cocoa and flour.
5. Blend well.
6. Pour batter into 4 ramekins and wrap in foil.
7. Pour 1 cup of water into your Power Pressure Cooker XL and lower in the trivet.
8. Put the wrapped ramekins on top of the trivet and seal the lid.
9. Select "Chicken/Meat" and adjust time to 21 minutes.
10. When the timer beeps, quick-release the pressure.
11. Take out the ramekins and wait a few minutes before unwrapping them.
12. Poke the center with a toothpick to make sure they're cooked to your liking.
13. Serve as is or with vanilla ice cream.

Nutritional Info (1 cake serving):

Total calories: 377
Protein: 6
Carbs: 56
Fat: 17
Fiber: 0

Raspberry Croissant Pudding

<u>Serves:</u> 7
<u>Time:</u> 49 minutes (5 minutes prep time, 20 minutes soak time, 24 minutes cook time)

This quick, creamy, and fruity "pudding" is a little like French Toast. You soak the croissants in a mixture of sugar, vanilla, eggs, milk, and cream cheese before cooking it in the Power Pressure Cooker XL for 24 minutes with the raspberries. If there are any leftovers, have the rest for a breakfast treat!

Ingredients:

- 3 large, cut-up croissants
- One 8-ounce package softened cream cheese
- 2 eggs
- 1 cup milk
- 1 cup raspberries
- ⅔ cup sugar
- 1 teaspoon vanilla extract

Directions:

1. Place raspberries and croissants in a bowl that's safe for the pressure cooker.
2. In another bowl, mix the vanilla, sugar, eggs, and cream cheese together.
3. Mix in milk.
4. Pour this mixture over the berry/croissants and soak for 20 minutes.
5. Put the bowl in the PPCXL.
6. Seal the lid.
7. Select "Chicken/Meat" and adjust time to 24 minutes.
8. When time is up, turn off the cooker and quick-release the pressure.
9. Serve hot!

Nutritional Info (1/7 recipe):
Total calories: 263
Protein: 8
Carbs: 40
Fat: 18
Fiber: 2

Key Lime Pie

<u>Serves:</u> 6-8

<u>Time:</u> 4 hours, 45 minutes (15 minutes prep time, 30 minutes cook time, 4 hours chill time)

Tart and refreshing with a buttery graham-cracker crust, key lime pie is one of my favorite summertime desserts. Key limes are smaller than regular limes and have a powerful, beautiful fragrance and taste, so you don't need to use much to get that pie flavor. Serve with fresh whipped cream on top.

<u>Ingredients:</u>

For the crust
- ☐ ¾ cup graham cracker crumbs
- ☐ 3 tablespoons melted butter
- ☐ 1 tablespoon sugar

For the filling
- ☐ 4 large egg yolks
- ☐ 14-ounces sweetened condensed milk
- ☐ ⅓ cup sour cream
- ☐ 2 tablespoons grated key lime zest
- ☐ ¼ cup fresh key lime juice
- ☐ ¼ cup fresh lemon juice

<u>Directions:</u>

1. Prepare a 7-inch springform pan with cooking spray.
2. Mix melted butter, sugar, and graham cracker crumbs in a bowl.
3. Press into the bottom of the pan and up the sides by 1-inch.
4. Put in the freezer.
5. Whisk egg yolks until blended.
6. Mix in the condensed milk
7. Gradually whisk in the lemon and lime juices.
8. Mix in the sour cream and lime zest before pouring the filling into the springform pan.
9. Wrap in foil.
10. Pour 1 cup of water into the PPCXL, adding the trivet on the bottom.

11. Put the wrapped pan on top of the trivet and seal the lid.
12. Select "Chicken/Meat" and adjust time, so you cook it for 18 minutes.
13. When the timer beeps, turn off the cooker and wait 10 minutes before quick-releasing.
14. Carefully remove the pan and look at the pie. The middle should be slightly jiggly, but mostly set.
15. If it isn't done yet, finish cooking under pressure for another 5 minutes and quick-releasing when it's done.
16. Let the pie cool completely before covering with saran wrap and chilling for 4 hours.

Nutritional Info (⅙ recipe):

Total calories: 553
Protein: 11
Carbs: 85
Fat: 21
Fiber: 1

Mango Syrup Cake

<u>Serves:</u> 8

<u>Time:</u> 1 hour, 23 minutes (5 minutes active time, 48 minutes cook time, 20 minutes natural pressure release, 10 minutes cooling time)

A gorgeous sunset color thanks to the mango syrup or puree, this cake is fluffy and fruity. It's a lower calorie option for summer evenings after a heavy meal or as a snack with a cup of coffee or tea.

Ingredients:

- ☐ 1 ¼ cups flour
- ☐ ¾ cup milk
- ☐ ½ cup granulated white sugar
- ☐ ¼ cup coconut oil
- ☐ 1 tablespoon fresh lemon juice
- ☐ 1 teaspoon baking powder
- ☐ 1 teaspoon mango syrup (½ cup pureed mango)
- ☐ ¼ teaspoon baking soda
- ☐ ⅛ teaspoon salt

Directions:

1. Prepare a pressure-cooker friendly baking pan with cooking spray.
2. In a bowl, mix coconut oil, milk, and sugar until the sugar dissolves smoothly.
3. Mix in the mango syrup or puree.
4. Sift in all the dry ingredients.
5. Add the lemon juice before mixing everything well.
6. Pour batter into your pan.
7. Pour 1 cup of water into the cooker, adding a trivet.
8. Put the pan, uncovered, on top of the trivet and seal the lid.
9. Hit "Chicken/Meat" and adjust time to 48 minutes.
10. When the timer beeps, turn off the cooker and wait for a natural pressure release.
11. Cool the cake for 10 minutes on the counter before removing it from the pan.
12. Serve right away!

Nutritional Info (⅛ recipe):

Total calories: 230
Protein: 2
Carbs: 39
Fat: 7
Fiber: 0

Mini Pumpkin Puddings

<u>Serves:</u> 4

<u>Time:</u> About 2 hours (5 minutes prep time, 18 minutes cook time, 15 minutes natural pressure release, 1 ½ hours cooling time)

Bursting with flavors like cinnamon, nutmeg, and pumpkin, and served in personal ramekins, these mini puddings are perfect for the fall season. They only take 18 minutes to cook; most of the overall time is cooling the ramekins for an hour and a half before serving with a generous dollop of fresh whipped cream.

Ingredients:

- ☐ 1 cup water
- ☐ 1 cup pumpkin puree
- ☐ ¼ cup half-and-half
- ☐ ¼ cup sugar
- ☐ 1 beaten whole egg
- ☐ 1 egg yolk
- ☐ 1 tablespoon butter
- ☐ ½ teaspoon vanilla extract
- ☐ ½ teaspoon ground cinnamon
- ☐ ¼ teaspoon ground ginger
- ☐ ¼ teaspoon salt
- ☐ Pinch of ground cloves

Directions:

1. Prepare your Power Pressure Cooker XL by pouring in 1 cup of water and inserting the trivet or steamer basket.
2. Spray four ramekins (safe for the pressure cooker) with cooking spray.
3. Whisk pumpkin, sugar, and ground spices together in a bowl.
4. Add the beaten egg, egg yolk, half-and-half, and vanilla until smooth.
5. Pour pudding into the ramekins.
6. Lower into the pressure cooker and seal the lid.
7. Press "Chicken/Meat" and adjust time to 18 minutes.
8. When the cooking time is up, hit "cancel" and let the pressure decrease naturally.
9. Remove the puddings and cool for 1 ½ hours on the counter.

Nutritional Info (1 ramekin of pudding):

Total calories: 174
Protein: 4
Carbs: 18
Fat: 6
Fiber: 1

Fruit Medley Upside-Down Cake

<u>Serves:</u> 6

<u>Time:</u> 1 hour, 22 minutes (10 minutes prep time, 22 minutes cook time, 10 minutes natural pressure release, 40 minutes cool time)

Upside-down cake takes me back to vintage cookbooks and potlucks. This slightly updated version is for vegans, and uses vegan butter, unsweetened almond milk, and zero eggs. It also replaces the traditional pineapple with a medley of fruit - peaches, nectarines, and strawberries. It's perfect for summer or anytime when you're favorite fruit is in season!

Ingredients:

- 1 ⅓ cups whole-wheat flour
- 1 large sliced peach
- 1 large sliced nectarine
- Handful of sliced strawberries
- ⅓ cup rapeseed oil
- ⅓ cup unsweetened almond milk
- ¾ cup + ¼ cup white sugar
- 3 ½ tablespoons vegan butter
- 1 teaspoon pure vanilla
- 1 teaspoon apple cider vinegar
- ½ teaspoon baking powder
- ¾ teaspoon baking soda
- ¼ teaspoon salt

Directions:

1. Mix ¼ cup of sugar and butter together.
2. Spread on the bottom of your cooker-safe cake dish, and up the sides, too.
3. Lay down fruit slices in the dish.
4. In a bowl, mix flour, baking soda, baking powder, and salt.
5. Mix milk and apple cider vinegar together.
6. Into that mixture, add rapeseed oil, vanilla, and the rest of the sugar.
7. Mix wet into dry until just combined.
8. Pour the batter into your dish and cover with foil.
9. Pour 1 cup of water into your pressure cooker and lower in trivet.
10. Set dish on trivet, and seal the lid.
11. Cook on "manual" for 22 minutes on high pressure.

12. When time is up, hit "cancel" and wait about 10 minutes for a natural pressure release.
13. Remove any excess pressure.
14. Unwrap the dish and let it cool for 30 minutes before inverting.
15. Cool another 10 minutes before slicing!

Nutritional Info (⅙ recipe per serving):

Total calories: 336
Protein: 4
Carbs: 42
Fat: 18
Fiber: 3.8

Pears Poached in Cinnamon with Chocolate Sauce

<u>Serves:</u> 6
<u>Time:</u> 10 minutes (5 minutes prep time, 3 minutes cook time, 2 minutes stovetop)

This really fast dessert is fresh, sweet, and chocolatey, which is a rare combination. You pressure-cook six whole, ripe pears in a liquid of cinnamon sticks, white wine, sugar, water, and lemon so they become juicy, tender, and saturated with flavor. The chocolate sauce only uses four ingredients, and is vegan-friendly to boot.

Ingredients:

Pears
- ☐ 6 cinnamon sticks
- ☐ 6 ripe + firm pears
- ☐ 3 cups water
- ☐ 2 cups white wine
- ☐ 2 cups sugar
- ☐ 1 halved lemon

Chocolate sauce
- ☐ 9-ounces chopped bittersweet chocolate
- ☐ ½ cup coconut milk
- ☐ 2 tablespoons maple syrup
- ☐ ¼ cup coconut oil

Directions:

1. Put water, sugar, wine, and cinnamon sticks into your Power Pressure Cooker XL.
2. Hit "Chicken/Meat" and heat until the sugar dissolves.
3. Turn off the cooker.
4. Prepare the pear by peeling off the skin, but keeping the stems.
5. Rub peeled flesh with the lemon half.
6. Squeeze the lemon into the cooker and drop it in.
7. Add pears. If you're worried they might burn, use a steamer basket, though they won't become infused as much with the cooking liquid.
8. Seal the lid.
9. Turn cooker to "Rice/Risotto" and adjust time down to 3 minutes.

10. When time is up, hit "cancel" and quick-release.

11. Take out the pears to cool.

12. While they cool, heat coconut milk, syrup, and coconut oil in a saucepan on the stove to make the chocolate sauce.

13. When beginning to boil, add chocolate and stir till smooth.

14. Quickly pour the pressure cooker liquid over the pears, followed by chocolate sauce.

Nutritional Info (⅙ recipe per serving):

Total calories: 210
Protein: 2.8
Carbs: 50
Fat: 1.6
Fiber: 7.5

Walnut Fudge Drops

<u>Makes:</u> 30 pieces
<u>Time:</u> 35 minutes (5 minutes cook time, 30 minutes freeze time)

Sweet and crunchy chocolate-and-nut candy is hard to resist, but it's hard to find store-bought candy that isn't packed with artificial ingredients. The solution is to make your own in the Power Pressure Cooker XL! It only takes four ingredients - sweetened condensed milk, walnuts, vanilla, and chocolate chips.

Ingredients:

- One 14-ounce can of sweetened condensed milk
- Two 6-ounce packages of semi-sweet chocolate chips
- 2 cups water
- 1 cup chopped walnuts
- 1 teaspoon vanilla

Directions:

1. Find a bowl that fits in your PPCXL, and pour in condensed milk and chocolate chips.
2. Wrap bowl in foil.
3. Pour water into the pressure cooker and add trivet.
4. Put the bowl on top and seal the lid.
5. Select "Rice/Risotto" and cook for 6 minutes.
6. When time is up, hit "cancel" and quick-release.
7. Mix the nuts and vanilla into the melted chocolate mixture.
8. Make drops of candy with a teaspoon unto a cookie sheet with wax paper.
9. Freeze for at least a half hour

Nutritional Info (1 piece of candy recipe per serving):

Total calories: 176
Protein: 4
Carbs: 19
Fat: 11
Fiber: 1

Conclusion

In a time where processed and packaged food is cheap and plentiful, and schedules are packed, it's easy to fall into bad eating habits. We all know that a home-cooked meal is better for us, but when it's nearly 7pm and everyone is tired and hungry, it just makes sense to grab something frozen or pick up the phone for takeout. The goal of this book was to show you how easy and convenient home-cooked meals can be when you use a Power Pressure Cooker XL pressure cooker, and I hope that my goal was achieved.

The concept of pressure cooking is old, but it has endured for a reason: it works. It's fast, it's the healthiest cooking method, and thanks to the technology featured in electric cookers like the Power Pressure Cooker XL, it's safe and easy for anyone. The opening chapters gave a full rundown of how a pressure cooker is constructed and how to clean it, so it runs properly and lasts as long as it should. There are also certain problems that commonly pop up, and the book explained what to do if you encounter them.

The recipes in this book explored just how versatile the pressure cooker is. You can cook anything from cheesy frittatas to flank steaks to curries to ribs to soups to cakes. You could literally only cook in the pressure cooker for the rest of your life, and always make satisfying, healthy, and most importantly, delicious meals. If you started out reading this book unsure if you wanted to start pressure cooking, I sincerely hope I've changed your mind. What recipe are you going to start with?

POWER PRESSURE
COOKER XL
COOKBOOK

200 Irresistible Electric Pressure Cooker
Recipes for Fast, Healthy, and Amazingly
Delicious Meals

VANESSA OLSEN

Power Pressure Cooker XL Cookbook:

200 Irresistible Electric Pressure Cooker Recipes for Fast, Healthy, and Amazingly Delicious Meals

Vanessa Olsen

TABLE OF CONTENTS

Introduction

If you want a long, happy, and healthy life, paying attention to what you eat is crucial. Years of studies have shown that people who eat good food like vegetables, whole grains, and lean proteins are more resistant to disease, get more from their workouts, have more energy, and so on. There are so many benefits to a healthy diet.

This probably doesn't come as a surprise to you, but eating healthy isn't a walk in the park. It can be expensive and take a lot of time. First, you have to get high-quality ingredients, and then preparing all those meals takes time away from other things, like your family. That's where pressure cooking comes in. By preparing your meals in a pot with a special airtight seal, you raise the boiling point of water, which speeds up cooking time and preserves nearly 100% of an ingredient's nutrients. Because the pressure cooker also produces really delicious and tender results, you can use cheaper cuts of meat and frozen vegetables, and still end up with professional-tasting results.

If you've never used a pressure cooker before, this cookbook will walk you through everything you need to know. The first chapters cover the history of the cooker, and more reasons why it's such a good choice. The Power Pressure Cooker XL is a particularly good choice, so the recipes - which make up the majority of the book - are written especially for that cooker. Whether you're a vegan or meat lover, you'll be able to find great recipes I hope you'll love. I know I love them.

Chapter 1

The When + Why of Pressure Cookers

You might be surprised to know how long pressure cookers have been around. The concept of sealing a lid to speed up the time water takes to boil is ancient, but that special seal that really contains the steam didn't exist until Denis Papin. He was a Frenchman from the 17th-century and seeing how the poor could not find good food, he decided to create a cooking tool capable of breaking down the toughest cuts of meat into meat "jelly." The invention he ended up calling "the bone digester" was large and to show it off, Papin prepared a meal for the king using his pressure cooker. The king loved the meal, but Papin's original intention for the pot to be used by the poor never came to pass. The cooker was expensive as well as big, and pretty dangerous, since it had a habit of exploding.

After Papin's pressure cooker idea was co-opted into the pressure canner, and used in more industrial capacities, a home stovetop pressure cooker finally appeared in 1939, at the World's Fair. It became very popular during WWII, when people had victory gardens and lots of produce they needed to use up. The pressure cooker also provided a way to cook more affordable foods into something tasty, since money was tight. The cookers were still dangerous, though. It would be decades until companies would finally make safety a priority.

You can see years of advances in technology and safety in today's modern pressure cooker. Better steam valves, better construction, and more have made cookers like the Power Pressure Cooker XL as safe as any piece of equipment you have in your kitchen right now.

Stovetop vs. electric cookers

There are stovetop cookers and electric cookers available, and they each have their own pros and cons. Stovetop cookers look like saucepans, but they have special lids and seals. Electric cookers look like your average crockpot. Which one is better?

Health benefits

The health benefits are the same no matter what type of pressure cooker you use. What are they exactly? Pressure cooking is actually the healthiest cooking method, even more than steaming. This is because the longer something cooks, the more nutrients are lost. Because pressure-cooking is so fast, minimal nutrient-loss occurs. Some people are worried that such high temperatures will be bad for food, but most food still holds onto its nutrients. Only a few ingredients - like vegetables - do need to be cooked at a lower temperature, so you adjust the heat to "low pressure."

Versatility

The other common trait between stovetop and electric cookers is that they are both very versatile and cook just about any meal, side dish, appetizer, or dessert. Anything that you would cook directly in a pot, like soup, stew, meat, and so on will work, and for anything that needs a separate dish like créme brûlée or casseroles, you can put down a trivet in the cooker and put the baking dishes right on the trivet. After sealing the lid, the heat effectively steams whatever is in the dish to completion.

Speed

Stovetop pressure cookers are faster than electric cookers. They come to pressure faster and finish the food faster. However, electric pressure cookers are still way faster than an ordinary saucepan or cooking in the oven.

Safety

While stovetop cookers are faster, electric cookers are safer, and for most people, it's a good trade. Stovetop pressure cookers are much safer than they used to be, but you still have to monitor the burner to maintain the right pressure, which means you can't leave the cooker by itself. With electric ones, you just set it, and go, and don't have to worry about it building too much pressure. Electric pressure cookers also have more safety features built-in, because of technological advances.

Price

Because stovetop cookers don't have all the safety features and convenience of electric cookers, they tend to be cheaper. For a good electric pressure cooker, it's not unusual to pay $100 or more. However, electric cookers last a long time, and eliminate the need to get a slow cooker. In terms of overall value, an electric cooker is a better choice for most people who want all the benefits of pressure cooking in a hassle-free package.

Chapter 2

Getting to Know the Power Pressure Cooker XL

Steam Release Valve

Large Arm Handle

Safe Lock Lid

Stainless Steel Housing

Non-Stick Inner pot
6 Qt. Capacity
(Not Shown)

Digital Display Panel

One Touch Preset Buttons

cooking time up to
70%
Faster
than conventional cooking

The image on the previous page is an electric pressure cooker known as the Power Pressure Cooker XL. If you're shopping for a good cooker, this is a great option. It has lots of safety features, as you can see, and an easy-to-use control panel. We'll go through each setting shortly.

The PPCXL is available in four models: the 6-quart, 8-quart, 8-quart deluxe, and the 10-quart. The 8-quart deluxe includes a steamer rack, canning lid, and three color choices. A 6-quart is a good size for a family of four, although for recipes that make enough food for eight plus people, an 8-quart does let you make everything in a single batch.

The most important thing to know about this particular cooker is what the PSI is. PSI is the abbreviation for "pounds per square inch," and the higher the PSI on a cooker, the faster it is. The Power Pressure Cooker XL has 7.2 PSI, which is significantly lower than what a stovetop pressure cooker can do (15 PSI) or other cookers, which top out about 11 or 12. This is important to know because it will affect cooking time. If you're following an electric pressure cooker recipe that is not specifically written for the PPCXL, you will probably need to add 20% of the time to it. The recipes in this book already take that into account, so just follow the time that's written.

While we're talking about time, elevation does affect pressure cookers, too. The higher you are above sea level, the longer water takes to boil, so the more time will be added to a recipe. For every 1,000 feet above sea level, you will need to increase the time by 5%. The time it takes for the cooker to actually reach pressure (which is when a recipe's time count begins) will be longer, too.

The display panel and cooking programs

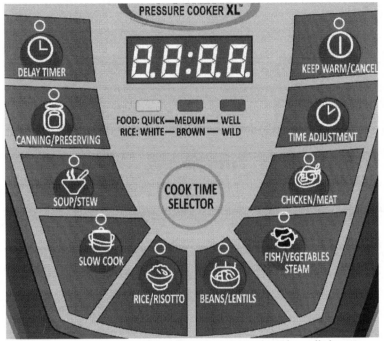

There are ten buttons on your control panel, so let's see what they all do.

DELAY TIMER - If you want to delay when the cooker starts building to pressure, you'll use this button. In this recipe book, you won't need to use it.

CANNING/PRESERVING - You won't be using this button for the recipes in this book either.

SOUP/STEW - The PSI on this setting is automatically 7.2, which is true for all the cooking programs. The default time for soup/stew is 10 minutes.

SLOW COOK - This turns your pressure cooker into a regular slow cooker. The default time is 2 hours, with options for 6 or 12 hours.

RICE/RISOTTO - Default time is 6 minutes.

KEEP WARM/CANCEL - If you push a button you didn't mean to, hitting this button will reset the cooker. You also hit it before you release the pressure. When a cooking cycle is complete, the cooker will switch on its own to the Keep Warm function.

TIME ADJUSTMENT - After selecting a cooking program, you can change the default time. You'll be using this button a lot, because you rarely use the default time.

CHICKEN/MEAT - The default time for this one is 15 minutes. This is the button you'll be using the most, just for simplicity's sake. Using it for ingredients that aren't chicken or meat doesn't make a difference, since the PSI is always the same.

FISH/VEGETABLES/STEAM - The default time is 2 minutes, which makes this the lowest amount of time you can use on the PPCXL.

COOK TIME SELECTOR - Push this button to adjust a program to "Medium" or "Well" on the chicken/meat setting, or "White," "Wild," or "Brown," for the rice/risotto setting. You won't be using this button at all in this cookbook

Setting up your cooker

Reading the manual is important for starting to use your cooker. You will need to do some assembly, and run your cooker through a simple cleaning routine before you actually cook any food in it. The rubber gasket looks like a ring and is what seals the lid to the cooker. Look to your manual to see how it should be fit into the lid. It will also tell you how to open and close the steam valve, which is a very easy process.

Using the PPCXL for the first time

Once your cooker is clean and ready to go, it's time to learn how to use it. We'll try out a simple mac 'n cheese recipe. Here are your ingredients:

o 16-ounces macaroni
o 4 cups water
o 1 ½ cups milk
o 1 ½ cups half-and-half
o 1 chopped onion
o 8-ounces shredded Monterey Jack cheese
o 8-ounces shredded cheddar cheese
o 1 teaspoon olive oil
o 1 teaspoon dry mustard
o 1 teaspoon salt

The first thing you're going to do is sauté the onion with a little olive oil. You use your cooker like a regular skillet, with the lid off. To turn it on, you're going to be hitting the "chicken/meat" setting and adding oil. When the oil is hot, add onion.

If a recipe has any aromatic ingredients (onion, celery, carrot, garlic, whole spices, etc.), odds are you're going to be cooking them before you add the rest of the ingredients and actually bring the cooker to pressure. This step is very important for creating really good flavors.

Once the onion has become clear, you're adding the macaroni, water, salt, and mustard into the cooker. Always make sure the cooker isn't more than ⅔ of the way full. Some recipes like oatmeal and pasta actually say to only fill ½ of the way, so be aware. Seal the lid. You're now going to hit the "time adjustment button and changing the default time of 15 minutes to just 5 minutes. The cooker takes about 10 minutes or so to get to pressure, and then the timer starts counting down. The time it takes for the cooker to get to pressure is not included in the recipes, since it will vary depending on where you live.

Once the timer beeps, it's time to release the pressure. This is a quick-release recipe, so you're going to hit "cancel" and then turn the steam valve so it's in the open position. Hot steam will pour out, so don't touch it. If this recipe was a "natural pressure release," you would just hit "cancel" and wait for the pressure to come down on its own. This can take anywhere from 10 minutes to 40+ minutes, depending on how long the cook time was.

Once it's safe to open the cooker, you're going to add in your half-and-half and milk.

Most recipes will have to add any dairy after the cooker has come to pressure and the pressure is released, because of how dairy can cause food and water to come out of the steam valve. Once the dairy is added, you're going to turn your cooker back on to "chicken/meat," but without closing the lid. A lot of recipes have you do this to simmer the food. In this recipe's case, it is to get the mac and cheese thickened. The last step is to stir in the cheese and seasonings, and that's it!

Cleaning the cooker

Once you've eaten your delicious pressure-cooked meal, it's time to clean up. There are a few parts to be concerned with: the lid, the inner pot, the gasket, and the exhaust valve. The lid should always be wiped down with some soap and water after using the cooker, because that's where all the food residue sticks. The inner pot always needs to be washed every time, since that's always where the food is. It can be washed like a regular pot; just don't use something abrasive because it will scratch. Most inner pots are dishwasher-safe, too.

The gasket should be removed and washed at least every 2-3 times you use it, because it absorbs smells. It isn't dishwasher-safe, so just soak it in regular dish soap and hot water for 10-15 minutes. For bad stains or smells, use baking soda and vinegar. Eventually, the gasket wears down and will need to be replaced.

The exhaust valve can be cleaned after you cook rice, pasta, or oats. These are foamy foods because of their starch, so the exhaust valve can get clogged. The valve cover is on the inside of the lid, and looks like a round metal hat. It pops off (don't twist), revealing the tiny valve hole. Use a needle or something else thin and metallic to clear it out. Don't use something that can break off in the valve.

Can the PPCXL be used as a canner?

The PPCXL can be used as a canner, but that is not something we will focus on in this book

Chapter 3

Common Problems + Solutions

Even the best pressure cooker can cause some headaches. The most common problems including undercooked food, overcooked food or leaky lids, all have easy solutions. Here's what to do if you encounter these issues:

PROBLEM #1: FOOD IS UNDERCOOKED

There are a few reasons why food isn't cooking completely. The cooker might have too much water, you're using frozen food, there's too much food in the cooker, or there's a thick liquid in the cooker. To make sure you're not using too much water, always measure, don't just splash it in there. Even ⅓-½ cup of extra liquid can cause problems. If you used frozen food, use thawed next time, or add up to 30 minutes to the recipe's time. Thick sauces increase cooking time, too. It's best to add thickeners (like flour or cornstarch) after you've cooked everything else. If you think the problem is too much food, make sure to only fill it ⅔ of the way, and only ½ of the way full for foamy foods.

PROBLEM #2: FOOD IS OVERCOOKED

To avoid overcooked food, never add time to a recipe. It's a common thing to do with an oven or saucepan, but even a few minutes can make a huge difference in a pressure cooker. If the food is burned, reducing the time might not be the solution. It might be because the food is in direct contact with the pot. Put the food in a steamer basket. Food that will burn if it's touching the pot include fish and vegetables. Burned food can also mean you need more water in your cooker, so look at the minimum required amount for your pressure cooker.

PROBLEM #3: COOKER ISN'T COMING TO PRESSURE

Sometimes the pressure cooker won't come to pressure and start the countdown. The first issue might be because the seal isn't tight on the lid. That's a problem with the rubber gasket. Look for any tears or food particles. If there's food, clean the gasket, but tears or cracks means you have to replace it.

PROBLEM #4: WATER OR STEAM IS LEAKING OUT

A leaky valve can usually be pinned down to a clogged valve. Just clean out the valve on a regular basis, so stuck food isn't causing a problem. Leaks can also indicate that your gasket is worn out, and you need a new one.

PROBLEM #5: COOKER IS SPRAYING OUT FOOD

When you quick-release the cooker, the valve should just release steam, but sometimes it can spray out water or food. This could be because there's some kind of thickener in the pot, like flour, which generates more foam. A natural pressure release for 10 minutes, followed by a quick-release, could stop the problem. Another reason might be because the cooker is too full. Next time, don't fill the cooker so much.

Cleaning stains

Over time, your cooker might show some stains that aren't easily cleaned with soap and water. Here's what to do:

⬇ Cleaning alkali stains

Cleaning solutions with ammonia or baking soda cause alkali stains. If the stains aren't bad, you can clean them off by cooking food with acids, like a batch of tomatoes for sauce. For deeper stains, boil 2-3 tablespoons of cream of tartar with a quart of water and vinegar, for just 10 minutes. Rub with a sponge, dish soap, and then rinse.

⬇ Cleaning Mineral Stains

Tap water with minerals can cause stains on the aluminum of the cooker. Vinegar and lemon juice is a good solution. Rub the stain with the mixture and wait 4-5 hours. Rinse well with water, and then polish the cooker with lemon juice. Rinse again in hot water, and dry well. When you're using a sponge or cloth, make sure they're soft, not abrasive.

Chapter 4

Converting Slow Cooker Recipes to the PPCXL

🞛🞛🞛

If you have favorite slow cooker recipes, you can start cooking those in the pressure cooker! Converting them to the PPCXL is not too difficult. There are four steps:

STEP 1: FIGURE OUT IF YOU NEED TO HALF OR COOK THE RECIPE IN BATCHES

Slow cookers can be filled more than pressure cookers, so you might need to cut the recipe in half and cook less food, or cook the food in batches. If the recipe is making enough food for just 4-6 people, odds are, it will fit in your pressure cooker. If it's for 8 or more people, you're probably going to need to cut the recipe down, or cook more than one batch.

STEP 2: REDUCE THE LIQUID

Unlike slow cookers, pressure cookers pretty much keep all the liquid preserved. That means the amount of liquid you put in at the beginning is the same amount you end up with. Slow cookers lose liquid, so you're going to need to reduce the amount you put in the pressure cooker at the beginning. Most recipes will only need enough liquid to just cover the food in the cooker. Always put in at least the minimum requirement, or the cooker won't reach pressure and/or food will burn. For an easy solution, just look up a pressure cooker recipe that's similar to your slow cooker one.

STEP 3: SAUTÉ AROMATICS FIRST

Slow cooker recipes have you add ingredients all at once, while with pressure cookers, you get better flavor by cooking aromatics first. This includes onions, fresh herbs, carrots, celery, and whole spices. Pick those out from the slow cooker recipe and use your pressure cooker like a skillet to get those nice and browned.

STEP 4: REDUCE COOKING TIME

You will definitely be reducing cooking time when you convert a slow cooker recipe to a pressure cooker one. In general, you'll be cooking the meal for less than 10% of the slow cooker recipe's time. For example, if the slow cooker recipe calls for 4 hours, 10% of 240 minutes is 24 minutes. You'll cook the meal for 24 minutes in your pressure cooker. That represents the lowest amount of time, so given the lower PSI of a PPCXL, you'll probably have to cook it for longer, but 24 minutes is a good place to start with so you don't overcook anything. The 24 minutes also doesn't include prep time, the time it takes the cooker to reach pressure, or a natural pressure release, if the recipe requires that. Cook time does not include any time changes due to the sea-level rule, so you'll have to factor that in yourself with each recipe.

Cooking charts

Cookbooks often include a chart at the end where it shows how long certain ingredients take to cook in the pressure cooker, but the Power Pressure Cooker XL has a copyright on the charts. Look to your manual in the "General Operating Instructions" section to find that information.

Chapter 5

Breakfasts

Hot Barley Cereal with Fresh Raspberries

Serves: 4

Time: 13 minutes (3 minutes cook time, 10 minutes natural pressure release)

Barley flakes are underused compared to oats, but they are packed with healthy vitamins and minerals, like fiber and B-1. In this recipe, the flakes are cooked in creamy vanilla almond milk. Once cooked, you melt in butter and top with fresh raspberries and cinnamon.

Ingredients:

- ☐ 2 cups of vanilla-flavored almond milk
- ☐ 1 cup of barley flakes
- ☐ 1 cup fresh raspberries
- ☐ 2 tablespoons butter
- ☐ A sprinkle of cinnamon

Directions:

1. Pour flakes and milk into the pressure cooker, making sure it's only filled ½ way full, because it will foam.
2. Close and seal the cooker lid.
3. Hit the Rice/Risotto button and adjust time to 3 minutes.
4. When time is up, hit "cancel" and wait 10 minutes for a natural pressure release.
5. Mix in the butter till melted.
6. Serve with raspberries and a sprinkle of cinnamon on top!

Nutritional Info (¼ of recipe):
Total calories: 88
Protein: 4
Carbs: 29
Fat: 8
Fiber: 3.5

Stone-Ground Grits

Serves: 4

Time: 32 minutes (5 minutes prep time, 12 minutes cook time, 15 minutes natural pressure release)

Grits are a classic Southern food that can be eaten any time of day. For breakfast, we're using cream, butter, and cheddar cheese. For best results, make sure to get stone-ground grits, which toast beautifully in coconut oil, and cook into a texture that's creamy, but never gluey.

Ingredients:

- ☐ 3 cups water
- ☐ 1 ¾ cups of cream
- ☐ 1 cup stone-ground grits
- ☐ 4-ounces of cheddar cheese
- ☐ 3 tablespoons butter
- ☐ 2 tablespoons coconut oil
- ☐ 2 teaspoons salt
- ☐ Black pepper to taste

Directions:

1. Turn your PPCXL to "chicken/meat" to preheat the pot.
2. Add the coconut oil, and when hot, stir the grits around to toast them.
3. Turn off the cooker and pour in the water, cream, salt, pepper.
4. Close the lid and hit "chicken/meat" again, adjusting the time to 12 minutes.
5. When the timer beeps, hit "cancel" and wait 15 minutes for the pressure to reduce.
6. Quick-release any remaining pressure.
7. Stir in the butter and cheese until melted.
8. Season to taste before serving!

Nutritional Info (¼ recipe)
Total calories: 532
Protein: 13
Carbs: 34
Fat: 38
Fiber: 0

Homemade Hash Browns with Bacon

Serves: 4
Time: 27 minutes (20 minutes prep time, 7 minutes cook time)

Making your own hash browns may seem hard, but it's actually very easy with a pressure cooker. The potatoes are grated or pulsed very thin, so they cook very quickly. First, you brown them with oil, salt, and pepper, before adding parsley and cooked bacon crumbles. The dish cooks under pressure for just 7 minutes followed by a quick-release.

Ingredients:

- 2 pounds of washed and peeled russet potatoes
- Just under 1 cup of cooked, crumbled bacon
- 2 tablespoons olive oil
- 2 tablespoons chopped parsley
- Salt and pepper to taste

Directions:

1. Pulse potatoes through a food processor, or grate them into strips.
2. Put potatoes in a strainer and rinse in cold water for 30 seconds.
3. Squeeze them dry with a paper towel.
4. Pour olive oil into pressure cooker and hit "chicken/meat."
5. When the oil is hot, add in potatoes with salt and pepper.
6. Brown for 5-6 minutes.
7. Add parsley and bacon.
8. Using a spatula, flatten the potatoes down together into a hash brown shape.
9. Close the pressure cooker lid.
10. Adjust the "chicken/meat" setting to 7 minutes.
11. When the timer beeps, hit "cancel" and quick-release.
12. Serve hot!

Nutritional Info (¼ recipe)
Total calories: 303
Protein: 16
Carbs: 34
Fat: 15
Fiber: 0

Gouda-Mushroom Oats with Thyme

Serves: 4

Time: 32 minutes (10 minutes prep time, 12 minutes cook time, 10 minutes natural pressure release)

Not all breakfast oats need to be sweet. This recipe embraces the fifth taste, known as umami, with mushrooms and smoked gouda. Other bold flavors like garlic and earthy thyme balance out the velvety mushrooms and melted cheese.

Ingredients:

- 14-ounces chicken broth
- 8-ounces sliced crimini mushrooms
- 1 cup steel-cut oats
- ½ cup water
- ½ cup finely-grated smoked gouda cheese
- ½ diced onion
- 2 minced garlic cloves
- 2 tablespoons butter
- 3 sprigs fresh thyme
- Salt and pepper to taste

Directions:

1. Turn your PPCXL to "chicken/meat" and add butter.
2. When melted, add mushrooms and onion.
3. After 3 minutes of cooking, add garlic and stir for another minute or so.
4. Add and toast steel-cut oats for one minute.
5. Pour in broth, water, salt, and thyme sprigs.
6. Seal the cooker lid.
7. Adjust cooking to 12 minutes.
8. When the timer beeps, hit "cancel" and wait 10 minutes for a natural pressure release.
9. Quick-release leftover pressure.
10. Stir in the cheese, salt, and pepper.
11. Serve!

Nutritional Info (¼ recipe)
Total calories: 266
Protein: 9
Carbs: 31
Fat: 12
Fiber: 5

Hard-Boiled Eggs

Serves: 12
Time: 16 minutes (6 minutes cook time, 10 minutes cool/peel time)

For a quick burst of energy on the go, it's hard to beat a boiled egg. In your Power Pressure Cooker XL, you can make 12 eggs in just 6 minutes. If you're eating one right away, let it cool before peeling. Save the rest of the unpeeled eggs in your fridge to enjoy later.

Ingredients:

☐   12 eggs
☐   1 ½ cups water

Directions:

1. Pour water into your cooker.
2. Lower in the steamer basket with the eggs inside.
3. Close and seal the lid.
4. Hit "Rice/Risotto" and cook for the default time, which is 6 minutes.
5. When the timer beeps, quick-release the pressure.
6. Carefully put eggs in a bowl of cold water with ice.
7. After a few minutes, peel and eat.
8. If you're going to be saving them, don't peel until ready to serve.

Nutritional Info (1 egg per serving):
Total calories: 78
Protein: 6.3
Carbs: .5
Fat: 5.3
Fiber: 0

Ginger-Apricot Oats

Serves: 4
Time: 12 minutes

Dried apricots are lusciously sweet with a hint of tartness, so by adding ginger, you get a sweet-spicy flavor going on. You cook the dried fruit right in the cooker with oats, water, and salt. To serve, you add cane sugar, ground ginger, and some candied ginger.

Ingredients;

- ☐ 3 ½ cups water
- ☐ 1 cup dried apricots
- ☐ 1 cup steel-cut oats
- ☐ ¼ cup organic cane sugar
- ☐ 3 tablespoons candied ginger
- ☐ ½ teaspoon ground ginger
- ☐ ¼ teaspoon salt

Directions:

1. Pour oats, water, apricots, and salt into the cooker.
2. Seal the lid.
3. Hit "chicken/meat" and adjust time to 12 minutes.
4. When time is up, hit "cancel" and carefully quick-release. If the vent spits at you, wait 5 minutes or so, and then try again.
5. Stir the oats, making sure the apricots are soft.
6. Add sugar and ground ginger.
7. Serve with candied ginger.

Nutritional Info (¼ recipe per serving):
Total calories: 233
Protein: 5
Carbs: 48
Fat: 3
Fiber: 5

Black Forest Oats

Serves: 4
Time: 12 minutes

Cherry and chocolate are one of my favorite flavor combinations, so of course, I welcome it for breakfast. You cook steel-oats and frozen pitted cherries in water for 12 minutes, so the cherries thaw and become very soft. To serve, just a little sugar is necessary, because the cherries are naturally sweet (unless you specifically use tart cherries, in which case you might need more sugar), along with dark chocolate chips.

Ingredients:

- ☐ 3 ½ cups water
- ☐ 1 cup steel-cut oats
- ☐ 1 cup frozen, pitted cherries
- ☐ 3 tablespoons dark chocolate chips
- ☐ ⅛ cup organic cane sugar
- ☐ ¼ teaspoon salt

Directions:

1. Pour oats, water, cherries, and salt into the cooker.
2. Close and seal the lid.
3. Hit "chicken/meat" and adjust time to 12 minutes.
4. When the timer beeps, hit "cancel" and carefully quick-release.
5. Stir in sugar and chocolate.
6. Serve!

Nutritional Info (¼ recipe per serving):
Total calories: 283
Protein: 5
Carbs: 54
Fat: 6
Fiber: 5.6

Banana French Toast

Serves: 6-8

Time: 51 minutes (15 minutes prep time, 30 minutes cook time, 6 minutes rest time)

Decadent and delicious, this banana French toast is a great weekend treat. You layer sliced French bread, bananas, brown sugar, cream cheese, pecans, and butter in a baking pan before pouring over an egg mixture. The toast cooks for a half hour, and then rests for 6 minutes before it's ready to be served.

Ingredients:

- ☐ 6 slices cubed French bread
- ☐ 4 sliced bananas
- ☐ 3 eggs
- ☐ ½ cup milk
- ☐ ¼ cup cream cheese
- ☐ ¼ cup chopped pecans
- ☐ 2 tablespoons brown sugar
- ☐ 2 tablespoons chilled, sliced butter
- ☐ 1 tablespoon white sugar
- ☐ 1 teaspoon vanilla extract
- ☐ ½ teaspoon cinnamon

Directions:

1. Spray a 1 ½-quart baking dish that fits in the PPCXL.
2. Add a layer of bread cubes to pan.
3. Layer sliced bananas on top of the bread, and sprinkle in 1 tablespoon of brown sugar.
4. In a separate bowl, microwave cream cheese for 30-45 seconds, or until it's soft enough to spread over the bread and bananas.
5. Add rest of the bread cubes to dish and layer on another banana.
6. Sprinkle rest of brown sugar and half of the pecans on top.
7. Lay down sliced butter as the final layer.
8. In another bowl, whisk eggs.
9. Add in white sugar, milk, vanilla, and cinnamon.
10. Pour over the French toast.
11. Prepare your cooker with ¾ cup of water and put in a trivet.
12. Put the baking dish on top of the trivet and seal the lid.

13. Select "chicken/meat" and adjust cook time to 30 minutes.
14. When time is up, hit "cancel" and quick-release the pressure.
15. Wait 5-6 minutes before serving with more sliced bananas and the rest of the pecans.

Nutritional Info (⅙ recipe per serving):
Total calories: 313
Protein: 8
Carbs: 39
Fat: 15
Fiber: 2

Ham + Hash Brown Bake

Serves: 8
Time: 11 minutes (5 minutes prep time, 6 minutes cook time)

By using frozen hash browns and cooked Canadian bacon, this breakfast is very fast. After browning the ham, you stir in hash browns and then pour over a mixture of eggs, cheese, milk, salt, and pepper. That all cooks together into a sliceable patty for just 6 minutes, and then a quick-release before serving!

Ingredients:

- ☐ 8 eggs
- ☐ 6 slices Canadian bacon
- ☐ 2 cups frozen hash browns
- ☐ 1 cup shredded mozzarella cheese
- ☐ ¼ cup milk
- ☐ 1 teaspoon salt
- ☐ ½ teaspoon black pepper

Directions:

1. Turn your PPCXL to "chicken/meat" and add bacon.
2. When nice and browned, add hash browns and stir until they begin to thaw.
3. In a separate bowl, whisk milk, eggs, cheese, salt, and pepper.
4. Pour over the hash browns.
5. Seal the lid.
6. Adjust cooking time to 6 minutes.
7. When the timer beeps, hit "cancel" and quick-release.
8. Slice and serve!

Nutritional Info (⅛ recipe per serving):
Total calories: 137
Protein: 15
Carbs: 8
Fat: 5
Fiber: 1

Bacon 'n Egg Breakfast Sandwich

Serves: 1

Time: 22 minutes (6 minutes prep time, 6 minutes cook time, 10 minutes natural pressure release)

Bacon and egg sandwiches are a fast-food classic, but did you know you can make your own in about 20 minutes? First, you cook the bacon, and then layer your sandwich fillings - bacon, egg, and cheese - in a ramekin. That goes on top of the trivet in the cooker and cooks for 6 minutes. After a natural pressure release, take out the ramekin, and scooch filling between two slices of bread!

Ingredients:

- ☐ 2 slices bread
- ☐ 2 slices bacon
- ☐ 1 egg
- ☐ 1 cup water
- ☐ 1 tablespoon grated cheddar cheese
- ☐ Drizzle of olive oil

Directions:

1. Turn your cooker to "chicken/meat" and cook the bacon.
2. Remove bacon, turn off the cooker, and carefully wipe out the grease.
3. Pour water into the cooker and add trivet.
4. Drizzle in a little olive oil.
5. In a ramekin, fold in cooked bacon and crack an egg on top.
6. Sprinkle on cheese and black pepper.
7. Wrap in foil and put on top of trivet in the cooker.
8. Seal the lid.
9. Hit "chicken/meat" again and adjust time to 6 minutes.
10. Toast your bread.
11. When the timer beeps, turn off the cooker and wait for a natural pressure release.
12. Assemble sandwich.

Nutritional Info (1 recipe per serving):
Total calories: 368
Protein: 20
Carbs: 31
Fat: 13
Fiber: 6

Easy Soft-Boiled Eggs

Serves: 4
Time: 4 minutes

One of the best and most simple breakfasts is a whole-grain English muffin, toasted, with a runny soft-boiled egg on top. To make soft-boiled eggs in the cooker, you pour 1 cup of water into the cooker and insert the steamer basket. To keep the eggs separated in the basket, canning lids are a great idea. Cook for 4 minutes and then quick-release before submerging eggs in a cold-water bath. Peel and serve!

Ingredients:

- ☐ 4 eggs
- ☐ 1 cup water
- ☐ Two toasted English muffins
- ☐ Salt and pepper to taste

Directions:

1. Pour 1 cup of water in your pressure cooker and lower in the steamer basket.
2. Lay four canning lids in the basket and put in the whole, un-cracked eggs - one egg per lid.
3. Seal the lid.
4. Hit "chicken/meat" and adjust time to 4 minutes.
5. When time is up, hit "cancel" and quick-release.
6. Remove eggs with tongs and dunk in a bowl of cold water.
7. After 1-2 minutes, peel.
8. Serve with toasted English muffins, salt, and pepper.

Nutritional Info (1 egg + ½ English muffin):
Total calories: 139
Protein: 9
Carbs: 14
Fat: 6
Fiber: 2

Sweet Breakfast Quinoa

Serves: 4-5
Time: 10 minutes

You've probably had quinoa as a savory side, but its naturally-nutty flavor goes really well with sweeteners like maple syrup. With just a few other seasonings like cinnamon and vanilla, you can turn heart-healthy quinoa into a breakfast. It only takes one minute to cook, and then you let it sit for 10 minutes before serving.

Ingredients:

- ☐ 2 ¼ cups water
- ☐ 1 ½ cups raw and rinsed quinoa
- ☐ 2 tablespoons maple syrup
- ☐ ½ teaspoon vanilla
- ☐ ¼ teaspoon cinnamon
- ☐ Pinch of salt

Directions:

1. Pour everything into your PPCXL and seal the lid.
2. Hit "rice/risotto" and adjust time to 1 minute.
3. When time is up, hit "cancel" and let it sit and steam for 10 minutes.
4. If there's any leftover pressure, quick-release.
5. Fluff quinoa before serving with a splash of milk or other toppings.

Nutritional Info (⅕ of recipe, no toppings):
Total calories: 213
Protein: 7
Carbs: 41
Fat: 3
Fiber: 2

Chapter 6

Poultry

Pulled Turkey with BBQ Mustard Sauce

Serves: 4

Time: 1 hour, 57 minutes (15 minutes prep time, 72 minutes cook time, 20 minutes natural pressure release, 10 minutes reduction time)

Turkey is underused compared to chicken, which is a shame, because it has more moisture. Take your next outdoor event to the next level with this pulled turkey tossed in a homemade barbeque mustard sauce. The turkey cooks in beer, which adds richness, and is under pressure for 72 minutes to give the turkey a long-roasted flavor.

Ingredients:

Turkey:
- ☐ 2-3 pounds of turkey breast
- ☐ ½ cup beer

BBQ sauce:
- ☐ ½ cup apple cider vinegar
- ☐ ½ cup yellow mustard
- ☐ 2 tablespoons honey
- ☐ 2 tablespoons olive oil
- ☐ 1 tablespoon Worcestershire sauce
- ☐ 1 tablespoon molasses
- ☐ 2 teaspoons hot sauce
- ☐ 1 teaspoon mustard powder
- ☐ 1 teaspoon liquid smoke
- ☐ 1 teaspoon garlic powder
- ☐ 1 teaspoon onion powder
- ☐ Salt and pepper to taste

Directions:

1. To make the BBQ sauce, mix mustard, vinegar, Worcestershire, molasses, honey, hot sauce, liquid smoke, mustard powder, onion powder, garlic powder, salt, and pepper.
2. Season turkey breast with salt.
3. Turn the PPCXL to "chicken/meat" and heat oil until shimmering.
4. Place the turkey in and brown on both sides.

5. Plate for now.
6. Pour beer into the pot and deglaze, which means using a wooden spoon or spatula to scrape off any stuck-on turkey bits.
7. Pour in the BBQ sauce and turkey, turning so it becomes coated.
8. Seal the lid.
9. Adjust time to 72 minutes, or 1 hour and 12 minutes.
10. When the timer beeps, hit "cancel" and wait for a natural pressure release.
11. When safe, remove the turkey.
12. Turn the cooker back to "chicken/meat" and wait for the sauce to reduce.
13. While that boils, pull the turkey apart with two forks.
14. When the sauce is the way you want it, stir the turkey back in and serve!

Nutritional Info (¼ recipe per serving):
Total calories: 504
Protein: 51
Carbs: 17
Fat: 25
Fiber: 0

Italian Garlic Chicken

Serves: 4

Time: 16 minutes (7 minutes prep time, 4 minutes cook time, 5 minutes simmer time)

With only a few ingredients, you can turn chicken into a creamy, flavor-packed dinner delicious enough for a special occasion. The stars of the dish are the heavy cream, Parmesan cheese, and sun-dried tomatoes, which are both full of umami and addicting. The other great thing about this dish? It takes less than 20 minutes.

Ingredients:

- ☐ 2 pounds boneless and skinless chicken breasts
- ☐ 1 cup chopped spinach
- ☐ ¾ cup heavy cream
- ☐ ½ cup chicken broth
- ☐ ½ cup Parmesan cheese
- ☐ ½ cup sun-dried tomatoes
- ☐ 2 minced garlic cloves
- ☐ 2 tablespoons olive oil
- ☐ 2 teaspoons Italian seasoning
- ☐ ½ teaspoon salt

Directions:

1. Pound the chicken breasts thin and cut in half.
2. Rub chicken with olive oil, garlic, Italian seasoning, and salt.
3. Throw a dash of salt into your cream and return to the fridge for now.
4. Turn your PPCXL to "chicken/meat," and once hot, add the chicken with its marinade.
5. Brown breasts on both sides.
6. Pour in broth and scrape up any stuck-on chicken bits.
7. Seal the lid.
8. Adjust time to 4 minutes.
9. When the timer beeps, turn off the cooker and quick-release the pressure.
10. Turn the cooker back to "chicken/meat" and add salted cream.
11. Simmer for 5 minutes or so before stirring in cheese.
12. Add sun-dried tomatoes and spinach, and simmer until spinach wilts.
13. Serve hot!

Nutritional Info (¼ recipe per serving):
Total calories: 455
Protein: 57
Carbs: 3
Fat: 26
Fiber: 2

Turkey-Stuffed Bell Peppers

Serves: 4
Time: 34 minutes (26 minutes prep time, 8 minutes cook time)

Make a dinner with a bowl you can eat! Stuffed peppers are a great way to get your veggies, and in this turkey-stuffed meal, there's also corn, onion, and mild green chiles. Stuffed peppers wouldn't be complete without cheese, so remember to sprinkle on sharp cheddar before devouring!

Ingredients:

- ☐ Four big bell peppers (red or green)
- ☐ 1 pound ground turkey
- ☐ One 4 1/2 -ounce can of mild green chiles
- ☐ 1 chopped yellow onion
- ☐ 1 cup shredded sharp cheddar cheese
- ☐ ½ cup corn kernels
- ☐ 2 tablespoons butter
- ☐ 2 teaspoons minced garlic
- ☐ 1 teaspoon dried oregano
- ☐ 1 teaspoon ground cumin
- ☐ ¼ teaspoon salt
- ☐ ¼ teaspoon (or less) cayenne

Directions:

1. Turn your PPCXL to "chicken/meat" and add butter.
2. When melted, cook onion for 3 minutes or until it softens.
3. Add ground turkey and cook for another 3 minutes, stirring.
4. Season with salt, garlic, oregano, cumin, and cayenne.
5. After stirring well, move pot contents to cool for 20 minutes in a bowl. Turn off the cooker.
6. In that time, prep the peppers. Cut off the tops and remove seedy membranes.
7. Stuff peppers with turkey.
8. Wipe out your cooker with a paper towel before pouring in 1 cup of water.
9. Lower in the steamer basket and put in the peppers.
10. Seal the lid.
11. Turn the cooker back to "chicken/meat" and adjust time to 8 minutes.

12. When time is up, hit "cancel" and quick-release.
13. Sprinkle on cheese and once melted, serve!

Nutritional Info (1 stuffed pepper per serving):
Total calories: 371
Protein: 35
Carbs: 17
Fat: 18
Fiber: 2

Whole Turkey with Cranberry Glaze

Serves: 8

Time: 1 hour, 6 minutes -not counting defrost time for the turkey (36 minutes cook time, 30 minutes natural pressure release)

Combine two Thanksgiving essentials with this recipe: turkey and cranberries. Cook a whole 9 ½ thawed bird in just 36 minutes with an amazing glaze made from cranberry jam, cumin, coriander, and black pepper, and make Thanksgiving hassle-free. Remember that turkey should be cooked to 160-degrees.

Ingredients:

- ☐ 9 ½ pound thawed turkey
- ☐ 5-ounces cranberry jam
- ☐ 1 cup chicken stock
- ☐ 1 peeled and diced onion
- ☐ 1 teaspoon salt
- ☐ 1 teaspoon black pepper
- ☐ ½ teaspoon turmeric
- ☐ ½ teaspoon cumin
- ☐ ½ teaspoon coriander

Directions:

1. Rinse the turkey with cool water and pat dry with paper towels.
2. Mix jam, coriander, cumin, coriander, and black pepper together.
3. Rub glaze on the bird.
4. Pour broth, carrot, and onion into the pressure cooker.
5. Put turkey on top and seal the lid.
6. Select "chicken/meat" and adjust time to 36 minutes.
7. When the timer beeps, hit "cancel" and let the pressure descend on its own.
8. Take out the turkey and serve!

Nutritional Info (⅛ recipe per serving):
Total calories: 880
Protein: 101
Carbs: 19
Fat: 43
Fiber: 0

Turkey Breast and Gravy

Serves: 4-6

Time: 51 minutes (5 minutes prep time, 36 minutes cook time, 10 minutes rest/gravy time)

If you don't want to make a whole turkey, how about a large turkey breast with skin? Six pounds is enough for 4-6 people. Using the pressure cooker also allows you make a gravy in the same pot once the turkey is cooked. The whole process takes less than an hour, leaving plenty of time to make other sides or just sit back and relax.

Ingredients:

Turkey:

- ☐ 6 pound bone-in, skin-on thawed turkey breast
- ☐ 4 cups chicken broth
- ☐ 3 smashed garlic cloves
- ☐ 1 halved onion
- ☐ 2 halved celery stalks
- ☐ 4 tablespoons butter
- ☐ 1 tablespoon chopped parsley
- ☐ 1 tablespoon chopped rosemary
- ☐ 1 tablespoon sage
- ☐ Salt and pepper to taste

Gravy:

- ☐ Leftover cooking liquid from turkey
- ☐ 2 tablespoons butter
- ☐ 2 tablespoons flour

Directions:

1. Pour chicken broth into the PPCXL and lower in the steamer basket.
2. Put garlic, carrot, celery, and onion into the basket.
3. In a bowl, mix parsley and rosemary with your fingers.
4. Rinse the bird and pat dry with paper towels.
5. Season well with salt and pepper.
6. Stretch up the skin from the breast's top, and rub in chopped herb mixture, and add four pats of butter beneath the skin with a few sage leaves.
7. Lower turkey into cooker.

8. Press "chicken/meat" and adjust cook time to 36 minutes.
9. When the timer beeps, turn off the cooker and wait for a natural pressure release.
10. Take out the turkey and put on a baking sheet.
11. Broil for a few minutes to get the skin crispy.
12. Tent in foil while you make the gravy.
13. Remove veggies and take 1 cup of liquid out from the cooker.
14. Melt 2 tablespoons of butter in a saucepan and whisk in flour until smooth.
15. Pour in 1 cup of turkey liquid and stir.
16. Turn cooker back to "chicken/meat" and pour roux into the rest of the turkey liquid.
17. When simmered to a thickened, gravy consistency, it's time to serve with the turkey breast!

Nutritional Info (⅙ recipe per serving):
Total calories: 637
Protein: 93
Carbs: 5
Fat: 27
Fiber: 2

Stuffed Turkey Breast

Serves: 4-6

Time: 1 hour, 10 minutes (25 minutes prep time, 30 minutes cook time, 15 minutes natural pressure release)

Why have stuffing on the side when you can roll it into your turkey? Made from breadcrumbs, cooked onions and celery, parsley, and milk, the stuffing is aromatic and earthy. For extra flavor, slather grainy mustard on the stuffed turkey before cooking for 30 minutes.

Ingredients:

2 ½-3 pound boneless and skinless turkey breast
2 cups veggie stock
2 cups breadcrumbs
1 cup whole milk
2 chopped red onions
2 chopped celery stalks
2 tablespoons butter
2 tablespoons chopped parsley
2 tablespoons chopped sage
1 tablespoon olive oil
2 minced garlic cloves
2 teaspoons grainy mustard
1 ½ teaspoons salt
Pinch of red pepper flakes

Directions:

1. Turn your cooker to "chicken/meat."
2. Once warm, add celery, onions, garlic, sage, and butter.
3. Cook until the onions and celery are softening, which should take about 5 minutes.
4. While that cooks, mix breadcrumbs with 1 teaspoon of salt and the parsley.
5. Pour milk and mix to get a batter-like texture.
6. When the veggies are done, hit "cancel" and move veggies to another bowl, and mix with the breadcrumb batter.
7. Butterfly the turkey breast and pound thin, so you are able to roll it.
8. Spoon breadcrumb mixture in the middle, and spread evenly, leaving the top edge and side of turkey bare.
9. Roll tightly and tie with kitchen string.

10. Turn your PPCXL to "chicken/meat" and add oil.
11. Brown turkey breast on both sides, for 5 minutes per side, until a rich golden.
12. Pour in the stock and spoon grainy mustard on top of turkey, so it's even on the top and sides.
13. Seal the lid.
14. Adjust cook time to 30 minutes.
15. When time is up, hit "cancel" and wait for a natural pressure release.
16. Serve with the cooking liquid as a sauce.

Nutritional Info (¼ recipe per serving):
Total calories: 495.8
Protein: 36.5
Carbs: 47
Fat: 17
Fiber: 3.7

Whole Chicken

Serves: 4-6

Time: 46-51 minutes (6 minutes prep time, 25-30 minutes cook time, 15 minutes natural pressure release)

Cooking a whole chicken is a great way to meal prep a protein for the week. You can use the meat in a lot of ways, from sandwiches to salad toppings to meat for soups and more. A simple seasoning blend of garlic, paprika, thyme, salt, black pepper, and lemon ensures that every bite is flavorful.

Ingredients:

- ☐ One 3-4 pound thawed whole chicken
- ☐ 2 cups chicken broth
- ☐ 4 garlic cloves
- ☐ 1 lemon
- ☐ 1 tablespoon olive oil
- ☐ 1 teaspoon paprika
- ☐ 1 teaspoon dried thyme
- ☐ ½ teaspoon black pepper
- ☐ ½ teaspoon salt

Directions:

1. Season chicken evenly with paprika, thyme, salt, and pepper.
2. Turn cooker to "chicken/meat" and add chicken, with the breast-side down, and brown for 5 minutes.
3. Turn over.
4. Pour in chicken broth.
5. Halve the lemon, squeeze in juice, and toss both halves in the pot with garlic.
6. Seal the lid.
7. Adjust cook time to 25 (for a 3-pounder) or 30 minutes (for a 4-pounder).
8. When time is up, hit "cancel" and wait for a natural pressure release.
9. Cool a bit before carving and serving!

Nutritional Info (¼ recipe per serving):
Total calories: 736
Protein: 58
Carbs: 4
Fat: 49
Fiber: 0

Sticky Ginger Chicken Thighs

Serves: 4
Time: 32 minutes (5 minutes prep time, 12 minutes cook time, 15 minutes broil time)

You'll be licking your fingers when you're done with this meal. Affordable chicken thighs are cooked in the pressure cooker with a marinade made from honey, hoisin, soy sauce, brown sugar, ginger, garlic, Sriracha, and chicken stock. To make those addicting flavors even stronger, you cook more of those ingredients down in a skillet to get a thick, sticky sauce that you slather on the cooked thighs before broiling.

Ingredients:

- ☐ 2-3 pounds boneless, skinless chicken thighs
- ☐ 1 ¾ cups chicken stock
- ☐ ½ cup honey
- ☐ ½ cup + 2 tablespoons hoisin sauce
- ☐ ½ cup + 2 tablespoons soy sauce
- ☐ 5 tablespoons brown sugar
- ☐ 4 tablespoons Sriracha hot sauce
- ☐ 2 tablespoons sesame oil
- ☐ 1 tablespoon + 1 teaspoon minced garlic
- ☐ 3 teaspoons grated ginger

Directions:

1. Pat chicken dry with paper towels and put in your cooker.
2. In a bowl, mix 1 teaspoon garlic, 1 teaspoon ginger, 2 tablespoons soy sauce, 2 tablespoons hoisin, 1 tablespoon brown sugar, 1 tablespoon Sriracha, and chicken stock.
3. Pour over chicken.
4. Seal the lid.
5. Hit "chicken/meat" and adjust time to 12 minutes.
6. In the meantime, add other ingredients to a skillet and mix.
7. On medium high, let the mixture come to a boil, and then reduce the heat and simmer to a thick sauce.
8. When the cooker timer beeps, hit "cancel" and quick-release the pressure.
9. Put chicken thighs on a cookie sheet lined with parchment and broil for 5-7 minutes per side.

10. Slather on sauce and broil again for 5 minutes.
11. Flip wings, slather, and broil one last time for 5 minutes or until charred.
12. Serve with green onions and rice.

Nutritional Info (¼ recipe per serving):
Total calories: 786
Protein: 74
Carbs: 80
Fat: 21
Fiber: 0

Spicy Peach Chicken

Serves: 4
Time: 21 minutes (10 minutes prep time, 11 minutes cook time)

Three parts to a meal - chicken, rice, and a peach - all cook in one pressure cooker. The chicken has a citrusy marinade made from orange juice and zest, soy sauce, peach schnapps, honey, soy sauce, and some red pepper flakes for heat. You layer rice and chicken in the pressure cooker, and set a whole peach on top. 11 minutes later, and you've got a unique and delicious dinner ready to go!

Ingredients:

- ☐ 4 chicken breasts
- ☐ 3 cups chicken stock
- ☐ 2 cups basmati rice
- ☐ 1 big peach
- ☐ ½ cup chopped onion
- ☐ 2 tablespoons soy sauce
- ☐ 2 tablespoons honey
- ☐ 1 tablespoon olive oil
- ☐ 1 tablespoon yellow mustard
- ☐ 1 tablespoon butter
- ☐ 1 tablespoon peach schnapps
- ☐ 2 teaspoons orange zest
- ☐ 1 teaspoon red pepper flakes
- ☐ 1 teaspoon salt
- ☐ Juice from 1 orange

Directions:

1. In a bowl, mix orange juice, orange zest, soy sauce, mustard, schnapps, honey, and red pepper flakes.
2. Coat chicken with marinade.
3. Store in a fridge for now, wrapped in saran wrap.
4. Turn your cooker to "chicken/meat" and warm up.
5. Add olive oil and heat.
6. Add salt and onions, and wait for 2-3 minutes.

7. Hit "cancel" and stir in butter.
8. Pour in stock and rice.
9. Put a trivet on top of the rice.
10. Put chicken in a pan that fits in the cooker, and put on top of the trivet.
11. Pour any leftover liquid on the chicken.
12. Lay a piece of parchment paper on chicken, and put peach on top.
13. Seal the lid.
14. Hit "chicken/meat" and adjust time to 11 minutes.
15. When time is up, hit "cancel" and quick-release the pressure.
16. Serve chicken with sliced peach and rice.

Nutritional Info (¼ recipe per serving):
Total calories: 604
Protein: 32
Carbs: 89
Fat: 13
Fiber: 1

Chicken Thighs with Pears, Golden Raisins, and Pine Nuts

Serves: 4-6
Time: 28 minutes (10 minutes prep time, 18 minutes cook time)

There are endless ways to serve cheap chicken thighs. This recipe uses fresh pears, sweet golden raisins, and pine nuts for a delicious, layered bite. The sauce is also a star with ingredients based in butter and balsamic vinegar. Make sure to toast the pine nuts while the chicken cooks in the pressure cooker.

Ingredients:

- 2 pounds boneless, skinless chicken thighs
- 2 large, firm peeled and sliced Bosc pears
- 1 chopped shallot
- 1 cup pine nuts
- ⅔ cup chicken broth
- ¼ cup golden raisins
- 2 tablespoons butter
- 2 tablespoons balsamic vinegar
- ½ teaspoon dried dill
- ½ teaspoon salt
- ½ teaspoon black pepper

Directions:

1. Turn your cooker to "chicken/meat" and melt butter.
2. Season chicken thighs well with salt and pepper.
3. Brown on both sides; you'll probably have to do brown in batches.
4. Move chicken to a bowl, and put shallot and pear in the cooker.
5. Cook and stir until the shallot softens.
6. Pour in vinegar, raisins, and dill.
7. Once the mixture is bubbling, pour in the broth.
8. Add the chicken thighs and seal the lid.
9. Adjust time to 18 minutes.
10. While the chicken and sauce cooks, put pine nuts in a skillet on medium-low (no oil)

and stir for 3 minutes or so until golden and fragrant.
11. When time is up, turn off the cooker and quick-release carefully.
12. Stir once before plating the thighs with plenty of sauce.
13. Garnish with pine nuts!

Nutritional Info (¼ recipe per serving):
Total calories: 632
Protein: 50
Carbs: 29
Fat: 38
Fiber: 3.5

Chicken with Creamy White Sauce

Serves: 4-5
Time: 33 minutes (15 minutes prep time, 18 minutes cook time)

In the mood for something creamy and rich that doesn't take all evening to prepare? Chicken pieces - ideally a mix of chicken thighs and wings - cook in the pressure cooker with wine, bacon, butter, garlic, broth, onion, and thyme to a beautiful tenderness. At the end, you stir in cream, and that brings the whole dish together.

Ingredients:

- ☐ 2 ½ pounds chicken pieces
- ☐ 2 cups dry white wine
- ☐ 1 cup chicken stock
- ☐ 1 cup finely-chopped onion
- ☐ ¾ cup cream
- ☐ 5-ounces chopped bacon
- ☐ 3 crushed garlic cloves
- ☐ 1 tablespoon olive oil
- ☐ 1 tablespoon butter
- ☐ 1 teaspoon dried thyme
- ☐ Salt and pepper to taste

Directions:

1. Season the chicken with salt and pepper.
2. Turn your cooker to "chicken/meat" and heat oil.
3. When shiny, brown the chicken (skin-side down first) till golden.
4. Flip and cook for just one minute.
5. Plate chicken for now.
6. Melt butter in pot.
7. Cook onion and garlic for 3 minutes.
8. Add bacon and cook until crispy.
9. Pour in wine and deglaze, scraping the cooker.
10. Bring to a simmer for 2 minutes.
11. Pour in broth and thyme, and add chicken back to cooker.
12. Close and seal the lid.
13. Adjust cook time to 18 minutes.

14. When time is up, hit "cancel" and quick-release. Chicken should be at 165-degrees. If not cooked through, hit "chicken/meat" again and cook with the lid off until the proper temperature is reached.
15. Stir in cream and season with more salt and pepper if necessary.
16. Serve!

Nutritional Info (¼ recipe per serving):
Total calories: 706
Protein: 74
Carbs: 7
Fat: 34
Fiber: 0

Chicken-Prosciutto Roll-Ups

Serves: 6
Time: 21 minutes (15 minutes prep time, 7 minutes cook time)

The secret to a good roll-up is to pound the meat thin enough. Once the chicken is thin, you roll in salty prosciutto, and stick in a toothpick with a sage leaf, so the herb infuses the meat with flavor. This recipe looks fancy, but they are actually very easy and only take 21 minutes to make!

Ingredients:

- ☐ 6 chicken breasts
- ☐ 6 prosciutto slices
- ☐ 10 sage leaves
- ☐ 1 cup frozen peas
- ☐ ¾ cup chicken stock
- ☐ ¼ cup dry white wine
- ☐ 2 tablespoons olive oil
- ☐ 1 teaspoon sea salt

Directions:

1. Pound out the chicken breasts so they're thin enough to roll.
2. Lay down one slice of prosciutto per chicken breast, and roll.
3. Secure your rolls with toothpicks with a sage leaf pressed against the chicken.
4. Turn your cooker to "chicken/meat" and add olive oil and the rest of the sage.
5. Add chicken to brown, starting on the side with the sage. You will have to push the toothpick nearly all the way into the roll in order for the chicken to touch the hot pot.
6. Once golden, pour in the wine.
7. When the alcohol smell has faded, add salt and broth.
8. Tumble peas on top of chicken rolls and seal the lid.
9. Adjust cook time to 7 minutes.
10. When the time is up, hit "cancel" and quick-release the pressure.
11. Serve chicken rolls with peas!

Nutritional Info (⅙ of recipe per serving):
Total calories: 266
Protein: 36
Carbs: 4
Fat: 8
Fiber: 0

Chicken and Cornbread Stuffing

Serves: 5-6
Time: 26 minutes cook time (divided into three times)

This dish is almost like a chicken pot pie, except that the crust was mixed in with the fillings, and that crust was made of cornbread. A lower-calorie comfort food option, your family will fall in love with this extremely-easy dish that cooks in three parts - first for 18 minutes, then 2, and then 5.

Ingredients:

- Four large frozen skinless and boneless chicken breasts
- 1 bag of frozen green beans
- 23-ounces of cream of chicken soup
- 14-ounce bag of cornbread stuffing
- 1 cup chicken broth

Directions:

1. Pour broth into pressure cooker and add chicken.
2. Seal the lid.
3. Select "chicken/meat" and cook for 18 minutes.
4. When time is up, hit "cancel" and quick-release.
5. Add green beans and seal lid again.
6. Select "chicken/meat" again and cook for 2 minutes.
7. Quick-release again.
8. Add cornbread stuffing and cream of chicken soup, but do not stir.
9. Seal lid and cook for another 5 minutes before quick-releasing one last time.
10. Stir everything well and season with salt and pepper.
11. Serve!

Nutritional Info (⅕ recipe per serving):
Total calories: 374
Protein: 34
Carbs: 36
Fat: 12
Fiber: 2

Marsala-Spiked Turkey and Mushrooms

Serves: 4
Time: 42 minutes (10 minutes prep time, 22 minutes cook time, 10 minutes rest/sauce time)

Marsala is a dry, sweet wine that is usually used with chicken, but for this recipe, we substitute turkey instead. White mushrooms join the party, and cook in shallot, garlic, and thyme for a mix of earthy and bright flavors. The sauce is probably my favorite part, since it involves cream, and I'm always a fan of creamy sauces.

Ingredients:

- ☐ 1 ¼ pound boneless and skinless turkey breasts
- ☐ 6-ounces sliced white mushrooms
- ☐ ⅔ cup chicken stock
- ☐ ⅓ cup dry marsala wine
- ☐ 1 minced garlic clove
- ☐ 3 tablespoons heavy cream
- ☐ 3 tablespoons chopped shallots
- ☐ 2 tablespoons olive oil
- ☐ 1 ½ tablespoons cornstarch
- ☐ ½ teaspoon dried thyme
- ☐ Salt and pepper to taste

Directions:

1. Remove the turkey's silvers sinews.
2. Tie breasts horizontally every 2 inches with kitchen string
3. Season well with salt and pepper.
4. Pour 1 tablespoon of olive oil into the cooker and heat.
5. Brown turkey breasts for 3 minutes on each side.
6. When brown, set aside on a plate.
7. Pour in the remaining oil and cook mushrooms with shallot, garlic, and thyme.
8. When the mushrooms are beginning to soften, pour in the wine and deglaze, scraping up any stuck-on bits.
9. Once the alcohol smell has faded, return the turkey to the cooker.
10. Hit "chicken/meat" and adjust time to 22 minutes.
11. When the timer beeps, hit "cancel" and quick-release the pressure.
12. Make sure turkey is 160-degrees before tenting with foil.

13. Turn your cooker back on to "chicken/meat" and bring the liquid to a boil.
14. In a separate bowl, mix heavy cream and cornstarch.
15. Pour into the cooker to thicken the sauce.
16. Season with salt and pepper before moving sauce to a gravy boat or other serving bowl.
17. Cut string off turkey breasts and slice.
18. Serve!

Nutritional Info (¼ recipe per serving):
Calories: 192
Protein: 15
Carbs: 5
Fat: 12
Fiber: 1

Crispy Chicken and Gravy

Serves: 4

Time: 26 minutes (11 minutes cook time, 5 minutes batter time, 10 minutes oven time)

It's possible to get crispy chicken without frying thanks to this recipe's combination of pressure-cooking and baking. First, you cook the chicken thighs with some garlic, onion, and rosemary for just 11 minutes, and then coat in a batter of panko, eggs, flour, butter, oil, and salt. While the chicken becomes crispy in the oven, you make the gravy from the liquid in the pressure cooker, along with soy sauce, salt, and pepper.

Ingredients:

Chicken:

- ☐ 6 large chicken thighs
- ☐ 4 chopped garlic cloves
- ☐ 1 sliced onion
- ☐ 1 cup cold water
- ☐ 2 tablespoons cornstarch + 2 ½ tablespoons cold water
- ☐ 1 tablespoon soy sauce
- ☐ Pinch of rosemary
- ☐ Salt and pepper to taste

Coating:

- ☐ ½ cups panko breadcrumbs
- ☐ big, beaten eggs
- ☐ 1 cup flour
- ☐ tablespoons olive oil
- ☐ 2 tablespoons butter
- ☐ Salt to taste

Directions:

1. Put garlic, rosemary, onion, and cold water into your cooker.
2. Lower in the steamer basket.
3. Put chicken thighs in the basket and seal the cooker lid.
4. Select "chicken/meat" and cook for 11 minutes.
5. In the meantime, preheat a skillet on the stove.

6. Mix in olive oil, butter, and breadcrumbs.
7. Salt and stir till the breadcrumbs have turned golden.
8. When time is up on the PPCXL, turn off the cooker and allow the pressure to come down on its own.
9. Preheat your oven to 400-degrees F while the cooker releases pressure.
10. Chicken should be 165-degrees before you begin to coat them. Keep the cooking liquid in the pot.
11. Pat chicken with a paper towel and then season with salt and pepper.
12. Coat chicken first with flour, then beaten eggs, and then toasted breadcrumbs.
13. Bake in the oven until the breadcrumbs have stuck on the chicken into a nice crust.
14. While that bakes, begin chicken gravy by turning your pressure cooker to "chicken/meat."
15. Pour 1 tablespoon of soy sauce, salt, and pepper into the cooker's liquid and bring to a bubble.
16. In a separate bowl, mix cornstarch and cold water till smooth, and pour into the cooker ⅓ at a time until it thickens to your liking.
17. Serve chicken thighs with gravy.

Nutritional Info (¼ recipe per serving):
Total calories: 548
Protein: 44
Carbs: 43
Fat: 23
Fiber: 1

Sweet 'n Sour Mango Chicken

Serves: 4

Time: 38 minutes (10 minutes prep time, 18 minutes cook time, 10 minute thickening time)

Fruit and chicken are a great combination, especially when you know how to add complementary and contrasting flavors. In this recipe, those flavors come from sharp, acidic red onion, spicy-sweet ginger, tangy lime juice, sweet honey, and salty fish sauce. The whole dish takes less than 40 minutes, and packs 38 grams of protein!

Ingredients:

- ☐ 8 boneless chicken thighs
- ☐ 1 chopped mango
- ☐ 4 chopped garlic cloves
- ☐ ½ cup chicken broth
- ☐ ½ chopped red onion
- ☐ ¼ cup chopped cilantro
- ☐ ¼ cup + 1 tablespoon coconut aminos
- ☐ 1-inch piece of chopped ginger
- ☐ 2 tablespoons apple cider vinegar
- ☐ 2 tablespoons lime juice
- ☐ 2 tablespoons honey
- ☐ 1 tablespoon olive oil
- ☐ 1 teaspoon fish sauce
- ☐ Salt to taste

Directions:

1. Pour oil into your PPCXL and heat on the "chicken/meat" setting.
2. When hot, add chicken thighs and brown on the skin side for 3 minutes.
3. Brown on the other side for just 2 minutes and move the chicken to a plate.
4. Add garlic, onion, and mango to the cooker.
5. When the onion has turned clear and the mango is browning, hit "cancel."
6. Return the chicken to the pot.
7. Add lime juice, ¼ cup aminos, honey, ginger, fish sauce, and 1 tablespoon of apple cider vinegar.
8. Close and seal the lid.

9. Hit "chicken/meat" again and adjust cook time to 18 minutes.
10. When the timer beeps, hit "cancel" and quick-release the pressure.
11. Remove the thighs.
12. Pour 1 tablespoon of aminos, 1 tablespoon of vinegar, and salt into the pot.
13. Hit "chicken/meat" and let the sauce reduce for 10-15 minutes, until thick.
14. Serve chicken with sauce and cilantro on top!

Nutritional Info (¼ recipe per serving):
Total calories: 379
Protein: 38
Carbs: 26
Fat: 13
Fiber: 4

Coconut Chicken Curry

Serves: 6

Time: 52 minutes (30 minutes prep time, 12 minutes cook time, 10 minutes natural pressure release)

Everyone with a pressure cooker should have at least one authentic curry recipe under their belt. Why? Curries teach you how amazing spice combinations can be, so you can keep recipes very low carb, low fat, and high in protein. You can get whole spices at good grocery stores like Whole Foods or Asian markets.

Ingredients:

Curry paste:

- ☐ 6 peeled and halved shallots
- ☐ 4 small dried red chilies
- ☐ 4 whole cloves
- ☐ 3 green cardamom pods
- ☐ ¾ cup grated, unsweetened coconut
- ☐ 1-inch cinnamon stick
- ☐ 4 teaspoons Chinese Five-Spice
- ☐ 2 teaspoons black peppercorns

Chicken:

- ☐ 3 pounds boneless, skinless chicken thighs (cut into pieces)
- ☐ 1 tablespoon coconut oil
- ☐ 1 tablespoon vinegar
- ☐ 2 sliced yellow onions
- ☐ 2 sliced tomatoes
- ☐ 2 minced garlic cloves
- ☐ 1-inch piece of minced ginger
- ☐ 3 teaspoons salt

Directions:

1. The first ingredient list is the coconut curry paste, which you make first.
2. Turn your cooker to "chicken/meat" and add chilies and shallots.
3. Cook until charred spots appear.

4. Remove with tongs and put in a food processor, but don't blend yet.
5. Add whole spices and coconut to cooker and stir for one minute.
6. Add turmeric and stir.
7. Move everything to the food processor and add 4-6 tablespoons of water.
8. Pulse until a paste forms, and set aside for now.
9. Add oil to cooker and heat until shiny.
10. Add onions, garlic, and ginger.
11. Cook until onions are soft and beginning to brown.
12. Add coconut paste and cook for one minute before adding tomatoes.
13. Cook for five minutes.
14. Add vinegar, salt, and chicken.
15. Stir once before sealing the lid.
16. Adjust cook time to 12 minutes.
17. When the timer beeps, turn off the cooker and wait for a natural pressure release.
18. Serve!

Nutritional Info (⅙ recipe per serving):
Total calories: 320
Protein: 47
Carbs: 5
Fat: 9
Fiber: 4

Balsamic + Sherry Chicken Thighs

Serves: 2
Time: 28 minutes (10 minutes prep time, 18 minutes cook time)

You can never have too many easy chicken recipes. With only 210 calories and 14 grams of protein per ½-pound serving, these chicken thighs are flavored with sweet and rich balsamic vinegar, sherry wine, and seasonings like basil, green onion, garlic, and black pepper. To make it a more complete meal, serve with rice or another starchy side.

Ingredients:

- ☐ 1 pound boneless + skinless chicken thighs
- ☐ ½ cup balsamic vinegar
- ☐ ⅓ cup sherry wine
- ☐ 2 tablespoons olive oil
- ☐ 2 tablespoons minced green onion
- ☐ 2 tablespoons chopped cilantro
- ☐ 1 ½ teaspoons minced garlic
- ☐ 1 teaspoon Worcestershire sauce
- ☐ 1 teaspoon dried basil
- ☐ 1 teaspoon garlic powder
- ☐ ½ teaspoon black pepper

Directions:

1. Mix balsamic, sherry, green onion, garlic powder, Worcestershire, basil, garlic powder, and black pepper in a plastic bag.
2. Put chicken in the bag and coat well.
3. Turn your cooker to "chicken/meat" and add oil.
4. Cook fresh garlic until fragrant.
5. Pour in chicken and sauce before sealing the lid.
6. Adjust cook time to 18 minutes.
7. When time is up, quick-release the pressure.
8. Serve with cilantro!

Nutritional Info (½ pound thighs per serving):
Total calories: 210
Protein: 14
Carbs: 10
Fat: 12
Fiber: 0

Chapter 7

Beef + Lamb

White Cheddar-Stuffed Hamburgers

Serves: 2

Time: 16 minutes (5 minutes prep time, 6 minutes cook time, 5 minutes natural pressure release)

If you've ever been to Minnesota, you may have heard of (or even tried) the Juicy Lucy burger. It's a hamburger stuffed with gooey, melty cheese. Making your own at home is surprisingly easy, especially when you use a pressure cooker. This recipe uses white cheddar cheese, though you can substitute any cheese you like. You envelop the cheese in raw hamburger meat, stick the patties in a steamer basket, and cook under pressure for just 6 minutes. Allow the pressure to come down naturally, and then serve with all your favorite burger toppings! Nutritional info is just for the patties and does not include a bun or extras.

Ingredients:

- ☐ 1 pound ground beef
- ☐ 2 slices of white cheddar cheese
- ☐ ½ cup beer
- ☐ 1 tablespoon Worcestershire sauce
- ☐ Garlic powder to taste
- ☐ Salt and pepper to taste

Directions:

1. In a bowl, mix beef, salt, pepper, garlic, and Worcestershire.
2. Form four balls and flatten with a plate.
3. Put a slice of cheese into the center of two of the hamburger patties.
4. Take the other flattened hamburger ball and smoosh it on top, pushing the edges together, so the cheese is completely enveloped.
5. Pour beer into the PPCXL and lower in the steamer basket.
6. Put the burgers in the basket and seal the lid.
7. Hit "chicken/meat" and adjust time to 6 minutes.
8. When time is up, hit "cancel" and wait for a natural pressure release.
9. Serve burgers on buns with all the fixin's!

Nutritional Info (½ recipe per serving):
Total calories: 620
Protein: 50
Carbs: 3
Fat: 43
Fiber: 0

Beef Shepherd's Pie

Serves: 8

Time: 54 minutes (10 minutes prep time, 14 minutes cook time, 5 minutes mash time, 20 minutes oven time, 5 minutes rest time)

Shepherd's pie is originally from England, which is known for its savory meat pies. This recipe uses beef, peas, carrots, onion, and fresh thyme. For the topping, it's homemade mashed potatoes. The pie starts off in the pressure cooker for 14 minutes before you finish off in the oven for 20 minutes. What's great about the recipe is that you prepare the filling and topping at the same time; the beef filling cooks in the actual pot while the potatoes stay separated in the steamer basket.

Ingredients:

Filling:

- ☐ 1 ½ pounds ground beef
- ☐ 1 cup chicken stock
- ☐ 1 cup frozen peas
- ☐ 2 diced carrots
- ☐ 1 diced onion
- ☐ 3 tablespoons butter
- ☐ 1 tablespoon tomato paste
- ☐ 1 tablespoon Worcestershire sauce
- ☐ 1 thyme sprig
- ☐ 1 teaspoon salt
- ☐ ½ teaspoon apple cider vinegar
- ☐ ¼ teaspoon pepper

Topping:

- ☐ 1 ½ pounds sliced (2-inch pieces) potatoes
- ☐ ½ cup milk
- ☐ ½ teaspoon salt

Directions:

1. Melt 1 tablespoon of butter in your PPCXL on the "chicken/meat" setting and add diced onion.

2. Cook until soft.
3. Move the onion to the side and add meat, breaking it up and browning for 5 minutes.
4. Add carrots, Worcestershire, tomato paste, salt, thyme, pepper, and stock.
5. Stir before adding the steamer basket filled with potatoes into the pot.
6. Seal the lid.
7. Adjust cook time to 14 minutes.
8. When time is up, hit "cancel" and quick-release the pressure.
9. Turn your oven to 4oo-degrees.
10. While that preheats, take out the steamer basket and add 1 cup of peas into the cooker.
11. Mix.
12. Move potatoes to a bowl and peel the skin off.
13. Add milk and salt.
14. Mash well.
15. Pour the meat filling into a 10x13 baking dish and scoop potato topping evenly on top.
16. Smash down with your fork so it's even.
17. Finish off with the rest of the butter (chopped) and put in the oven.
18. Bake for 20 minutes.
19. Wait 5 minutes before serving!

Nutritional Info (⅛ recipe per serving):
Total calories: 403.3
Protein: 17.8
Carbs: 22.3
Fat: 27.5
Fiber: 3.4

Sloppy Joe's with Tangy Dijon Slaw

Serves: 6-8
Time: 37 minutes (20 minutes prep time, 12 minutes cook time, 5 minutes thickening time)

Sloppy Joe's are a childhood favorite and so easy to make that they can become a weekly staple. This recipe uses lots of veggies in addition to lean ground beef, so there's red onion, pepper, and carrots. There's even ½ cup of rolled oats which add some fiber and help bulk up the dish. Also included is a recipe for a fresh, tangy Dijon coleslaw that you can eat on the side or in the sloppy Joe sandwich.

Ingredients:

Joe's:
- ☐ 1 pound lean ground beef
- ☐ 1 cup chopped tomatoes
- ☐ 1 cup water
- ☐ ½ cup rolled oats
- ☐ 1 chopped red onion
- ☐ 1 chopped green bell pepper
- ☐ 1 grated carrot
- ☐ 4 tablespoons tomato paste
- ☐ 4 tablespoons apple cider vinegar
- ☐ 1 tablespoon olive oil
- ☐ 1 tablespoon Worcestershire sauce
- ☐ 2 teaspoons garlic powder
- ☐ 1 ½ teaspoons salt

Slaw:
- ☐ ½ head sliced cabbage
- ☐ 2 grated carrots
- ☐ ½ chopped red onion
- ☐ 2 tablespoons apple cider vinegar
- ☐ 1 tablespoon Dijon mustard
- ☐ 1 tablespoon honey

Directions:

1. Pour olive oil in your PPCXL and heat on the "chicken/meat" setting.
2. Add beef and brown on both sides, which for frozen meat, will take about 8 minutes per side.
3. Move beef to one side of the pot and add onions, carrots, bell pepper, salt, and garlic powder.
4. When soft, stir in Worcestershire sauce, tomatoes, vinegar, tomato paste, and water.
5. When everything is boiling, add oats (don't stir) and seal the lid.
6. Adjust cook time to 12 minutes.
7. When time is up, hit "cancel" and gradually quick-release the pressure.

8. With the lid off, hit "chicken/meat" and stir for 5 minutes so the sauce thickens.
9. To make the slaw, mix vinegar, honey, and mustard in a bowl.
10. Add carrots, onion, and cabbage.
11. Serve!

Nutritional Info (¾ cup meat w/ ¾ cup slaw per serving):
Total calories: 179.8
Protein: 15
Carbs: 18
Fat: 5.9
Fiber: 3.5

Barbacoa Beef

Serves: 9

Time: 1 hour, 53 minutes (15 minutes prep time, 78 minutes cook time, 20 minutes natural pressure release)

Barbacoa is essentially Mexican barbeque and is known for being extremely tender. Traditionally, the meat is steamed and smoked at the same time, so when you use a pressure cooker, you're performing half of that process. For smoky flavors, there's chipotles in adobo sauce and spices like cumin and clove. A four-ounce serving is only 153 calories with 24 grams of protein.

Ingredients:

- ☐ 3 pounds trimmed bottom round roast
- ☐ 5 garlic cloves
- ☐ 1 cup water
- ☐ ½ onion
- ☐ 3 bay leaves
- ☐ 2-4 tablespoons chipotles in adobo sauce
- ☐ Juice of 1 lime
- ☐ 1 tablespoon ground oregano
- ☐ 1 tablespoon ground cumin
- ☐ 2 ½ teaspoons salt
- ☐ 1 teaspoon olive oil
- ☐ ½ teaspoon ground cloves
- ☐ Black pepper to taste

Directions:

1. Put onion, garlic, lime juice, oregano, cumin, cloves, chipotles, and water in a blend and puree.
2. Cut the meat into 3-inch pieces.
3. Season with salt and black pepper.
4. Heat the PPCXL on "chicken/meat" and add oil.
5. When shiny, add meat and brown in batches for 5 minutes per side.
6. Add blender sauce and bay leaves.
7. Seal the lid.
8. Adjust cook time to 78 minutes.

9. When time is up, hit "cancel" and wait 20 minutes for a natural pressure release.
10. Quick-release any leftover pressure.
11. Save 2 ½ cups of the cooking liquid before shredding the meat.
12. Mix meat with saved cooking liquid, along with ½ teaspoon salt and ½ teaspoon cumin.

Nutritional Info (4-ounces meat per serving):
Total calories: 153
Protein: 24
Carbs: 2
Fat: 4.5
Fiber: 0

Brandy-Thyme Short Ribs

Serves: 4

Time: 1 hour, 30 minutes (15 minutes prep time, 1 hour cook time, 10 minutes natural pressure release, 5 minutes simmer time)

Rich and addicting, these short ribs are flavored with brandy, maple syrup, and thyme. For added aromatic properties, there's onion, garlic, and carrot, of course. The meat cooks under pressure for 1 hour, followed by a 10 minute natural pressure release and quick-release. To make the sauce thicker, you simmer it by itself until it's reduced.

Ingredients:

- ☐ 2 pounds short ribs
- ☐ 2 cups chicken broth
- ☐ 1 chopped onion
- ☐ 1 chopped carrot
- ☐ 2 minced garlic cloves
- ☐ 2 tablespoons butter
- ☐ 2 tablespoons brandy
- ☐ 1 tablespoon maple syrup
- ☐ 1 teaspoon dried thyme
- ☐ 1 teaspoon salt
- ☐ ½ teaspoon black pepper

Directions:

1. Turn your PPCXL to "chicken/meat" and add butter.
2. When melted, add ribs in batches and cook for 3 minutes per side.
3. When the ribs are done, plate.
4. Add onion and carrot to the pot, cooking until softened, for about 5 minutes.
5. Add garlic and cook for just another minute.
6. Spoon in maple syrup, along with brandy, salt, thyme, and black pepper.
7. When the liquid has evaporated and the smell of alcohol has subsided, pour in broth.
8. Scrape up any stuck-on foods and add ribs.
9. Seal the lid.
10. Adjust the cook time to 60 minutes.
11. When the timer beeps, hit "cancel" and wait 10 minutes.
12. Quick-release the pressure and take out the ribs.

13. Tent with foil.
14. Pour the liquid from the pressure cooker into a blender and process till smooth.
15. Return to the pot and hit "chicken/meat" to simmer.
16. Reduce by ¼, which takes about 5 minutes.
17. Taste and season with salt and pepper.
18. Serve ribs with sauce.

Nutritional Info (¼ recipe per serving):
Total calories: 586
Protein: 45
Carbs: 7
Fat: 50
Fiber: 3

Beef Brisket with Veggies

Serves: 4

Time: 1 hour, 47 minutes (30 minutes prep time, 72 minutes cook time, 5 minutes additional time)

Prepare a full meal in your Power Pressure Cooker XL with this recipe, which has you cooking beef brisket with potatoes, carrots, onion, and celery. Flavors from the Worcestershire, garlic, and bay leaf warm up the soul, making this a great recipe for fall and winter.

Ingredients:

- ☐ 2 pounds brisket
- ☐ 2 ½ cups beef broth
- ☐ 6 red potatoes
- ☐ 4 bay leaves
- ☐ 1 big yellow onion
- ☐ 2 cups chopped carrots
- ☐ 2 chopped celery stalks
- ☐ 3 tablespoons chopped garlic
- ☐ 3 tablespoons Worcestershire sauce
- ☐ 2 tablespoons olive oil
- ☐ Black pepper to taste
- ☐ Knorr Demi-Glace sauce to taste

Directions:

1. Turn your pressure cooker to "chicken/meat" and add 1 tablespoon of oil.
2. Add onion and cook until very brown.
3. Move to a bowl.
4. Season the meat well on both sides with black pepper.
5. Pour another tablespoon of oil in your cooker and sear meat on both sides.
6. Seal the lid.
7. Adjust cook time to 60 minutes.
8. When time is up, hit "cancel" and quick-release.
9. Take off the lid and put in all the veggies and bay leaves, including onions.
10. Hit "chicken/meat" again and adjust time to 12 minutes.
11. When time is up, turn off the cooker and quick-release.

12. Remove veggies and meat.
13. Pick out the bay leaves.
14. Turn the pot back to "chicken/meat" and bring to a boil.
15. Stir in 1 tablespoon of Demi-Glace before serving.

Nutritional Info (⅕ recipe per serving):
Total calories: 400
Protein: 28
Carbs: 10
Fat: 18
Fiber: 1

Swiss Steak with Sauce

Serves: 4
Time: 38 minutes (20 minutes prep time, 18 minutes cook time)

Cooked in a delicious sauce made from condensed tomato soup with horseradish, beef round steak becomes extremely tender in the pressure cooker. Since one serving is just 253 calories, serve with a side like a salad or grain dish to make this a complete meal.

Ingredients:

- ☐ 1 ½ pounds boneless beef round steak
- ☐ One 10 ¾-ounce can of condensed tomato soup
- ☐ 1 cup chopped green pepper
- ☐ ¾ cup chopped celery
- ☐ ½ cup cold water
- ☐ 2 chopped carrots
- ☐ 1 chopped onion
- ☐ 2 tablespoons flour
- ☐ 2 tablespoons canola oil
- ☐ 1 teaspoon cornstarch
- ☐ 1 teaspoon horseradish
- ☐ ½ teaspoon salt
- ☐ ¼ teaspoon pepper

Directions:

1. Chop steak into smaller pieces.
2. In a bowl, mix flour, pepper, and salt.
3. Rub both sides of the steak pieces.
4. Pour oil into your PPCXL and hit "chicken/meat."
5. When hot, brown the steak on both sides.
6. Add vegetables.
7. In another bowl, mix water and cornstarch.
8. Add horseradish and tomato soup into this bowl before pouring it all into the pressure cooker.
9. Seal the lid.
10. Adjust cook time to 18 minutes.
11. When time is up, hit "cancel" and quick-release.

12. Serve!

Nutritional Info (¼ recipe per serving):
Total calories: 253
Protein: 28
Carbs: 16
Fat: 8
Fiber: 3

Beef Taco Pie

Serves: 4
Time: 17 minutes (5 minutes prep time, 12 minutes cook time)

Beef tacos are one of my favorite summertime dishes, but when the weather gets colder, I need something a bit more hearty. This beef taco pie layered with beans, meat, and cheese is the answer. For the full taco experience, serve the savory pie with tomatoes, lettuce, sour cream, and any other favorite toppings.

Ingredients:

- ☐ 1 package of flour or corn tortillas
- ☐ 1 pound lean ground beef
- ☐ 12-ounces Mexican-style cheese
- ☐ ¼ cup refried beans
- ☐ 1 package taco seasoning

Directions:

1. Pour 1 cup of water into your PPCXL.
2. Mix beef with taco seasoning.
3. Lay 1 tortilla in the bottom of a springform pan.
4. Cover with beans, and then cheese.
5. Add another tortilla, then beans, beef, and lastly, more cheese.
6. When all the ingredients are gone, lower your pan in the pressure cooker.
7. Seal the lid.
8. Hit "chicken/meat" and adjust time to 12 minutes.
9. When the timer beeps, turn off the cooker and quick-release the pressure.
10. Remove the pie from the springform pan.
11. Serve with lettuce, tomatoes, sour cream, and other taco fixin's!

Nutritional Info (¼ recipe per serving):
Total calories: 363
Protein: 25
Carbs: 29
Fat: 19
Fiber: 6

Shredded Steak with Banana Peppers

Serves: 8
Time: 2 hours, 4 minutes (84 minutes cook time, 40 minutes natural pressure release)

Serve this versatile steak in tacos, sandwiches, or even over salad. Just pick up four pounds of steak, a can of banana peppers, and beef broth. There's little to no prep time, and then you just wait 84 minutes before letting the cooker release its pressure naturally. It's a great recipe for when you're too busy to spend time chopping or stirring.

Ingredients:

- ☐ 4 pounds steak (any cut)
- ☐ One 16-ounce can of banana peppers
- ☐ ½ cup beef broth
- ☐ 1 tablespoon garlic powder
- ☐ Salt and black pepper to taste

Directions:

1. Season steak with garlic, salt, and pepper.
2. Put in the pressure cooker.
3. Pour in jar of banana peppers and broth.
4. Seal the lid.
5. Hit "chicken/meat" and adjust time to 84 minutes.
6. When time is up, hit "cancel" and wait for a natural pressure release.
7. When safe, open the cooker and shred the meat.
8. Serve!

Nutritional Info (⅙ recipe per serving)
Total calories: 442
Protein: 65
Carbs: 3
Fat: 18
Fiber: 0

Brown Sugar +Mustard-Glazed Meatloaf

Serves: 4

Time: 1 hour, 14 minutes (10 minutes prep time, 54 minutes cook time, 10 minutes rest time)

Spicy and sweet are two of the best contrasting flavors. In this recipe, the sweet is coming from brown sugar and the spicy is brown mustard. You mix the two ingredients with ketchup and brush it over the meatloaf, which includes the classic beef and bread crumbs mixture, as well as basil, garlic, and black olives.

Ingredients:

Meafloaf:

- ☐ 1 pound lean ground beef
- ☐ ⅔ cup diced onion
- ☐ ⅔ cup bread crumbs
- ☐ 6 sliced black olives
- ☐ 1 egg white
- ☐ 2 tablespoons ketchup
- ☐ 2 fresh, chopped basil leaves
- ☐ 1 teaspoon minced garlic
- ☐ ½ teaspoon salt
- ☐ Black pepper

Glaze:

- ☐ ¼ cup ketchup
- ☐ 1 tablespoon spicy brown mustard
- ☐ 1 tablespoon brown sugar

Directions:

1. Grease a one-quart round baking dish.
2. In a bowl, mix all the ingredients from the first list and form a loaf.
3. In a second bowl, mix glaze ingredients.
4. Brush glaze on loaf and cover dish with foil.
5. Pour 1 cup of water into your PPCXL and add trivet.
6. Put the meatloaf dish on the trivet.
7. Seal the lid.
8. Hit "chicken/meat" and adjust time to 54 minutes.

9. When time is up, hit "cancel" and quick-release.
10. Remove the dish and tilt it into the sink, pouring out excess liquid.
11. Let the meat rest for 10 minutes or so before serving.

Nutritional Info (¼ recipe per serving):
Total calories: 261
Protein: 25
Carbs: 19.2
Fat: 7.5
Fiber: 0

Pressure-Cooker Pot Roast

Serves: 8

Time: 1 hour, 9 minutes (15 minutes prep time, 54 minutes cook time)

Pot roast is one of those meals every home cook should be familiar with. In the pressure cooker, it couldn't be easier, and the only real "work" involved is browning the meat and pouring in some broth and soy sauce. Adding apples, garlic, ginger, and fresh orange juice to the roast helps infuse it with lots of flavor that your whole family will love.

Ingredients:

- ☐ 4 pounds bottom roast cut into cubes
- ☐ 1 peeled and chopped Granny Smith apple
- ☐ 5 minced garlic cloves
- ☐ 1 cup beef broth
- ☐ ½ cup soy sauce
- ☐ 1 thumb of grated ginger
- ☐ Juice of one large orange
- ☐ 2 tablespoons olive oil
- ☐ Salt and pepper to taste

Directions:

1. Season roast with salt and pepper.
2. Turn your PPCXL to "chicken/meat."
3. Add oil and heat up.
4. When hot, add roast and brown evenly.
5. Plate.
6. Pour broth in the pot and scrape up any burnt-on food bits.
7. Stir in soy sauce.
8. Return the meat to the pot.
9. Put the apple, garlic, and ginger on the roast.
10. Pour in orange juice and seal the lid.
11. Adjust cook time to 54 minutes.
12. When time is up, hit "cancel" and quick-release the pressure.
13. Serve!

Nutritional Info (⅛ recipe per serving):
Total calories: 492
Protein: 46
Carbs: 3
Fat: 37
Fiber: 0

Top Round Beef with Bourbon, Bacon, + Potatoes

Serves: 6

Time: 2 hours, 14 minutes (15 minutes prep time, 84 minutes cook time, 30 minutes natural pressure release, 5 minutes rest time)

With only 15 minutes of prep time, this top round recipe is top-notch. Richly flavored with bacon and bourbon, you also cook 1 ½ pounds of Yukon Golds in the cooker for a new take on meat-and-potatoes. Relatively low in carbs and fat, this meal is high-protein as well as delicious.

Ingredients:

- ☐ 3 pounds beef top round
- ☐ 1 ½ pounds Yukon Gold potatoes
- ☐ 1 ½ cups beef broth
- ☐ ¼ cup bourbon
- ☐ 4 chopped bacon slices
- ☐ 1 stemmed, cored, and chopped green bell pepper
- ☐ One 6-inch rosemary sprig
- ☐ 2 teaspoons black pepper

Directions:

1. Season beef with black pepper.
2. Turn your PPCXL to "chicken/meat" and cook the bacon.
3. Plate bacon before adding the roast to the cooker.
4. Brown evenly.
5. Add bell pepper and cook for 3 minutes until softened.
6. Pour broth and bourbon into the pot, scraping up any stuck-on food bits.
7. Add rosemary sprig, bacon, and beef.
8. Seal the lid.
9. Adjust cook time to 66 minutes.
10. When the timer beeps, hit "cancel" and quick-release the pressure.
11. Add potatoes and seal the lid again.
12. Hit "chicken/meat" again and adjust time to 18 minutes.
13. When time is up, turn off the cooker and wait for a natural pressure release.
14. Remove the rosemary sprig and plate meat for 5 minutes.

15. Slice and serve with potatoes and sauce!

Nutritional Info (⅙ recipe per serving):
Total calories: 553
Protein: 73
Carbs: 21
Fat: 13
Fiber: 1.6

Lamb Roast with Potatoes and Herbs

Serves: 8

Time: 1 hour, 30 minutes (15 minutes prep time, 72 minutes cook time (divided), 3 minutes thickening time)

What can you do with a big leg of lamb? Make a pot roast, of course! With plenty of potatoes and dried herbs, this lamb pot roast only takes an hour and a half from start to finish, and offers little to no carbs and lots of protein. By adding arrowroot and water at the very end, you thicken the cooking liquid into a delicious gravy, making this a true one-pot meal.

Ingredients:

- ☐ 6-pound leg of lamb
- ☐ 3 pounds peeled and cut potatoes
- ☐ 2 cups chicken broth
- ☐ ⅓ cup water
- ☐ 3 minced garlic cloves
- ☐ 2 tablespoons olive oil
- ☐ 3 tablespoons arrowroot powder
- ☐ 1 crushed bay leaf
- ☐ 1 teaspoon ginger
- ☐ 1 teaspoon dried thyme
- ☐ 1 teaspoon dried marjoram
- ☐ 1 teaspoon dried sage
- ☐ Salt and pepper to taste

Directions:

1. Turn your PPCXL to "chicken/meat" and add oil.
2. When shimmering and hot, add roast, moving it around so it becomes coated in oil.
3. Lift it up and flip it over to brown.
4. Brown it on the other side, too.
5. Sprinkle on salt, pepper, and the dried herbs.
6. Pour in the broth and seal the lid.
7. Adjust cook time to 60 minutes.
8. When time is up, hit "cancel" and carefully quick-release.
9. Add the potatoes and seal the lid again.
10. Hit "chicken/meat" and adjust cook time to 12 minutes.

11. When time is done, quick-release again.
12. If potatoes are tender, move to a plate, along with the meat.
13. In a separate bowl, mix water and arrowroot powder till smooth.
14. Pour into the broth and stir immediately.
15. Sauce should become thicker and become a gravy.
16. Serve with the lamb and potatoes!

Nutritional Info (⅛ recipe per serving):
Total calories: 796
Protein: 214
Carbs: 32
Fat: 45
Fiber: 3.8

Tuscan Lamb Shanks

Serves: 4
Time: 56 minutes (20 minutes prep time, 36 minutes cook time)

Flavored with the essence of Italy (tomatoes, garlic, and rosemary), these lamb shanks are a great idea for a small dinner party with people you want to impress. White navy beans, carrots, and celery cook in the pot at the same time as the meat, so you get both a main dish and a side simultaneously. Serve with the cooking liquid, which transforms into a flavorful sauce.

Ingredients:

- ☐ Two 1-pound lamb shanks
- ☐ 3 ½ cups water
- ☐ One 14-ounce can of tomatoes with juice
- ☐ 1 cup dried navy beans
- ☐ 2 chopped carrots
- ☐ 2 chopped celery ribs
- ☐ 3 sliced garlic cloves
- ☐ 2 rosemary sprigs
- ☐ 2 tablespoons olive oil
- ☐ Salt and pepper

Directions:

1. Dry lamb shanks with a paper towel and season with salt and pepper.
2. Pour oil into your pressure cooker and heat on the "chicken/meat" setting until shiny.
3. Add shanks one at a time and brown on both sides.
4. Move to a plate.
5. Add celery, onion, garlic, and carrots to the cooker and cook for 6 minutes, or until brown.
6. Pour in tomatoes with juice, and toss in the rosemary.
7. Stir for one minute before adding beans, water, ½ teaspoon salt, and ¼ teaspoon pepper.
8. Put the meat back into the cooker and bring to a boil.
9. Immediately seal the lid and adjust cook time to 36 minutes.
10. When time is up, hit "cancel" and quick-release.
11. Pick out the rosemary and check the lamb's temperature. For medium, it should be 160-degrees. If it isn't cooked through yet, put under pressure for the minimum time,

which is 2 minutes.

12. When ready, move shanks to a cutting board and shred.
13. Serve with cooking liquid as a sauce with the beans and veggies.

Nutritional Info (¼ recipe per serving):
Total calories: 547
Protein: 42
Carbs: 43
Fat: 28
Fiber: 16

Lamb with Red Wine Sauce and Gremolata

Serves: 4
Time: 51 minutes (15 minutes prep time, 36 minutes cook time)

Red wine and lamb were meant to be together. The alcohol all burns off in this sauce, but the rich flavors remain intact, and are accented by garlic, onion, and tomato puree. The gremolata, which is just another word for a garnish or dressing, is fresh parsley, garlic, and bright grated lemon zest. You'll only spent about 15 minutes actually working on the dish before it cooks under pressure for 36 minutes, followed by a quick-release.

Ingredients:

Lamb:
Four ½-pound lamb shanks
One 700-gram jar of tomato puree
1 cup red wine
½ cup flour
2 peeled and sliced onions
4 crushed garlic cloves
3 tablespoons olive oil
Salt and pepper to taste

Gremolata:
½ cup chopped parsley
2 crushed garlic cloves
Grated rind of one lemon

Directions:

1. Coat shanks in flour, salt, and pepper.
2. Pour oil into the pressure cooker and heat on the "chicken/meat" setting.
3. Add shanks and brown evenly all over before moving to a plate.
4. Put onion and garlic in the cooker and cook for 2-3 minutes.
5. Pour in wine and deglaze, scraping up any stuck-on food, and cooking off the alcohol for 2 minutes.
6. Stir in tomato puree and return shanks.
7. Bring to a boil before sealing the lid.
8. Adjust cook time to 36 minutes.
9. Meanwhile, mix parsley, lemon rind, and garlic.

10. When time is up on the cooker, hit "cancel" and quick-release.
11. Serve shanks with gremolata on top with some of the cooking liquid as sauce.

Nutritional Info (¼ recipe per serving):
Total calories: 708
Protein: 42
Carbs: 54
Fat: 32
Fiber: 1

Chapter 8

Pork

Cafe Rio Brown-Sugar Pork

Serves: 8

Time: 43 minutes (3 minutes prep time, 30 minutes cook time, 10 minutes natural pressure release)

This shredded pork will make you a BBQ hero at every gathering. It only needs nine ingredients, including plenty of brown sugar, lemon juice, butter, soy sauce, and garlic. If you love BBQ on the sweet side, this is the recipe for you.

Ingredients:

- ☐ 3 pounds cubed (1-inch) pork roast
- ☐ 1 ¼-1-½ cups brown sugar
- ☐ ½ cup lemon juice
- ☐ 1 chopped yellow onion
- ☐ 3 tablespoons butter
- ☐ 2 tablespoons soy sauce
- ☐ 2 minced garlic cloves
- ☐ 1 teaspoon sea salt
- ☐ ½ teaspoon black pepper

Directions:

1. Turn your PPCXL to "chicken/meat."
2. Add butter, onion, and garlic.
3. Once the onion has become soft, which is about 3 minutes, add pork roast and ¾ cup of water.
4. Stir and seal the lid.
5. Adjust time to 30 minutes.
6. When time is up, hit "cancel" and wait 10 minutes.
7. Release any remaining pressure.
8. Pour pot contents into a colander, saving ½ cup of liquid.
9. Shred the meat and return to pot.
10. Pour in brown sugar, lemon juice, soy sauce, salt, pepper, and saved liquid.
11. Serve with tacos or hamburger buns.

Nutritional Info (⅛ recipe)
Total calories: 551
Protein: 34
Carbs: 43
Fat: 28
Fiber: 0

Garlic Pork Loin with Veggies

Serves: 4

Time: 1 hour, 2 minutes (15 minutes prep time, 36 minutes cook time, 6 minutes additional cook time, 5 minutes cool time)

In this recipe, you poke garlic right into the pork loin, which infuses the meat with rich flavor. Aromatic seasonings like a bay leaf, carrots, celery, and onion add to the earthy, hearty dish that also includes russet potatoes. It's a one-pot meal that takes just over an hour from start to finish.

Ingredients:

- ☐ 2 pounds trimmed boneless pork loin top roast
- ☐ 4-6 small garlic cloves
- ☐ 2 cups water
- ☐ 3 quartered russet potatoes
- ☐ 1 quartered onion
- ☐ 3 chopped carrots
- ☐ 2 chopped celery stalks
- ☐ 1 bay leaf
- ☐ 2 tablespoons olive oil
- ☐ Salt and pepper to taste

Directions:

1. Cut slits into the top of each pork loin, about 1 ½-inch deep.
2. Cut one hole every inch on the top, and poke the garlic inside.
3. Season pork with salt and pepper.
4. Pour oil into pressure cooker and brown meat all over on the "chicken/meat" setting.
5. Drain extra oil and add water.
6. Toss in the bay leaf.
7. Put pork on rack and put inside the cooker.
8. Seal the lid.
9. Adjust cook time to 36 minutes.
10. When time is up, hit "cancel" and quick-release.
11. Take out the meat.
12. Add veggies and potatoes on the rack.
13. Put meat back on top of the veggies and seal the lid again.

14. Hit "chicken/meat" again and adjust time to 6 minutes.
15. When time is up, hit "cancel" and quick-release.
16. Cool for 5 minutes before serving.

Nutritional Info (¼ recipe)
Total calories: 724
Protein: 41
Carbs: 28
Fat: 7
Fiber: 2

Pork Roast with Apple Gravy

Serves: 6

Time: 2 hours, 7 minutes (15 minutes prep time, 72 minutes cook time, 30 minutes natural pressure release, 10 minutes gravy time)

One of the great things about the pressure cooker is that you can cook gravy right in the pot with the main protein, which in this dish, is a bone-in pork shoulder roast. The gravy embodies the flavors of autumn, with plenty of apples, apple juice, sage, and onion. You strain the gravy before adding the thickener, making a smooth sauce you will want to eat with a spoon.

Ingredients:

- [ ] 4 pounds bone-in pork shoulder roast
- [ ] 2 cored and sliced apples
- [ ] 1 cup apple juice
- [ ] 1 cup chicken broth
- [ ] 1 sliced yellow onion
- [ ] 3 sage leaves
- [ ] 1 bay leaf
- [ ] 1 sprig rosemary
- [ ] 3 tablespoons flour
- [ ] 3 tablespoons butter
- [ ] 1 tablespoon olive oil
- [ ] 1 teaspoon salt
- [ ] ½ teaspoon black pepper

Directions:

1. Rinse and dry roast.
2. Season with salt and pepper on both sides.
3. Turn your pressure cooker to "chicken/meat" and add oil.
4. When hot, brown the pork roast for 5 minutes on each side.
5. Add the broth, juice, herbs, onion, and apples.
6. Seal the lid.
7. Adjust cook time to 72 minutes.
8. When time is up, hit "cancel" and wait for a natural pressure release.

9. Take out the meat and tent with foil on a plate.
10. Strain the liquid into a bowl and throw out the solids.
11. Add butter to your PPCXL and hit "chicken/meat" again.
12. Whisk in flour and stir for 3-5 minutes until a golden brown.
13. Whisk in strained broth to thicken into a gravy.
14. Shred the pork and return to the pot, stirring into the gravy.

Nutritional Info (¼ recipe)
Total calories: 638
Protein: 41
Carbs: 15
Fat: 45
Fiber: 1.3

Honey-Orange Pork

Serves: 2-3

Time: 1 hour, 55 minutes (15 minutes prep time, 1 hour cook time, 30 minutes natural pressure release, 10 minutes simmer time)

Honey and orange go beautifully together. The honey brings out the natural sweetness of the orange, while it simultaneously contrasts the orange's tartness. Garlic, cloves, cinnamon, ginger, and maple syrup add deep, spicy-sweet flavors, making this a favorite for kids and adults alike.

Ingredients:

- [ ] 1 ½-pounds pork shoulder meat
- [ ] 3 minced garlic cloves
- [ ] ½ cup water
- [ ] 1 orange
- [ ] 1 cinnamon stick
- [ ] 1 sliced onion
- [ ] 2 cloves
- [ ] 2 tablespoons soy sauce
- [ ] 1 tablespoon honey
- [ ] 1 tablespoon maple syrup
- [ ] 1 tablespoon olive oil
- [ ] 1 ½ tablespoons cornstarch
- [ ] 1 tablespoon water
- [ ] 1 tablespoon sliced ginger
- [ ] Pinch of dried rosemary
- [ ] Salt and pepper to taste

Directions:

1. Season meat with salt and pepper.
2. Turn your PPCXL to "chicken/meat" and add olive oil.
3. When hot, brown pork shoulder for 3-5 minutes on each side.
4. When brown, plate.
5. Add ginger, onions, a bit of salt, and pepper into the pressure cooker.
6. Cook for 1 minute before adding garlic, and stirring for 30 seconds.
7. Cut the orange in half and squeeze into the pot, deglazing and scraping up any burnt-

on bits.

8. Pour in water, soy sauce, honey, cloves, maple syrup, the cinnamon stick, rosemary, and cut-up orange.
9. Put the pork into the pot and seal the lid.
10. Adjust cook time to 1 hour.
11. When time is up, hit "cancel" and wait for a natural pressure release.
12. Take out the pork and hit "chicken/meat" again.
13. Remove the orange pieces, cinnamon stick, and cloves.
14. Taste and season with more salt, pepper, or honey to your liking.
15. In a separate bowl, mix water and cornstarch.
16. Add gradually into the pot, until you get the thickness you want.
17. Hit "cancel" and return the pork, coating it in the sauce.

Nutritional Info (½ recipe)
Total calories: 839
Protein: 64
Carbs: 38
Fat: 43
Fiber: 1

Pork in a Peach-Mustard Sauce

Serves: 8

Time: Overnight + 1 hour, 10 minutes (55 minutes cook time, 15 minutes rest time)

With only a few key ingredients, you can make a party-worthy pork dish that will have your guests "oohing" and "ahhing." The pork marinates overnight in a dry rub of just salt and brown sugar. The next day, you just throw it in the pressure cooker for 55 minutes. While that cooks, you make the sauce on the stove with white wine, peaches, sugar, rice wine vinegar, thyme, and grainy mustard.

Ingredients:

Pork:

- ☐ 4 pounds pork shoulder
- ☐ ⅓ cup salt
- ☐ ⅓ cup brown sugar

Peach sauce:

- ☐ 2 cups dry white wine
- ☐ 2 cups sliced peaches
- ☐ ½ cup sugar
- ☐ 2 ½ tablespoons rice wine vinegar
- ☐ 2 tablespoons chicken broth
- ☐ 2 sprigs of thyme
- ☐ 1 tablespoon grainy mustard

Directions:

1. The night before you plan on making the meal, mix brown sugar and salt in a bowl.
2. Rub on pork before wrapping in plastic wrap and refrigerating overnight.
3. When ready to cook, pour the minimum requirement of liquid into your PPCXL.
4. Add pork and seal the lid.
5. Hit "chicken/meat" and adjust time to 55 minutes.
6. When there's a half hour left on the pressure cooker, put broth, peaches, wine, 2 tablespoons vinegar, sugar, and thyme into a saucepan.
7. Simmer and reduce for 30 minutes.
8. When the sauce is reduced, stir in mustard and rest of the vinegar.
9. When the pressure cooker is done, hit "cancel" and quick-release.

10. Take out the pork and tent with foil for 15 minutes.
11. Serve pork with sauce and enjoy!

Nutritional Info (⅛ recipe)
Total calories: 665
Protein: 44
Carbs: 38
Fat: 32
Fiber: 0

Easiest Southern Pork-Sausage Gravy

Serves: 8

Time: 36 minutes (20 minutes prep time, 6 minutes cook time, 10 minutes thickening time)

Get ready to make the easiest gravy ever. It's only eight total ingredients - including salt and pepper - and thanks to the pressure cooker, it tastes like it's been simmering way longer than just 16 minutes. Serve with biscuits, naturally!

Ingredients:

- ☐ 1 pound pork sausage
- ☐ 2 cups milk
- ☐ 1 chopped onion
- ☐ ¼ cup flour
- ☐ 4 minced garlic cloves
- ☐ 1 tablespoon olive oil
- ☐ Salt and pepper to taste

Directions:

1. Heat olive oil in the pressure cooker on the "chicken/meat" setting.
2. Add onion and cook until clear.
3. Add garlic and stir until fragrant.
4. Add meat and brown.
5. Add 1 1/2 cups milk before sealing the lid.
6. Hit the "rice/risotto" setting and cook for default time.
7. When time is up, hit "cancel" and quick-release.
8. In a separate bowl, mix flour and remaining milk.
9. Hit "chicken/meat" on the pressure cooker and gradually add in the flour/milk mixture to thicken the gravy.
10. Serve with biscuits!

Nutritional Info (⅛ recipe)
Total calories: 268
Protein: 11
Carbs: 8
Fat: 22
Fiber: 0

Pork Loin Stuffed with Apples + Walnuts

Serves: 4

Time: 40 minutes (15 minutes prep time, 20 minutes cook time, 5 minutes thickening time)

Stuffed pork is one of my favorite "fancy" meals, especially when the filling is made from ingredients like tart green apples and walnuts, one of the best brain foods. The nuts and apples cook with onions first before you stuff them into the pork and sear the meat. The chops cook for just 20 minutes under pressure, and then you thicken the cooking liquid into a gravy with potato flakes.

Ingredients:

- 3 pounds center-cut pork loin
- 2 cored, peeled, and sliced green apples
- 1 cup apple cider
- 1 cup chicken stock
- 1 cup potato flakes
- ½ cup chopped toasted walnuts
- 1 sliced onion
- 6-ounces diced mushrooms
- 2-ounces butter
- 2 tablespoons olive oil
- 1 teaspoon sea salt
- 1 teaspoon black pepper

Directions:

1. Slice the pork longways so there's an open slit where you will stuff the filling.
2. Season well with salt and pepper.
3. Turn your pressure cooker to "chicken/meat" and add half of the onions, all the apples, and all the walnuts.
4. Cook for just 2-3 minutes and turn off the cooker.
5. Fill the pork before rolling up as best as you can and tying with kitchen string.
6. Turn the cooker back to "chicken/meat" and sear pork on both sides.
7. Remove and add the rest of the onions, cooking until they release their juices.
8. Add everything else (except potato flakes) including the pork, and seal the lid.
9. Adjust cook time to 20 minutes.

10. When time is up, hit "cancel" and quick-release the pressure.
11. Take out the pork.
12. Add potato flakes and butter to gravy.
13. When thickened, serve with pork.

Nutritional Info (¼ recipe)
Total calories: 543
Protein: 24
Carbs: 39
Fat: 31
Fiber: 4

Mexican-Braised Pork

Serves: 4
Time: 40 minutes (10 minutes prep time, 20 minutes cook time, 10 minutes rest time)

For a healthy but hearty meal, pork loin and sweet potatoes are a great combination. On their own, these two ingredients have a similar flavor profile that's on the sweet, nutty side, so we need to add spices. For a Mexican flare, try tomato salsa, cilantro, cumin, and tomatillos, which taste a little like lime. Garnish with cilantro or parsley, if you don't like cilantro.

Ingredients:

- ☐ 3 pounds pork loin
- ☐ 2 peeled and diced sweet potatoes
- ☐ 1 cup tomato salsa
- ☐ ½ cup diced tomatillos
- ☐ ½ cup chicken stock
- ☐ ¼ cup cilantro
- ☐ 1 teaspoon salt
- ☐ 1 teaspoon pepper
- ☐ ½ teaspoon cumin

Directions:

1. Turn your PPCXL to "chicken/meat."
2. Season pork with salt, pepper, and cumin.
3. Add oil to your pressure cooker.
4. When hot, sear the pork on both sides, and leave them in the pot.
5. Add salsa, half the cilantro, diced tomatillos, and chicken stock.
6. Put the sweet potatoes on one side of the pot.
7. Seal the lid and adjust cook time to 20 minutes.
8. When time is up, hit "cancel" and quick-release.
9. Take out the pork and rest for 8-10 minutes before slicing.
10. Serve with sweet potatoes, sauce, and the rest of the cilantro.

Nutritional Info (¼ recipe)
Total calories: 520
Protein: 73
Carbs: 22

Fat: 15
Fiber: 2.2

Baby-Back Ribs

Serves: 4

Time: 43 minutes (18 minutes cook time, 15 minutes natural pressure release, 10 minutes oven time)

Skip going out tonight and make the family homemade baby-back ribs. It's a simple recipe that uses common ingredients like salt, liquid smoke, black pepper, apple cider, and BBQ sauce. Four teaspoons of pure vanilla add a bourbon-like flavor.

Ingredients:

- ☐ 2 racks of pork baby-back ribs
- ☐ 2 chopped onions
- ☐ 2 cups of your favorite BBQ sauce
- ☐ 2 cups apple cider
- ☐ 1 cup water
- ☐ 4 teaspoons pure vanilla extract
- ☐ 3 teaspoons salt
- ☐ 2 teaspoons liquid smoke
- ☐ 2 teaspoons black pepper

Directions:

1. Put water, apple cider, vanilla, onions, and liquid smoke into your pressure cooker.
2. Season well with salt and pepper and seal the lid.
3. Hit "chicken/meat" and adjust time to 18 minutes.
4. When time is up, hit "cancel" and wait 15 minutes.
5. Preheat oven to 400-degrees.
6. Quick-release any remaining pressure.
7. Remove ribs and put on a baking sheet lined with foil.
8. Brush on BBQ sauce and stick in the oven.
9. Bake for 5 minutes before turning over ribs, slathering on more sauce, and returning to the oven for another 5 minutes.
10. Serve!

Nutritional Info (¼ recipe)
Total calories: 608
Protein: 19
Carbs: 19
Fat: 18
Fiber: .9

Pork Medallions + Dijon Mushrooms

Serves: 2

Time: 43 minutes (15 minutes prep time, 18 minutes cook time, 10 minutes mushroom time)

Make a rich and earthy date-night dinner complete with side dish in just over 40 minutes. The pork is seasoned simply with salt, pepper, and fresh herbs, and go under pressure for 18 minutes while the mushrooms cook with a chicken broth and Dijon mustard sauce.

Ingredients:

Pork:

- ☐ 2 pork tenderloins
- ☐ 2 ½ cups chicken stock
- ☐ ½ cup flour
- ☐ 3 sprigs fresh thyme
- ☐ 2 sprigs fresh rosemary
- ☐ Olive oil
- ☐ Salt and pepper

Dijon mushrooms:

- ☐ 3 cups sliced cremini mushrooms
- ☐ ½ cup chicken stock
- ☐ 1 ½ tablespoons Dijon mustard
- ☐ Enough oil to coat skillet

Directions:

1. Cut the pork into medallions.
2. In a bowl, mix salt, pepper, and ½ cup flour.
3. Heat olive oil in the PPCXL on "chicken/meat."
4. Coat pork in flour and put in the pressure cooker.
5. Brown on both sides before plating.
6. Add fresh herbs to cooker and deglaze with the chicken stock, scraping up any burnt-on pork bits.
7. Return pork to cooker and seal the lid.
8. Adjust cook time to 18 minutes.
9. While that cooks, brown mushrooms in a skillet with a little oil.

10. Once browned, remove.
11. Pour chicken broth into skillet and whisk in mustard.
12. After 1 minute, return mushrooms to skillet and stir.
13. Season with salt and pepper.
14. When the pressure cooker beeps, hit "cancel" and quick-release the pressure.
15. Remove herbs.
16. Serve!

Nutritional Info (½ recipe)
Total calories: 343
Protein: 35
Carbs: 34
Fat: 9
Fiber: 1

Pork Shoulder with Dr. Pepper BBQ Sauce

Serves: 10-12

Time: 1 hour, 24 minutes (10 minutes prep time, 54 minutes cook time, 10 minutes natural pressure release, 10 minutes simmer time)

Dr. Pepper or another cola is a great base for a homemade BBQ sauce. In this recipe, it is cooked with pork shoulder that's been seasoned with paprika, brown sugar, chili powder, and a pinch of cayenne. It's a perfect mix of sweet and spicy.

Ingredients:

For the rub
- ☐ 3-4 pounds of pork shoulder
- ☐ 3 tablespoons brown sugar
- ☐ 2 tablespoons paprika
- ☐ 2 tablespoons chili powder
- ☐ ½ teaspoon salt
- ☐ ¼ teaspoon cayenne pepper

For the BBQ sauce
- ☐ ½ cup Dr. Pepper
- ☐ ½ cup ketchup
- ☐ 1 teaspoon liquid smoke
- ☐ Salt and pepper to taste

Directions:

1. Cut pork into 4 parts.
2. Mix rub ingredients in a bowl.
3. Coat pork in rub.
4. Mix soda and ketchup together in the PPCXL.
5. Put pork inside and seal the lid.
6. Hit "chicken/meat" and adjust time to 54 minutes.
7. When the timer beeps, turn off the cooker and wait 10 minutes.
8. Quick-release any remaining pressure.
9. Remove meat and tent with foil on a plate.
10. Turn the pot back to "chicken/meat" and simmer to reduce.
11. Add salt, pepper, and liquid smoke.

12. When the sauce has thickened nicely, shred pork and mix into the sauce.
13. Serve!

Nutritional Info (1 / 10 recipe)
Total calories: 245
Protein: 16
Carbs: 7.3
Fat: 16
Fiber: 0

Honey-Ginger Pork Chops

Serves: 6

Time: 33 minutes (15 minutes prep time, 18 minutes cook time)

These quick pork chops are perfect for busy weeknights. Seasoned simply with salt, pepper, and garlic, they cook in a finger-lickin' sauce made from maple syrup, ginger, cinnamon, cloves, mustard, and honey. Low-carb and low-fat, you get over 25 grams of protein per chop.

Ingredients:

- ☐ 6 boneless pork chops
- ☐ ¼ cup honey
- ☐ 2 tablespoons maple syrup
- ☐ ½ teaspoon peeled and minced fresh ginger
- ☐ ½ teaspoon cinnamon
- ☐ ½ teaspoon sea salt
- ☐ ½ teaspoon ground garlic
- ☐ ¼ teaspoon ground cloves
- ☐ ¼ teaspoon black pepper
- ☐ Splash of apple cider vinegar

Directions:

1. Begin by seasoning the chops with salt, pepper, and garlic.
2. Turn your pressure cooker to "chicken/meat" and add meat.
3. Brown till golden on both sides.
4. In a bowl, mix mustard, honey, ginger, maple syrup, cloves, and cinnamon.
5. Pour into pressure cooker, coating the pork.
6. Seal the lid.
7. Adjust cook time to 18 minutes.
8. When the timer beeps, hit "cancel" and quick-release.
9. Serve!

Nutritional Info (⅙ recipe)

Total calories: 239

Protein: 25.8

Carbs: 10.6

Fat: 10

Fiber: 0

Sweet + Gingery Pork Belly

Serves: 4

Time: 1 hour, 3 minutes (13 minutes prep time, 30 minutes cook time, 10 minutes natural pressure release, 10 minutes simmer time)

With only eight ingredients, create one of your new favorite dishes. Pork belly is like bacon, but better. The addicting sauce is sherry, maple syrup, coconut aminos, molasses, and ginger. ½ pound of the meal is almost 800 calories, so it isn't a low-calorie meal, but it does pack in 64 grams of protein.

Ingredients:

- ☐ 2 pounds fatty pork belly, cut into 1.5-inch cubes
- ☐ ⅓ cup water
- ☐ 1-inch piece of peeled and smashed ginger
- ☐ 3 tablespoons sherry
- ☐ 2 tablespoons maple syrup
- ☐ 2 tablespoons coconut aminos
- ☐ 1 tablespoon blackstrap molasses
- ☐ Pinch of sea salt

Directions:

1. Pour water into your PPCXL and turn to "chicken/meat."
2. Bring to a boil.
3. Add pork, making sure the cubes are covered by the water.
4. After 3 minutes of boiling, hit "cancel" and pour the whole pot through a colander, rinsing the meat with cool water.
5. Put the pot back into the cooker (without pork) and add maple syrup.
6. Turn back to "chicken/meat" and warm up.
7. When warm, return the pork back to the pot and brown evenly for 10 minutes.
8. Add the rest of the ingredients before sealing the lid.
9. Adjust cook time to 30 minutes.
10. When the timer beeps, hit "cancel" and let the pressure decrease naturally.
11. Remove the lid and hit "chicken/meat" to reduce the sauce.
12. Serve when it looks good!

Nutritional Info (¼ recipe per serving):
Total calories: 783
Protein: 64
Carbs: 11
Fat: 55
Fiber: 0

Pork Chops with Cherry-Jam Sauce

Serves: 4-6
Time: 39 minutes (10 minutes prep time, 29 minutes cook time)

Pork and sour cherry go very well together, thanks to the natural sweetness of pork and tartness of the jam. Asian-inspired spices like cardamom, cinnamon, ginger, and coriander help bind all the flavors together. This is a great recipe for smaller dinner parties or family meals.

Ingredients:

- ☐ Two 1 ¼-2 inch thick bone-in pork loin chops
- ☐ 1 cup pearl onions
- ☐ ½ cup sour cherry jam
- ☐ ¼ cup medium-dry red wine
- ☐ 2 tablespoons olive oil
- ☐ 1 tablespoon butter
- ☐ ½ teaspoon ground cinnamon
- ☐ ¼ teaspoon ground cardamom
- ☐ ¼ teaspoon ground ginger
- ☐ ¼ teaspoon ground coriander
- ☐ ¼ teaspoon salt

Directions:

1. Mix cinnamon, cardamom, ginger, coriander, and salt in a bowl.
2. Coat pork chops all over.
3. Add butter into the pot and hit "chicken/meat" to melt.
4. Add chops one at a time to brown on both sides, making sure to not burn the spices.
5. Plate the browned chops and add in onions.
6. Cook for 4 minutes, stirring, until brown.
7. Add wine and jam, scraping up any burnt-on food bits.
8. When the jam has dissolved, add chops and coat.
9. Seal the lid.
10. Adjust the cook time to 29 minutes.
11. When time is up, hit "cancel" and quick-release.
12. Serve!

Nutritional Info (¼ per serving):
Total calories: 425
Protein: 47
Carbs: 22
Fat: 19
Fiber: 1

Pork Tenderloin with Apples & Onions

Serves: 5-6

Time: 1 hour, 52 minutes (10 minutes prep time, 72 minutes cook time, 30 minutes natural pressure release)

Apples, onion, and pork are a classic combination, and couldn't be easier to make. There's just pork, apples, apple juice, broth, onion, bay leaves, salt, and pepper. The pork takes 72 minutes in the pressure cooker followed by a natural pressure release, and it's ready!

Ingredients:

- ☐ 4 pounds of pork rump roast
- ☐ 3 sliced apples
- ☐ 2 cups apple juice
- ☐ 1 cup chicken broth
- ☐ 1 sliced onion
- ☐ 2 bay leaves
- ☐ Salt and pepper to taste

Directions:

1. Trim the excess fat from the pork and season well with salt and pepper.
2. Put apples and onion in the cooker, and pour over apple juice and broth.
3. Add pork before sealing the lid.
4. Hit "chicken/meat" and adjust time to 72 minutes.
5. When time is up, hit "cancel" and wait for a natural pressure release.
6. Cut pork and serve with gravy.

Nutritional Info (⅕ recipe per serving):
Total calories: 215
Protein: 23
Carbs: 15
Fat: 7
Fiber: 3

Bacon-Wrapped Ribeye Steak

Serves: 4

Time: 43 minutes (15 minutes prep time, 18 minutes cook time, 10 minutes natural pressure release)

Pork wrapped in bacon: what could be better? It's a simple, but hearty recipe. You wrap ribeye steaks in bacon and cook them with potatoes, mushrooms, and green pepper. The result is a protein-heavy, one-pot meal with only 400 calories.

Ingredients:

- ☐ 4 ribeye pork steaks
- ☐ 6-8 strips of bacon
- ☐ 3-4 peeled and quartered potatoes
- ☐ 1 ½ cups water
- ☐ 4-ounces sliced mushrooms, any kind
- ☐ ½ chopped green pepper
- ☐ 1 tablespoon olive oil
- ☐ Salt to taste

Directions:

1. Season the pork well with salt.
2. If they're thick, flatten before rolling and wrapping bacon around them.
3. Secure fold with a toothpick.
4. Hit "chicken/meat" and heat oil.
5. Add pork and brown evenly.
6. Add veggies and pour in water.
7. Seal the lid.
8. Adjust cook time to 18 minutes.
9. When the timer beeps, turn off the cooker and wait 10 minutes before quick-releasing.
10. Remove meat and veggies.
11. Strain broth and serve!

Nutritional Info (¼ recipe)
Total calories: 399
Protein: 26
Carbs: 21

Fat: 25
Fiber: 0

Pork-Rib Stew

Serves: 4

Time: 1 hour, 22 minutes (15 minutes prep time, 42 minutes cook time, 5 minutes natural pressure release, 10 minutes additional cook time, 10 minutes reduction time)

A good stew can take hours, but with a pressure cooker, it's less than 1 hour and a half before you can dip your spoon in. Two pounds of pork ribs cook with a mixture of ginger, garlic, soy sauce, sugar, sherry, rice wine, and vinegar, creating sweet, salty, and savory flavors. The radish and pork are perfectly tender, and the taste only gets better as leftovers.

Ingredients:

- 2 pounds of pork ribs
- ¾ pound peeled and chopped radish
- 1 cup water + 1 tablespoon
- 4 slices of fresh ginger
- 1 minced garlic clove
- 3 tablespoons soy sauce
- 2 tablespoons sherry
- 1 tablespoon rice wine
- ½ tablespoon raw sugar
- 3 teaspoons white vinegar
- 2 teaspoons cornstarch
- Salt to taste

Directions:

1. Bring a large pot of water to a boil on your stovetop (or use your pressure cooker).
2. When a rolling boil is reached, put pork ribs in water for a few seconds.
3. Quickly drain into a colander and plate the ribs.
4. Turn the PPCXL to "chicken/meat," and coat the bottom with olive oil.
5. When hot, add pork ribs and brown on both sides.
6. Add garlic, ginger, soy sauce, sugar, vinegar, 1 cup of water, sherry, and wine.
7. Close and seal the lid.
8. Adjust cook time t0 42 minutes.
9. When time is up, turn off the cooker and wait 5 minutes before quick-releasing the leftover pressure.

10. Add radish and seal the lid again.
11. Hit "chicken/meat" and cook for another 12 minutes.
12. When time is up, hit "cancel" again and quick-release.
13. Take off the lid and select "chicken/meat" to reduce the sauce.
14. While that simmers, mix 1 tablespoon of cold water with the cornstarch.
15. Pour into pot.
16. When thickened to your taste, season well with salt.

Nutritional Info (¼ recipe)
Total calories: 336
Protein: 22
Carbs: 17
Fat: 18
Fiber: 1.9

Chapter 9

Seafood

Seafood Paella

Serves: 4

Time: 28 minutes (6 minutes prep time, 7 minutes cook time, 15 minutes natural pressure release)

This paella, which is basically a stew with rice, has tons of delicious seafood, like shrimp, clams, scallops, and white fish. You can pretty much put any seafood you like in there, and leave out what you don't. For flavor-building, there's onion, and both red and green bell pepper. Paella traditionally uses saffron, which is where it gets that distinct yellow color. However, saffron is expensive, so we're substituting with paprika and turmeric, which has a similar flavor profile.

Ingredients:

- ☐ 2 cups short-grain rice
- ☐ 2 cups mixed shellfish (shrimp, clams, etc.)
- ☐ 1 ¾ cups veggie stock
- ☐ 1 cup seafood (scallops and white fish)
- ☐ 1 diced yellow onion
- ☐ 1 diced green bell pepper
- ☐ 1 diced red bell pepper
- ☐ 4 tablespoons olive oil
- ☐ 2 teaspoons sea salt
- ☐ ½ teaspoon paprika
- ☐ ¼ teaspoon ground turmeric

Directions:

1. Turn your cooker to "chicken/meat" and add oil.
2. When hot and shiny, add onion and peppers.
3. Cook for 4 minutes until the onions are soft.
4. Add paprika, seafood, and rice.
5. Stir for 2 minutes.
6. Add stock, salt, and turmeric and stir.
7. Add mixed shellfish, but don't stir.
8. Close and seal lid.
9. Adjust cook time to 7 minutes.
10. When time is up, hit "cancel" and wait for a natural pressure release.

11. Stir and wait just one minute before serving!

Nutritional Info (¼ recipe per serving):
Total calories: 637
Protein: 29
Carbs: 90
Fat: 17
Fiber: 4

Steamed Mussels in a Tomato Broth

Serves: 2

Time: 25 minutes (11 minutes prep time, 4 minutes cook time, 10 minutes pressure release)

If you want to impress your seafood-loving significant other, this is a creative, yet simple dish to make. It's all about perfectly-steamed mussels and a savory broth made from tomatoes, garlic, lemon juice, white wine, and red pepper flakes. The broth is strong enough to offset too much of any "fishy" flavor, while parsley at the very end adds freshness.

Ingredients:

- ☐ 2 pounds mussels
- ☐ 1 (14.5-ounce) can of undrained and chopped stewed tomatoes
- ☐ 1 (8-ounce) bottle of clam juice
- ☐ ¼ cup dry white wine
- ☐ 2 tablespoons chopped parsley
- ☐ 2 teaspoons minced garlic
- ☐ 2 teaspoons extra-virgin olive oil
- ☐ 1 teaspoon lemon juice
- ☐ ¼ teaspoon red pepper flakes

Directions:

1. Scrub your mussels with a kitchen brush.
2. To debeard a mussel, look for the thin, string-like membrane on the mussel's "mouth," and pull it off.
3. Set aside mussels.
4. Turn your PPCXL to "chicken/meat" and add oil.
5. Add garlic and cook till it becomes fragrant.
6. Add wine, clam juice, tomatoes, lemon juice, and red pepper flakes.
7. Once the liquid is boiling, add the mussels, and seal the lid.
8. Adjust cook time to 4 minutes.
9. When the timer goes off, hit "cancel" and wait for a natural pressure release.
10. Stir in parsley and serve mussels with the broth.

Nutritional Info (15 mussels + 1 cup broth per serving):
Total calories: 295
Protein: 25.4
Carbs: 21.4
Fat: 8.9
Fiber: 3.6

Lemon-Ginger Cod with Broccoli

Serves: 4
Time: About 5 minutes (3 minutes prep time, 2 minutes cook time)

If I had to pick two ingredients that always go with white fish, I would have to say lemon and ginger. Lemon is bright and acidic, which cuts through any of the fish fattiness, while ginger packs a two-punch of sweet yet spicy. Both of those flavors also happen to go really well with broccoli, which cooks in your PPCXL right with a pound of cod fillets.

Ingredients:

- ☐ 1 pound, 1-inch thick frozen cod fillets
- ☐ 2 cups chopped broccoli
- ☐ 1 cup water
- ☐ 1 teaspoon ginger
- ☐ 1 teaspoon cumin
- ☐ 1 teaspoon lemon pepper
- ☐ Salt to taste

Directions:

1. Cut fish so there are four pieces.
2. Season with cumin, ginger, lemon pepper, and salt.
3. Put fish and broccoli into the steamer basket.
4. Before lowering in the basket, pour 1 cup of water into the pressure cooker.
5. Once the steamer basket is in the cooker, seal the lid.
6. Hit "chicken/meat" and adjust time to 2 minutes.
7. When the timer beeps, hit "cancel" and quick-release pressure.
8. Serve!

Nutritional Info (¼ recipe per serving):
Total calories: 113
Protein: 23
Carbs: 4
Fat: 1
Fiber: 1.2

Spicy Mahi-Mahi with Honey + Orange

Serves: 2
Time: 11 minutes (5 minutes prep time, 6 minutes cook time)

Even people who claim to not like fish like mahi-mahi. It's flaky, bites a bit like a steak, and with the citrus juices, honey, and sriracha sauce, it's a dish you'll want to make over and over again. To make the meal complete, serve with veggies or rice.

Ingredients:

Two mahi-mahi fillets
Juice of ½ lime
2 minced garlic cloves
1-inch grated ginger piece
2 tablespoons sriracha
2 tablespoons honey
1 tablespoon orange juice
1 tablespoon Nanami Togarashi
Salt and pepper

Directions:

1. Season fillets with salt and pepper.
2. Mix honey, juices, garlic, ginger, Nanami, and sriracha together in a bowl.
3. Pour 1 cup of water into the PPCXL and lower in the steamer basket with the fish inside.
4. Pour bowl of sauce on top of the fish.
5. Seal the lid.
6. Hit "chicken/meat" and adjust time to 6 minutes.
7. When time is up, quick-release.
8. Serve!

Nutritional Info (½ recipe per serving):
Total calories: 229
Protein: 32
Carbs: 23
Fiber: 0
Fat: 1

Creole-Style Shrimp with White Beans

Serves: 8

Time: 4 hours, 58 minutes (4 hours soak time, 15 minutes prep time, 18 minutes cook time, 15 minutes natural pressure release, 10 minutes shrimp time)

Don't be deterred by the cook time - that four hours is reserved for soaking the dry beans, so once you actually start cooking, this full-flavored shrimp dish rich with Creole influence takes just under an hour. To make things convenient, we're using Creole seasoning, which big spice brands like McCormick sells. If you don't have seafood stock on hand, chicken or vegetable will work just fine, too.

Ingredients:

1 pound peeled and cleaned shrimp
1 pound Great Northern dried beans
2 cups seafood stock
2 diced onions
2 bay leaves
1 diced celery rib
1 small diced green bell pepper
1 chopped garlic clove
Handful of chopped parsley
Creole seasoning to taste

Directions:

1. Pick through beans for any stones and rinse.
2. Soak in water for at least 4 hours in a bowl on the counter.
3. When ready, pour oil into your cooker and hit "chicken/meat."
4. When hot, add onion and seasonings.
5. Stir until onions are translucent.
6. Add garlic and cook for another 5 minutes.
7. Add celery and bell pepper.
8. After 5 minutes, drain beans and add to cooker with stock and water, so everything is covered.
9. Toss in bay leaves and parsley.
10. Seal the lid.
11. Adjust cook time to 18 minutes.
12. When time is up, turn off the cooker and let the pressure descend naturally.

13. Stir in the shrimp and close (but don't seal) the lid for 10 minutes.
14. Once the shrimp is solid and pink, serve!

Nutritional Info (⅛ recipe per serving):
Total calories: 530
Protein: 36
Carbs: 40
Fat: 25
Fiber: 10

Clam Chowder

Serves: 4-6

Time: 21 minutes (10 minutes prep time, 6 minutes cook time, 5 minutes simmer time)

Clam chowder is a staple of the coast, and once you've tasted it, you'll know why. It's amazing how combining cream, bacon, clams, and white potatoes makes each ingredient stand out. The secret to good clam chowder's magic is a roux - flour and butter - that you add after you've brought the cooker to pressure.

Cooking tip: Using fresh clams is important. The tighter the clam, the better. If they're open a little, and you tap them on the counter, and they close, you can use them. If any of the clams are open, throw them out. If you aren't making the chowder right away, you can store clams in the fridge, in a bowl covered by a wet towel, for up to two days.

Ingredients:

- ☐ 12-24 fresh clams
- ☐ 2 cubed potatoes, skin on
- ☐ 2 cups clam juice
- ☐ 1 cup chopped bacon
- ☐ 1 cup cream
- ☐ 1 cup 2% milk
- ☐ ½ cup white wine
- ☐ 1 bay leaf
- ☐ 1 chopped onion
- ☐ 1 tablespoon flour
- ☐ 1 tablespoon butter
- ☐ 1 sprig of thyme
- ☐ Pinch of red pepper flakes

Directions:

1. Turn your PPCXL to "chicken/meat" and add bacon.
2. Once cooked, take out the bacon, but leave the grease.
3. Cook the onion with salt and pepper in the cooker.
4. Once the onion is softening, pour in wine.

5. Deglaze the pot, scraping up any stuck-on bits.
6. Cook until the onion is beginning to soften.
7. Once the wine has evaporated, add potatoes, clam juice, bay leaf, thyme, and red pepper flakes.
8. Seal the lid.
9. Adjust cook time to 6 minutes.
10. While that cooks, melt butter in a skillet on low heat.
11. Whisk in flour until smooth to make a roux.
12. When the pressure cooker has finished its cycle, hit "cancel" and quick-release the pressure.
13. Add the roux, clams, cream, and milk.
14. Turn the cooker back to "chicken/meat" and simmer without the lid for 5 minutes.
15. Stir and serve!

Nutritional Info (¼ recipe per serving):
Total calories: 265
Protein: 16
Carbs: 20
Fat: 14
Fiber: 6

Sockeye Salmon with Chili Pepper + Lemon

Serves: 4
Time: 9 minutes (3 minutes prep time, 6 minutes cook time)

Sockeye salmon is wild salmon, and most people would say it's the best you can get, in terms of taste and health benefits. It couldn't be easier to put together: just season fish generously with black pepper, salt, lemon juice, and an assorted chili pepper seasoning. Cook for 6 minutes in a steamer basket, and quick-release. For an extra lemon kick, serve with slices of lemon.

Ingredients:

- ☐ Four wild sockeye salmon fillets
- ☐ 1 juiced lemon
- ☐ 1 sliced lemon
- ☐ 1 cup water
- ☐ 2 tablespoons assorted chili pepper seasoning
- ☐ Salt and pepper to taste

Directions:

1. Season salmon with chili pepper, black pepper, salt, and lemon juice.
2. Put fish in the steamer basket, being careful not to overlap much.
3. Pour 1 cup of water into pressure cooker and lower in the basket.
4. Seal the lid.
5. Hit "chicken/meat" and adjust time to 6 minutes.
6. When the timer beeps, turn off the cooker and quick-release.
7. Serve salmon with lemon slices.

Nutritional Info (¼ recipe per serving):
Total calories: 194
Protein: 24
Carbs: 1
Fat: 10
Fiber: 0

Salmon Steaks with Homemade Tartar Sauce

Serves: 4
Time: 11 minutes (6 minutes prep time, 5 minutes cook time)

You won't miss beef when you taste these salmon steaks. They're cooked between layers of onion and lemon, and seasoned with just salt, pepper, and dill. The homemade tartar sauce adds so much to the dish; don't be tempted to settle for store-bought. Make sure to prepare the sauce at least an hour before serving with the fish, it gets really chill and the flavors have blended.

Ingredients:

Salmon:
- ☐ 4 skin-on salmon steaks
- ☐ 1 cup water
- ☐ ¾ cup dry white wine
- ☐ 1 peeled and sliced onion
- ☐ 1 sliced lemon
- ☐ 1 teaspoon dried dill
- ☐ Salt and pepper to taste

Tartar sauce:
- ☐ ¾ cup mayo
- ☐ ¾ cup plain Greek yogurt
- ☐ ⅓ cup dill pickle relish
- ☐ ¼ cup chopped green onions
- ☐ 3 tablespoons chopped parsley
- ☐ 3 tablespoons rinsed and chopped capers
- ☐ 3 tablespoons lemon juice
- ☐ 1 teaspoon Dijon mustard
- ☐ Pinch of turmeric
- ☐ Pinch of black pepper

Directions:

1. Mix everything in the tartar sauce ingredient list.
2. Store in the fridge for at least an hour.

3. Put trivet and steamer basket in your PPCXL.
4. Overlap onion slices in the basket.
5. Add steaks on top and pour over wine.
6. Add dill, salt, and pepper.
7. Lay down lemon slices on top of that, and pour in water on the side, so it doesn't drain off the seasonings.
8. Turn cooker on to "chicken/meat" and boil for 1 minute.
9. Seal the lid.
10. Adjust cook time to 5 minutes.
11. When the timer beeps, turn off cooker and quick-release the pressure.
12. Serve salmon with the onions, if desired, and tartar sauce.

Nutritional Info (¼ recipe per serving):
Total calories: 495
Protein: 24
Carbs: 7
Fat: 39
Fiber: 0

Easy Alaskan Cod with Cherry Tomatoes

Serve: 2-3
Time: 8 minutes (2 minutes prep time, 6 minutes cook time)

This under-10 minute fish dish is based on two ingredients: wild-caught Alaskan cod and cherry tomatoes. Butter slices on top keep the fish moist and tasty. If the fish is thawed, it only takes 6 minute in the pressure cooker. If you're using frozen fish, cook for 11 minutes in the pressure cooker.

Ingredients:

- ☐ 1 large wild Alaskan cod fillet
- ☐ 1 cup cherry tomatoes
- ☐ 2 tablespoons butter cut into pats
- ☐ Drizzle of olive oil
- ☐ Salt and pepper to taste

Directions:

1. Cut fish into 2-3 even pieces, depending on how many you're serving.
2. Put the tomatoes in a pressure-cooker safe baking dish and put the fish on top.
3. Season well with salt and pepper.
4. Lay pats of butter on top of fish and drizzle on olive oil.
5. Pour 1 cup of water into your PPCXL and insert trivet.
6. Put baking dish on trivet and seal the lid.
7. Select "chicken/meat," and adjust to 6 minutes.
8. When time is up, quick-release the pressure.
9. Serve!

Nutritional Info (½ recipe per serving)
Total calories: 174
Protein: 14
Carbs: 3
Fat: 12
Fiber: 0

Halibut with Olives, Jalapenos, and Tomatoes

Serves: 4-6
Time: 13 minutes (5 minutes prep time, 8 minutes cook time)

Halibut is a great source for omega-3 and protein, and as a white fish, it doesn't have a strong "ocean" flavor. This recipe cooks the fish with a salsa-like mixture of diced tomatoes, green olives, onion, capers, and jalapeno rings.

Ingredients:

- ☐ Two 1-pound skinless halibut fillets
- ☐ One 28-ounce can of diced tomatoes
- ☐ 16 chopped and pitted green olives
- ☐ 1 chopped yellow onion
- ☐ 2 tablespoons minced pickled jalapeno rings
- ☐ 2 tablespoons brine (from pickled jalapeno jar)
- ☐ 2 tablespoons drained and chopped capers
- ☐ 2 tablespoons lime juice
- ☐ 2 tablespoons olive oil
- ☐ 1 tablespoon minced garlic
- ☐ Two rosemary sprigs
- ☐ Two oregano sprigs

Directions:

1. Pour oil into the PPCXL and heat on the "chicken/meat" setting.
2. Add onion and stir for about 3 minutes, until it's clear.
3. Add garlic and cook for just 30 seconds until it becomes fragrant.
4. Pour in olives, capers, jalapenos, jalapeno brine, and lime juice.
5. Stir in fresh herbs.
6. Seal the lid.
7. Adjust cook time to 6 minutes.
8. When time is up, quick-release.
9. Open the lid and add fish, so it's surrounded by sauce.
10. Seal the lid again.
11. Hit "chicken/meat" and cook for just 2 minutes.
12. When the timer beeps, hit "cancel" and quick-release again.

13. Fish should read at 145-degrees.
14. Serve with plenty of sauce!

Nutritional Info (¼ recipe per serving)
Total calories: 642
Protein: 61
Carbs: 21
Fat: 35
Fiber: 4

Lobster Ziti Casserole

Serves: 4

Time: 36 minutes (1 minute prep time, 10 minutes cook time, 15 minutes cool time, 10 minutes simmer/thickening time)

Rich and creamy, this lobster pasta dish elevates your normal casseroles up a notch. The pressure cooker prepares lobster tails and pasta in just 10 minutes. Once those are cooked, you cook the cream sauce, which has Gruyere, dry white wine, Worcestershire, and half-and-half. Mix all of it together, and you're ready to eat!

Ingredients:

- ☐ 6 cups water
- ☐ 8-ounces dried ziti
- ☐ Three 6-ounce lobster tails
- ☐ 1 cup half-and-half
- ☐ ¾ cup Gruyere cheese
- ☐ ½ cup dry white wine
- ☐ 1 tablespoon Worcestershire sauce
- ☐ 1 tablespoon flour
- ☐ 1 tablespoon chopped tarragon
- ☐ ½ teaspoon black pepper

Directions:

1. Pour cups of water into your PPCXL.
2. Lower in the lobster tails and add pasta.
3. Seal the lid.
4. Select "chicken/meat," and adjust to 10 minutes.
5. When the timer beeps, hit "cancel" and quick-release.
6. Drain pasta and lobster, and cool.
7. When cool enough to touch, remove the meat from the lobster tails, chop, and stir into the pasta. Do not return to the pot just yet.
8. Turn the empty cooker back to "chicken/meat."
9. Add in wine, Worcestershire sauce, flour, half-and-half, tarragon, and black pepper.
10. Simmer until the flour has dissolved.
11. Add pasta and lobster, and stir for half a minute or so.
12. Stir in cheese until melted.

13. Hit "cancel" and cover the pot halfway with the lid, so the casserole can thicken.
14. Once it has reached a good texture, serve!

Nutritional Info (¼ recipe per serving):
Total calories: 441
Protein: 28
Carbs: 44
Fiber: 0
Fat: 15

One-Pot Shrimp Scampi with Rice

Serves: 4

Time: 21 minutes (6 minutes cook time, 15 minutes cool time)

Shrimp scampi is usually made with pasta, but this recipe uses tender Jasmine rice, almost like a risotto. It's very easy to make, too, you just throw everything in the cooker, seal lid, and cook for 6 minutes.

Ingredients:

1 pound frozen, wild-caught shrimp, shells on
1 ½ cups water
1 cup jasmine rice
4 minced garlic cloves
¼ cup butter
¼ cup chopped parsley
Juice of 1 lemon
Salt and pepper to taste
1 pinch turmeric
1 pinch of paprika
Sprinkle of red pepper flakes

Directions:

1. Add everything in your PPCXL and seal the lid.
2. Select "chicken/meat," and adjust time to 6 minutes.
3. When the timer beeps, hit "cancel" and quick-release the pressure.
4. When the shrimp is cool enough, peel off the shells.
5. Serve!

Nutritional Info (¼ recipe per serving):
Total calories: 225
Protein: 14
Carbs: 10
Fat: 12
Fiber: 0

Packet Salmon

Serves: 4

Time: 28 minutes/two packets (10 minutes prep time, 13 minutes cook time, 5 minutes steam time)

Packet salmon, or "hobo salmon," is an easy and tidy way to serve a fish dinner. Everything cooks together in a layer of parchment paper and then foil, infusing the salmon with flavors from onion, lemon, and herbs. The potato slices become buttery and melt in your mouth. If you cook only two packets at once in the pressure cooker, the cook time will be longer.

Ingredients:

- ☐ Four ½-pound salmon fillets
- ☐ 2 cups water
- ☐ 2 sliced potatoes
- ☐ 1 sliced lemon
- ☐ 1 shaved onion
- ☐ 4 thyme sprigs
- ☐ 4 parsley sprigs
- ☐ Olive oil
- ☐ Salt and pepper to taste

Directions:

1. Cut four pieces of parchment paper, each big enough to wrap one salmon fillet and fillings.
2. Drizzle on some olive oil, then add potato slice, salt, pepper, more olive oil, salmon fillet, salt, pepper, olive oil, a sprig of thyme, a sprig of parsley, onion shavings, lemon slice, salt, and end with another drizzle of oil.
3. Fold packet, and then wrap in aluminum foil.
4. Repeat until you have four salmon packets.
5. Pour water into your pressure cooker and lower in the steamer basket.
6. Put two packets in the basket, unless you can fit more and they don't overlap.
7. Seal the lid.
8. Hit "chicken/meat" and cook for 13 minutes.
9. When time is up, hit "cancel" and quick-release, but wait 5 minutes before removing the packets.
10. Repeat if necessary with the remaining salmon packets.
11. Serve!

Nutritional Info (1 packet per serving):
Total calories: 310
Protein: 30
Carbs: 9
Fat: 14
Fiber: 3

Clams with Golden Butter, Lemon, and Dill

Serves: 4
Time: 10 minutes (5 minutes prep time, 5 minutes cook time)

Making clams in a pressure cooker is extremely easy. Just scrub them up and toss them in the cooker with wine, water, butter, garlic, and dill. Cook for 5 minutes, and then quick-release! That's it! It can be served with crusty bread and some pasta for a heartier meal, or as an appetizer.

Cooking tip: To make golden butter, melt it in a saucepan over medium heat and wait until it becomes a deep golden and smells nutty. It might have little brown speckles in it; keep them. Let the butter cool to room temperature before using.

Ingredients:

- ☐ 28 scrubbed littleneck clams
- ☐ ½ cup dry white wine
- ☐ ¼ cup water
- ☐ 2 tablespoons brown butter
- ☐ 2 tablespoons lemon juice
- ☐ 1 tablespoon fresh minced dill
- ☐ 1 tablespoon minced garlic

Directions:

1. Pour water, wine, golden butter, lemon juice, garlic, and dill into the cooker.
2. Turn the cooker to "chicken/meat" and bring to a simmer.
3. Add in clams and seal the lid.
4. Adjust cook time to 5 minutes.
5. When the timer beeps, hit "cancel" and quick-release.
6. The clams should be open, but not gaping open, as that means they're overcooked.
7. Serve clams with the golden-butter broth.

Nutritional Info (¼ recipe per serving):
Total calories: 149
Protein: 13
Carbs: 3
Fat: 7
Fiber: 0

Shrimp Fried Rice

Serves: 6

Time: 43 minutes (10 minutes prep time, 18 minutes cook time, 10 minutes natural pressure release, 5 minutes warm time)

Chinese takeout is all well and good, but with some pre-cooked shrimp, rice, eggs, and veggies, you can make your own with very little effort. First, you scramble the eggs, and set them aside. The rice is what actually goes under pressure, along with veggies, garlic, onion, and seasonings. Once that's cooked, you stir in the shrimp and eggs.

Ingredients:

- ☐ 4 cups water
- ☐ 12-ounce bag of peeled and thawed pre-cooked shrimp
- ☐ 4 garlic cloves
- ☐ 2 beaten eggs
- ☐ 2 cups brown rice
- ☐ 1 ½ cups frozen peas and carrots
- ☐ 1 cup chopped onion
- ☐ 3 tablespoon sesame oil
- ☐ ¼ cup soy sauce
- ☐ ½ teaspoon ginger
- ☐ ¼ teaspoon cayenne pepper
- ☐ Salt and pepper to taste

Directions:

1. Turn your PPCXL to "chicken/meat" and add oil.
2. When hot, add eggs and scramble.
3. Take out of the cooker for now, and pour in a little more oil.
4. Cook onion and garlic until clear and fragrant.
5. Turn off the cooker before adding veggies.
6. Rinse rice before adding to cooker.
7. Pour in ginger, salt, pepper, water, and soy sauce.
8. Stir and then seal the lid.
9. Hit "chicken/meat" button and adjust time to 18 minutes.
10. When time is up, hit "cancel" and wait 10 minutes before quick-releasing.

11. Open the lid and stir in shrimp and scrambled eggs, letting the heat of the rice warm them through.
12. Add cayenne before serving.

Nutritional Info (⅙ recipe per serving)
Total calories: 221
Protein: 13
Carbs: 22
Fat: 10
Fiber: 1

Cheesy Tuna 'n Noodles

Serves: 4
Time: 8 minutes (5 minutes cook time, 3 minutes broil time)

A homemade take on Tuna Helper, this dinner just involves putting everything in a cooker and cooking for 5 minutes. When it's done, you can broil bread crumbs on top for 3 minutes, and serve!

Ingredients:

- ☐ 1 can drained tuna
- ☐ 28-ounce can of cream of mushroom soup
- ☐ 16-ounces egg noodles
- ☐ 4-ounces shredded cheddar cheese
- ☐ 3 cups water
- ☐ 1 cup frozen peas
- ☐ ¼ cup breadcrumbs
- ☐ Salt and pepper to taste

Directions:

1. Pour water and pasta into your PPCXL.
2. Add soup, peas, and tuna on top.
3. Seal the lid.
4. Hit "chicken/meat" and adjust time to 5 minutes.
5. When time is up, hit "cancel" and quick-release.
6. Stir in cheese until melted.
7. Move food to a baking dish and cover with breadcrumbs.
8. Broil for just 2-3 minutes for a crunchy topping.
9. Season and serve!

Nutritional Info (¼ recipe per serving)
Total calories: 430
Protein: 18
Carbs: 42
Fat: 22
Fiber: 2

Chapter 10

Soups + Stews

Marsala Mushroom Soup

Serves: 4-6
Time: 18 minutes (10 minutes prep time, 3 minutes cook time, 5 minutes blend time)

Marsala wine is usually paired with chicken, but limiting the ingredient to that one dish would be underusing this delicious sweet wine. This mushroom soup uses a chicken stock and whipping cream base with sautèed onions and garlic. For thickening, you just make a basic roux with butter and flour while the soup is under pressure for 3 minutes. Before serving, you puree the soup.

Ingredients:

- ☐ 1 pound chopped baby Portobello mushrooms
- ☐ 4 cups chicken stock
- ☐ 2 cups heavy whipping cream
- ☐ 1 cup diced onion
- ☐ ½ cup dry marsala wine
- ☐ 2 chopped garlic cloves
- ☐ 2 tablespoons butter
- ☐ 2 tablespoons flour
- ☐ 2 teaspoons chopped thyme
- ☐ 2 teaspoons chopped rosemary
- ☐ 1 teaspoon salt
- ☐ Dash of black pepper

Directions:

1. Turn your PPCXL to "chicken/meat" and add a small pat of butter.
2. When melted, add onion and salt.
3. After two minutes, add garlic, mushrooms, and black pepper.
4. Toss in herbs, and pour in wine and stock.
5. Seal the lid.
6. Adjust cook time to 3 minutes.
7. While that cooks, melt 2 tablespoons of butter in a saucepan.
8. Whisk in flour until smooth.
9. After a minute, remove from the heat.
10. When time on the pressure cooker is up, hit "cancel" and quick-release.

11. Blend the soup to a smooth texture before stirring in cream.
12. Add roux and hit "chicken/meat" again, heating until the soup has thickened.
13. Serve with parmesan cheese!

Nutritional Info (¼ recipe per serving):
Total calories: 560
Protein: 15
Carbs: 16
Fat: 51
Fiber: 1

Creamy Enchilada Soup

Serves: 8

Time: 39 minutes (24 minutes cook time, 15 minutes natural pressure release)

Turning favorite dishes into soups is a great way to use up a lot of ingredients and make the meal more portable for lunch leftovers. This enchilada soup uses all the fixins' like beans, green chilies, garlic, bell pepper, and lots of seasonings. For the creaminess, you've got butternut squash and potatoes, which when pureed, mimic the texture of cream.

Ingredients:

- ☐ Three 1-pound boneless + skinless chicken breasts
- ☐ 8 cups peeled and cubed butternut squash
- ☐ 4 cups chicken broth
- ☐ Two 15-ounce rinsed and drained cans of cannellini beans
- ☐ One 8-ounce can tomato sauce
- ☐ One 3.5-ounce can of chopped green chilies
- ☐ 3 big peeled and quartered russet potatoes
- ☐ 3 garlic cloves
- ☐ 1 chopped onion
- ☐ 1 cored, seeded + chopped red bell pepper
- ☐ 2 tablespoons taco seasoning
- ☐ 2 teaspoons cumin
- ☐ 2 teaspoons salt

Directions:

1. Pour broth, chicken, onion, green chilies, tomato sauce, potatoes, butternut squash, garlic, cumin, and salt into your pressure cooker.
2. Seal the lid and hit "chicken/meat," adjusting cook time to 24 minutes.
3. When time is up, hit "cancel" and wait for a natural pressure release.
4. Take out the chicken and tent with foil on a cutting board.
5. Blend the soup in the cooker till smooth.
6. Shred the chicken and return to the pot along with the cannellini beans.
7. Serve with cheese and fresh parsley!

Nutritional Info (⅛ recipe per serving):
Total calories: 397
Protein: 45
Carbs: 46
Fat: 5
Fiber: 3

Chunky Potato Soup

Serves: 6-8

Time: 23 minutes (7 minutes prep time, 5 minutes cook time, 5 minutes natural pressure release, 6 minutes simmer time)

A good chunky potato soup can be a lifesaver on cold nights. Made with tender chunks of potatoes, corn, onion, cheese, and bacon, the soup has a rich broth of chicken stock, butter, and Greek yogurt, which replaced cream cheese.

Ingredients:

- ☐ 6 cups peeled and cubed potatoes
- ☐ Two 14-ounce cans of chicken broth
- ☐ 6 slices cooked, crumbled bacon
- ☐ 2 cups half-and-half
- ☐ 1 cup frozen corn
- ☐ 1 cup shredded cheddar cheese
- ☐ ½ cup chopped onion
- ☐ 6 tablespoons Greek yogurt
- ☐ 2 tablespoons water
- ☐ 2 tablespoons butter
- ☐ 2 tablespoons dried parsley
- ☐ 1 teaspoon salt
- ☐ ½ teaspoon black pepper
- ☐ Pinch of red pepper flakes

Directions:

1. Turn your PPCXL to "chicken/meat" and melt butter.
2. Add onion and stir for 5 minutes, or until onion has softened.
3. Add 1 can of broth, bell pepper, salt, black pepper, and parsley.
4. Lower in the steamer basket with potatoes.
5. Seal the lid and adjust cook time to 5 minutes.
6. When time is up, hit "cancel" and wait 5 minutes.
7. Quick-release the pressure.
8. Remove the basket.
9. In a cup, dissolve cornstarch with 2 tablespoons of water.
10. Turn your cooker back to "chicken/meat" and pour in cornstarch/water, whisking.

11. Add yogurt and shredded cheese.
12. Stir till melted before adding half-and-half, corn, other can of chicken broth, potatoes, and crumbled bacon.
13. Stir until everything is warmed through.
14. Serve!

Nutritional Info (⅙ recipe per serving):
Total calories: 390
Protein: 16
Carbs: 34
Fat: 24
Fiber: 2

Quick Miso Soup

Serves: 4
Time: 12 minutes (7 minutes cook time, 5 minutes dissolve time)

Miso soup is a simple, savory introduction to an Asian meal. Carrots, celery, corn, onion, sweet seaweed (wakame) and tofu cook in water for 7 minutes before you add miso paste, which is fermented soybean. It provides amazing flavor as well as important enzymes. Serve with soy sauce for additional saltiness.

Ingredients:

- [ ] 4 cups water
- [ ] 1 cup cubed firm silken tofu
- [ ] ½ cup fresh corn
- [ ] 2 chopped celery stalks
- [ ] 2 chopped carrots
- [ ] 2 tablespoons miso paste
- [ ] 1 small onion sliced into half moons
- [ ] 1 teaspoon wakame flakes
- [ ] Soy sauce to taste

Directions:

1. Mix everything (minus soy sauce and miso) in your PPCXL.
2. Seal the lid.
3. Hit "chicken/meat" and adjust time to 7 minutes.
4. When time is up, hit "cancel" and quick-release the pressure.
5. Ladle out one cup of broth and mix in miso paste.
6. When dissolved, pour back into the cooker.
7. Stir in soy sauce and serve!

Nutritional Info (¼ recipe per serving):
Total calories: 46
Protein: 3.8
Carbs: 3.7
Fat: 1.7
Fiber: 1

Chicken Wild Rice Soup

Serves: 4
Time: 34 minutes (27 minutes cook time, 7 minutes simmer time)

Chicken wild rice soup is a deli classic, and packed with protein. It's a fast-cooking soup at only 34 minutes from start to finish, so it's good to keep in your back pocket for busy evenings. Standout ingredients like dry sherry, whipping cream, thyme, and nutmeg ensure complex flavors and a beautiful smooth broth that's perfect for the chicken, wild rice, mushrooms, and other veggies.

Ingredients:

- ☐ 4 cups chicken stock
- ☐ 1 large chicken breast cut into cubes
- ☐ 6-ounces sliced mushrooms
- ☐ 4 diced carrots
- ☐ 2 diced celery stalks
- ☐ 1 cup heavy whipping cream
- ☐ ½ cup wild rice
- ☐ ¼ cup dry sherry
- ☐ 2 tablespoons flour
- ☐ 2 tablespoons softened butter
- ☐ ¼ teaspoon ground thyme
- ☐ Salt, pepper, and nutmeg to taste

Directions:

1. Pour stock and rice into the cooker.
2. Seal the lid and hit "chicken/meat," adjusting cook time to 24 minutes.
3. When time is up, turn off cooker and quick-release.
4. Add in celery, carrots, onion, and chicken.
5. Seal lid and hit "chicken/meat," again, adjusting to 3 minutes.
6. While that cooks, mix butter and flour into a paste.
7. Mix mushrooms and sherry into the paste.
8. When time is up on the cooker, hit "cancel" and quick-release.
9. Add your mushroom mixture into the cooker and cook on "chicken/meat" with the lid off for 5 minutes.

10. Mix in cream.
11. Season with salt, pepper, and nutmeg!

Nutritional Info (2 cups per serving):
Total calories: 381
Protein: 18
Carbs: 24
Fat: 21
Fiber: 1

Tomato Basil Soup

Serves: 8

Time: 26 minutes (10 minutes prep time, 6 minutes cook time, 5 minutes natural pressure release, 5 minutes blend time)

Tomato soup is another essential recipe everyone should know. This pressure cooker recipe is fast and doesn't use that many ingredients. Cooking celery, onions, carrots, and garlic first in butter is necessary to bring out the deeper flavors that mimic what happens when you cook for longer. Then you add the stock, tomatoes, basil, salt, and pepper. Cook for just 6 minutes, then wait 5 minutes before quick-releasing. Puree before adding Parmesan and half-and-half.

Ingredients:

- ☐ 3 pounds cored, peeled, and quartered tomatoes
- ☐ Two 14.5-ounces cans chicken broth
- ☐ 2 diced celery stalks
- ☐ 1 diced onion
- ☐ 1 diced carrot
- ☐ 1 cup half & half
- ☐ ½ cup shredded Parmesan cheese
- ☐ ¼ cup fresh basil
- ☐ 3 tablespoons butter
- ☐ 1 tablespoon tomato paste
- ☐ ½ teaspoon ground pepper
- ☐ ½ teaspoon salt

Directions:

1. Melt butter in your pressure cooker and cook celery, carrots, and onion.
2. When tender, stir in garlic for 1 minute.
3. Pour in chicken stock, and add tomatoes, basil, salt, and pepper.
4. Seal the lid and hit "chicken/meat," adjusting time to 6 minutes.
5. When the timer beeps, hit "cancel" and wait 5 minutes.
6. After that time, quick-release the pressure.
7. Puree the soup until smooth.
8. Stir in half-and-half and cheese.

Nutritional Info (⅛ recipe per serving):
Total calories: 314
Protein: 11
Carbs: 16
Fat: 23
Fiber: 2

Chicken Wing & Pork Ramen

Serves: 8

Time: 2 hours, 58 minutes (30 minutes prep time, 108 minutes cook time, 40 minutes natural pressure release)

The longest soup in this collection, chicken and pork ramen takes so long because you need to cook the meat in garlic, onion, and ginger for over an hour and a half. That ensures a really richly-flavored broth, which is essential for the dish. Traditionally, you would add ramen noodles once you've completed the recipe.

Ingredients:

- ☐ 2 ½ pound pork spareribs cut in 2-inch pieces
- ☐ 1 ½ pounds chicken wings
- ☐ 3 smashed garlic cloves
- ☐ 2 sliced onions
- ☐ 2 tablespoons cooking oil
- ☐ Thumb-sized ginger piece
- ☐ Soy sauce to taste
- ☐ Water

Optional toppings: Minced scallions, bean sprouts, cooked bamboo shoots, seaweed, sesame seeds

Directions:

1. Boil water in a large stockpot and add ribs and wings.
2. Let the meat boil for 7 minutes.
3. Dump out the water and rinse meat.
4. Plate for now.
5. Put oil in your PPCXL and heat.
6. Cook onions for 8 minutes.
7. Add garlic, ginger, and meat.
8. Pour water into the pressure cooker, so it reaches the "max" line.
9. Seal the lid and hit "chicken/meat," adjusting time to 108 minutes.
10. When time is up, hit "cancel" and wait for a natural pressure release.
11. Remove meat and pull off the bones.
12. Strain broth through a fine-mesh strainer, throwing out any solids.

13. Add meat back into broth, season with soy sauce, and serve with any toppings you like.

Nutritional Info (⅛ recipe per serving):
Total calories: 552
Protein: 18
Carbs: 75
Fat: 20
Fiber: 2

Lasagna Soup with Ricotta Balls

Serves: 4-6
Time: 29 minutes (15 minutes prep time, 12 minutes cook time, 2 minutes pasta time)

Here's another meal that's converted into delicious soup form. You use spicy Italian sausage, Mafalda pasta, chopped tomatoes, and traditional seasonings like onion and garlic. The best part of the soup is the ricotta balls, which just use ricotta and mozzarella cheese. You serve them in the soup like Matzo balls.

Ingredients:

Soup:
- ☐ 2 pounds spicy Italian sausage
- ☐ 4 cups chicken broth
- ☐ 1 package Mafalda pasta
- ☐ 32-ounces of chopped tomatoes
- ☐ 1 chopped yellow onion
- ☐ 3 minced garlic cloves
- ☐ 2 tablespoons Italian seasoning

Ricotta balls:
- ☐ 2-3 tablespoons fresh ricotta
- ☐ Shredded mozzarella to taste

Directions:

1. Turn your cooker to "chicken/meat" and heat oil until shiny.
2. Add meat, breaking it up with a wooden spoon.
3. Once evenly browned, toss in Italian seasoning.
4. Turn off the cooker.
5. Add chopped onions, tomatoes, and garlic.
6. Pour in broth and close the cooker lid
7. Hit "chicken/meat" again and adjust time to 12 minutes.
8. In the meantime, make ricotta balls.
9. Mix 2-3 tablespoons of ricotta with mozzarella (as little or as much as you want) and roll into a ball.
10. Store in the fridge until you're ready to serve the soup.
11. When the cooker timer beeps, hit "cancel" and quick-release.

12. Pour in 1-2 cups of pasta and seal the lid again.
13. Cook on the "chicken/meat" setting for 2 minutes.
14. When time is up, turn off cooker and carefully quick-release.
15. Serve with ricotta balls.

Nutritional Info (¼ recipe per serving):
Total calories: 557
Protein: 34
Carbs: 52
Fat: 23
Fiber: 4

Sausage + Lentil Soup

Serves: 6-8
Time: 28 minutes (10 minutes prep time, 18 minutes cook time)

Lentils are one of the healthiest foods out there and are a good source of just about everything, from protein to fiber. However, some people aren't too fond of them, so in this soup, we hide their flavor using sausage, tomatoes, a trio of aromatic veggies, and rich beef broth. The soup takes 18 minutes under pressure, followed by a quick release.

Ingredients:

- ☐ 6 cups water
- ☐ 2 cups beef broth
- ☐ 2 cups crushed tomatoes
- ☐ 1-2 cups cooked and chopped sausage
- ☐ 1 cup chopped celery, carrots, and onions
- ☐ ¾ cup dried lentils
- ☐ 4 minced garlic cloves
- ☐ 2 bay leaves
- ☐ 1 tablespoon olive oil
- ☐ Salt and pepper to taste

Directions:

1. Turn the cooker to "chicken/meat" and heat olive oil.
2. When shiny, cook carrots, celery, onion, and garlic until beginning to soften and become fragrant.
3. Hit "cancel" and add the rest of the ingredients.
4. Seal the cooker lid.
5. Hit "chicken/meat" again and adjust cook time to 18 minutes.
6. When time is up, hit "cancel" and quick-release the pressure.
7. Stir the soup.
8. Season with salt and pepper before serving.

Nutritional Info (⅙ recipe per serving):
Total calories: 313.9
Protein: 14.7
Carbs: 16.6
Fat: 21.1
Fiber: 5.8

Chicken Corn Chowder with Pumpkin Puree

Serves: 4-5
Time: 15 minutes (10 minutes prep time, 5 minutes cook time)

Pumpkin in chicken corn chowder? Absolutely! The pumpkin puree adds a rich smoothness that would usually be accomplished with cream, and it adds a nutty sweetness that doesn't overwhelm the other flavors. At only 15 minutes from start to finish, this is one of the fastest soups.

Ingredients:

- ☐ 2 large diced chicken breasts
- ☐ Two 14.5 cans of chicken broth
- ☐ One 15-ounce can of pumpkin puree
- ☐ 2 cubed russet potatoes
- ☐ 2 cups frozen corn
- ☐ 1 cup diced onion
- ☐ ½ cup half-and-half
- ☐ 1 minced garlic clove
- ☐ 2 tablespoons butter
- ☐ ½ teaspoon Italian seasoning
- ☐ ¼ teaspoon black pepper
- ☐ ⅛ teaspoon nutmeg
- ☐ ⅛ teaspoon red pepper flakes

Directions:

1. Add butter to your PPCXL and melt it on the "chicken/meat" setting.
2. Cook onion until it becomes clear.
3. Add garlic and cook for just another minute.
4. Mix in broth, pumpkin puree, and seasonings.
5. Put in potatoes and chicken.
6. Seal the lid and adjust cook time to 5 minutes.
7. When time is up, hit "cancel" and quick-release.
8. Stir in corn and half-and-half.
9. Serve!

Nutritional Info (2 cups per serving):
Total calories: 321
Protein: 19.4
Carbs: 36
Fat: 13
Fiber: 4.4

Beef + Potato Soup with Kale

Serves: 6

Time: 30 minutes (15 minutes prep time, 5 minutes cook time, 10 minutes natural pressure release)

With 23 grams of protein, this soup is great for a lunchtime pick-me-up. It uses russet potatoes, kale, ground beef, and bacon. After cooking onion and browning the meat, the soup goes under pressure with water, potato, and bacon for only 5 minutes. Dicing the potatoes is what allows them to cook so quickly. Cream and kale go in at the very end.

Ingredients:

- ☐ 3 quarts of water
- ☐ 1 pound ground beef
- ☐ 5 diced russet potatoes
- ☐ 8 chopped kale leaves
- ☐ 12-ounces of cooked bacon
- ☐ 1 chopped onion
- ☐ 1 cup heavy cream
- ☐ 3 minced garlic cloves
- ☐ 1 tablespoon butter
- ☐ 2 teaspoon sea salt
- ☐ 1 teaspoon red pepper flakes
- ☐ ½ teaspoon basil
- ☐ ½ teaspoon oregano

Directions:

1. Preheat your cooker on the "chicken/meat" setting before adding butter and onion.
2. Stir and cook until onion becomes translucent.
3. Add garlic, seasonings, and ground beef.
4. When the beef has cooked through, add cooked bacon and potatoes.
5. Pour in enough water, so it's at the 3-quarts line, and stir before sealing the lid.
6. Adjust cook time to 5 minutes.
7. When time is up, hit "cancel" and wait for a natural pressure release.
8. Stir in cream and kale.
9. When kale has wilted, season with salt and pepper.

10. Serve!

Nutritional Info (⅙ recipe per serving)
Total calories: 506
Protein: 23
Carbs: 34
Fat: 31
Fiber: 4

Chicken Chili with White Beans

Serves: 10

Time: 2 hours, 12 minutes (10 minutes prep time, 1 hour 12 minutes cook time, 30 minutes natural pressure release, 10 minutes cool time, 10 minutes simmer time)

Another longer recipe, this chili needs the time to blend flavors like green chilies, jalapeno, garlic, onion, beans, and broth. This recipe is a little unusual because the chicken is already cooked and added toward the end. It's a great way to use up leftover chicken. For thickening, you use milk and cornmeal. Season generously with salt and pepper.

Ingredients:

- ☐ 8 cups chicken broth
- ☐ 1 pound rinsed and dried Great Northern beans
- ☐ 2 cans chopped green chilies
- ☐ 3 cups cooked, diced chicken
- ☐ ½ cup whole milk
- ☐ 1 sliced onion
- ☐ 4 minced garlic cloves
- ☐ 2 sliced Jalapenos
- ☐ 2 tablespoons butter
- ☐ 1 tablespoon cornmeal
- ☐ 1 ½ tablespoons ground cumin
- ☐ ½ teaspoon cayenne pepper
- ☐ ½ teaspoon paprika
- ☐ White pepper and salt to taste
- ☐ Splash of olive oil

Directions:

1. Turn your PPCXL to "chicken/meat" and add oil and butter.
2. When hot, add jalapenos, garlic, chilies, and onions.
3. When they've softened, turn off the cooker.
4. Mix in beans.
5. Pour in chicken broth and lock the lid.
6. Hit "chicken/meat" again and adjust to 1 hour and 12 minutes.
7. When time is up, hit "cancel" and wait for a natural pressure release.
8. When safe, open the lid and stir in seasonings and chicken.

9. Wait 10 minutes before hitting "chicken/meat" again.
10. In a separate bowl, mix half a cup of milk with 1 tablespoon of cornmeal.
11. Pour into pot and simmer (with the lid off) for 5-10 minutes to thicken.
12. Season to taste and serve!

Nutritional Info (1 cup per serving):
Total calories: 358
Protein: 46
Carbs: 33
Fat: 2
Fiber: 7

Zuppa Toscana

Serves: 8

Time: 20 minutes (10 minutes prep time, 5 minutes cook time, 5 minutes simmer time)

Spicy and savory, this soup has less than 250 calories per serving and 9 grams of protein. You use chicken sausage for leanness and evaporated milk for reduced carbs. Bacon adds saltiness, while spinach provides important minerals and vitamins. Top with Parmesan cheese before serving.

Ingredients:

- ☐ 1 pound ground chicken sausage
- ☐ Three 14.5-ounce cans of chicken broth
- ☐ One 12-ounce can of evaporated milk
- ☐ 6 diced slices of cooked bacon
- ☐ 3 cubed russet potatoes
- ☐ 2 cups chopped spinach
- ☐ 1 cup of diced onion
- ☐ 1 cup shredded parmesan cheese
- ☐ 3 minced garlic cloves
- ☐ 3 tablespoons cornstarch
- ☐ 1 tablespoon butter
- ☐ ½ teaspoon red pepper flakes
- ☐ ½ teaspoon black pepper
- ☐ ½ teaspoon salt

Directions:

1. Brown the sausage in your PPCXL and plate over a paper towel, so it absorbs excess grease.
2. Add butter to pot and melt.
3. Add onion and cook for 5 minutes until soft.
4. Add garlic and cook for just one more minute.
5. Pour in one can of broth and add seasonings.
6. Put diced potatoes in the steamer basket and lower into cooker.
7. Close the lid.
8. Select "chicken/meat" and adjust time to 5 minutes.

9. When the timer beeps, hit "cancel" and quick-release the pressure.
10. Pour in remaining two cans of broth.
11. In a separate bowl, whisk cornstarch with a little evaporated milk until smooth.
12. Add into the rest of the evaporated milk.
13. Pour into pot and hit "chicken/meat" again.
14. Simmer the soup until boiling.
15. When the soup has thickened, add ¾ cup of cheese, sausage, potatoes, spinach, and three pieces of the bacon.
16. Top with remaining cheese and bacon before serving.

Nutritional Info (⅛ serving per serving):
Total calories: 233
Protein: 9
Carbs: 18.5
Fat: 14.3
Fiber: 2.4

Cheese-and-Bacon Cauliflower Soup

Serves: 4

Time: 1 hour, 1 minute (10 minutes prep time, 36 minutes cook time, 15 minutes natural pressure release)

At over 1000 calories, this isn't the lowest-calorie recipe in this book. However, it does offer over 40 grams of protein and healthy carbs, so it's a great option for runners and other athletes. Using cauliflower helps reduce the amount of cream and sour cream in the rest of the recipe while also adding fiber, vitamin C, and folate. You can also use less cheese and bacon to help cut down on the fat content, if you want, it won't affect the overall taste or texture of the soup too much.

Ingredients:

- ☐ 32-ounces chicken broth
- ☐ 16-ounces sharp shredded cheddar cheese
- ☐ 12 strips of bacon
- ☐ 1 head's worth of cauliflower florets
- ☐ 2 shredded carrots
- ☐ 2 diced celery stalks
- ☐ 1 diced onion
- ☐ 1 cup heavy cream
- ☐ 1 cup sour cream
- ☐ 4 tablespoons flour
- ☐ ¼ cup butter
- ☐ Salt and pepper to taste

Directions:

1. Turn your PPCXL on and hit "chicken/meat."
2. Cook bacon until crispy.
3. Add butter and veggies, and stir for 5 minutes.
4. Add the other ingredients, minus half of the cheese.
5. Seal the lid and adjust cook time to 36 minutes.
6. When the timer beeps, hit "cancel" and wait for a natural pressure release.
7. Serve with the rest of the cheese.

Nutritional Info (¼ per serving):
Total calories: 1048
Protein: 43
Carbs: 31
Fat: 82
Fiber: 4.5

Chapter 11

Rice and Pasta

Italian Mac + Cheese

Serves: 4
Time: 11 minutes (6 minutes cook time, 5 minutes melt time)

Homemade mac + cheese is one of life's little pleasures. There's just something magical about cheese and pasta. For this recipe, we're taking a little more inspiration from Italy than usual. We're using three kinds of cheese - mozzarella, provolone, parmesan - and adding cottage cheese instead of ricotta. They are very similar texture-wise. The pasta cooks in water, salt, pepper, and 1 cup of spaghetti sauce for just 6 minutes, and then you stir in everything else.

Ingredients:

- ☐ 1 pound small pasta shells
- ☐ 8-ounces shredded Mozzarella cheese
- ☐ 6-ounces shredded provolone cheese
- ☐ 4-ounces cottage cheese
- ☐ 2-ounces shredded parmesan
- ☐ 2 cups water
- ☐ 1 cup spaghetti sauce
- ☐ 2 teaspoons dried oregano
- ☐ Salt and pepper to taste

Directions:

1. Add pasta, water, spaghetti sauce, salt, and pepper to your pressure cooker.
2. Seal the lid.
3. Hit the "rice" button, which sets a default time of 6 minutes.
4. When time is up, hit "cancel" and quick-release the pressure.
5. Stir in cheese, with the cottage cheese first, then mozzarella, provolone, and lastly, parmesan.
6. Season with oregano and then serve!

Nutritional Info (¼ recipe per serving):
Total calories: 753
Protein: 42
Carbs: 95
Fat: 25
Fiber: 0

Cajun Chicken Pasta

Serves: 4

Time: 26 minutes (10 minutes prep time, 6 minutes cook time, 10 minutes natural pressure release)

Rich, creamy, and brimming with spices, this chicken pasta is fantastic after a hard day with lots of physical activity. You brown the chicken first in oil, before adding the bell pepper, garlic, onion, and a Cajun spice blend. After simmering for a bit, you add water, pasta, and cream. Notice that we're subbing out heavy cream for full-fat coconut cream. Allow time for a 10-minute natural pressure release, and it's ready!

Ingredients:

- ☐ 1 pound bowtie pasta
- ☐ 12-ounces full fat coconut cream
- ☐ 8-ounces diced chicken breast
- ☐ 2 cups water
- ☐ ½ cup diced red bell pepper
- ☐ 1 diced onion
- ☐ 3 tablespoons Cajun spice blend
- ☐ 1 tablespoon olive oil
- ☐ 1 tablespoon minced garlic

Directions:

1. Turn your PPCXL to "chicken/meat" and add oil.
2. When hot, brown the chicken well.
3. Add garlic, pepper, onion, and Cajun spice.
4. After two minutes of stirring, add water, cream, and pasta.
5. Seal the lid.
6. Adjust cook time to 6 minutes.
7. When the timer beeps, hit "cancel" and wait for a natural pressure release.
8. When ready, open the lid and stir before serving.

Nutritional Info (¼ recipe per serving):

Total calories: 684

Protein: 30

Carbs: 89

Fat: 25

Fiber: 0

Homemade "Hamburger Helper"

Serves: 6

Time: 21 minutes (10 minutes prep time, 6 minutes cook time, 5 minutes thickening/melt time)

Remember hamburger helper? This is similar, but better. It's basically just pasta, meat, and cheese, but that simple combination is so delicious. For creaminess, we're adding one cup of Greek yogurt at the very end instead of sour cream. This adds protein without all the fat.

Ingredients:

- 1 pound lean ground beef
- 2 cups chicken stock
- 16-ounces elbow macaroni
- 16-ounces cheddar cheese
- 4-ounces mozzarella cheese
- 1 cup plain Greek yogurt
- 1 tablespoon onion powder
- 1 tablespoon garlic powder
- Black pepper to taste

Directions:

1. Season the beef with onion powder, garlic, powder, and black pepper.
2. Turn your PPCXL to "chicken/meat" and add meat.
3. Brown for 5-7 minutes or so, until the meat isn't pink.
4. Pour in stock and pasta.
5. Seal the lid.
6. Adjust cook time to 6 minutes.
7. When time is up, hit "cancel" and carefully quick-release.
8. Stir in Greek yogurt, which should thicken up the dish.
9. Add cheeses to melt and season more to taste, if necessary.
10. Serve!

Nutritional Info (⅙ recipe per serving):
Total calories: 765
Protein: 51
Carbs: 59

Fat: 37
Fiber: 0

Traditional Spaghetti & Meatballs

Serves: 4

Time: 38 minutes (10 minutes prep time, 13 minutes cook time, 10 minutes natural pressure release, 5 minutes rest time)

A true one-pot meal, this pasta recipe has you cook meatballs and pasta in one pressure cooker. You put the meatballs, which are just ground beef, breadcrumbs, milk, and seasonings, on top of the pasta. Cook for 13 minutes, making sure the beef ends up at 165-degrees, and stir. That's it!

Ingredients:

- ☐ 1 pound of ground beef
- ☐ 14-ounces spaghetti sauce
- ☐ 10-ounces of spaghetti pasta
- ☐ 2 eggs
- ☐ 2 minced garlic cloves
- ☐ ¼ cup bread crumbs
- ☐ ¼ cup milk
- ☐ Salt and pepper to taste

Directions:

1. Let's start with the meatballs. In a bowl, mix the beef with eggs, bread crumbs, minced garlic, salt, and pepper.
2. Add noodles and spaghetti sauce into your pressure cooker.
3. Fill the jar with water and pour in cooker, too.
4. Form the meat into balls, and nestle on top of the noodles and sauce.
5. Seal the lid.
6. Hit "chicken/meat" and adjust cook time to 13 minutes.
7. When time is up, hit "cancel" and wait 10 minutes for a natural pressure release.
8. If there's leftover pressure, quick-release it.
9. Meatballs should be at 165-degrees.
10. Stir the spaghetti, and wait for 5 minutes or so for the flavors to really blend. If you like a saucier spaghetti, go with a bigger jar of sauce.

Nutritional Info (¼ recipe)
Total calories: 703
Protein: 32
Carbs: 71
Fat: 29
Fiber: 0

Pressure Cooker Lasagna

Serves: 8
Time: 21 minutes (10 minutes prep time, 6 minutes cook time, 5 minutes simmer time)

Lasagna is one of America's favorite comfort dishes, but it can take a long time. Make a super speedy version in the pressure cooker at only 21 minutes. This recipe uses 15-ounces of three ingredients - tomato sauce, stewed tomatoes, and cottage cheese, which we use in place of ricotta. We also throw in some spinach for extra vitamins. The recipe makes enough for 8 people.

Ingredients:

- ☐ 1 pound lean ground beef
- ☐ 16-ounces bowtie pasta
- ☐ 15-ounces tomato sauce
- ☐ 15-ounces stewed tomatoes
- ☐ 15-ounces cottage cheese
- ☐ 10-ounces thawed frozen spinach
- ☐ 1 chopped onion
- ☐ 1 cup shredded Mozzarella
- ☐ 1 minced garlic clove
- ☐ 1 teaspoon oregano
- ☐ 1 teaspoon Italian seasoning

Directions:

1. Turn the PPCXL to "chicken/meat" and add beef.
2. Brown for 3-5 minutes.
3. Add onion and stir until it becomes clear.
4. Add pasta, sauce, tomatoes, garlic, oregano, Italian seasoning, and the spinach.
5. Mix and pour in enough water to cover everything.
6. Seal the lid.
7. Adjust cook time to 6 minutes.
8. When time is up, hit "cancel" and quick-release.
9. Open the lid, hit "chicken/meat" again, and stir in cottage cheese with the lid off.
10. Simmer for 5 minutes or so.
11. Serve with mozzarella on top.

Nutritional Info (⅛ recipe per serving):
Total calories: 407
Protein: 29
Carbs: 55
Fat: 9
Fiber: 1

Thai Chicken Peanut Noodles

Serves: 4
Time: 9 minutes (3 minutes prep time, 6 minutes cook time)

If you're tired of tomato-based pastas, try out this Thai chicken noodle dish. Egg noodles cook faster, so the whole recipe just takes about 9 minutes. The star of the dish is the sweet-salty peanut sauce. The brand Thai Kitchen makes a great peanut satay sauce. You're also using cooked chicken, so it's a great way to use up leftovers.

Ingredients:

- ☐ 1 pound egg noodles
- ☐ 12-ounces Thai peanut sauce
- ☐ 8-ounces cooked chicken
- ☐ 2 ½ cups water
- ☐ 1 sliced onion
- ☐ 3 minced garlic cloves
- ☐ 1 tablespoon olive oil
- ☐ 1 tablespoon chopped scallions
- ☐ Juice from ½ lime
- ☐ Salt and pepper to taste

Directions:

1. Turn your cooker to "chicken/meat" and add oil.
2. When shiny and hot, cook the onion and garlic for about a minute.
3. Pour in water and peanut sauce along with the chicken, and stir.
4. Add noodles.
5. Seal the lid.
6. Adjust cook time to 6 minutes.
7. When time is up, hit "cancel" and quick-release the pressure.
8. Stir in the scallions.
9. Serve with a squeeze of lime juice on top.

Nutritional Info (¼ recipe per serving):

Total calories: 725
Protein: 19
Carbs: 92

Fat: 25
Fiber: 0

Chicken-Broccoli Alfredo

Serves: 4

Time: 25 minutes (10 minutes prep time, 10 minutes cook time, 5 minutes simmer time)

After a long day at work, this is a great recipe to throw together. From start to finish, it takes less than a half hour. You just need chicken breasts, pasta, broccoli, cheese, cream, and some flavoring essentials like garlic, salt, and pepper. Cut the chicken into cubes and brown with the garlic and oil. Deglaze the pot with white wine before pouring in the water and pasta. That cooks for just 10 minutes. The cream and cheese finish off the dish in style.

Ingredients:

- ☐ 1 pound of cubed boneless + skinless chicken breasts
- ☐ 16-ounces of pasta
- ☐ 16-ounces of frozen broccoli
- ☐ 16-ounces of Asiago cheese
- ☐ 8-ounces of heavy cream
- ☐ 2 cups water
- ☐ 1 cup white wine
- ☐ 2 minced garlic cloves
- ☐ 1 tablespoon olive oil
- ☐ Salt and pepper to taste

Directions:

1. Turn your PPCXL to "chicken/meat" and add oil.
2. When hot, add garlic and cook until fragrant.
3. Add the chicken cubes to brown for 1-2 minutes on each side.
4. Pour in the wine with the browned chicken and deglaze, scraping up any food bits that have stuck to the bottom of the cooker.
5. Pour in water and pasta.
6. Mix in broccoli and seal the lid.
7. Adjust cook time to 10 minutes.
8. When the timer beeps, hit "cancel" and quick-release the pressure. If water sprays out at you, wait 5 minutes before trying again.
9. Open the lid, hit "chicken/meat" again, and stir in heavy cream.
10. Sauce will begin to thicken, so add cheese to melt.
11. Enjoy!

Nutritional Info (¼ recipe per serving)
Total calories: 309
Protein: 8.5
Carbs: 21
Fat: 20.9
Fiber: 2.6

Easy Chicken + Rice

Serves: 4

Time: 49 minutes (36 minutes chicken time, 7 minutes broil time, 6 minutes rice time)

Because it's so full of protein (73 grams!), this easy recipe is a great dinner after you've been working out a long time. The rice is full of carbs to replace what you've lost, and the protein in the chicken helps the body repair and build muscle. You can use any seasoning blend you want; I like Herbes de Provence, because it gives the meal a fresh, French twist.

Ingredients:

- ☐ 3-pound chicken thighs
- ☐ 2 cups water
- ☐ 1 ½ cups long-grain white rice
- ☐ 2 tablespoons Herbes de Provence
- ☐ Salt and pepper to taste

Directions:

1. Season chicken with salt, pepper, and Herbes de Provence.
2. Pour water into your pressure cooker and add chicken.
3. Seal the lid.
4. Hit "chicken/meat" and adjust cook time to 36 minutes.
5. When the timer beeps, hit "cancel" and remove chicken.
6. Put chicken on a cookie sheet and broil for 5-7 minutes, until the skin becomes crispy.
7. Strain the broth in the cooker into a bowl, so you have 3 cups total.
8. Pour broth and rice into the pressure cooker.
9. Seal the lid and hit the "rice" function, to the default time of 6 minutes.
10. When time is up, hit "cancel" and carefully quick-release.
11. Serve rice with chicken on top

Nutritional Info (¼ recipe per serving):

Total calories: 698

Protein: 73

Carbs: 67

Fat: 14

Fiber: 0

Kale and Sweet Potato Brown Rice

Serves: 12

Time: 55 minutes (6 minutes prep time, 39 minutes cook time, 10 minutes natural pressure release)

Need a side dish that can feed a crowd? This healthy brown rice bowl is spiced to perfection with fresh ginger, nutmeg, coriander, salt, and pepper. Kale is chock full of fiber and iron, and any bitterness is balanced by the sweet potato. Butter is added at the very end to ensure the rice isn't dry.

Ingredients:

- ☐ 4 cups chicken broth
- ☐ 4 cups chopped kale
- ☐ 2 cups long-grain brown rice
- ☐ ½ cup chopped onion
- ☐ 1 peeled and diced sweet potato
- ☐ 2 tablespoons butter
- ☐ 2 tablespoons minced chives
- ☐ 2 tablespoons minced fresh ginger
- ☐ 1 teaspoon ground coriander
- ☐ ¼ teaspoon ground nutmeg
- ☐ Salt and pepper to taste

Directions:

1. Spray your pressure cooker pot with a coconut oil-based cooking spray and turn the cooker to "chicken/meat."
2. Add onion and 1 ½ tablespoons ginger.
3. After 4 minutes or so, add potato and rice.
4. Stir for 1 minute before adding nutmeg, coriander, salt, and pepper.
5. Pour in the broth and stir.
6. Put kale on top, don't stir, and seal the lid.
7. Adjust cook time to 39 minutes.
8. When time is up, hit "cancel" and wait 10 minutes before quick-releasing remaining pressure.
9. Add chives, butter, and the rest of the ginger.
10. Stir and serve!

Nutritional Info (⅔ cup per serving):
Total calories: 159
Protein: 4
Carbs: 29
Fat: 3
Fiber: 1

Mediterranean Rice

Serves: 6
Time: 15 minutes (5 minutes prep time, 10 minutes cook time)

Bring the flavors of the Mediterranean islands to your dinner table. Made from a combination of quinoa and basmati rice, this side dish is full of fresh flavors like lemon, garlic, and herbs. It's a great option for a side with fish or chicken, or if you want an easy lunch, add some leftover sliced chicken breast, and you've got a new salad recipe.

Ingredients:

- ☐ 2 ¾ cups chicken stock
- ☐ 1 cup basmati rice
- ☐ 1 cup chopped spinach
- ☐ ½ cup quinoa
- ☐ 1 diced onion
- ☐ 2 minced garlic cloves
- ☐ 2 tablespoons butter
- ☐ 2 teaspoons lemon zest
- ☐ 2 teaspoons chopped oregano
- ☐ 1 teaspoon chopped rosemary
- ☐ Juice from one lemon
- ☐ Salt and pepper to taste

Directions:

1. Hit "chicken/meat" on your cooker and add butter.
2. When melted, cook the onion for two minutes before adding garlic.
3. After a minute of stirring, add quinoa, rice, herbs, zest, lemon juice, and chicken stock.
4. Seal the lid.
5. Adjust cook time to 10 minutes.
6. When time is up, hit "cancel" and quick-release the pressure.
7. Add in spinach, salt, and pepper before serving.

Nutritional Info (⅙ recipe per serving):
Total calories: 211
Protein: 5
Carbs: 37
Fat: 5
Fiber: 0

Easy Mexican Rice

Serves: 6

Time: 24 minutes (5 minutes prep time, 4 minutes cook time, 15 minutes natural pressure release)

The perfect side for any Mexican-inspired dish, this easy rice recipe only uses six ingredients. Adding tomato paste to the water helps infuse the rice with a heartier flavor. Feel free to add more spices like cumin or fresh herbs to the final product; they won't add enough calories to make a difference.

Ingredients:

- [ ] 2 cups long-grain white rice
- [ ] 2 cups water
- [ ] ½ cup tomato paste
- [ ] ½ chopped onion
- [ ] 3 minced garlic cloves
- [ ] 2 teaspoons salt

Directions:

1. Hit "chicken/meat" on your PPCXL and pour in a little water.
2. Cook onion, garlic, rice, and salt for 3-4 minutes.
3. Mix tomato paste and water in a bowl, then stir into the pressure cooker.
4. Seal the lid.
5. Adjust cook time to 4 minutes.
6. When time is up, hit "cancel" and wait 15 minutes before releasing any leftover pressure.
7. Open the lid, fluff, season more if necessary, and serve!

Nutritional Info (⅙ recipe per serving):
Total calories: 299
Protein: 7
Carbs: 65
Fat: 1
Fiber: 0

Kale + Spinach Risotto

Serves: 6
Time: 22 minutes (10 minutes prep time, 7 minutes cook time, 5 minutes additional time)

This is one of the healthier risottos you could make. Spinach and kale are two of the best greens, and go wonderfully with sun-dried tomatoes and a little nutmeg. Since greens don't need to be pressure-cooked, you cook the rice on its own first with browned onions. Polish everything off with 3 tablespoons of butter and parmesan cheese, and it's ready to serve!

Ingredients:

- ☐ 3 ½ cups vegetable stock
- ☐ 1 ½ cups Arborio rice
- ☐ 1 cup baby kale leaves
- ☐ 1 cup baby spinach leaves
- ☐ 4 chopped sun-dried tomato halves (packed in oil)
- ☐ ¼ cup parmesan cheese
- ☐ ¼ cup minced onion
- ☐ 3 tablespoons butter
- ☐ 2 teaspoons olive oil
- ☐ Salt and pepper to taste
- ☐ Pinch of nutmeg

Directions:

1. Hit "chicken/meat" on your PPCXL and pour in olive oil.
2. When shiny and hot, add onions.
3. When softened and a golden color, stir in rice, coating in the hot oil.
4. Toast for 4-5 minutes and then hit "cancel" on the cooker.
5. Pour in broth and seal the lid.
6. Hit "chicken/meat" again and adjust time to 7 minutes.
7. When the timer beeps, hit "cancel" and carefully quick-release the pressure.
8. When the pressure is all gone, open the lid, and if there isn't any liquid, add ½ cup water.
9. Stir in nutmeg and tomatoes.
10. Add spinach and kale to wilt.
11. Whisk in butter.
12. When melted, add cheese and black pepper.

13. Season to taste with salt before serving.

Nutritional Info (⅙ recipe):
Total calories: 272
Protein: 6
Carbs: 40
Fat: 11
Fiber: 3

Chicken Sausage + Mushroom Risotto

Serves: 5-6
Time: 22 minutes (15 minutes prep time, 7 minutes cook time)

I love risottos that are also full meals. There's just something about digging into a hot bowl that warms the soul. This recipe has chicken sausage and cremini mushrooms. The sausage should already be fully-cooked; you just brown it a bit on its own before plating it. The onion and mushrooms go in the pot next, followed by salt, pepper, and fresh thyme. You cook this mixture with the rice for just 7 minutes, and then stir in the sausage along with parmesan cheese.

Ingredients:

- ☐ 1 pound sliced cremini mushrooms
- ☐ 10-ounces cooked and sliced chicken sausage
- ☐ 4 cups chicken stock
- ☐ 2 cups Arborio rice
- ☐ 1 chopped yellow onion
- ☐ 3 minced garlic cloves
- ☐ ½ cup white wine
- ☐ ¼ cup parmesan cheese
- ☐ 3 fresh thyme sprigs
- ☐ 3 tablespoons butter
- ☐ 2 tablespoons olive oil
- ☐ 1 tablespoon soy sauce
- ☐ Salt and pepper to taste

Directions:

1. Turn your cooker to "chicken/meat" and pour in olive oil.
2. When shimmering, add sausage and stir for 5 minutes to brown.
3. Move sausage to a plate.
4. Add butter to the hot oil to melt.
5. Add onion and mushrooms, stirring and cooking for 6 minutes.
6. Cook the garlic for a minute or so.
7. Add salt, pepper, and thyme.
8. Pour in wine and soy sauce, scraping the bottom of the cooker to break up any food particles.

9. When the wine has evaporated, add stock and rice.
10. Seal the lid.
11. Adjust cook time to 7 minutes.
12. When the timer beeps, turn off the cooker and quick-release the pressure.
13. Stir in browned sausage, cheese, and more salt and pepper if needed.

Nutritional Info (⅕ per serving):
Total calories: 415
Protein: 16
Carbs: 50
Fat: 6
Fiber: 2

Roasted Shrimp Risotto with Fresh Rosemary

Serves: 4
Time: 17 minutes (10 minutes prep time, 7 minutes cook time)

We're making bistro-quality risotto with this recipe. You use the pressure cooker for the rice part of the meal, and roast the shrimp in the oven with oil, salt, garlic, and fresh rosemary. If you've never had roasted shrimp, it might just become your new favorite way to eat it. Since the cooker takes about 10 minutes to reach pressure before the 7-minute countdown begins, you have plenty of time to get the shrimp baked and ready while the pressure cooker does its thing.

Ingredients:

- ☐ 1 pound peeled and cleaned shrimp
- ☐ 4 cups chicken broth
- ☐ 2 cups Arborio rice
- ☐ ¼ cup Parmesan cheese
- ☐ ½ diced yellow onion
- ☐ 3 minced garlic cloves
- ☐ 2 tablespoons butter
- ☐ 2 tablespoons +1 tablespoon olive oil
- ☐ 1 tablespoon chopped fresh rosemary sprigs
- ☐ ½ teaspoon salt

Directions:

1. Hit "chicken/meat" on your pressure cooker and add onions, and oil.
2. Stir until the onions have become soft.
3. Add rice, and stir to coat in the oil.
4. Pour in the chicken broth and seal the lid.
5. Adjust cook time to 7 minutes.
6. While that cooks, preheat your oven to 400-degrees.
7. Mix 1 tablespoon of olive oil, salt, garlic, and rosemary in a bowl.
8. Toss shrimp in the bowl, so they become coated.
9. Bake on a cookie sheet for 5 minutes in the oven.
10. When the pressure cooker is ready, hit "cancel" and quick-release the pressure.
11. Add cheese and butter to the rice.
12. Serve with shrimp on top!

Nutritional Info (¼ recipe)
Total calories: 544
Protein: 26
Carbs: 75
Fat: 18
Fiber: 3

Fried Rice with Pork

Serves: 4

Time: 35 minutes (12 minutes prep time, 7 minutes cook time, 10 minutes natural pressure release, 6 minutes additional time)

You can make this fried rice recipe in about the same amount of time it would take to wait for take-out. The key is to slice the pork pretty thin, so it browns quickly. You cook the rice separately, which takes just 7 minutes, and then scramble the egg right in the pot by making a little hole in the rice. Add in the frozen peas, browned pork, onion, carrot, and soy sauce!

Ingredients:

- ☐ 8-ounces thin pork loin, sliced into ½-inch pieces
- ☐ 3 cups + 2 tablespoons water
- ☐ 2 cups white rice
- ☐ ½ cup frozen peas
- ☐ 1 beaten egg
- ☐ 1 chopped onion
- ☐ 1 peeled and chopped carrot
- ☐ 3 tablespoons soy sauce
- ☐ 3 tablespoons olive oil
- ☐ Salt and pepper to taste

Directions:

1. Turn your PPCXL to the "chicken/meat" setting and add 1 tablespoon of olive oil.
2. When hot, cook the onion and carrot for about 2 minutes.
3. Season the pork with salt and pepper.
4. Add to pot and brown for 5 minutes till golden.
5. Turn off the cooker and remove the pork, onion, and carrot.
6. Pour a little bit of water into the cooker (the minimum for the cooker) and scrape up any stuck-on bits.
7. Add rice and a dash of salt.
8. Seal the lid.
9. Hit "chicken/meat" again and adjust cook time to 7 minutes.
10. When time is up, hit "cancel" and wait 10 minutes before quick-releasing.
11. Stir the rice, forming a well in the middle, so the bottom of the pot is visible.
12. Hit "chicken/meat" again and pour 2 tablespoons of oil into the well.

13. Crack the egg in the well, scrambling it until it's cooked.
14. Add peas, onion, carrot, and pork.
15. Stir until everything is warmed through
16. Add soy sauce before serving!

Nutritional Info (¼ recipe):
Total calories: 547
Protein: 22
Carbs: 81
Fiber: 3
Fat: 2

Duck Fat Risotto

Serves: 4
Time: 21 minutes (10 minutes prep time, 6 minutes cook time, 5 minutes simmer time)

You only use 3 tablespoons of duck fat in this risotto, but it makes all the difference. Duck fat is a unique animal fat because of its amazingly-savory flavor and silky texture. It's perfect for risotto, which should be incredible all on its own, and not just about what's mixed in. We love those mix-ins, too, though, which are white mushrooms, prosciutto, shallot, and orange zest.

Ingredients:

- ☐ 4 cups warmed-up chicken broth
- ☐ 2 cups Arborio rice
- ☐ ½ cup dry white wine
- ☐ 8-ounces sliced white mushrooms
- ☐ 2 minced garlic cloves
- ☐ 4-ounces chopped prosciutto
- ☐ 3 tablespoons duck fat
- ☐ 2 tablespoons chopped shallot
- ☐ 1 tablespoon chopped parsley
- ☐ 1 tablespoon orange zest
- ☐ Salt and pepper to taste

Directions:

1. Hit "chicken/meat" on your PPCXL and add duck fat.
2. When hot, cook the shallots for 3 minutes.
3. Add garlic, and cook for just half a minute.
4. Add mushrooms and cook for 4 minutes.
5. Add rice, and stir to coat in the oil.
6. When the rice has become toasty, pour in wine and deglaze by scraping off any stuck food bits.
7. Once the alcohol smell has faded, stir in the broth.
8. Seal the cooker lid.
9. Adjust cook time to 6 minutes.
10. When time is up, turn off the cooker and quick-release.
11. Remove the lid and hit "chicken/meat" again, but keep the lid off.

12. Stir risotto for 3-5 minutes to let the liquid absorb even more into the rice.
13. Add prosciutto, parsley, orange zest, salt, and pepper before serving.

Nutritional Info (¼ recipe per serving):
Total calories: 437
Protein: 8
Carbs: 77
Fat: 11
Fiber: 1

Chapter 12

Sides + Snacks

Soft Green Beans with Mushrooms + Bacon

Serves: 4
Time: 15 minutes

If you like your green beans "country-style," which means soft instead of crunchy, this is a good recipe for you. You cook the green beans for 15 minutes with flavorful mushrooms, bacon, garlic, and chicken stock. They would be a great accompaniment to chicken or pork.

Ingredients:

- ☐ 1 ½ pounds fresh green beans
- ☐ 4-5 sliced mushrooms
- ☐ 1 cup chicken stock
- ☐ 1 slice bacon
- ☐ 1 teaspoon minced garlic
- ☐ ½ teaspoon salt
- ☐ Black pepper to taste

Directions:

1. Put everything in your pressure cooker and stir.
2. Seal the lid.
3. Hit "chicken/meat" and cook for the default time of 15 minutes.
4. When time is up, hit "cancel" and quick-release.
5. Serve!

Nutritional Info (¼ recipe per serving):
Total calories: 80
Protein: 5
Carbs: 14
Fat: 1
Fiber: 6

Spiced Sweet Potatoes with Pineapple

Serves: 8
Time: 24 minutes (14 minutes cook time, 10 minutes spice/smash time)

This sweet potato dish tastes a bit like the filling of a pumpkin pie, but without all the added sugar. It's all about natural sweetness and spices like cinnamon, nutmeg, and ginger. Sweet potatoes take 14 minutes to cook under pressure, and then you make the sauce with butter, pineapple juice, and spices. Mash everything together, and you have a delicious, high-fiber side!

Ingredients:

- ☐ 4 pounds peeled sweet potatoes, cut into 1 ½-inch chunks
- ☐ 3 cups water
- ☐ 3 tablespoons butter
- ☐ 2 tablespoons thawed, unsweetened pineapple juice concentrate
- ☐ 1 teaspoon salt
- ☐ ½ teaspoon ground ginger
- ☐ ¼ teaspoon ground cinnamon
- ☐ ¼ teaspoon grated nutmeg

Directions:

1. Pour water into your PPCXL along with the sweet potatoes.
2. Seal the lid.
3. Hit "chicken/meat" and adjust cook time to 14 minutes.
4. When time is up, hit "cancel" and quick-release the pressure.
5. Drain the potatoes, and when cool enough, pull off the skin.
6. Turn your cooker back to "chicken/meat" and melt the butter.
7. Stir in ginger, nutmeg, and cinnamon for one minute.
8. Pour in pineapple juice and salt.
9. Hit "cancel."
10. Add potatoes and smash using a wooden spoon.
11. When you have the texture you want, serve!

Nutritional Info (⅛ of recipe):
Total calories: 241
Protein: 4
Carbs: 48
Fat: 5
Fiber: 6.8

Spicy Cauliflower, Broccoli, + Citrus Salad

Serves: 4
Time: 11 minutes (5 minutes dressing time, 6 minutes cook time)

High in fiber, this salad is a nice change from caesar or cobbs. You cook broccoli and two kinds of cauliflower in the pressure cooker, making them very tender, and dress them in a fresh and slightly-spicy dressing made from capers, orange juice, anchovies, one hot pepper, salt, and pepper. For a sweet and juicy garnish, you've got fresh orange slices.

Ingredients:

Salad:
- ☐ 1 pound of broccoli florets
- ☐ 2 sliced seedless oranges
- ☐ Florets of 1 small Romanesco cauliflower
- ☐ Florets of 1 small regular cauliflower

Dressing:
- ☐ 4 anchovies
- ☐ 4 tablespoons olive oil
- ☐ 1 tablespoon capers
- ☐ The juice and zest of one orange
- ☐ 1 chopped hot pepper
- ☐ Salt and pepper to taste

Directions:

1. Put all the dressing ingredients in a container and shake. Store in the fridge for now.
2. Pour 1 cup of water into your PPCXL and add steamer basket.
3. Put all the florets in the basket and seal the lid.
4. Hit "rice/risotto" and cook for 6 minutes.
5. When time is up, hit "cancel" and quick-release.
6. Plate florets and arrange orange slices.
7. Pour over dressing and enjoy!

Nutritional Info (¼ of recipe per serving):
Total calories: 260
Protein: 6
Carbs: 33
Fat: 14
Fiber: 11

Mashed Acorn Squash

Serves: 4
Time: 49 minutes (24 minutes cook time, 20 minutes cool time, 5 minutes mash time)

Acorn squash is sometimes neglected in favor of butternut, because it's less sweet. However, by adding brown sugar and nutmeg, the acorn squash is wonderfully-flavored, and any "gritty" texture that some have complained about isn't noticeable when you cook the squash in the pressure cooker.

Ingredients:

- ☐ 2 halved and seeded acorn squash
- ☐ ½ cup water
- ☐ 2 tablespoons brown sugar
- ☐ 2 tablespoons butter
- ☐ 1 teaspoon salt
- ☐ ½ teaspoon grated nutmeg
- ☐ ¼ teaspoon baking soda
- ☐ Salt and pepper to taste

Directions:

1. Sprinkle the cut side of the squash with baking soda and salt.
2. Pour water into the pressure cooker.
3. Put squash in the steamer basket and lower into cooker.
4. Seal the lid.
5. Hit "chicken/meat" and adjust cook time to 24 minutes.
6. When time is up, hit "cancel" and quick-release the pressure.
7. Wait for the squash to cool.
8. When ready, use a fork to scrape out the flesh.
9. Mix with butter, brown sugar, and nutmeg.
10. Mash well.
11. Season to taste with salt and pepper before serving.

Nutritional Info (¼ of recipe per serving):
Total calories: 166
Protein: 2
Carbs: 30

Fat: 6
Fiber: 3

Spicy Black Bean Brown Rice Salad

Serves: 4-8

Time: 44 minutes (29 minutes cook time, 10 minutes natural pressure release, 5 minutes dressing time)

Brown rice is a whole grain with fiber, and makes a great foundation for this flavorful, spicy salad. You cook the rice first with just water and salt for 29 minutes. Next, you add your fresh ingredients - the grape tomatoes, avocado, beans, and cilantro. As for the dressing, it's garlic, oil, lime juice, hot sauce, and agave nectar. One serving is just 140 calories.

Ingredients:

Rice:

- ☐ 1 ½ cups of water
- ☐ One 14-ounce can drained and rinsed black beans
- ☐ 12 quartered grape tomatoes
- ☐ 1 cup brown rice
- ☐ 1 diced avocado
- ☐ ¼ cup minced cilantro
- ☐ ⅛ teaspoon salt

Dressing:

- ☐ 2 minced garlic cloves
- ☐ 3 tablespoons fresh lime juice
- ☐ 3 tablespoons extra-virgin olive oil
- ☐ 2 teaspoons Tabasco sauce
- ☐ 1 teaspoon agave nectar
- ☐ ¼ teaspoon salt

Directions:

1. Mix rice, salt, and water in the PPCXL.
2. Seal the lid and hit "chicken/meat," adjusting time to 29 minutes.
3. When time is up, hit "cancel" and wait 10 minutes before quick-releasing.
4. Fluff rice and cool.
5. Mix with tomato, avocado, beans, and cilantro.
6. To make dressing, mix Tabasco, garlic, agave, salt, and lime juice.
7. Gradually add olive oil and whisk.
8. Pour dressing on rice and serve!

Nutritional Info (¼ recipe per serving):
Total calories: 140
Protein: 3.5
Carbs: 28
Fat: 2.8
Fiber: 2

Pine-Nut Polenta with Honey

Serves: 6

Time: 21 minutes (6 minutes prep time, 14 minutes cook time, 1 minute rest time)

With only six ingredients, you can make the perfect polenta that's good and sweet enough to eat for breakfast. You first bring water, honey, and pine nuts to a boil in your pressure cooker, and then cook with polenta under pressure for 14 minutes. Add cream and salt after you've quick-released the pressure.

Ingredients:

- ☐ 5 cups water
- ☐ 1 cup stone-ground polenta
- ☐ ½ cup honey
- ☐ ½ cup heavy cream
- ☐ ¼ cup pine nuts
- ☐ Salt to taste

Directions:

1. Mix water, honey, and pine nuts in your PPCXL.
2. Hit "chicken/meat" and bring to a boil, stirring.
3. Add polenta and stir.
4. Seal the lid.
5. Adjust cook time to 14 minutes.
6. When the timer beeps, hit "cancel" and carefully quick-release the pressure.
7. Open the lid and stir in cream.
8. After waiting one minute, season with salt and serve!

Nutritional Info (⅙ recipe per serving):

Total calories: 282

Protein: 1

Carbs: 25

Fat: 11

Fiber: 1.5

Spaghetti Squash with an Apple Juice Glaze

Serves: 4-6
Time: 50 minutes (24 minutes cook time, 20 minutes cool time, 6 minutes glaze time)

Embrace the flavors of autumn with this easy spaghetti squash recipe. The real star is the apple juice glaze, which is made just by reducing apple juice into a syrup-like texture, and adding some olive oil. Serve with literally anything, from chicken to pork to fish.

Ingredients:

- ☐ One 3-lb spaghetti squash
- ☐ ¾ cup 100% apple juice
- ☐ 2 tablespoons olive oil
- ☐ Salt to taste

Directions:

1. Pour 1 cup of water into your PPCXL and insert the steamer basket.
2. Put the spaghetti squash in the basket and seal the lid.
3. Hit "chicken/meat" and adjust cook time to 24 minutes.
4. When the timer beeps, hit "cancel" and quick-release the pressure.
5. Take out the squash (it's hot!) and cool enough so you can cut it in half.
6. Leave it on a plate to keep cooling.
7. Pour the water out of your pressure cooker and replace with the apple juice.
8. Hit "chicken/meat" again and simmer until the juice becomes to thicken.
9. When the juice is more syrupy, stir in olive oil.
10. Scoop out seeds from the squash and scrape flesh into the cooker.
11. Stir well and season with salt.
12. Serve!

Nutritional Info (¼ recipe per serving):
Total calories: 188
Protein: 1
Carbs: 29
Fat: 9
Fiber: 6

Butternut Squash with Sage Brown Butter

Serves: 4
Time: 17 minutes (5 minutes prep time, 12 minutes cook time)

Butternut squash is an incredibly delicious and versatile winter vegetable. For this recipe, you serve it simply, with an amazing brown butter sauce that's been cooked in sage. Brown butter is what happens to regular butter when you cook it until solids begin to form. It's almost like a savory caramel, and it's one of my favorite easy sauces to prepare.

Ingredients:

- ☐ One medium-sized butternut squash
- ☐ 1 cup water
- ☐ 8 sliced sage leaves
- ☐ 4 tablespoons butter
- ☐ Salt and pepper to taste
- ☐ Dash of nutmeg

Directions:

1. Peel and seed the squash before chopping into 1-inch pieces.
2. Pour water into your pressure cooker and lower in the steamer basket.
3. Put the squash pieces in the basket and seal the lid.
4. Hit "chicken/meat" and adjust cook time to 12 minutes.
5. In the meantime, cook butter and sage together in a saucepan until the butter begins to darken and smell nutty.
6. When time is up on the pressure cooker, hit "cancel" and quick-release.
7. Serve squash with brown butter poured on top, and seasoned with nutmeg, salt, and pepper.

Nutritional Info (¼ recipe per serving):
Total calories: 267
Protein: 5
Carbs: 42
Fat: 12
Fiber: 6.7

Ricotta-Stuffed Zucchini

Serves: 6
Time: 21 minutes (15 minutes prep time, 6 minutes cook time)

These bite-sized zucchinis are filled with ricotta, which is one of my favorite indulgent dishes. It's just so creamy and irresistible, especially when mixed with nutmeg and thyme. The stuffed zucchinis cook along with a sauce made from crushed tomatoes, garlic, and onion, so when you serve, don't forget a spoon.

Ingredients:

- ☐ 3 large zucchinis
- ☐ 1 ¾ cups crushed tomatoes
- ☐ 1 cup ricotta
- ☐ 1 large egg yolk
- ☐ ½ cup breadcrumbs
- ☐ 1 yellow onion
- ☐ 2 tablespoons olive oil
- ☐ 1 tablespoon minced fresh oregano
- ☐ 2 teaspoons fresh thyme
- ☐ 2 teaspoons minced garlic
- ☐ ¼ teaspoon grated nutmeg
- ☐ Salt + pepper

Directions:

1. Mix ricotta, egg yolk, breadcrumbs, nutmeg, and thyme in a bowl.
2. Cut the zucchinis into 2-inch long pieces, and hollow out the middle so there's about ¼-inch flesh on the sides, and ½-inch on the bottom.
3. Fill hollows with 2 tablespoons each of the ricotta.
4. Turn your pressure cooker to "chicken/meat" and add oil.
5. Cook onion till soft before adding garlic, cooking that for just 30 seconds.
6. Add tomatoes, salt, pepper, and oregano.
7. Put the zucchinis in the cooker, with the stuffed-side facing up.
8. Seal the lid.
9. Adjust cook time to 6 minutes.
10. When the timer beeps, hit "cancel" and quick-release the pressure.

11. Serve with cooking liquid as sauce!

Nutritional Info (⅙ recipe per serving):
Total calories: 209
Protein: 10
Carbs: 18
Fat: 11
Fiber: 2

Bacon-Wrapped Asparagus

Serves: 6

Time: 9 minutes (5 minutes prep time, 4 minutes cook time)

Perfect for parties, this dish will make even people who aren't crazy about asparagus coming back for more. You just wrap the spears in bacon, stick in a steamer basket, and cook for 4 minutes. You quick-release the pressure, and that's it!

Ingredients:

- ☐ 1 pound of asparagus
- ☐ 8-ounces bacon
- ☐ 1 cup of water

Directions:

1. Pour water into your PPCXL.
2. Wrap asparagus in the raw bacon.
3. If there are any leftover asparagus, put them in the bottom of a steamer basket.
4. Top with the wrapped asparagus and lower into cooker.
5. Seal the lid.
6. Hit "chicken/meat" and adjust cook time to 4 minutes.
7. When the timer beeps, turn off the cooker and quick-release.
8. Remove the basket.
9. Serve!

Nutritional Info (⅙ recipe per serving):

Total calories: 183

Protein: 12

Carbs: 3

Fat: 15

Fiber: 1.4

Carrots with Butter, Bacon, and Leeks

Serves: 4-6
Time: 18 minutes (10 minutes prep time, 8 minutes cook time)

Got some baby carrots lying around that you don't know what to do with? Make a buttery, lip-smacking side dish with some white wine, bacon, butter, and a leek. You cook the bacon first, followed by the leek, and then a deglaze with the sweet wine. You add carrots right into the pot, but you're actually cooking everything in a baking dish that sits on a trivet in the pressure cooker. Cover the dish with parchment paper first, and then wrap the whole thing in foil.

Ingredients:

- ☐ 1 pound baby carrots
- ☐ ¼ cup sweet white wine
- ☐ 4-ounces diced bacon
- ☐ 1 sliced leek
- ☐ 2 tablespoons chopped butter
- ☐ Black pepper to taste

Directions:

1. Turn your cooker to "chicken/meat" and add bacon.
2. Cook until crisp.
3. Add white and green parts of the leek and cook for just one minute.
4. Pour in wine and scrape up any stuck-on bits.
5. Stir in a bit of pepper and carrots before hitting "cancel."
6. Pour the pressure cooker contents into a 1-quart baking dish.
7. Add pats of butter and layer a piece of parchment paper on top.
8. Wrap the whole dish with foil.
9. Wipe out the cooker with a paper towel and pour in 2 cups of water.
10. Lower in trivet and put baking dish on top.
11. Seal the lid.
12. Hit "chicken/meat" again and adjust cook time to 8 minutes.
13. When the timer beeps, hit "cancel" and quick-release.
14. Stir dish and serve!

Nutritional Info (¼ recipe per serving):
Total calories: 201
Protein: 6
Carbs: 13
Fat: 14
Fiber: 3

Vegetable Rice Pilaf with Toasted Almonds

Serves: 8-10

Time: 13 minutes (5 minutes prep time, 3 minutes cook time, 5 minutes natural pressure release)

Full of aromatic veggies and topped with toasted almonds, this side dish is great when you need something light. Thanks to the pressure cooker, rice cooks very quickly, so you're actually only putting the dish under pressure for 3 minutes. The rest is preparing the vegetables and then waiting for a natural pressure release.

Ingredients:

- ☐ 2 cups long-grain white rice
- ☐ One 14-ounce can of chicken broth
- ☐ 1 ¼ cups water
- ☐ 1 cup thawed frozen peas
- ☐ ½ cup toasted and sliced almonds
- ☐ 1 chopped celery stalk
- ☐ 1 chopped carrot
- ☐ 1 chopped white onion
- ☐ 2 tablespoons chopped fresh parsley
- ☐ 1 tablespoon butter
- ☐ Salt and pepper to taste

Directions:

1. Add butter to your PPCXL and hit "chicken/meat."
2. When melted and hot, toss in the celery, carrot, and onion.
3. Stir for 3-5 minutes, until the veggies are becoming tender.
4. Pour in the rice and toast for 1-2 minutes.
5. Pour in water and broth.
6. Throw in a dash of salt before sealing the cooker lid.
7. Adjust cook time to 3 minutes.
8. When the timer beeps, wait 5 minutes, then quick-release any leftover pressure.
9. Stir in parsley and peas, letting the peas warm through.
10. Top with toasted almonds and serve!

Nutritional Info (¹/₈ recipe):
Calories: 277
Protein: 6
Carbs: 51
Fat: 4
Fiber: 2

Scalloped Potatoes

Serves: 6
Time: 15 minutes (5 minutes prep time, 6 minutes cook time, 4 minutes simmer/broil time)

Scalloped potatoes are a favorite dish around the holidays, especially Thanksgiving. They're super easy to prepare in the pressure cooker because of how fast the cooker is with potatoes. Slicing the potatoes thin helps speed up the process, too. After the potatoes are cooked in broth, chives, salt, and pepper, you move them to a baking dish. Mix a thickening sauce of milk, sour cream, and potato starch in the cooker, and then pour over the potatoes. Broil for a few minutes to brown the top.

Note: If you don't like using sour cream because of the fat content, use plain Greek yogurt instead.

Ingredients:

- ☐ 6 peeled and thinly-sliced potatoes
- ☐ 1 cup chicken broth
- ☐ ⅓ cup sour cream
- ☐ ⅓ cup milk
- ☐ 2 tablespoons potato starch
- ☐ 1 tablespoon chopped chives
- ☐ 1 teaspoon salt
- ☐ Dash of black pepper
- ☐ Dash of paprika

Directions:

1. Pour broth into cooker.
2. Tumble in potatoes, along with salt, pepper, and chives.
3. Seal the lid.
4. Hit "chicken/meat," adjusting time to 6 minutes.
5. When the timer beeps, hit "cancel" and quick-release.
6. Move potatoes (leave the cooking liquid in the pot) to a dish that's safe under the broiler.
7. Pour sour cream, milk, and potato starch into your pressure cooker.
8. Hit "chicken/meat" again and whisk for one minute.
9. Pour over the potatoes and mix well.

10. Sprinkle on paprika, and cook under the broiler until the top browns.

Nutritional Info (⅙ recipe per serving):
Calories: 168
Protein: 4
Carbs: 31
Fat: 3
Fiber: 3

Savoy Cabbage with Coconut Milk + Bacon

Serves: 4-6

Time: 20 minutes (10 minutes prep time, 5 minutes cook time, 5 minutes simmer time)

This isn't your ordinary cabbage. Cooked in a pressure cooker with onion and bacon, Savoy cabbage becomes extremely tender flavorful. Add in some full-fat coconut milk and nutmeg, and you've got a creamy, salty, and spicy-sweet side dish that goes with just about any entree.

Ingredients:

- ☐ 1 chopped, medium-sized head of Savoy cabbage
- ☐ 2 cups beef or chicken bone broth
- ☐ 1 cup diced bacon
- ☐ ½ can of full-fat coconut milk
- ☐ 1 chopped onion
- ☐ 1 bay leaf
- ☐ 2 tablespoons parsley flakes
- ☐ ¼ teaspoon nutmeg
- ☐ Salt to taste

Directions:

1. Cut round piece of parchment paper sized to fit the bottom of the pot, but don't put it in just yet.
2. Turn the cooker to "chicken/meat," and add onion and bacon.
3. When the onion is brown and bacon cooked, pour in broth, scraping up any stuck-on bits.
4. Add cabbage and bay leaf.
5. Put the parchment paper on top of the food.
6. Seal the lid.
7. Adjust cook time to 5 minutes.
8. When the timer beeps, turn off the cooker and quick-release the pressure.
9. Take off the paper and hit "chicken/meat" again.
10. Once the pot is boiling, add coconut milk and nutmeg.
11. Simmer for 5 minutes.
12. Serve with parsley!

Nutritional Info (¼ recipe per serving):
Total calories: 234
Protein: 11
Carbs: 11
Fat: 15
Fiber: 4

Cabbage with Chicken Sausage

Serves: 4
Time: 13 minutes (10 minutes prep time, 3 minutes cook time)

Cabbage is bland on its own; it loves salty, fatty additions like sausage. We're going with chicken sausage for this recipe, along with a sauce made from balsamic vinegar, sugar, mustard, and garlic. As a relatively tender vegetable, cabbage doesn't need to cook for very long. Three minutes under pressure should do the trick.

Ingredients:

- ☐ 1 pound chicken sausage
- ☐ 1 head's worth of cabbage
- ☐ 1 diced onion
- ☐ 3 minced garlic cloves
- ☐ 2 teaspoons balsamic vinegar
- ☐ 2 teaspoons Dijon mustard
- ☐ 2 teaspoons sugar
- ☐ Enough olive oil to coat your pressure cooker
- ☐ Salt and pepper to taste

Directions:

1. Pour just enough oil into your PPCXL to coat the bottom.
2. Hit "chicken/meat" and heat.
3. Add onion and sausage, and cook until brown.
4. Stir in rest of the ingredients and seal the lid.
5. Adjust cook time to 3 minutes.
6. When time is up, hit "cancel" and quick-release.
7. Serve!

Nutritional Info (¼ recipe per serving):
Total calories: 219
Protein: 25
Carbs: 19
Fat: 6
Fiber: 6

Corn with Cilantro Butter

Serves: 4
Time: 3 minutes (3 minutes cook time)

Summer is corn season, and it's great to have a really fast, really simple recipe to lean on. The corn is cooked in water, sugar, salt, chili powder, and butter, so the flavor is really locked in. When it's done, you just serve with melted butter that's been mixed with cilantro, and that's it!

Ingredients:

- ☐ 4 ears of shucked corn
- ☐ 1 ⅕ cups of water
- ☐ 6 tablespoons butter, divided
- ☐ 2 tablespoons minced cilantro
- ☐ ½ teaspoon salt
- ☐ ½ teaspoon chili powder
- ☐ ¼ teaspoon sugar

Directions:

1. Mix water, salt, chili powder, and sugar in your PPCXL.
2. Add corn and 2 tablespoons butter.
3. Seal the lid.
4. Hit "chicken/meat," adjusting time to 3 minutes.
5. In the meantime, add the rest of the butter to a saucepan and heat until it melts.
6. Add cilantro.
7. When the pressure cooker beeps, hit "cancel" and quick-release.
8. Serve corn with butter!

Nutritional Info (1 ear of corn + butter per serving):
Total calories: 309
Protein: 5
Carbs: 32
Fat: 21
Fiber: 12

Easy Baked Beans

Serves: 6

Time: 8 hours soak time/88 minutes (15 minutes prep time, 48 minutes cook time, 10 minutes natural pressure release, 15 minutes additional cook time)

Homemade baked beans are so much better than what you get in a can. The problem is dry beans take forever to cook. Well, they used to, until you started using the pressure cooker. Dry navy beans (that have been soaked for 8 hours) cook in a mixture of broth, balsamic vinegar, molasses, brown sugar, onion, and some other ingredients. There's also bacon, which makes everything better.

Ingredients:

- ☐ 2 cups dry navy beans
- ☐ 1 cup water
- ☐ 1 cup chicken broth
- ☐ 1 cup diced bacon
- ☐ ⅓ cup molasses
- ☐ ⅓ cup dark brown sugar
- ☐ ½ diced onion
- ☐ 2 tablespoons tomato paste
- ☐ 1 tablespoon balsamic vinegar
- ☐ 1 tablespoon Worcestershire sauce
- ☐ 1 teaspoon dry mustard
- ☐ 1 teaspoon salt
- ☐ 1 teaspoon black pepper

Directions:

1. Soak beans in water for at least 8 hours.
2. When the beans are soaked and you've thrown out any stones, turn your PPCXL to "chicken/meat."
3. Add bacon and cook until crispy.
4. Plate, leaving the fat in the cooker.
5. Add onions next, cooking until softened.
6. Hit "cancel" and stir in chicken stock, scraping up any stuck-on food particles.
7. Add in the rest of the ingredients (minus bacon), including beans, and stir. Make sure

the beans are just covered by liquid.

8. Seal the lead.
9. Hit "chicken/meat" again and adjust time to 48 minutes.
10. When time is up, hit "cancel" and wait 10 minutes before quick-releasing, because beans are a foamy food.
11. Add bacon and seal the lid again.
12. Hit "chicken/meat" and adjust time to 15 minutes.
13. When time is up, hit "cancel" and quick-release.
14. Serve!

Nutritional Info (⅙ recipe per serving):
Total calories: 238
Protein: 13
Carbs: 59
Fat: 2
Fiber: 10.5

Chapter 13

Paleo

BBQ Chicken + Sweet Potatoes

Serves: 4

Time: 37 minutes - not counting 1 hour for paleo BBQ sauce (15 minutes prep time, 22 minutes cook time)

The BBQ sauce is homemade in this recipe, so you know it's Paleo-friendly. The sauce needs to simmer for an hour, so plan accordingly. Once the sauce is done, you brown an onion and then throw beef and sweet potatoes in the cooker with some butter, spices, and BBQ sauce. 22 minutes later, and you're ready to eat!

Ingredients:

Chicken and sweet potatoes:
1 pound thawed chicken breasts
16-ounces diced sweet potatoes
1 diced onion
3 tablespoons grass-fed butter
3 tablespoons BBQ sauce
½ teaspoon onion powder
½ teaspoon garlic powder
Salt and pepper to taste

Paleo BBQ sauce (makes 1 ½ cups):
16-ounces tomato sauce
1 cup water
½ cup apple cider vinegar
5 tablespoons raw honey
2 tablespoons tomato paste
½ tablespoon onion powder
½ tablespoon pepper
½ teaspoon ground mustard
1 tablespoon lemon juice
1 teaspoon paprika

Directions:

1. To make the BBQ sauce, put all the ingredients in a saucepan over medium-high.
2. Bring to a boil, and then reduce heat to low.
3. Simmer for 1 hour.

4. Turn your PPCXL on to "chicken/meat" and heat 1 tablespoon of butter.
5. Add onion and cook until browned.
6. Add the sweet potatoes, rest of the butter, seasonings, and 3 tablespoons of your BBQ sauce.
7. Seal the lid.
8. Adjust cook time to 22 minutes.
9. When the timer beeps, hit "cancel" and quick-release the pressure.
10. Serve!

Nutritional Info (¼ of recipe per serving):
Total calories: 298
Protein: 20
Carbs: 25
Fat: 12
Fiber: 3.7

Beef + Plantain Curry with Coconut Milk

Serves: 5-6

Time: 1 hour, 47 minutes (40 minutes prep time, 42 minutes cook time, 20 minutes natural pressure release, 5 minute simmer time)

If you aren't a huge fan of very spicy curries, this one is very mild and tasty. The marinade is just a little coconut oil and dry spices - garlic, ginger, turmeric, and salt. You cook the beef with a cinnamon stick first after sautéing some onion, and then add a very ripe - practically black - plantain at the very end.

Ingredients:

Beef and plantains:

- ☐ 2 pounds cubed bottom blade pot roast
- ☐ 1 very ripe/black sliced and chopped plantain
- ☐ 2 peeled and sliced onions
- ☐ 1 cup coconut milk
- ☐ 1 tablespoon chopped coriander leaves
- ☐ 1 stick cinnamon
- ☐ 3 teaspoons coconut oil
- ☐ Sea salt to taste

Marinade:

- ☐ 2 teaspoons coconut oil
- ☐ 1 teaspoon ground garlic
- ☐ 1 teaspoon ground ginger
- ☐ 1 teaspoon ground turmeric
- ☐ 1 teaspoon sea salt

Directions:

1. Mix the marinade ingredients in a plastic bag, and add beef.
2. Shake to distribute evenly and store in fridge for half-hour.
3. When ready, turn your pressure cooker to "chicken/meat."
4. Add three teaspoons coconut oil and warm up.
5. Add onion and cook until translucent.
6. Move onions to a plate and add meat.
7. Brown evenly before plating with the onions.

8. Pour coconut milk into the pot, and stir to break up any stuck-on food bits.
9. Return meat and onions to the pot, with the cinnamon stick.
10. Seal the lid.
11. Adjust cook time to 42 minutes.
12. When time is up, hit "cancel" and wait for the pressure to come down.
13. Open the lid and hit "chicken/meat" again.
14. Add salt and plantain.
15. Keep stirring until the plantain is soft and cooked, and the curry has thickened.
16. Remove the cinnamon stick and sprinkle on coriander before serving.

Nutritional Info (⅕ of recipe per serving):
Total calories: 360
Protein: 41
Carbs: 14
Fat: 15
Fiber: 1.6

Easy Paleo Meatballs

Serves: 2
Time: 35 minutes (5 minutes prep time, 30 minutes cook time)

Meatballs are a great protein bomb for those on the Paleo diet. You can eat them as is or in zoodles with a good sauce. This recipe goes with grass-fed beef, grape jelly for sweetness, and an egg and arrowroot powder for structure. Cook under pressure for just a half-hour.

Ingredients:

- ☐ 1 pound grass-fed ground beef
- ☐ 1 egg
- ☐ 5 tablespoons 100% grape jelly
- ☐ ½ cup chili sauce
- ☐ ¼ cup arrowroot powder
- ☐ 1 teaspoon garlic salt
- ☐ ½ teaspoon chili powder
- ☐ ½ teaspoon paprika
- ☐ Black pepper to taste

Directions:

1. Mix beef, egg, arrowroot, garlic salt, and black pepper in a bowl.
2. Form meatballs.
3. Pour jelly, chili sauce, paprika, and chili powder into the cooker.
4. Add meatballs, coating in the sauce, and seal the lid.
5. Hit "chicken/meat" and adjust time to 30 minutes.
6. When the timer beeps, hit "cancel" and quick-release.
7. Serve with the sauce!

Nutritional Info (½ of recipe per serving):
Total calories: 583
Protein: 51
Carbs: 26
Fat: 19
Fiber: 0

Cashew Chicken

Serves: 4

Time: 32 minutes (10 minutes prep time, 12 minutes cook time, 10 minutes natural pressure release)

Chinese food is really tasty, but not always very healthy. This Paleo-friendly recipe sticks to real ingredients like organic ketchup, palm sugar, and rice wine vinegar. The raw cashews are added at the very end along with chopped green onions for a crunchy texture. Serve with rice.

Ingredients:

- ☐ 1 ½ pounds chopped skinless, boneless chicken breast
- ☐ ½ cup chopped raw cashews
- ☐ 1 chopped green onion
- ☐ 3 tablespoons coconut aminos
- ☐ 2 tablespoons rice wine vinegar
- ☐ 2 tablespoons arrowroot powder
- ☐ 2 tablespoons coconut palm sugar
- ☐ 1 tablespoon organic ketchup
- ☐ 1 tablespoon coconut oil
- ☐ 2 minced garlic cloves
- ☐ 1 teaspoon minced garlic
- ☐ ½ teaspoon black pepper

Directions:

1. Put arrowroot powder and black pepper in a bag, and shake with the chicken.
2. Add coconut oil to your PPCXL and warm on "chicken/meat."
3. Brown the chicken evenly.
4. Mix everything else in a bowl, minus cashews, and pour over chicken.
5. Stir and seal the lid.
6. Adjust cook time to 12 minutes.
7. When time is up, hit "cancel" and wait 10 minutes for a natural pressure release before quick-releasing.
8. Chicken's internal temperature should be 165-degrees. If it isn't ready, hit "chicken/meat" and cook until done with the lid off.
9. Serve with sauce, cashews, and green onions on top. For a full meal, serve with rice,

too.

Nutritional Info (¼ of recipe per serving):
Total calories: 346
Protein: 38
Carbs: 18
Fat: 13
Fiber: 1

Buffalo Chicken Wings

Serves: 4

Time: 22 minutes (5 minutes prep time, 12 minutes cook time, 5 minutes broil time)

You can never have too many chicken wing recipes. Pick up a Paleo-friendly hot sauce and a few pantry staples, and you'll be ready to make this easy meal. The dipping sauce made from whole milk yogurt and parsley is fresh and cool, which is perfect for the spiced wings.

Ingredients:

Wings:

- ☐ 2 pounds chicken wings
- ☐ 4 tablespoons Paleo-friendly hot sauce
- ☐ ¼ cup tomato puree
- ☐ ¼ cup honey
- ☐ 3 teaspoons salt

Sauce:

- ☐ 1 cup whole milk yogurt
- ☐ 1 tablespoon parsley

Directions:

1. Pour 1 cup of water into your pressure cooker and lower in steamer basket.
2. Slice the wings by cutting through the skin to the joint, and bending apart, so you have two pieces.
3. Put wings in the steamer basket.
4. Seal the lid.
5. Hit "chicken/meat" and adjust cook time to 12 minutes.
6. While that cooks, whisk hot sauce, tomato puree, honey, and salt in a bowl till smooth.
7. When the timer beeps, hit "cancel" and quick-release.
8. Mix wings with the sauce.
9. Line a cookie sheet with parchment paper and broil for 5 minutes, or until the wings become crispy.
10. Mix dipping sauce.
11. Serve!

Nutritional Info (¼ of recipe per serving):
Total calories: 543
Protein: 44
Carbs: 22
Fat: 32
Fiber: 0

Pina Colada Chicken

Serves: 4

Time: 33 minutes (18 minutes cook time, 10 minutes natural pressure release, 5 minutes thickening time)

This recipe reminds me of being in Hawaii, so what's not to love? You use affordable, tender chicken thighs, which are cooked with pineapple, coconut aminos, and full-fat coconut cream. After the pressure is down, you thicken the sauce with Paleo-friendly arrowroot powder and water.

Ingredients:

- ☐ 2 pounds chopped chicken thighs
- ☐ 1 cup pineapple chunks
- ☐ ½ cup full-fat coconut cream
- ☐ ½ cup chopped green onions
- ☐ 2 tablespoons coconut aminos
- ☐ 1 tablespoon water
- ☐ 1 teaspoon arrowroot
- ☐ 1 teaspoon cinnamon
- ☐ ⅛ teaspoon salt

Directions:

1. Put everything (except the green onions, arrowroot, and water) in the pressure cooker.
2. Seal the lid.
3. Hit "chicken/meat" and adjust time to 18 minutes.
4. When time is up, hit "cancel" and wait 10 minutes for a natural pressure release.
5. Mix arrowroot with water in a small bowl till smooth.
6. Hit "chicken/meat" again on your cooker and pour in bowl.
7. Stir until thickened.
8. Turn off cooker and serve with green onions.

Nutritional Info (¼ of recipe per serving):

Total calories: 531

Protein: 41

Carbs: 11

Fat: 36

Fiber: 0

Italian Stuffed Peppers

Serves: 4

Time: 33 minutes (10 minutes prep time, 18 minutes cook time, 5 minutes broil time)

Stuffed peppers are a great way to get in your much-needed servings of protein and vegetables. The filling is beef, bacon, zucchini, carrots, and more. It cooks in a tomato-based sauce in the PPCXL, before you broil them, so the mozzarella cheese topping becomes deliciously-melted and browned.

Ingredients:

Peppers:

- ☐ 1 pound ground beef
- ☐ 4 big yellow or red bell peppers
- ☐ ¾ cup cooked diced bacon
- ☐ 1 cup minced onion
- ☐ 2 shredded zucchinis
- ☐ 2 shredded carrots
- ☐ 2 minced garlic cloves
- ☐ 1 tablespoon dried basil
- ☐ 1 teaspoon dried parsley
- ☐ 1 teaspoon ground oregano
- ☐ 1 teaspoon black pepper
- ☐ 1 teaspoon salt
- ☐ Mozzarella cheese to taste

Sauce:

- ☐ ½ can tomato paste
- ☐ 1 teaspoon dried oregano
- ☐ 1 teaspoon dried basil
- ☐ Salt and pepper to taste

Directions:

1. Wring out veggies to get out excess moisture.
2. Mix carrots, zucchini, onion, garlic, bacon, and ground beef in a big bowl.
3. Add in spices. Leave filling in the bowl for now.
4. Stir the sauce ingredients in your pressure cooker.

5. Cut off the peppers stems and take out the seeds to create a hollow.
6. Stuff with filling.
7. Put inside the PPCXL, so the peppers are not touching the sides, and seal.
8. Hit "chicken/meat" and adjust cook time to 18 minutes.
9. When done, hit "cancel" and quick-release. Filling should read at 160-degrees, since they will finish cooking under the broiler.
10. Remove peppers and put in a baking dish.
11. Top with mozzarella cheese.
12. Broil for 2-3 minutes, until cheese is melted and beginning to brown.
13. Serve!

Nutritional Info (¼ of recipe per serving):
Total calories: 458
Protein: 34
Carbs: 20
Fat: 26
Fiber: 4

Blueberry-Coconut Pork Roast

Serves: 6
Time: 1.5 hours

Give your pork roast a fruity, tropical flare with fresh blueberries and rich coconut milk. Balsamic vinegar helps cut through the sweet creaminess, while a garnish of green onions brings a pop of acid to the party. The whole recipe only uses six ingredients, and takes about an hour and a half.

Ingredients:

- ☐ 3-4 pounds pork shoulder roast
- ☐ 2 cups fresh blueberries
- ☐ 1 cup full-fat coconut milk
- ☐ ⅓ cup chopped green onion
- ☐ 2 tablespoons balsamic vinegar
- ☐ 1 teaspoon salt

Directions:

1. Put everything except green onions in your pressure cooker and seal the lid.
2. Hit "chicken/meat" and adjust time to 1 hour, 30 minutes.
3. When time is up, hit "cancel" and carefully quick-release.
4. Garnish with green onions and serve!

Nutritional Info (¼ of recipe per serving):
Total calories: 872
Protein: 71
Carbs: 13
Fat: 52
Fiber: 1.8

Mocha-Rubbed Chuck Roast

Serves: 4

Time: 70 minutes (10 minutes prep time, 40 minutes cook time, 15 minutes natural pressure release, 5 minutes thickening time)

Are you a fan of coffee? If the answer is yes, you're going to love this chuck roast recipe. Even if you don't love coffee, you'll be happy, too. A 2 pound-chuck roast is chopped up, and then coated in 4 tablespoons of rub that includes finely-ground coffee, cocoa powder, ginger, and other spices. The beef cooks in a sauce with coffee, broth, figs, balsamic vinegar, and onion. The result is hearty and full of rich, deep flavor.

Ingredients:

Beef:
- ☐ 2 pounds cubed beef chuck roast
- ☐ 1 cup beef broth
- ☐ 1 cup brewed coffee
- ☐ 6 chopped, dried figs
- ☐ 1 chopped onion
- ☐ 3 tablespoons balsamic vinegar
- ☐ Salt and pepper to taste

Mocha rub:
- ☐ 2 tablespoons finely-ground coffee
- ☐ 2 tablespoons smoked paprika
- ☐ 1 tablespoon cocoa powder
- ☐ 1 tablespoon black pepper
- ☐ 1 teaspoon red pepper flakes
- ☐ 1 teaspoon ground ginger
- ☐ 1 teaspoon chili powder
- ☐ 1 teaspoon salt

Directions:

1. Mix the rub ingredients together.
2. Toss beef in 4 tablespoons of the rub.
3. In a blender, pulse brewed coffee, figs, vinegar, onion, and broth.
4. Put the beef in your PPCXL and pour over the sauce.

5. Seal the lid.
6. Select "chicken/meat" and adjust time to 40 minutes.
7. When time is up, hit "cancel" and wait 15 minutes before quick-releasing.
8. Internal temperature should be at 145-degrees.
9. Remove the meat and let it rest for at least 3 minutes.
10. To thicken sauce, hit "chicken/meat" again and bring to a boil.
11. Simmer until thickened to your liking.
12. Serve meat with plenty of sauce!

Nutritional Info (¼ of recipe per serving):
Total calories: 342
Protein: 33
Carbs: 13
Fat: 8
Fiber: 2.3

Duck Glazed in Key Lime

Serves: 6

Time: 1 hour, 5 minutes (30 minutes cook time, 5 minutes glaze time, 30 minutes oven time)

Duck is a protein that loves citrus, because it's fatty on its own. Key limes, orange, and lemon add much-needed acid and beautiful fruity flavor to a whole duck, while spices like cloves, cinnamon, and paprika add some sweet-and-spiciness. The whole dish takes just over an hour from start to finish, so it's a great option for a dinner party meal where you don't want to spend all your time cooking.

Ingredients:

- ☐ 1 large, whole duck
- ☐ 8-10 key limes
- ☐ 16-ounces orange marmalade
- ☐ 4 cups water
- ☐ 3 lemons
- ☐ 3 oranges
- ☐ ¼ cup orange juice
- ☐ 1 cinnamon stick
- ☐ 1 tablespoon brown sugar
- ☐ 1 teaspoon ground cloves
- ☐ 1 teaspoon paprika
- ☐ Dash of pepper

Directions:

1. Pour water into your pressure cooker.
2. Add one sliced lemon, one sliced orange, the cinnamon, and ground cloves.
3. Put the duck on top and seal the lid.
4. Hit "chicken/meat" and adjust cook time to 30 minutes.
5. When done, quick-release the pressure. As the duck cools, make the glaze by whisking together the marmalade, ½ cup fresh-squeezed orange juice from the remaining oranges, ¼ cup fresh-squeezed lemon juice, the zest of the lemon, ½ cup key lime juice and their zest, and brown sugar.
6. Pour ¾ cup of this glaze on the duck, getting it under the skin, too.
7. Put duck in a baking dish and cook for 15 minutes in a 400-degree oven.

8. Add the rest of the orange juice to the glaze and brush on the duck.
9. Cook for another 15 minutes to get a crispy skin.
10. Duck should be 170-degrees for medium-well.

Nutritional Info (⅙ of recipe per serving):
Total calories: 703
Carbs: 63
Protein: 54
Fat: 25
Fiber: 0

Chicken Pho

Serves: 4

Time: 1 hour, 2 minutes (5 minutes prep time, 17 minutes cook time, 20 minutes natural pressure release, 5 minutes rest time, 10 minutes soak time, 5 minutes assembly time)

Pho, the classic Vietnamese dish, can be prepared with several proteins. This recipe is for chicken pho, with apple, onion, ginger, and whole cloves. The broth is amazing; it's good enough to drink on its own, but for the sake of satisfying your hunger, you pour it over a bed of zoodles. You actually only use half of a pressure-cooked, 4-pound whole chicken, which you can use for lunch in another dish.

Ingredients:

Broth:

- ☐ 4-pound whole chicken
- ☐ 7 cups water
- ☐ 3 whole cloves
- ☐ 1 peeled, cored, and chopped Fuji apple
- ☐ 1 yellow onion
- ☐ ¾ cup chopped cilantro
- ☐ 2-inch thumb of peeled and sliced ginger
- ☐ 1 ½ tablespoons fish sauce
- ☐ 1 ½ teaspoons salt
- ☐ 1 teaspoon ground coriander

Extras:

- ☐ 4 spiralized zucchinis
- ☐ 2 thinly-sliced green onions
- ☐ ½ sliced yellow onion

Directions:

1. Hit "chicken/meat" on your PPCXL and add whole cloves.
2. Toast for a few minutes.
3. Stir in ginger and onion and cook for another minute or so.
4. Pour in 4 cups water and add chicken, the breast facing up.
5. Add cilantro, apple, salt, coriander, and rest of the water.

6. Seal the lid.
7. Adjust cook time to 17 minutes.
8. When time is up, hit "cancel" and wait 20 minutes.
9. Quick-release any leftover pressure.
10. Open the lid and wait 5 minutes.
11. Remove chicken and run cold water over it.
12. Soak in water for 10 minutes.
13. Pour out water, and put in a bowl.
14. Strain the broth in the pressure cooker and throw out the solids.
15. Season broth with salt and fish sauce.
16. Shred half of the meat, saving the rest for another meal.
17. Hit "chicken/meat" on the cooker to let the broth simmer.
18. Assemble bowls by adding a layer of zoodles on the bottom, adding chicken, and then pouring over 2 cups of broth per bowl.
19. Add green onion, yellow onion, salt, and pepper.
20. Serve hot!

Nutritional Info (⅙ of recipe per serving):
Total calories: 712
Protein: 59
Carbs: 14
Fat: 46
Fiber: 1

Thai Carrot Soup

Serves: 6

Time: 29 minutes (10 minutes prep time, 14 minutes cook time, 5 minutes puree time)

Not every soup needs to have meat to be delicious and satisfying. This soup recipe is creamy, sweet, spicy, and salty. The sweetness comes from over a pound of carrots and honey, the spicy is from jalapeno and Indian spices, while the salty is from fish sauce. Coconut milk gets stirred in at the very end, after you've pureed the soup, for a creamy finish.

Ingredients:

- ☐ 4 cups chicken broth
- ☐ 1 ¼ pounds chopped carrots
- ☐ ½ cup full-fat coconut milk
- ☐ 1 chopped yellow onion
- ☐ 1 seeded and chopped jalapeno
- ☐ 3 tablespoons raw honey
- ☐ 1 tablespoon olive oil
- ☐ 1 tablespoon fish sauce
- ☐ 2 teaspoons grated ginger
- ☐ ½ teaspoon curry powder
- ☐ ¼ teaspoon turmeric
- ☐ ¼ teaspoon garam masala

Directions:

1. Turn your PPCXL to "chicken/meat" and heat the oil.
2. Add onion and cook for 3-5 minutes, just before the onion is browning.
3. Add in carrot and jalapeno, stirring for a few minutes.
4. Pour in broth and all the spices.
5. Seal the lid.
6. Adjust cook time to 14 minutes.
7. When the timer beeps, hit "cancel" and quick-release.
8. Puree the soup till smooth.
9. Stir in honey and coconut milk.
10. Serve!

Nutritional Info (⅙ of recipe per serving):
Total calories: 127
Protein: 2
Carbs: 18
Fat: 6
Fiber: 2.3

Spiced Cauliflower Rice

Serves: 4
Time: 12 minutes (5 minutes prep time, 2 minutes cook time, 5 minutes toast time)

Paleo side dishes can be tricky, because you don't want meat as a side for a meat entree. This "rice" made from pressure-cooked cauliflower is toasted with a variety of spices for a tasty and healthy side anyone will enjoy. You can play with any spice you like; this recipe uses turmeric and cumin, which are easy to find, and pack in a lot of flavor.

Ingredients:

- 1 big head of cauliflower
- 2 tablespoons olive oil
- 1 lime
- ½ teaspoon dried parsley
- ¼ teaspoon salt
- ¼ teaspoon turmeric
- ¼ teaspoon cumin

Directions:

1. Wash cauliflower and chop, discarding the leaves.
2. Put in the steamer basket and lower into cooker.
3. Pour 1 cup of water into the cooker.
4. Seal the lid.
5. Hit "chicken/meat" and adjust cook time to just 2 minutes.
6. When time is up, hit "cancel" and quick-release.
7. Take out the cauliflower and pour out water.
8. Add oil and hit "chicken/meat" again, without putting on the lid.
9. Return the cauliflower to the pot, breaking it up with a wooden spoon or potato masher.
10. Throw in seasonings and stir, toasting everything together.
11. Squeeze on the lime before serving!

Nutritional Info (¼ of recipe per serving):

Total calories: 115
Protein: 4
Carbs: 12

Fat: 7
Fiber: 3

Chapter 14

Vegan

Vegetable Bolognese

Serves: 8

Time: 28 minutes (10 minutes prep time, 8 minutes cook time, 10 minutes natural pressure release)

Perfect for pasta or zoodles, this totally-vegan bolognese is made by pulsing small pieces of vegetables into even smaller bits. This helps them cook really quickly, so the whole recipe comes together in less than a half-hour. The veggies of choice are cauliflower, tomatoes, mushrooms, eggplant, and carrots.

Ingredients:

- ☐ Florets from ½ cauliflower head
- ☐ Two 28-ounce cans of crushed tomatoes
- ☐ One 10-ounce container of mushrooms
- ☐ 2 cups chopped eggplant
- ☐ 2 cups shredded carrots
- ☐ 1 cup water
- ☐ 6 minced garlic cloves
- ☐ 2 tablespoons balsamic vinegar
- ☐ 2 tablespoons agave nectar
- ☐ 2 tablespoons tomato paste
- ☐ 1 tablespoon dried basil
- ☐ 1 ½ tablespoons dried oregano
- ☐ 1 ½ teaspoons dried rosemary
- ☐ Salt and pepper to taste

Directions:

1. Pulse the cauliflower florets into a food processor until it has a rice-like texture.
2. Put into the PPCXL.
3. Add mushrooms to food processor and chop up.
4. Put in the PPCXL, too.
5. Pulse carrots and eggplant, and put in the pot.
6. Stir in water, tomatoes, garlic, agave, oregano, balsamic, basil, and rosemary.
7. Seal the lid.
8. Hit "chicken/meat" and adjust cook time to 8 minutes.

9. When time is up, hit "cancel" and wait for a natural pressure release.
10. Season to taste before serving.

Nutritional Info (⅛ recipe per serving):
Total calories: 139
Protein: 7
Carbs: 32
Fat: 1
Fiber: 5.7

Steamed Vegetable Dumplings

Serves: 4
Time: 32 minutes (25 minutes prep time, 7 minutes cook time)

Making homemade dumplings is like wrapping birthday presents, but they're for you, too. After cooking the gingery filling - cabbage, mushrooms, and carrots - in rice wine vinegar, olive oil, and tamari, you make the dumplings, which I think is really fun. You make 12, which isn't so many that you feel like the prep is taking forever. They steam in the pressure cooker for only 7 minutes.

Ingredients:

- 12 vegan dumpling wrappers (round)
- 1 ½ cups minced cabbage
- 1 cup minced shiitake mushrooms
- ½ cup shredded carrots
- 2 tablespoons tamari
- 1 tablespoon olive oil
- 1 tablespoon rice wine vinegar
- 1 teaspoon grated ginger

Directions:

1. Turn your pressure cooker to "chicken/meat" and add oil.
2. When shiny and hot, cook mushrooms until they begin to release their juice.
3. Add carrot, cabbage, tamari, and rice wine vinegar.
4. When the liquid has evaporated, hit "cancel" and carefully remove the pot and set on a pot holder. This stops the cooking process completely.
5. Mix in ginger.
6. Spray your steamer basket with a little vegan-friendly cooking oil.
7. Cut out a piece of parchment paper that will fit on top of the steamer.
8. Pour water into a small bowl.
9. Time to make the dumplings.
10. Put a wrapper on a cutting board and with a wet fingertip, swivel around the edge of the wrapper.
11. Add 1 tablespoon of filling in the center of the wrapper, and fold in half, pressing down, so the water acts like a glue on the dough.
12. When you've sealed all the dumplings, put in your steamer basket.

13. Wash out the pressure cooker pot and fill with 1 ½ cups water.
14. Return to the actual cooker and lower in the steamer basket, the parchment paper on top of it.
15. Seal the lid.
16. Hit "chicken/meat" and adjust time to 7 minutes. Since the PPCXL is a low-pressure cooker, this setting is okay for steaming the dumplings.
17. When time is up, hit "cancel" and quick-release the pressure.
18. Serve tamari as a dipping sauce.

Nutritional Info (3 dumplings per serving):
Total calories: 143
Protein: 5
Carbs: 25
Fat: 4
Fiber: 0

Chickpea Curry

Serves: 4

Time: 42 minutes (25 minutes prep time, 7 minutes cook time, 10 minutes natural pressure release)

Curry is one of a vegan's go-to meals, because there are so many ways to make it. This recipe is for a chickpea curry, with lots of flavors from just a few ingredients, like a garam masala spice blend, cumin, turmeric, and fresh ginger. Using canned chickpeas cuts down on cooking time. You can serve the curry as is, or put it on top of rice.

Ingredients:

- ☐ One 15-ounce can of washed and drained chickpeas
- ☐ 1 ½ cups water
- ☐ 3 chopped tomatoes
- ☐ 6 peeled and chopped garlic cloves
- ☐ ½ chopped red bell pepper
- ☐ 1 teaspoon lemon juice
- ☐ 1 teaspoon garam masala spice blend
- ☐ ½ teaspoon cumin
- ☐ ¼ teaspoon turmeric
- ☐ ½-inch thumb of ginger
- ☐ Salt and pepper to taste

Directions:

1. Hit "chicken/meat" on your pressure cooker and add oil.
2. When hot, add the red bell pepper and cook until it begins to brown.
3. Add garlic and ginger, and cook for just a minute.
4. Add spices and stir.
5. Pour in tomatoes and cook for 10-15 minutes, or until the tomatoes have become mushy.
6. With a wooden spoon, mash tomatoes a little, and add chickpeas, salt, black pepper, and 1 ½ cups water.
7. Seal the lid.
8. Adjust cook time to 7 minutes.
9. When the timer beeps, hit "cancel" and wait for a natural pressure release.
10. Taste and season more if necessary.

11. To serve, ladle on top of rice, or eat as is.

Nutritional Info (¼ recipe per serving):
Total calories: 511
Protein: 31
Carbs: 80
Fat: 8
Fiber: 5.7

Sweet Potato + Peanut Butter Soup

Serves: 4

Time: 20 minutes (10 minutes prep time, 5 minutes cook time, 5 minutes natural pressure release)

Peanut butter may seem like an odd choice for soup, but it adds a lovely creaminess and nutty flavor that is perfectly-suited to sweet potatoes. The sweetness of those two ingredients is cut with lime juice, garlic, onion, and green chiles. This may be a new cooking adventure for you, but rest assured, it is a delicious one.

Ingredients:

- ☐ 3 large cubed sweet potatoes
- ☐ One 15-ounce can of diced tomatoes (liquid saved)
- ☐ One 14-ounce can of full-fat coconut milk
- ☐ 2 cups veggie broth
- ☐ 3 chopped garlic cloves
- ☐ 1 chopped onion
- ☐ One 4-ounce can of green chilis
- ☐ ½ cup peanut butter
- ☐ 1 tablespoon lime juice
- ☐ ½ teaspoon allspice
- ☐ ¼ teaspoon ground cilantro

Directions:

1. Turn your PPCXL to "chicken/meat" and add oil.
2. When hot and shimmery, add onion and garlic.
3. When softened, turn off the cooker.
4. Stir in the rest of the ingredients.
5. Seal the lid.
6. Hit "chicken/meat" again and adjust cook time to 5 minutes.
7. When time is up, hit "cancel" and wait for a natural pressure release.
8. When the pressure is all gone, stir and then puree until silky-smooth.
9. Serve!

Nutritional Info (¼ recipe per serving):
Total calories: 286
Protein: 8
Carbs: 29
Fat: 16
Fiber: 6

Vegan Chocolate Cheesecake

Serves: 8

Time: 6 hours, 16 minutes (10 minutes prep time, 66 minutes cook time, 1 hour cool time, 4 hours chill time)

Desserts for vegans can be tricky, because so many baked goods use dairy. In this recipe, the filling is made from soaked cashews, chocolate nut milk, and non-dairy chocolate chips. You'll be using two types of flour - almond and coconut. To save on time the day of making the cake, soak the cashews in water for at least four hours in advance. The recipe takes over 6 hours, but the majority of that time is taken up by chilling the completed cheesecake, so plan accordingly.

Ingredients:

Crust:

- ☐ 1 ½ cups almond flour
- ☐ ¼ cup melted coconut oil
- ☐ ¼ cup agave syrup

Filling:

- ☐ 1 ½ cups soaked and drained cashews
- ☐ 1 cup chocolate nut milk
- ☐ ⅔ cups sugar
- ☐ ¼ cup non-dairy chocolate chips
- ☐ 2 tablespoons coconut flour
- ☐ 2 teaspoons pure vanilla
- ☐ ½ teaspoon salt

Directions:

1. Mix the crust ingredients and press with clean fingers into the bottom of a 7-inch cheesecake pan (pressure cooker safe, like silicone) and about halfway up the sides.
2. Put in the fridge for now.
3. Pulse all the filling ingredients (minus chocolate chips) in a blender until smooth.
4. Stir in the chips.
5. Pour batter into the pan.
6. Pour 1 ¾ cups water into your pressure cooker and insert trivet.
7. Put the pan on top of the trivet and close the cooker lid.
8. Hit "chicken/meat" and adjust time to 66 minutes

9. When time is up, hit "cancel" and allow a 10-minute natural pressure release.
10. Release the remaining pressure through the valve.
11. Take out the pan and cool on the counter for 1 hour.
12. Chill in the fridge covered in saran wrap for at least 4 hours before serving.

Nutritional Info (⅛ recipe per serving):
Total calories: 396
Protein: 8
Carbs: 36
Fat: 26
Fiber: 1

Black-Eyed Pea Lunch Cakes

Serves: 4

Time: 1 hour, 45 minutes (1 hour soak time, 15 minutes prep time, 30 minutes cook time)

The ideal portable lunch food, these black-eyed pea cakes are only 158 calories for two cakes, and pack in 29 grams of protein! The flavors from a roasted red pepper, Old Bay seasoning, and onion are bold and inviting. In addition to being vegan, the recipe is also oil free.

Ingredients:

- ☐ 1 cup dried black-eyed peas
- ☐ ¼ cup veggie broth
- ☐ 1 chopped onion
- ☐ 1 roasted red pepper
- ☐ 1 tablespoon tomato paste
- ☐ 1 ½ - 2 teaspoons Old Bay seasoning
- ☐ 1 teaspoon salt
- ☐ ¼ teaspoon white pepper

Directions:

1. Pick out any stones from the dried peas.
2. Soak in a bowl of hot water (2-inches above peas) for one hour.
3. Drain and pulse in a food processor until they've just broken apart.
4. Move to a bowl and cover in clean, cool water.
5. With your fingers, peel off the skins by rubbing, until they're white.
6. Return peas to food processor, along with tomato paste, 2 tablespoons of broth, onion, and red pepper.
7. Pulse until smooth.
8. Move to a bowl and add seasonings. If the mixture is too thick to pour, add a bit more broth.
9. Grease eight ramekins with a vegan-friendly spray and pour batter into them, so they're ½ full.
10. Wrap tightly in foil.
11. Pour 1 cup of water into the pressure cooker and lower in trivet.
12. Put ramekins on top and seal lid.
13. Hit "chicken/meat" and adjust time to 30 minutes.

14. When the timer goes off, hit "cancel" and quick-release the pressure.
15. To make sure the cakes are done, poke a toothpick in the center. If it's mostly clean, it's done. They'll keep cooking just a little longer after they're out of the cooker, so a crumb or two is okay.
16. Eat!

Nutritional Info (2 cakes per serving):
Total calories: 158
Protein: 29
Carbs: 9
Fat: 1
Fiber: 5

Personal Vegetable Pot Pies

Serves: 5
Time: 48 minutes (15 minutes biscuit time, 30 minutes prep time, 3 minutes cook time)

Homemade biscuits and savory vegetable filling make up a fantastic cool-weather meal and lunch leftovers, if there are any. You make your own vegan biscuits from scratch with just five ingredients, before cooking onion and garlic in your pressure cooker. Whisk in flour, broth, almond milk, and bay leaves for flavor. Since you use frozen vegetables, the cook time is cut down, so the ramekins with filling and biscuit on top takes only 3 minutes to cook.

Cooking Tip: If you don't want to bother washing your pressure cooker in the middle of the recipe, cook your sauce in a separate skillet.

Ingredients:

Biscuits:
- ☐ 2-2 ¼ cups unbleached all-purpose flour
- ☐ 1 ¼ cups cold, full-fat coconut milk
- ☐ 1 tablespoon vinegar
- ☐ 1 tablespoon cane sugar
- ☐ 3 teaspoons baking powder
- ☐ ½ teaspoon salt

Filling:
- ☐ 2 cups veggie broth
- ☐ 2 cups mixed, frozen veggies
- ☐ 2 bay leaves
- ☐ 1 minced garlic clove
- ☐ ½ medium yellow onion
- ☐ ¼ cup unsweetened almond milk
- ☐ ¼ cup flour
- ☐ Salt and pepper to taste

Directions:

1. To make the biscuits, mix the flour, sugar, salt, and baking powder in a bowl.
2. In a separate bowl, mix coconut milk and vinegar.

3. Form a well in the dry ingredients, and pour in contents of the wet bowl.

4. Slowly mix until just combined; don't overmix.

5. Dust a cutting board with flour, as well as your hands, and pat dough until it's ¾-inch thick. If it's too wet to work with, add flour 1 tablespoon at a time.

6. Wet a cookie cutter or rim of a glass, and cut out five biscuits. Store in the fridge for now.

7. Now it's time for the filling. Turn your PPCXL to "chicken/meat" and add garlic and onion.

8. Cook until the onion has softened.

9. Whisk in flour, quickly, and gradually pour in broth, still whisking.

10. Add bay leaves and almond milk.

11. Simmer for 10 minutes.

12. Prepare 5 ramekins with cooking spray.

13. When the filling has thickened in the cooker, throw in frozen vegetables and cook for another 5 minutes.

14. Season with salt and pepper.

15. Hit "cancel" and pick out bay leaves.

16. Carefully pour filling into your ramekins.

17. Wash your pressure cooker pot.

18. When clean and dry, pour in 1 cup of water and the steamer basket.

19. Put one raw biscuit on top of each ramekin and wrap loosely in foil to allow the biscuits to rise.

20. Put the cooker in the basket, and seal the lid.

21. Hit "chicken/meat" again and adjust cook time to just 3 minutes.

22. When the timer beeps, hit "cancel" and quick-release the pressure.

23. Cool a few minutes and serve!

Nutritional Info (1 ramekin with biscuit per serving):
Total calories: 307
Protein: 8.3
Carbs: 41
Fiber: 4.7
Fat: 12

Mexican Casserole

Serves: 4

Time: 35 minutes cook time (+ 2-hours soak time for beans)

When you don't have much in your pantry, this casserole made from vegan staples like brown rice and black beans is extremely easy to throw together. The spices are what make this dish so good - onion powder, chili powder, minced garlic, and salt. The only thing you have to remember is since you're using dry black beans, you need to soak them at least two hours beforehand. If you don't have time or only have canned beans, that's just fine, too.

Ingredients:

- ☐ 5 cups water
- ☐ 2 cups uncooked brown rice
- ☐ 1 cup soaked black beans
- ☐ 6-ounces tomato paste
- ☐ 2 teaspoons onion powder
- ☐ 2 teaspoons chili powder
- ☐ 1 teaspoon garlic
- ☐ 1 teaspoon salt

Directions:

1. At least two hours before dinner, submerge beans in water and soak.
2. When two hours is done, drain and put in the PPCXL.
3. Add everything else and seal the lid.
4. Hit "chicken/meat" and adjust cook time to 35 minutes.
5. When the timer beeps, hit "cancel" and quick-release the pressure.
6. Taste and season if needed before serving.

Nutritional Info (¼ recipe per serving):

Total calories: 322

Protein: 6

Carbs: 63

Fat: 2

Fiber: 9

Maple Syrup Carrots

Serves: 4
Time: 25 minutes (5 minutes prep time, 15 minutes cook time, 5 minutes simmer time)

One of the best vegan sweeteners, maple syrup turns carrots into deliciously-caramelized treats with only 117 calories per cup. Even kids (or adults, for that matter) who hate vegetables will get addicted to this side dish and keep asking you to make it again and again.

Ingredients:

- ☐ 4 cups carrots
- ☐ 1 cup water
- ☐ 2 tablespoons maple syrup
- ☐ 1 tablespoon vegan butter
- ☐ Dash of salt

Directions:

1. Put the butter, syrup, salt, and water into your pressure cooker.
2. Hit "chicken/meat" and stir until the butter is melted and incorporated into the syrup.
3. Stir in carrots to coat.
4. Seal the lid.
5. Cook the default setting for "chicken/meat," which is 15 minutes.
6. When the timer goes off, press "cancel" and quick-release the pressure.
7. Open the lid and hit "chicken/meat" again.
8. Cook until all the liquid has evaporated.
9. Serve!

Nutritional Info (1 cup per serving):
Total calories: 117
Protein: 2
Carbs: 23
Fat: 2
Fiber: 3.4

Sweet Potato Chili

Serves: 4

Time: 32 minutes (10 minutes prep time, 12 minutes cook time, 10 minutes natural pressure release)

One of the comfort dishes a lot of vegans miss is chili. Its filling meatiness was designed for cold days, so when winter comes rolling around, you need a vegan-friendly version ready to go. Packed with spices and hearty vegetables like sweet potatoes, two kinds of beans, and bell pepper, you won't even notice the meat is missing. You might notice that the recipe also calls for 2 teaspoons of cocoa powder; you read that right. A bit of unsweetened chocolate adds a deep richness that mimics the long-cooked taste that slow-simmered chili usually has.

Ingredients:

- ☐ 2 cups vegetable broth
- ☐ One 28-ounce can of diced tomatoes (liquid saved)
- ☐ One 15-ounce can rinsed and drained kidney beans
- ☐ 1 15-ounce can rinsed and drained black beans
- ☐ 1 medium-sized peeled and chopped sweet potato
- ☐ 4 minced garlic cloves
- ☐ 1 chopped green bell pepper
- ☐ 1 chopped red onion
- ☐ 1 chopped red bell pepper
- ☐ 1 tablespoon chili powder
- ☐ 1 tablespoon olive oil
- ☐ 2 teaspoons unsweetened cocoa powder
- ☐ 1 teaspoon cayenne pepper
- ☐ 1 teaspoon ground cumin
- ☐ ¼ teaspoon ground cinnamon
- ☐ Sea salt and pepper to taste

Directions:

1. Turn your PPCXL to "chicken/meat."
2. Heat oil and add sweet potato, onion, and the bell peppers.
3. Stir until the onions are beginning to turn translucent.
4. Toss in spices and beans, and pour in tomatoes with their liquid, and broth.
5. Stir well before sealing the lid.

6. Adjust cook time to 12 minutes.
7. When the timer beeps, hit "cancel" and allow the pressure to come down naturally.
8. You'll know the potatoes are done when they fall apart easily under your fork.
9. Season more if needed.
10. Serve!

Nutritional Info (¼ of recipe per serving):
Total calories: 297
Protein: 16
Carbs: 53
Fat: 4
Fiber: 35

Sesame-Broccoli Tofu with Sweet Potato

Serves: 4
Time: 15 minutes (10 minutes prep time, 5 minutes cook time)

No collection of vegan recipes would be complete without tofu. Tofu is made from soy milk, and provides a blank canvas where a myriad of spices can play. For this recipe, it's only fitting that we look to Asia, and go with flavors from tamari (gluten-free soy sauce), tahini, which is made from sesame seeds, sriracha, and toasted sesame oil. The tofu is served with sweet potato and broccoli, and offers 17 grams of protein.

Ingredients:

- ☐ 1 pound extra-firm + cubed tofu
- ☐ 2 cups broccoli florets
- ☐ 2 cups sliced yellow onion
- ☐ 1 cup peeled, diced sweet potato
- ☐ ⅓ cup veggie broth
- ☐ 3 minced garlic cloves
- ☐ 1-2 tablespoons tamari
- ☐ 2 tablespoons sesame seeds
- ☐ 2 tablespoons tahini
- ☐ 2 tablespoons sriracha
- ☐ 1 tablespoon rice vinegar
- ☐ 2 teaspoons toasted sesame oil

Directions:

1. Turn your cooker to "chicken/meat" and pour in toasted sesame oil.
2. When warm, cook the sweet potato and onion for just 2 minutes.
3. Toss in minced garlic along with 1 tablespoon of the sesame seeds.
4. After just a minute, add tamari, vinegar, broth, and tofu in the cooker.
5. Seal the lid.
6. Adjust cook time to 3 minutes.
7. When the timer beeps, hit "cancel" and quick-release.
8. Add the broccoli and seal the lid again.
9. Hit "chicken/meat" and adjust cook time to 2 minutes.
10. When that cycle is done, hit "cancel" and quick-release.
11. Stir in tahini and sriracha.
12. Serve with the rest of the sesame seeds sprinkled on top.

Nutritional Info (¼ recipe per serving):
Total calories: 250
Protein: 17
Carbs : 22
Fat: 12
Fiber: 2

Lentil Sloppy Joe's

Serves: 6

Time: 57 minutes (10 minutes prep time, 32 minutes cook time, 15 minutes natural pressure release)

In terms of fiber and folate, lentils are a superfood. They're extremely good for your heart and cook faster than most dried beans. You'll see them often in soup, but what are some other ways you can prepare them? This Sloppy Joe recipe takes out the meat, and replaces it with green lentils. All the other Joe ingredients - like crushed tomatoes, onion, and mustard - remain intact, so you get that classic Joe flavor with added nutritional benefits!

Ingredients:

- ☐ One 14-ounce can of crushed tomatoes
- ☐ 3 cups veggie broth
- ☐ 2 cups green lentils
- ☐ 1 stemmed and chopped red bell pepper
- ☐ 1 chopped yellow onion
- ☐ 2 tablespoons soy sauce
- ☐ 1 tablespoon olive oil
- ☐ 1 tablespoon coconut sugar
- ☐ 1 tablespoon Dijon mustard
- ☐ 1 teaspoon black pepper

Directions:

1. Hit "chicken/meat" on your PPCXL and heat the oil.
2. Cook onion and pepper until they're softened.
3. Pour in broth and soy sauce, and add lentils, brown sugar, tomatoes, Dijon, and black pepper.
4. Stir well, so the sugar dissolves.
5. Seal the lid.
6. Adjust cook time to 32 minutes.
7. When the timer beeps, hit "cancel" and wait for a natural pressure release.
8. Stir and serve.

Nutritional Info (⅙ of recipe per serving):
Total calories: 164
Protein: 9
Carbs: 38
Fat: 3
Fiber: .3

Seitan Slices with Italian Seasonings

Makes: 1 pound
Time: 29 minutes (10 minutes prep time, 19 minutes cook time)

Seitan is a meat substitute made from wheat gluten and nutritional yeast. It's kind of an odd food if you haven't had it before, but it contains a lot of protein and in the pressure cooker, is pretty easy to prepare. If you've ever made homemade bread, seitan will be a breeze, and if you haven't, it's easy to pick up quickly. You can add any seasonings you like to a plain seitan recipe; in this one, we're going with Italian flavors. Serve as the main protein in spaghetti, over zoodles, or even in sandwiches with tomato sauce and vegan cheese.

Note: Store extra seitan in a Tupperware with some veggie broth to prevent drying. It lasts in the fridge for one week. If you want to freeze, wrap the slices in saran wrap. It lasts 2 months frozen.

Ingredients:

- [ ] 1 cup vital wheat gluten
- [ ] ¾ cup vegetable broth
- [ ] 3 tablespoons nutritional yeast
- [ ] 1 tablespoon smoked paprika
- [ ] 2 teaspoons Italian seasoning
- [ ] 1 teaspoon garlic powder

Directions:

1. Mix everything in a bowl and form a sticky dough ball.
2. Knead with your hands for a few minutes.
3. Form the dough into the shape of a sausage or long bread loaf.
4. Cut into slices with a sharp, wet knife.
5. Grease the inside of your pressure cooker with a vegan-friendly spray.
6. Put the seitan slices inside and pour in water, so they're covered.
7. Seal the lid.
8. Hit "chicken/meat" and adjust time to 19 minutes.
9. When the timer beeps, hit "cancel" and quick-release.
10. Serve!

Nutritional Info (⅓ recipe per serving)
Total calories: 195
Protein: 26
Carbs: 15
Fat: 2
Fiber: 1.6

Fast Baked Potatoes

Serves: 4

Time: 27 minutes (12 minutes cook time, 15 minutes natural pressure release)

A baked potato is what could be called "peasant" food in that it's cheap, easy, and satisfying. In the pressure cooker, four big potatoes only take 12 minutes to cook to perfection. For seasoning, you can add anything you like. In this recipe, we're just going to use simple salt, pepper, and vegan butter.

Ingredients:

- ☐ 4 large potatoes
- ☐ 1 cup of water
- ☐ Salt and pepper to taste
- ☐ Vegan butter

Directions:

1. Pour water into the PPCXL and insert steamer rack or basket.
2. Put the whole potatoes in.
3. Seal the lid.
4. Hit "chicken/meat" and adjust time to 12 minutes.
5. When the timer beeps, hit "cancel" and wait for a natural pressure release.
6. To serve potatoes, cut open and serve with salt, pepper, and vegan butter. You can add any other spices or herbs you would like.

Nutritional Info (1 potato per serving):
Total calories: 110
Protein: 4
Carbs: 26
Fat: 0
Fiber: 2

Turmeric-Spiced Mashed Cauliflower

Serves: 4

Time: 13 minutes (6 minutes cook time, 2 minutes natural pressure release, 5 minutes mash time)

A much healthier alternative than mashed potatoes, this simple vegan side dish is creamy and savory in all the right ways. It just takes a few dashes of black pepper, salt, and turmeric to make plain-tasting cauliflower sing. Vegan butter adds creaminess, while a sprinkle of chives adds some freshness. This recipe is a great way to use up a whole head of cauliflower.

Ingredients:

- ☐ 1 whole cauliflower
- ☐ 1 ½ cups water
- ☐ 1 tablespoon vegan butter
- ☐ 3 chopped chives
- ☐ ½ teaspoon black pepper
- ☐ ½ teaspoon turmeric
- ☐ ¼ teaspoon salt

Directions:

1. Pour water into your PPCXL and insert steamer basket.
2. Put the cauliflower in the basket and seal the lid.
3. Hit "chicken/meat" and cook for 6 minutes.
4. When time is up, hit "cancel" and wait 2 minutes before quick-releasing.
5. The cauliflower should be soft enough to mash easily with a potato masher.
6. Mix with butter and seasonings.
7. Garnish with chives before serving.

Nutritional Info (¼ recipe per serving):
Total calories: 75
Protein: 4
Carbs: 12
Fat: 3
Fiber: 5.2

Chapter 15

Holiday Food

Cranberry-Spiced Beef Roast

Serves: 4-6

Time: 2 hours, 15 minutes (25 minutes prep time, 90 minutes cook time, 20 minutes natural pressure release)

Christmas is a popular time to make a fancy beef recipe, but you don't want to spend all day on it. Taking 2 hours and 15 minutes from start to finish, preparing this roast won't eat up all your day, but you will want to eat it all up. Cooked with whole cranberries, whole garlic, cinnamon, honey, and just a pinch of horseradish powder, your pressure cooker will look like you went foraging in the forest for all the best ingredients. Your taste buds will definitely agree.

Ingredients:

- ☐ 3-4 pounds beef roast
- ☐ 2 cups bone broth
- ☐ 1 cup whole cranberries
- ☐ 6 whole cloves
- ☐ ½ cup water
- ☐ ½ cup white wine
- ☐ ¼ cup honey
- ☐ 2 peeled whole garlic cloves
- ☐ One 3-inch cinnamon stick
- ☐ 2 tablespoons olive oil
- ☐ 1 teaspoon horseradish powder
- ☐ Salt and pepper to taste

Directions:

1. Pat your roast dry with paper towels.
2. Season evenly with salt and pepper.
3. Turn your cooker to "chicken/meat" and add olive oil.
4. When hot, add the roast and brown all over for 8-10 minutes.
5. Remove the meat and plate.
6. Pour in wine and deglaze, scraping up the burnt-on food bits.
7. Stir for 4-5 minutes to burn off the alcohol.
8. Add water, honey, garlic, whole cloves, cranberries, cinnamon, and horseradish

powder.

9. After 4-5 minutes of stirring, the cranberries will begin to burst.
10. Return the meat to the pot and pour in bone broth.
11. Seal the lid.
12. Adjust cook time to 90 minutes.
13. When time is up, hit "cancel" and wait 20 minutes for a natural pressure release.
14. Quick-release any leftover pressure.
15. Remove the meat, put it on a plate, and pour on some of the sauce.
16. Pour the rest of the sauce in a pitcher to serve at dinner.

Nutritional Info (¼ recipe per serving)

Total calories: 362
Protein: 25
Carbs: 31
Fat: 15
Fiber: 1

Braised Lamb Shanks

Serves: 4-6

Time: 55 minutes (20 minutes prep time, 30 minutes cook time, 5 minutes thickening time)

Packed with high-quality protein, this lamb recipe is the definition of "savory." Browning the lamb and cooking aromatic carrots, onion, garlic, tomatoes, and lemon zest ensure a broth that's full of rich flavor. The meat only takes about a half hour to cook perfectly, and then you quick-release the pressure. For a thicker gravy, add water and flour.

Ingredients:

- ☐ 4-6 trimmed lamb shanks
- ☐ 2 quartered tomatoes
- ☐ 3 peeled and sliced carrots
- ☐ ¾ cup red wine
- ☐ ¼ cup beef stock
- ☐ ¼ cup flour
- ☐ 1 chopped onion
- ☐ 1 crushed garlic clove
- ☐ 1 tablespoon chopped oregano
- ☐ 8 teaspoons olive oil
- ☐ 8 teaspoons cold water
- ☐ 4 teaspoons flour
- ☐ 1 teaspoon grated lemon zest
- ☐ Salt and black pepper to taste

Directions:

1. Put the lamb shanks in a plastic baggie, and add ¼ cup flour.
2. Shake well.
3. Turn your pressure cooker to "chicken/meat" and add 4 teaspoons oil.
4. Brown the shanks on both sides and plate.
5. Pour in the rest of the oil, along with the garlic, carrots, and onion.
6. Cook for 5 minutes, stirring, so the food doesn't stick.
7. Add tomatoes, oregano, lemon zest, and pour in beef stock and wine.
8. Once boiling, add the meat and sprinkle with salt and pepper.
9. Seal the lid.
10. Adjust cook time to 30 minutes.

11. When time is up, hit "cancel" and quick-release. Meat should have an internal temp of at least 145-degrees to be medium-rare.
12. Remove the meat and hit "chicken/meat" again.
13. Mix water and flour in a small bowl, and pour into the cooker to thicken the gravy.
14. Serve!

Nutritional Info (¼ recipe):
Total calories: 804
Protein: 73.7
Carbs: 19
Fat: 42.9
Fiber: 2.9

Lamb Stew with Dates + Walnuts

Serves: 4

Time: 1 hour, 30 minutes (20 minutes prep time, 45 minutes cook time, 25 minutes natural pressure release)

If you've been wanting to try something a bit different for a holiday dinner, how about lamb stew? It's more common in the Middle East than the United States, but the ingredients are just as easily found over here. You coat a leg of lamb in cinnamon, ginger, allspice, and salt, and brown it with red onion. The cooking liquid is apple juice and chicken broth with dates and walnuts. It all cooks together for just 45 minutes followed by a natural pressure release, and you've got a dish with complex flavors that's easy to throw together.

Ingredients:

- ☐ 2 ½ pounds boneless leg of lamb
- ☐ 1 cup halved and pitted dried dates
- ☐ ½ cup chicken broth
- ☐ ½ cup walnuts
- ☐ ½ cup unsweetened apple juice
- ☐ 1 thinly-sliced red onion
- ☐ 2 tablespoons olive oil
- ☐ ½ tablespoon ground cinnamon
- ☐ 1 teaspoon ground ginger
- ☐ ½ teaspoon salt
- ☐ ¼ teaspoon allspice

Directions:

1. Mix cinnamon, ginger, allspice, and salt in a bowl.
2. Coat lamb evenly in the rub.
3. Turn your PPCXL to "chicken/meat" and add oil.
4. When hot and shimmering, cook onion for 5 minutes.
5. Add meat and brown all over.
6. Pour in apple juice, broth, dates, and walnuts.
7. Scrape the pot to break up any stuck-on food.
8. Seal the lid.
9. Adjust cook time to 45 minutes.
10. When time is up, hit "cancel" and wait for a natural pressure release.

11. Stir before serving.

Nutritional Info (¼ recipe):
Total calories: 897
Protein: 76
Carbs: 23
Fat: 57
Fiber: 1

Cranberry Turkey Wings

Serves: **4**

Time: 50 minutes (15 minutes prep time, 30 minutes cook time, 5 minutes broil/simmer time)

Autumn is cranberry season, and if you've only ever used dried ones, you're missing out. Try your hand at a recipe with fresh berries that are tart and full of juices. They cook with walnuts, onion, and thyme to flavor tender turkey wings. When the wings are done, you broil them for a few minutes to get a crispy skin while you simmer the sauce in the pressure cooker, creating a sweet-sour, buttery gravy.

Ingredients:

- 4 meal-sized turkey wings
- 1 ½ cups fresh cranberries
- 1 cup chopped walnuts
- 1 cup natural (no sugar added) orange juice
- 1 sliced onion
- 1 handful of fresh thyme
- 2 tablespoons butter
- 2 tablespoons olive oil
- Salt and pepper to taste

Directions:

1. Turn your PPCXL to "chicken/meat" and add butter and oil.
2. Once those have melted together and are hot, add turkey wings.
3. Brown on both sides, seasoning with salt and pepper.
4. Remove turkey and add onions, before putting the turkey back on top of the onions in the cooker.
5. Toss in walnuts, thyme, and cranberries.
6. Pour orange juice over everything and seal the lid.
7. Adjust cook time to 30 minutes.
8. When time is up, hit "cancel" and wait 10 minutes before quick-releasing any remaining pressure.
9. Pick out the bunch of thyme.
10. Move the turkey to a baking dish and stick under the broiler for 5 minutes to get a crispy skin.

11. While that broils, turn the cooker back to "chicken/meat" to let the sauce simmer.
12. Once it's reduced by about half, it's ready.
13. Pour sauce over turkey wings and serve!

Nutritional Info (1 wing per serving):
Total calories: 340
Protein: 6
Carbs: 16
Fat: 19
Fiber: 0

Ginger-Spiced Duck with Dried Apples

Serves: 4

Time: 59 minutes (15 minutes prep time, 44 minutes cook time)

If you haven't cooked duck before, the holiday season provides an excellent excuse to give it a try. Duck's naturally "wild" taste is sweetened with white wine, dried apples, and candied ginger. In a switch from most recipes, you brown the duck first, so it releases some of its fat. That's what you cook the onion in, giving the onion an even richer, sweeter taste.

Note: The FDA recommends that all poultry should be cooked to 165-170°F, but duck is more like steak, and isn't as prone to salmonella as other poultry. Top chefs tend to cook duck so it's still a little pink, which is around the 135-145° range.

Ingredients:

- ☐ 4 duck leg-and-thigh quarters
- ☐ 1 ¼ cups dry, fruity white wine
- ☐ 1 cup packed + chopped dried apples
- ☐ 1 chopped yellow onion
- ☐ 2 tablespoons minced candied ginger
- ☐ 1 tablespoon olive oil
- ☐ ¼ teaspoon ground ginger
- ☐ ¼ teaspoon salt
- ☐ ¼ teaspoon pepper

Directions:

1. Add olive oil in your pressure cooker on the "chicken/meat" setting.
2. Season duck with salt, pepper, and ginger.
3. Add to the cooker and brown for 4 minutes on each side.
4. Plate and hit "cancel" on the cooker.
5. Drain fat from the cooker, leaving a few tablespoons.
6. Turn cooker back to "chicken/meat" and add onion, cooking in the duck fat for 3 minutes.
7. Pour in wine and deglaze, scraping up any stuck-on duck and onion bits.
8. Add apples and candied ginger.
9. Return the duck, too, with the skin-side facing up.
10. Seal the lid.

11. Adjust cook time to 44 minutes.
12. When the timer beeps, hit "cancel" and quick-release.
13. Duck should have an internal temp of at least 135-degrees to be medium-rare, which is how good duck should be served.
14. Serve with the pressure-cooker sauce.

Nutritional Info (¼ of recipe per serving):
Total calories: 388
Protein: 28
Carbs: 26
Fat: 15
Fiber: 1

Brown-Sugar Baked Ham

Serves: 6

Time: 1 hour, 43 minutes (5 minutes prep time, 38 minutes cook time, 1 hour oven time)

A classic spring holiday dish, sweet baked ham is easy and tasty. It makes great leftovers, too. It's hard to find someone who doesn't like it. You'll notice that it does take an hour in the oven to finish cooking, but without a pressure cooker, you'd have to boil ham for 2-3 hours first. The PPCXL cuts down significantly on that time.

Ingredients:

- ☐ 3 pounds ham
- ☐ Water
- ☐ White distilled vinegar
- ☐ 1 cup brown sugar
- ☐ 1 ½ tablespoons ground mustard

Directions:

1. Cut ham into chunks and put in the PPCXL.
2. Cover with water, being careful not to exceed the max line, and add vinegar. The ratio of water to vinegar is 2:1.
3. Seal the lid.
4. Hit "chicken/meat" and adjust time to 38 minutes.
5. When time is up, hit "cancel" and wait for a natural pressure release.
6. Remove the ham and shred into smaller pieces.
7. In a small bowl, mix with brown sugar and mustard.
8. Put half of ham in a baking dish, sprinkle on brown sugar/mustard, and add the rest of the ham, finishing the sugar/mustard sprinkle on top.
9. Wrap dish in foil and bake in a 325-degree oven for 60 minutes.

Nutritional Info (¼ recipe):
Total calories: 740
Protein: 37
Carbs: 40
Fat: 47
Fiber: 0

Maple Brisket

Serves: 4

Time: 2 hours, 25 minutes (30 minutes counter time, 15 minutes prep time, 1 hour cook time, 30 minutes natural pressure release, 10 minutes thickening time)

The highlight of this beef brisket recipe is the maple sugar, which forms a sticky, caramelized coating on the meat. Maple sugar is made by boiling tree sap until the sugar crystallizes. It has an intense maple syrup flavor. That sweetness is balanced with liquid smoke and spices like mustard powder, smoked paprika, and smoked sea salt. You can use regular sea salt and paprika, but the flavor isn't as deep. Since this is a holiday recipe, I say spring for the smoked spices. It's worth it.

Ingredients:

- ☐ 1 ½ pounds beef brisket
- ☐ 2 cups bone broth
- ☐ 3 sprigs fresh thyme
- ☐ 2 tablespoons maple sugar
- ☐ 1 tablespoon liquid smoke
- ☐ 2 teaspoons smoked sea salt
- ☐ 1 teaspoon onion powder
- ☐ 1 teaspoon mustard powder
- ☐ 1 teaspoon black pepper
- ☐ ½ teaspoon smoked paprika

Directions:

1. Take out the brisket 30 minutes before you plan to begin cooking.
2. When you're ready to start, mix sea salt, pepper, maple sugar, mustard, onion powder, and smoked paprika.
3. Dry the brisket with paper towels, and coat in the rub.
4. Put a little olive oil in your PPCXL and turn to "chicken/meat."
5. When warm, add meat and brown on both sides to a golden color.
6. Turn the brisket so the fatty side is facing up, and pour in liquid smoke and broth, scraping up any stuck-on food bits.
7. Toss in thyme and seal the lid.
8. Adjust cook time to one hour.
9. When time is up, hit "cancel" and wait for a natural pressure release.

10. When ready, remove the meat and tent with foil on a plate.
11. Turn the cooker back to "chicken/meat" and simmer for 10 minutes.
12. Slice brisket and serve with plenty of sauce!

Nutritional Info (¼ recipe):
Total calories: 565
Protein: 33
Carbs: 4
Fat: 46
Fiber: 0

Vegan Holiday Roast

Serves: 8
Time: 18 minutes (10 minutes prep time, 8 minutes cook time)

Vegans love the holidays, too, but it can be hard to find a main dish that isn't just a ton of vegetables. Luckily, lots of brands make vegan-friendly roasts. The roast we've chosen has a lot of flavor already; the "meat" is flavored with hazelnuts, and it's stuffed with sausages, apples, cranberries, and candied ginger.

Ingredients:

- One Field Roast roast (Hazelnut Cranberry Roast En Croute is great)
- 1 cup veggie broth
- 4 garlic cloves
- 1 chopped yellow onion
- 1 chopped celery stalk
- Salt and pepper to taste
- Enough olive oil to coat cooker bottom

Directions:

1. Turn your cooker to "chicken/meat" and add oil.
2. When hot and shiny, add onion and stir until it becomes softened.
3. Add celery and garlic, and stir until garlic is fragrant.
4. Add roast and pour over the veggie broth.
5. Sprinkle in salt and pepper before sealing the lid.
6. Adjust cook time to 8 minutes.
7. When time is up, hit "cancel" and quick-release.
8. Serve!

Nutritional Info (⅛ recipe):
Total calories: 354
Protein: 22
Carbs: 24
Fat: 19
Fiber: 9

Sweet Potato Puree

Serves: 6
Time: 17 minutes (12 minutes cook time, 5 minutes blend time)

An almost sauce-like side dish that would go really well with pork, this sweet potato puree is just white sweet potatoes, bone broth, and some salt. The potatoes only take 12 minutes to cook, and then you blend everything together till smooth. That's literally all there is to it! If you find them a little too one-note, add some spices like ginger or cumin.

Ingredients:

- ☐ 1 ½ cups bone broth
- ☐ 2 pounds peeled and chopped white sweet potatoes
- ☐ ½ teaspoon salt

Directions:

1. Pour broth and potatoes into your PPCXL.
2. Press "chicken/meat" and adjust cook time to 12 minutes.
3. When the timer beeps, hit "cancel" and quick-release the pressure.
4. Poke the potatoes with a fork; if they fall apart easily, they're done.
5. Pulse in a blender with pressure-cooker liquid, until very smooth.
6. Add salt and serve!

Nutritional Info (⅙ recipe per serving):
Total calories: 176
Protein: 5
Carbs: 32
Fat: 2
Fiber: 4

Pinto Beans with Bacon + Pecans

Serves: 4
Time: 25-30 minutes (not counting an overnight bean soak)

Beans might seem like an unusual side dish for the holidays, depending on where you're from, but they're a great canvas for all kinds of spices, regardless of the season. The dry beans need an overnight soak, and then you cook them in water for 21 minutes. Remember to save 1 cup of the liquid when they're done. Cooked bacon and pecans toast in butter for a little while, before you add the ground spices. It all comes together when you add the beans back into the pressure cooker with chiles and the reserved cooking liquid. The dish is nutty, spicy, salty, and oh-so savory.

Ingredients:

- ☐ 1 cup soaked pinto beans
- ☐ 3 slices chopped, cooked bacon
- ☐ 1 chopped onion
- ☐ ½ cup chopped pecans
- ☐ ½ cup chopped mild green chiles
- ☐ 1 tablespoon butter
- ☐ ½ teaspoon dried oregano
- ☐ ½ teaspoon ground cumin
- ☐ ¼ teaspoon ground coriander

Directions:

1. The night before you plan on making the dish, submerge the beans in water and leave overnight.
2. When you're ready to make the dish, drain the beans and pour into the pressure cooker.
3. Add enough water so the beans are covered by 2-inches.
4. Seal the lid.
5. Hit "chicken/meat" and adjust cook time to 21 minutes.
6. When time is up, hit "cancel" and wait 10 minutes before quick-releasing.
7. Ladle out 1 cup of the cooker liquid and pour into a bowl.
8. Drain beans, throwing out the rest of the liquid.
9. Turn your cooker to "chicken/meat" again and add butter.
10. When melted, add bacon and pecans.

11. Stir for 3 minutes.
12. Add onion and stir for another 3 minutes.
13. Toss in cumin, coriander, and oregano.
14. When toasty, add beans, ¼ of the cooking liquid from the bowl you set aside, and green chiles.
15. Stir and cook for a few minutes.
16. If the liquid starts to evaporate too much, add in liquid ¼ cup of a time.
17. When everything is hot, serve!

Nutritional Info (¼ of recipe per serving):
Total calories: 240
Protein: 9
Carbs: 17
Fat: 16
Fiber: 4.3

Cinnamon-Balsamic Brussels Sprouts with Bacon

Serves: 4

Time: 19 minutes (10 minutes prep time, 4 minutes cook time, 5 minutes dressing time)

Not a fan of Brussels sprouts? This recipe will change your mind. By adding just a few key ingredients, turn bland sprouts into a holiday treat complete with salty bacon, wine-like balsamic vinegar, pops of fine sea salt, and spicy-sweet cinnamon. Sprouts are packed with folic acid, fiber, and Vitamin C, so you know you're eating healthy and deliciously with this dish.

Ingredients:

- ☐ 1 pound halved and trimmed Brussels sprouts
- ☐ 1 cup water
- ☐ 4 slices bacon
- ☐ 1 tablespoon olive oil
- ☐ 1 teaspoon balsamic vinegar
- ☐ ½ teaspoon fine sea salt
- ☐ ½ teaspoon cinnamon

Directions:

1. Turn your cooker to "chicken/meat" and add bacon.
2. Cook until it becomes crispy.
3. Move to a plate and pat with paper towels.
4. Pour 1 cup of water into the pot after hitting "cancel."
5. Tear off the outer leaves of the sprouts and trim the stems.
6. Cut in half.
7. Put into the steamer basket and lower into the cooker.
8. Seal the lid.
9. Hit "chicken/meat" and adjust cook time to 4 minutes.
10. When the timer beeps, hit "cancel" and quick-release.
11. In a bowl, whisk balsamic vinegar and oil together slowly, by pouring the oil into the vinegar gradually.
12. Toss cooked sprouts in the dressing and crumble on the bacon.
13. Season with salt and cinnamon, and serve!

Nutritional Info (¼ of recipe):
Total calories: 139
Protein: 6
Carbs: 9
Fat: 7
Fiber: 4.25

Butternut Squash + Apple Mash

Serves: 6
Time: 13 minutes (10 minutes cook time, 3 minutes mash time)

A sweeter alternative to mashed potatoes, mashed butternut squash and apples only take 10 minutes to cook in the pressure cooker. To keep the mash from blending into a one-note dish, don't forget to add cinnamon, salt, and ginger. You can play with the amount of spices to your taste (I personally love going a bit more ginger-heavy), all while keeping the dish just above 100 calories per serving with almost 4 grams of fiber.

Ingredients:

- ☐ 1.5-pounds of cubed butternut squash
- ☐ 2 cored and diced apples
- ☐ 1 chopped onion
- ☐ 1 cup water
- ☐ 2 tablespoons coconut oil
- ☐ ¼ teaspoon cinnamon
- ☐ ½ teaspoon salt
- ☐ ⅛ teaspoon ginger

Directions:

1. Pour water into the PPCXL.
2. Put squash, apple, and onion into the steamer basket.
3. Sprinkle on salt and lower into cooker.
4. Seal the lid.
5. Hit "chicken/meat" and adjust cook time to 10 minutes.
6. When the timer beeps, turn off the cooker and quick-release the pressure.
7. Move pot contents to a bowl and mash.
8. Stir in oil and spices.
9. Serve!

Nutritional Info (⅙ of recipe per serving):
Total calories: 118
Protein: 2
Carbs: 21
Fat: 5
Fiber: 3.6

Whole White Beets with Greens

Serves: 2

Time: 55 minutes (30 minutes soak time, 15 minutes cook time, 10 minutes additional time)

When you go looking for white beets, you'll see they have full tops of greens. Those are the ones you want, because you'll be serving the greens, as well. They look a bit like turnips. You're going to be picking up three, and soaking just the white part for a half hour. This will help them cook faster in the pressure cooker. You finish cooking everything in a skillet with hot oil, garlic, and salt, and serve with a squirt of fresh lemon juice. This recipe is a bit more hands-on than some of the other ones, since you cook the beets and greens at different stages, as well as soak, cook, soak, drain, and then fry, but it's nothing too complicated. The result is a very tasty, fresh, and healthy side dish that goes with everything.

Ingredients:

- ☐ 3 whole white beets (with their greens separated)
- ☐ 2 minced garlic cloves
- ☐ 1 tablespoon olive oil
- ☐ 1 teaspoon lemon juice
- ☐ 1 teaspoon salt

Directions:

1. Soak the beets for 30 minutes.
2. Put beets in the pressure cooker with enough water to cover them.
3. Salt.
4. Seal the lid.
5. Hit "chicken/meat" and adjust cook time to 15 minutes.
6. When time is up, hit "cancel" and quick-release.
7. Add greens and let them soak for 5 minutes, closing the lid, but not bringing to pressure.
8. Put beets and greens in a strainer, and cool until you can touch them.
9. Cut beets.
10. Heat olive oil in a pan and add beets, letting them sit for a minute or so.
11. Add garlic and beet greens.
12. When the greens are wilted and the garlic fragrant, move everything to a serving plate.
13. Squeeze on some fresh lemon juice and serve!

Nutritional Info (½ recipe per serving):
Total calories: 105
Protein: 3
Carbs: 15
Fat: 11
Fiber: 3

Picnic Potato Salad

Serves: 4

Time: 1 hour, 15 minutes (5 minutes cook time, 10 minutes cool time, 1 hour chill time)

Summer means picnics and BBQs, which for a lot of people, means potato salad. Cooking six cubed potatoes and four eggs only takes 5 minutes in the pressure cooker. Normally, you would have to cook those two ingredients separately, but not anymore. The dressing is just mayo, parsley, mustard, pickle juice, salt, and pepper. If you don't like mayo or want to make the salad a bit healthier, sub in plain Greek yogurt.

Ingredients:

- ☐ 6 peeled and cubed medium-sized potatoes
- ☐ 1 ½ cups water
- ☐ 4 large eggs
- ☐ 1 cup mayonnaise
- ☐ 2 tablespoons fresh chopped parsley
- ☐ 1 tablespoon mustard
- ☐ 1 tablespoon pickle juice
- ☐ Salt and pepper

Directions:

1. Pour water into your PPCXL.
2. Add raw eggs and potatoes into the steamer basket, and lower into the cooker.
3. Seal the lid.
4. Hit "chicken/meat" and adjust cook time to 5 minutes.
5. When time is up, hit "cancel" and quick-release the pressure. If your potatoes are not tender enough, cook them by themselves for another 2 minutes under pressure.
6. Move eggs to a bowl of ice water.
7. In a separate bowl, mix the onion, mayo, parsley, mustard, and pickle juice together.
8. Fold in the cooked potato cubes.
9. Peel the cooled eggs, chop, and add to potato salad.
10. Season with salt and pepper.
11. Chill in the fridge for at least one hour before serving.

Nutritional Info (1 cup per serving):
Total calories: 358

Protein: 6.7
Carbs: 20.5
Fat: 5.9
Fiber: 3.3

Mexican Street Corn

Serves: 6
Time: 8 minutes (3 minutes cook time, 5 minutes additional time)

Another summer favorite, corn on the cob may be messy, but it's incredibly refreshing and delicious. This version adds what could be described as a "dressing" made from plain Greek yogurt, garlic powder, and lime juice. A sprinkle of chipotle chili powder and parmesan adds a final spicy, salty kick.

Ingredients:

- ☐ 6 ears unhusked sweet corn
- ☐ 2 cups water
- ☐ 2 limes
- ☐ 1 teaspoon chipotle chili powder
- ☐ 1 cup parmesan cheese
- ☐ 6 tablespoons plain Greek yogurt
- ☐ ½ teaspoon garlic powder

Directions:

1. Pour water into your pressure cooker.
2. Stick unhusked corn in the steamer basket and lower into the cooker.
3. Hit "chicken/meat" after sealing the lid, and cook for just 3 minutes.
4. In the meanwhile, mix yogurt, the juice of two limes, and garlic powder in a bowl.
5. When time is up, hit "cancel" and quick-release.
6. When corn is cooled a little, remove the husks.
7. Brush with the yogurt mixture.
8. Sprinkle on chipotle powder, brush with more yogurt, and then sprinkle on cheese.
9. Serve!

Nutritional Info (1 ear per serving):
Total calories: 130
Protein: 9
Carbs: 16
Fat: 5
Fiber: 2.4

From-Scratch Cornbread

Serves: 8

Time: 34 minutes (5 minutes prep time, 19 minutes cook time, 10 minutes natural pressure release)

Cornbread is a great side dish that can be served as a snack, side, or even a quick breakfast with some butter, honey, and/or fresh jam. This from-scratch recipe doesn't use Jiffy mix, but it manages to only use eight total ingredients. The water and vinegar just generate the steam. You mix the milk, butter, and egg together first, and then add the dry ingredients. The whole thing gets wrapped in foil and steams for just 19 minutes, followed by a natural pressure release. So easy!

Ingredients:

- ☐ 1 ¼ cups fine cornmeal
- ☐ 2 cups water
- ☐ 1 cup white flour
- ☐ 1 cup milk
- ☐ 1 large egg
- ☐ ½ cup white sugar
- ☐ ¼ cup melted butter
- ☐ 1 tablespoon baking powder
- ☐ ½ teaspoon salt
- ☐ Splash of white vinegar

Directions:

1. Pour water and a splash of vinegar into your PPCXL.
2. Lower in metal trivet.
3. Grease a round bread pan.
4. In a bowl, whisk the milk, butter, and egg together.
5. Gently stir in remaining ingredients until just moistened.
6. Pour into pan and wrap tightly in foil.
7. Put on top of the trivet in the cooker and seal the lid.
8. Hit "chicken/meat" and adjust cook time to 19 minutes.
9. When time is up, hit "cancel" and wait for a natural pressure release.
10. Serve!

Nutritional Info (⅛ recipe per serving):
Total calories: 183
Protein: 4
Carbs: 27
Fat: 6
Fiber: 2

Candied Yams

Serves: 4
Time: 6 minutes (5 minutes cook time, 1 minute broil time)

Sweet potato casserole is a common side dish around Thanksgiving and Christmas. This version is less of a casserole, and skips the marshmallow topping, which may be tasty, but isn't necessary. You just cook cubed, cornstarch-coated yams in the pressure cooker, with butter, brown sugar, water, maple syrup, cinnamon, and salt. ½ cup chopped pecans are added at the very end, and it's ready to serve!

Ingredients:

- ☐ 3 peeled and cubed yams
- ☐ 1 cup water
- ☐ ½ cup brown sugar
- ☐ ½ cup chopped pecans
- ☐ ¼ cup maple syrup
- ☐ 4 tablespoons butter
- ☐ 2 ½ tablespoons cornstarch
- ☐ 1 teaspoon cinnamon
- ☐ ½ teaspoon salt

Directions:

1. Put the yams in a plastic bag with cornstarch and shake.
2. Put in the pressure cooker, along with the rest of the ingredients, minus pecans.
3. Seal the lid.
4. Hit "chicken/meat" and adjust time to 5 minutes.
5. When time is up, hit "cancel" and quick-release.
6. Stir in pecans before tumbling into a serving dish.
7. Season again to taste and serve!

Nutritional Info (¼ recipe):
Total calories: 561
Protein: 89
Carbs: 89
Fat: 22
Fiber: 7.2

Chipotle-Cranberry Sauce

Serves: 4

Time: 1 hour, 52 minutes (30 minutes prep time, 12 minutes cook time, 10 minutes natural pressure release, 1 hour chill time)

This isn't your average cranberry sauce. It's far from what you'll get in a can, and probably pretty different from what you've made in the past. For one, it's got the heat from chipotle in it, which brings out the natural sweetness of the cranberries. Another thing that's different is that you don't puree the sauce, or add pectin, so it's truly a sauce as opposed to a jello.

Note: The prep time isn't set in stone; it depends on how long it takes you to pick through the cranberries.

Ingredients:

- ☐ 12-ounces fresh cranberries
- ☐ 2 limes
- ☐ 1 cup water
- ☐ 1 small can of chipotle chilis in adobo sauce
- ☐ ½ cup dark brown sugar
- ☐ ¼ cup red wine
- ☐ 1 teaspoon cumin
- ☐ ½ teaspoon chili powder
- ☐ ½ teaspoon cinnamon

Directions:

1. Rinse cranberries and pick through them to get rid of any small squishy ones.
2. Zest a lime over the good cranberries.
3. In a separate bowl, add a few chipotle chilis with a spoonful of sauce.
4. Pour in red wine.
5. Squeeze in the juice of both limes and puree with a blender.
6. Pour over the cranberries.
7. Stir in brown sugar, cumin, cinnamon, and chili powder.
8. Pour 1 cup of water into your PPCXL and put the trivet down inside.
9. Put cranberry bowl, uncovered, and seal the lid.
10. Hit "chicken/meat" and adjust time to 12 minutes.
11. When time is up, hit "cancel" and wait for a natural pressure release.

12. Take out the bowl and mash the cranberries a bit.
13. Cool slightly before storing in the fridge, if you want it chilled for serving. It's also good warm.

Nutritional Info (¼ recipe):
Total calories: 157
Protein: 0
Carbs: 31
Fat: 0
Fiber: 3.9

Cranapple (Cranberry + Apple) Sauce

Serves: 4

Time: 19 minutes + 1 hour chill time (6 minutes cook time, 10 minutes natural pressure release, 3 minutes simmer time, 1 hour chill time)

If you find cranberry sauce to be a bit too tart, this version adds a Honeycrisp apple, cider, ½ maple syrup, and some citrus. Everything cooks together in the pressure cooker for just 6 minutes, before you wait 10 minutes and then quick-release. The sauce will thicken up as it cools, so store in the fridge for at least 1 hour before serving.

Ingredients:

- ☐ 12-ounces cranberries, fresh or frozen
- ☐ 1 peeled and chopped Honeycrisp apple
- ☐ ½ cup maple syrup
- ☐ ½ cup apple cider
- ☐ Zest and juice of one big orange

Directions:

1. Put everything in your PPCXL and stir.
2. Seal the lid.
3. Hit "chicken/meat" and adjust cook time to 6 minutes.
4. When time is up, hit "cancel" and wait 10 minutes before quick-releasing leftover pressure.
5. Turn back to "chicken/meat" to simmer the sauce for 2-3 minutes.
6. Store in the fridge until completely chilled and thickened.

Nutritional Info (¼ recipe):
Total calories: 173
Protein: 1
Carbs: 43
Fat: 0
Fiber: 4.5

Chapter 16

Stocks + Sauces

Beef Bone Broth

Makes: 8 cups
Time: 1 hour, 1 minute (36 minutes cook time, 25 minutes natural pressure release)

Bone broth is very "in" these days, and the best way to prepare it is to make it yourself. It's a great way to use up bones. You can sip it hot in a mug, or use it as the base for all kinds of sauces and other dishes.

Ingredients:

- ☐ 2 ½ pounds of beef bones
- ☐ 8 cups of water
- ☐ 2 leeks
- ☐ 1 peeled carrot
- ☐ 2 tablespoons fish sauce
- ☐ 1 teaspoon apple cider vinegar

Directions:

1. Begin by putting carrots and leeks into the pot.
2. Add bones on top and pour in water.
3. Pour in fish sauce and vinegar.
4. Seal the lid.
5. Hit "chicken/meat' and adjust time to 36 minutes.
6. When time is up, hit "cancel" and wait for a natural pressure release.
7. Open the cooker and pour the broth through a strainer.
8. Throw out the solids.
9. Store in the fridge.
10. Use within 2-3 days or freeze for up to one year.

Nutritional Info (1 cup):
Total calories: 160
Protein: 8
Carbs: 0
Fat: 9
Fiber: 0

Mushroom Stock

Makes: About 4 cups
Time: 44 minutes (24 minutes cook time, 20 minutes natural pressure release)

For vegetarians and vegans, stock can be tricky. For a richer option than just vegetable broth, this mushroom broth uses dried shiitakes, celery, carrots, thyme, and bay leaves for a truly savory, flavorful base for any dish.

Ingredients:

- ☐ 4 cups water
- ☐ 2-ounces dried shiitake mushrooms
- ☐ 2 bay leaves
- ☐ 2 thyme sprigs
- ☐ 2 peeled and chopped carrots
- ☐ 2 chopped celery stalks

Directions:

1. Rinse the mushrooms under cool water.
2. Put in the cooker, along with everything else.
3. Seal the lid.
4. Hit "chicken/meat" and adjust time to 24 minutes.
5. When time is up, hit "cancel" and wait for the pressure to release on its own.
6. Strain stock and throw out the solids.
7. Use within 2-3 days or freeze for 3 months.

Nutritional Info (¼ recipe per serving):
Total calories: 65
Protein: 2
Carbs: 15
Fat: 0
Fiber: 0

Pork Stock

Makes: 16 cups

Time: 2 hours, 28 minutes (30 minutes roast time, 24 minutes cook time (2x), 20 minutes natural pressure release (2x), 30 minutes cool time)

You're going to be making two batches with 4 pounds of pork bones, so this is a great meat stock recipe if you know you're going to be needing a lot of broth for meals within a week. You can also freeze it, and it will last up to 6 months.

Ingredients:

- ☐ 16 cups water (divided)
- ☐ 4 pounds pork bones
- ☐ 6 chopped celery stalks
- ☐ 6 chopped carrots
- ☐ 2 sliced onions
- ☐ 4 bay leaves
- ☐ 1 tablespoon black peppercorns

Directions:

1. Preheat your oven to 450-degrees.
2. Put bones on a foil-lined cookie sheet brushed with oil.
3. Put the celery, onion, and carrots on another sheet lined in foil, also brushed with some oil.
4. Put sheets in the oven and roast for a half hour.
5. When they're done, put the veggies, garlic, peppercorns, and bay leaves in the pressure cooker with the bones.
6. Pour in 8 cups of water.
7. Seal the lid.
8. Hit "chicken/meat" and adjust cook time to 24 minutes.
9. When time is up, hit "cancel" and wait for a natural pressure release.
10. Strain stock, putting the bones and veggies back in the cooker for a second batch.
11. Pour in remaining 8 cups of water and cook for 24 minutes, just like the first batch.
12. Cool to room temperature before storing in the fridge.
13. Use within a week or freeze.

Nutritional Info (1 cup per serving):
Total calories: 31
Protein: 6
Carbs: 0
Fat: 1
Fiber: 0

Fish Stock

Makes: 1 liter

Time: 1 hour, 11 minutes (6 minutes cook time, 5 minutes natural pressure release, 45-60 minutes cool time)

Fish stock makes any seafood dish way better than if you used another meat stock. It's a great base for sauces, rices, and risottos. A lot of fish stocks use fish bones, but this one only needs dried anchovies and water.

Ingredients:

- ☐ 4 cups cold water
- ☐ 30 grams of dried anchovies

Directions:

1. Pour water and anchovies into your pressure cooker.
2. Seal the lid.
3. Hit "chicken/meat" and adjust time to 6 minutes.
4. When the timer beeps, hit "cancel" and wait 5 minutes before quick-releasing.
5. Strain and discard the solids.
6. Wait until the broth is completely cool before storing in the fridge in an airtight container.
7. Use within a week or freeze up to 3 months.

Nutritional Info (1 cup serving):
Total calories: 3
Protein: 1
Carbs: 0
Fat: 0
Fiber: 0

Chicken Stock

Makes: About 4 liters

Time: 1 hour, 31 minutes (36 minutes cook time, 25 minutes natural pressure release, 30 minutes cool time)

This is one of those ingredients you always need in your fridge, especially for pressure cooker recipes. Save the bones from one of your chicken meals, and all you need is water, peppercorns, garlic, onion, carrot, and celery. The broth is unsalted, so you can salt as much as you need for each individual dish.

Ingredients:

- [ ] 4 liters cold water
- [ ] 1 chicken carcass
- [ ] 15 whole black peppercorns
- [ ] 10 garlic cloves
- [ ] 1 big onion
- [ ] 1 big carrot
- [ ] 1 celery stalk

Directions:

1. Put everything in the cooker and seal the lid. Make sure the cooker isn't more than ⅔ of the way full.
2. Hit "chicken/meat" and adjust cook time to 36 minutes.
3. When time is up, hit "cancel" and wait for a natural pressure release.
4. When ready, strain the stock and throw out the solids.
5. Cool to room temperature and store in the fridge in an airtight container. Use within 1 week or freeze for up to 6 months.

Nutritional Info (1 cup per serving):
Total calories: 86
Protein: 6
Carbs: 8
Fiber: 0
Fat: 3

Essential Vegetable Stock

Makes: 5 cups

Time: 1 hour, 8 minutes (18 minutes cook time, 20 minutes natural pressure release, 30 minutes cool time)

Just like chicken stock is necessary for most meals, vegetable stock is essential for vegetarians and vegans. Organic stocks can be expensive at the store. Making your own is easy, healthy, and more affordable.

Ingredients:

- ☐ 4 ½ cups water
- ☐ 10 whole peppercorns
- ☐ 3 halved celery stalks
- ☐ 2 peeled and chopped carrots
- ☐ 1 peeled and halved onion
- ☐ 1 bay leaf
- ☐ 1 minced garlic clove

Directions:

1. Layer onions, celery, carrots, bay leaf, garlic, peppercorns, and water into your pressure cooker.
2. Seal the lid.
3. Hit "chicken/meat" and adjust cook time to 18 minutes.
4. When the timer beeps, hit "cancel" and wait for a natural pressure release.
5. Strain the broth, throwing out the solids.
6. Cool to room temperature before storing in the fridge for 2-3 days, or in the freezer for 3 months.

Nutritional Info (⅕ recipe per serving):
Total calories: 17.8
Protein: .7
Carbs: 4
Fat: 0
Fiber: .9

Garlic Broth

Makes: About 6 cups

Time: 1 hour, 8 minutes (18 minutes cook time, 20 minutes natural pressure release, 30 minutes cool time)

Do you love garlic? This broth is the definition of "savory." Fresh herbs like sage, thyme, and parsley help keep things aromatic and fresh. Use this broth in place of any stock for a garlicky infusion.

Ingredients:

- ☐ 6 cups water
- ☐ 4-6 chopped celery stalks with leaves
- ☐ 1 full head of garlic
- ☐ 1 quartered onion
- ☐ ½ cup parsley with stems
- ☐ 1 teaspoon dried thyme
- ☐ ¼ teaspoon rubbed sage

Directions:

1. Remove the garlic cloves from their bulb, but don't peel.
2. Add to the pressure cooker along with onion, celery, sage, thyme, and parsley.
3. Pour in the water and seal the lid.
4. Hit "chicken/meat" and adjust time to 18 minutes.
5. When the beeper goes off, hit "cancel" and let the pressure decrease naturally.
6. Strain the broth, pressing down on everything to get the most liquid out.
7. Throw out the solids.
8. Cool the broth to room temperature and use within 3 days, or freeze for up to 6 months.

Nutritional Info (⅙ recipe per serving):
Total calories: 3
Protein: 0
Carbs: 0
Fat: 0
Fiber: 0

Turkey Gravy

Serves: 4

Time: 1 hour, 22 minutes (6 minutes prep time, 43 minutes cook time, 20 minutes natural pressure release, 3 minutes roux time, 10 minutes simmer time)

Using some ignored parts of the turkey (neck, heart, gizzard, butt), this gravy is rich and high in protein. It is fantastic with homemade biscuits or waffles. The process is pretty easy, too - just brown the meat and onion together, pour in wine and cook down, and pressure cooker with water, bay leaf, and thyme. To make the roux, whisk melted butter and flour together, and then whisk in broth and diced meat.

Ingredients:

- ☐ 1 quart chicken broth
- ☐ Turkey neck, heart, butt, and gizzard (no liver)
- ☐ 1 quartered onion
- ☐ ½ cup dry white wine
- ☐ 2 sprigs thyme
- ☐ 1 bay leaf
- ☐ 4 tablespoons flour
- ☐ 4 tablespoons butter
- ☐ 1 tablespoon olive oil
- ☐ Salt and pepper to taste

Directions:

1. Add olive oil to pressure cooker on the "chicken/meat" setting.
2. Add turkey and onion.
3. Cook for 3 minutes until nice and brown.
4. Flip and cook another 3 minutes.
5. Add white wine and bring to a boil, scraping up any stuck food bits.
6. Pour in water, thyme, and bay leaf before sealing the lid.
7. Adjust cook time to 43 minutes.
8. When time is up, hit "cancel" and wait for a natural pressure release.
9. Strain the broth, saving the gizzard and heart.
10. When cool, take the gristle off the gizzard and dice, along with the heart.
11. In a saucepan, melt butter and whisk in flour.
12. Stir and cook until the flour has become golden, which should take 3 minutes.
13. Pour broth into the saucepan, whisking.

14. Bring to a boil and then reduce the heat to a simmer until the sauce has reduced by a third.
15. Stir in gizzard and heart.
16. Season with salt and pepper.
17. If you're eating right away, simmer for one minute. If you're going to use it later, let it cool before storing in the fridge up to 1 week.

Nutritional Info (¼ recipe per serving):
Total calories: 350
Protein: 29
Carbs: 6
Fat: 22
Fiber: 0

Bolognese Sauce

Serves: 6-8
Time: 34 minutes (22 minutes prep time, 12 minutes cook time)

Also known as good ol' meat sauce, this usually long-cooking sauce only takes 34 minutes in the pressure cooker. Browning the aromatics (celery, carrot, and onion) in the pancetta fat deepens the flavors and gives the sauce that slow-cooked taste. Don't forget to add that bit of cream at the very end for added smoothness and richness.

Ingredients:

- ☐ 11-ounces lean ground beef
- ☐ 4-ounces cubed pancetta
- ☐ 1 ½ cups hot water
- ☐ 1 cup beef stock
- ☐ ½ cup red wine
- ☐ 1 chopped carrot
- ☐ 1 chopped onion
- ☐ 1 chopped celery stalk
- ☐ 5 tablespoons tomato paste concentrate
- ☐ 1 tablespoon heavy cream
- ☐ 1 teaspoon salt
- ☐ ¼ teaspoon black pepper

Directions:

1. Turn your PPCXL to "chicken/meat" and add pancetta cubes.
2. Stir until the meat has released its fat and starts sizzling, which should take about 5 minutes.
3. Toss in carrot, onion, and celery.
4. Cook for 10 minutes, stirring occasionally.
5. Add the beef next, and brown.
6. Pour in wine and hot water, and deglaze by scraping the bottom of the cooker.
7. After 7 minutes, mix beef stock, tomato paste, salt, and pepper in a bowl, and pour into the cooker.
8. Seal the lid.
9. Adjust cook time to 12 minutes.
10. When the timer beeps, hit "cancel" and quick-release the pressure.
11. Mix in heavy cream and serve!

Nutritional Info (⅛ recipe per serving):
Total calories: 209.3
Protein: 9.5
Carbs: 6.7
Fat: 14.8
Fiber: 1.3

Caramelized Onions

Makes: 2 cups
Time: 34 minutes (10 minutes prep time, 24 minutes cook time)

Caramelized onions are one of my favorite toppings for burgers, but they take so long. That's where the pressure cooker comes in. You can make 3 pounds worth of caramelized yellow onions in just 34 minutes. Coating the raw onions in baking soda before pouring in water and bringing to pressure helps speed up the cook time even more, and ensures really beautiful golden-brown results.

Ingredients:

- ☐ 3 pounds thin-sliced yellow onions
- ☐ 6 tablespoons butter
- ☐ ½ teaspoon baking soda
- ☐ Salt and pepper to taste

Directions:

1. Add butter to pressure cooker and hit "chicken/meat."
2. Stir in baking soda and onions.
3. Season well with salt and pepper.
4. Cook until the onions are starting to soften and release their liquid.
5. Seal the lid.
6. Adjust cook time to 24 minutes.
7. When time is up, hit "cancel" and wait for a natural pressure release.
8. Take off the lid and hit "chicken/meat" again, simmering for about 5 minutes or until the onions are sticky and a beautiful deep-brown color.
9. Use within 10 days or freeze for 3-4 months.

Nutritional Info (½ cup per serving):
Total calories: 297
Protein: 3
Carbs: 35
Fat: 18
Fiber: 5.7

Butternut Squash-Sage Sauce

Serves: 4

Time: 32 minutes (10 minutes prep time, 12 minutes cook time, 10 minutes natural pressure release)

Tired of tomato sauces? Sweet, nutty, and infused with fresh sage, this butternut squash sauce is perfect for autumn and can be used in a variety of ways, from mixing with pasta to serving on top of pork tenderloin. Serve right away or store in the fridge no longer than 4 days.

Ingredients:

- ☐ 2 pounds chopped butternut squash
- ☐ 1 cup vegetable stock
- ☐ 1 chopped onion
- ☐ 2 tablespoons olive oil
- ☐ 2 chopped garlic cloves
- ☐ 1 tablespoon chopped fresh sage
- ☐ Pinch of red pepper flakes
- ☐ Salt and pepper to taste

Directions:

1. Hit "chicken/meat" on your cooker and add oil.
2. When hot and shiny, stir in the sage and coat in the hot oil.
3. When crispy, move to a plate.
4. Add the onion and cook until it becomes clear.
5. Add garlic and cook for a minute or so.
6. Pour in 1 cup of broth and deglaze, scraping up any onion or garlic that's stuck.
7. Pour in squash and seal the lid.
8. Adjust cook time to 12 minutes.
9. When time is up, hit "cancel" and wait 10 minutes before quick-releasing the pressure.
10. Let the squash cool with the lid off.
11. Add sage before pureeing sauce till smooth, adding more broth if necessary to get the right texture.
12. Eat within 3-4 days, storing in the fridge.

Nutritional Info (¼ recipe per serving):
Total calories: 179
Protein: 3
Carbs: 30
Fat: 7
Fiber: 5

Zucchini-Basil Pesto

Serves: 4-6
Time: 13 minutes (10 minutes prep time, 3 minutes cook time)

Zucchini season can be overwhelming if you grow your own, and even if you don't, you want to use as much of that awesome vegetable while you can. In this pesto recipe, the zucchini adds a touch of sweetness to the normal basil flavor, as well as fiber and other nutrients. This isn't a sauce that stores well, so plan on using it right away.

Ingredients:

- [ ] 1 ½ pounds fresh chopped zucchini
- [ ] ¾ cup water
- [ ] 1 bunch of fresh basil leaves
- [ ] 1 chopped onion
- [ ] 2 minced garlic cloves
- [ ] 2 tablespoons olive oil
- [ ] 1 ½ teaspoons salt
- [ ] Crack of black pepper

Directions:

1. Turn your PPCXL to "chicken/meat" and add 1 tablespoon of olive oil.
2. When hot, add onion and cook until they've softened.
3. Pour in water, and add zucchini and salt.
4. Seal the lid.
5. Adjust cook time to just 3 minutes.
6. When the timer beeps, hit "cancel" and quick-release.
7. Add garlic and basil.
8. Puree sauce.
9. Serve right away with a crack of black pepper and 1 tablespoon of olive oil drizzled on top.

Nutritional Info (⅙ recipe per serving):
Total calories: 71.4
Protein: 1.2
Carbs: 7.5

Fat: 4.7
Fiber: 2.3

Everyday Marinara

Makes: 2 quarts

Time: 35 minutes (5 minutes prep time, 15 minutes cook time, 15 minutes natural pressure release)

Marinara is a good vehicle for getting in your vegetables. You can hide a lot in there without anyone knowing. This recipe uses lentils and sweet potatoes for fiber. It's also less sweet than storebought sauces, which are often packed with unnecessary sugars. Serve with pasta, as a base for other sauces, and so on.

Ingredients:

- ☐ Two 28-ounce cans of crushed tomatoes
- ☐ 2 cups cubed sweet potatoes
- ☐ 1 ½ cups water
- ☐ ½ cup red lentils
- ☐ 3 minced garlic cloves
- ☐ 2 teaspoons ground basil
- ☐ 1 teaspoon salt

Directions:

1. Rinse lentils and pick out any stones.
2. Turn your pressure cooker to "chicken/meat" and add garlic, lentils, basil, sweet potatoes, and salt.
3. Simmer for a few minutes before pouring in water and tomatoes.
4. Stir to break up any stuck lentils.
5. Seal the lid.
6. Adjust cook time to 15 minutes.
7. When the timer goes off, turn off the cooker and let the pressure come down naturally.
8. Puree till smooth before serving.

Nutritional Info (⅛ recipe per serving):
Total calories: 145
Protein: 7
Carbs: 28
Fat: 2

Fiber: 9

Chapter 17

Desserts

Chocolate Chip Bread Pudding

Serves: 2
Time: 49 minutes (35 minutes prep time, 14 minutes cook time)

Bread pudding is simple and so satisfying. It's amazing what bread can become when you soak it in a bath of milk, egg, sugar, vanilla, and butter. This recipe also adds instant espresso powder and chocolate chips to the party, which provides a decadent kick to this classic comfort food.

Ingredients:

- ☐ 3-ounces Challah bread
- ☐ 1 big egg
- ☐ 1 cup water
- ☐ ½ cup milk
- ☐ ⅓ cup chocolate chips
- ☐ 3 tablespoons sugar
- ☐ 1 tablespoon butter
- ☐ ¼ teaspoon vanilla
- ☐ ¼ teaspoon instant espresso powder

Directions:

1. In a bowl, mix the eggs, milk, vanilla, and sugar until foamy.
2. Melt the butter with the espresso powder, and mix into the bowl.
3. Soak the bread in this mixture for 30 minutes.
4. Fold in chocolate chips.
5. Grease 2 ramekins with butter.
6. Pour pudding evenly into both ramekins.
7. Pour water into your pressure cooker and insert the trivet.
8. Put the ramekins on the trivet and seal the lid.
9. Hit "chicken/meat" and adjust cook time to 14 minutes.
10. When time is up, hit "cancel" and quick-release the pressure.
11. If you want a really crispy top, stick the ramekins under the broiler for a few minutes.

Nutritional Info (½ of recipe per serving):
Total calories: 509
Protein: 10
Carbs: 46
Fat: 24
Fiber: 1

Chocolate-Orange Bread Pudding

Serves: 4-5

Time: 48 minutes (10 minutes prep time, 18 minutes cook time, 20 minutes natural pressure release)

I associate orange and chocolate with Christmas, so this bread pudding is a great holiday treat. You use cubed French bread, which soaks in the classic mixture of cream, milk sugar, and egg, with some extras like almond extract, orange juice, and orange zest. That really infuses the pudding with citrus. The last thing you add before cooking is chopped dark chocolate, and then it goes in the cooker for 18 minutes, followed by a natural pressure release.

Ingredients:

- ☐ 3 ½ cups stale + cubed French bread
- ☐ 2 cups water
- ☐ 3 big eggs
- ☐ 3-ounces chopped dark chocolate
- ☐ ¾ cup heavy cream
- ☐ ½ cup whole milk
- ☐ ⅓ cup sugar + 1 tablespoon
- ☐ 2 tablespoons orange juice
- ☐ 1 teaspoon butter
- ☐ 1 teaspoon almond extract
- ☐ Zest of one orange
- ☐ Pinch of salt

Directions:

1. Pour 2 cups of water into your PPCXL and insert trivet.
2. Grease a 7-inch baking dish with some butter.
3. In a separate bowl, whisk the eggs with ⅓ cup of white sugar.
4. Pour in the cream, milk, orange zest and juice, almond extract, and pinch of salt.
5. Stir well before soaking the bread, for 5 minutes, turning at least once.
6. Mix in chocolate.
7. Pour batter into the dish and sprinkle 1 tablespoon of sugar evenly on top.
8. Put dish inside your cooker and seal the lid.
9. Hit "chicken/meat" and adjust time to 18 minutes.

10. When time is up, turn off the cooker and wait for the pressure to come down on its own.
11. Take out the dish and cool before serving!

Nutritional Info (¼ recipe per serving):
Total calories: 467
Protein: 12
Carbs: 51
Fat: 14
Fiber: 1

Apricot-Bourbon Bread Pudding

Serves: 6

Time: 1 hour (15 minutes prep time, 25 minutes cook time, 5 minutes saucepan time, 15 minutes cool time)

Upgrade your bread pudding into something that will wow your family and friends. With a few additions, like dried apricots, and an addicting bourbon sauce, you turn a simple dessert into something special. We're going to be using 3 cups of bread crumbs instead of whole pieces of bread, which gives the pudding a unique texture. That also means you don't need to take the time to soak the pudding, because the crumbs quickly absorb your egg and milk mixture. You make the sauce on the stovetop while the pudding cooks in the pressure cooker. Serve the pudding warm or chilled for up to 24 hours.

Ingredients:

For pudding

- ☐ 3 cups dry bread crumbs
- ☐ 4 beaten eggs
- ☐ 2 cups milk
- ☐ 1 ½ cups water
- ☐ ½ cup sugar
- ☐ ⅓ cup dried apricots
- ☐ 1 teaspoon vanilla

For sauce

- ☐ 1 egg yolk
- ☐ ¼ cup butter
- ☐ ½ cup sugar
- ☐ 2 tablespoons bourbon
- ☐ 2 tablespoons water

Directions:

1. Grease a 1 ½-quart soufflé dish.
2. Whisk milk, sugar, eggs, and vanilla.
3. Layer bread crumbs and apricots in a greased baking dish.
4. Pour over the egg mixture and wrap tightly in foil.
5. Pour 1 ½ cups water into the pressure cooker and add trivet.
6. Put the dish on the trivet and seal the lid.

7. Hit "chicken/meat" and adjust time to 30 minutes.
8. While that cooks, melt butter in a saucepan.
9. Remove from heat and whisk in sugar.
10. In another bowl, mix water and egg yolk.
11. Pour into saucepan and return to the stove.
12. Simmer and stir for 4-5 minutes until everything is mixed.
13. When it begins to boil, remove from heat and pour in bourbon.
14. When the pressure cooker cycle is done, hit "cancel" and wait for a natural pressure release.
15. Remove the dish and cool for 15 minutes before serving!

Nutritional Info (⅙ recipe per serving):
Total calories: 227
Protein: 9
Carbs: 36
Fat: 6
Fiber: .9

Peanut Butter Blondies

Serves: 6

Time: 56 minutes (10 minutes prep time, 36 minutes cook time, 10 minutes natural pressure release)

If you need a break from chocolate, but you still want something sweet, these peanut butter blondies are the answer. The recipe uses powdered peanut butter, which ensures the blondies doesn't end up too doughy. Oats help hold the blondies together, as well, and also provide some fiber. Serve as is or with vanilla ice cream.

Ingredients:

- ☐ 1 ½ cups water
- ☐ 1 room temperature egg
- ☐ 1 cup flour
- ☐ 1 cup regular oats
- ☐ ½ cup brown sugar
- ☐ ½ cup white sugar
- ☐ ½ cup softened butter
- ☐ ⅓ cup powdered peanut butter
- ☐ ½ teaspoon salt
- ☐ ½ teaspoon baking soda

Directions:

1. Grease a 7-inch springform pan with butter.
2. Cut a piece of parchment paper so it is round and fits in the bottom of your pan. Having this on the bottom helps you remove the baked blondies.
3. Cream powdered PB, butter, egg, salt, and both sugars together in a bowl.
4. Gently fold in the flour, baking soda, and oats.
5. Push this batter into the pan, so it's even.
6. Cover with a paper towel, and then a piece of foil, sealing it around the edges.
7. Pour water into the pressure cooker and lower in the trivet.
8. Put the pan on top of the trivet and seal the lid.
9. Hit "chicken/meat" and adjust cook time to 36 minutes.
10. When time is up, hit "cancel" and wait 10 minutes before quick-releasing.
11. Carefully remove the pan, wearing oven mitts.
12. Cool for 10-15 minutes before taking off the springform pan's sides.

13. Invert on a plate and cut into individual servings.

Nutritional Info (⅙ of recipe per serving):
'Total calories: 561
Protein: 8
Carbs: 61
Fat: 18
Fiber: 1.5

Mascarpone Cheesecake

Serves: 12-16

Time: 1 hour, 25 minutes + 4 hours (15 minutes prep time, 30 minutes cook time, 10 minutes natural pressure release, 30 minutes cool time, 4 hours chill time)

There are so many varieties of cheesecake, it's delightfully overwhelming. For a really sophisticated, but still easy take on the classic, we're making an amazing crust from ladyfinger cookies, espresso, and Kahlua liquor. The filling has cream cheese, of course, and mascarpone, which is how Italians make their cheesecake. As with all the cheesecakes in the book, the longest part of the preparation is the chill before the serve, which takes about 4 hours.

Ingredients:

Crust:

- ☐ 1 ½ cups crushed ladyfingers
- ☐ 1 tablespoon melted butter
- ☐ 1 tablespoon Kahlua liquor
- ☐ 1 tablespoon instant granulated espresso

Filling:

- ☐ 16-ounces softened cream cheese
- ☐ 8-ounces softened mascarpone
- ☐ 2 room temperature eggs
- ☐ ½ cup white sugar
- ☐ 2 tablespoons powdered sugar
- ☐ 1 teaspoon vanilla
- ☐ Dusting of cocoa powder

Directions:

1. In a bowl, mix melted butter, Kahlua, and crushed cookies.
2. In a separate bowl, mix white sugar, mascarpone, and cream cheese.
3. Add eggs, vanilla, and powdered sugar until just incorporated.
4. Grease an 8-inch springform pan with butter.
5. Press crust into the bottom.
6. Pour filling, smoothing out the top with a knife.
7. Cover pan with a paper towel, and then a piece of foil, sealing it at the sides.
8. Pour the minimum requirement of water into your PPCXL and lower in trivet.
9. Put wrapped pan on the trivet and seal the lid.

10. Hit "chicken/meat" and adjust time to 30 minutes.
11. When time is up, hit "cancel" and wait 10 minutes before quick-releasing.
12. Remove the cheesecake and unwrap.
13. Wait to cool before putting in the fridge for at least 4 hours.
14. To serve, dust with cocoa powder.

Nutritional Info (1/12 of recipe per serving):
Total calories: 426
Protein: 8
Carbs: 47
Fat: 23
Fiber: 0

Lighter Yogurt Cheesecake

Serves: 8

Time: 1 hour, 10 minutes + 6 hours cooling time (15 minutes prep time, 30 minutes cook time, 25 minutes natural pressure release)

This lightened-up cheesecake uses less cream cheese and adds Greek yogurt, specifically whole milk yogurt, which has more protein and less fat. The crust is a graham-cracker crust that uses cinnamon crackers and butter. If you love cheesecake, but don't love the fat and calories, make this recipe your go-to.

Ingredients:

- ☐ 1 ½ cups whole-milk Greek yogurt
- ☐ 1 ½ cups finely-ground cinnamon graham cracker crumbs
- ☐ 2 big eggs
- ☐ ¼ cup sugar
- ☐ 4-ounces softened, regular cream cheese
- ☐ 4 tablespoons melted butter
- ☐ 1 teaspoon vanilla

Directions:

1. Mix butter with cracker crumbs.
2. With your fingers, press down into the bottom of a 7-inch springform pan and halfway up the sides.
3. Mix yogurt, sugar, cream cheese, and vanilla.
4. Add eggs one at a time and mix until just combined.
5. Pour batter into the pan.
6. Pour 1 cup of water into your pressure cooker and insert a trivet.
7. Put the pan in the pressure cooker and seal the lid.
8. Hit "chicken/meat" and adjust time to 36 minutes.
9. When the timer beeps, hit "cancel" and wait for a natural pressure release.
10. Open the lid and remove the cake.
11. Blot any excess moisture off the top of the cheesecake.
12. Cool on a counter for 1-2 hours before chilling in the fridge for another 4 hours.

Nutritional Info (⅛ recipe per serving):
Total calories: 280
Protein: 6
Carbs: 26
Fat: 9
Fiber: 1

Oatmeal Chocolate Chip Cookies

Serves: 2
Time: 30 minutes (15 minutes prep time, 15 minutes cook time)

Sometimes you just need a quick dessert that can feed two people, and you don't want to take up an hour or more making a whole batch of cookies. These oatmeal chocolate chip cookies for two just takes 15 minutes in the pressure cooker, and don't use any eggs. If you like, you can add nuts, toffee chips, and so on to make the cookies your own. Don't leave out the oats, though, they help hold the dough together.

Ingredients:

- ¼ cup oats
- ¼ cup whole wheat flour
- 2-3 tablespoons chocolate chips
- 2 tablespoons sugar
- 2 tablespoons milk
- 1 tablespoon butter
- 1 tablespoon honey
- 2 teaspoons coconut oil
- ½ teaspoon vanilla extract
- 2 pinches of salt

Directions:

1. Mix flour, oatmeal, honey, sugar, vanilla, butter, one pinch of salt, milk, and chocolate chips together.
2. Add oil and knead.
3. You should get a cookie dough that's not sticky. If it is, add some more flour. If it's too hard to hold together, add more milk.
4. Take the gasket out of the lid; you won't be bringing the cooker to pressure yet.
5. Put the lid on the cooker and hit "chicken/meat" to heat up the cooker for 5 minutes.
6. Form cookies with your dough, about the size of a lemon, and flatten them slightly, just so they aren't perfect balls.
7. Grease a cake pan (or a big plate that fits in the pressure cooker) with some butter.
8. Put the cookies on the pan, about ¼-inches apart.
9. Put the pan in the cooker on a trivet, being careful not to touch the sides, so be sure to wear an oven mitt.

10. Put the lid back on the cooker (still without its gasket) and wait 15 minutes.
11. Cookies should be golden-brown and crispy. Move to a rack and cool.
12. Eat or store in a Tupperware for 4-5 days.

Nutritional Info (½ of recipe per serving):
Total calories: 412
Protein: 6
Carbs: 59
Fat: 20
Fiber: 1

Lemon Poppy Seed Cake

Serves: 8

Time: 44 minutes (10 minutes prep time, 24 minutes cook time, 10 minutes cool time)

Heavy cheesecakes and chocolate desserts are great, of course, but sometimes you want something a little lighter and fresher. Fragrant and tasting of spring, this lemon poppy seed cake only takes 44 minutes from start to finish, and satisfies any sweet tooth without making you feel too guilty. To cut the sugar content down, just leave off the glaze

Ingredients:

- ☐ 2 room temperature, separated eggs
- ☐ 1 stick butter
- ☐ 1 ¼ cups flour
- ☐ 1 cup sugar
- ☐ ⅔ cup milk
- ☐ ⅓ cup poppy seeds
- ☐ Juice and zest from one lemon
- ☐ 1 teaspoon baking powder
- ☐ 1 teaspoon baking soda
- ☐ ½ teaspoon salt

Glaze:
- ☐ ½ cup powdered sugar
- ☐ Juice and zest from one lemon

Directions:

1. Cream the sugar and butter together.
2. Beat in yolks and vanilla.
3. Add in lemon juice and zest.
4. Mix the dry ingredients together first, and then add ⅓ to wet ingredients, pour in some milk, then another ⅓ of the dry, and so on.
5. Fold in poppy seeds.
6. In another bowl, beat the egg whites until they form peaks.
7. Fold this into the batter until just incorporated.
8. Grease a 1-liter soufflé dish and sprinkle in a little flour.

9. Pour in cake batter.
10. Wrap foil around the dish.
11. Pour water into your pressure cooker and lower in trivet.
12. Put the dish in the cooker and seal the lid.
13. Hit "chicken/meat" and adjust cook time to 24 minutes.
14. When time is up, hit "cancel" and wait for a natural pressure release.
15. Remove the pan and cool before inverting on a serving plate.
16. To make the glaze, mix powdered sugar, lemon juice, and zest.
17. Serve cake with glaze on top.

Nutritional Info (⅛ of recipe per serving):
Total calories: 351
Protein: 6
Carbs: 50
Fat: 16
Fiber: 1

Tart Cherry Pie

Serves: 4-6

Time: 46 minutes (18 minutes prep time, 18 minutes cook time, 10 minutes natural pressure release)

When cherries are in season, it's time to make pies. Buy a double crust from the store, and make your own filling from pitted tart cherries, sugar, quick-cooking tapioca, butter, vanilla, and almond extract, which compliments the sour cherry flavor beautifully. The tapioca mimics gelatin without using any animal products, so vegans can make this, provided they also replace the butter with a vegan spread.

Ingredients:

- ☐ One 9-inch double crust pie crust
- ☐ 4 cups pitted tart cherries
- ☐ 2 cups water
- ☐ 1 cup sugar
- ☐ 4 tablespoons quick tapioca
- ☐ 1 ½ tablespoons butter
- ☐ ½ teaspoon vanilla extract
- ☐ ¼ teaspoon almond extract
- ☐ ⅛ teaspoon salt

Directions:

1. Pour water into your PPCXL and insert trivet.
2. Put one crust in a 7-inch springform pan; cover the other crust for now.
3. In a bowl, mix sugar, cherries, both extracts, salt, and tapioca.
4. Rest for 15 minutes.
5. Pour into the bottom crust and add cubes of butter on top.
6. Put the other crust on top.
7. Lower the springform pan into the cooker on the trivet.
8. Seal the lid.
9. Hit "chicken/meat" and adjust time to 18 minutes.
10. When time is up, hit "cancel" and wait 10 minutes before quick-releasing.
11. Cool before serving.

Nutritional Info (¼ of recipe per serving):
Total calories: 590
Protein: 3
Carbs: 106
Fat: 18
Fiber: 2.5

Cherry-Almond Pudding Cake

Serves: 6

Time: 1 hour, 27 minutes (10 minutes prep time, 42 minutes cook time, 30 minutes natural pressure release, 5 minutes cool time)

Full of fragrant, rich flavors like Amaretto, cherry jam, and brown sugar, this pudding cake is fantastic for the Christmas season. For even more almond flavor, you use finely-ground almonds that help with structure. The almonds also add fiber and protein to the dessert. For a cold contrast, serve warm with vanilla ice cream. Cherry Garcia ice cream would also be delicious.

Ingredients:

- ☐ 8 tablespoons butter
- ☐ 2 large room-temperature eggs
- ☐ ¾ cup finely-ground almonds
- ☐ ½ cup all-purpose flour
- ☐ ⅓ cup cherry jam
- ☐ ¼ cup packed dark brown sugar
- ☐ ¼ cup white sugar
- ☐ 3 tablespoons Amaretto (or almond-flavored syrup)
- ☐ 1 tablespoon pure vanilla extract
- ☐ ¼ teaspoon salt

Directions:

1. Grease a 2-quart baking dish with high sides with butter.
2. Spread the cherry jam on the bottom.
3. Pour 2 cups of water into your pressure cooker and add trivet.
4. Cream butter and both sugars in a heavy mixer for 5 minutes.
5. Add eggs one at a time and mix till smooth.
6. Add vanilla and Amaretto.
7. Add flour, almonds, and salt, and mix on low speed.
8. Pour batter into baking dish.
9. Brush butter on one side of a 12-inch piece of foil and put it butter-side down on the dish.
10. Put dish in the cooker and seal the lid.
11. Hit "chicken/meat" and adjust time to 42 minutes.

12. When time is up, hit "cancel" and let the pressure come down by itself.
13. Remove the dish and cool for 5 minutes.
14. Serve warm with a good vanilla ice cream.

Nutritional Info (⅙ of recipe per serving):
Total calories: 382
Protein: 5
Carbs: 39
Fat: 22
Fiber: 2

Applesauce with Ginger

Serves: 4
Time: 14 minutes (4 minutes cook time, 10 minutes natural pressure release)

Applesauce can take a long time. You usually have to simmer it over the stove for a few hours, at least, but in the pressure cooker, apples break down quickly. There are a lot of ways you can flavor applesauce, and crystallized ginger infuses a unique spicy-sweetness that gives the sauce a lot of depth. Depending on the kind of apples you use, you can make the sauce sweeter or tarter.

Ingredients:

- ☐ 4 pounds chopped apples
- ☐ ½ cup water
- ☐ 3-4 tablespoons crystallized ginger

Directions:

1. Pour water into your pressure cooker.
2. Add crystallized ginger and all the apples.
3. Hit "chicken/meat" and cook for 4 minutes.
4. When time is up, hit "cancel" and wait 10 minutes for a natural pressure release.
5. Mix the applesauce or puree, if you want it smooth.
6. Cool to room temperature before storing in glass jars or eating.
7. Store up to 10 days in the fridge.

Nutritional Info (1 cup per serving):
Total calories: 258
Protein: 5
Carbs: 66
Fat: 1
Fiber: 5.5

French Lemon Creme Pots

Serves: 6

Time: 1 hour, 37 minutes (40 minutes prep time, 12 minutes cook time, 45 minutes cool time)

Are you a fruit lover? This dessert was designed for you. The creme is made from cream, whole milk, sugar, egg, and lemon, so it's essentially a citrus mousse. It embodies freshness. For serving, we've used raspberries, but you can substitute any fruit you like, like blackberries, blueberries, or strawberries.

Ingredients:

- [ ] 6 egg yolks
- [ ] 1 cup whole milk
- [ ] 1 cup fresh cream
- [ ] ⅔ cup white sugar
- [ ] ½ cup fresh raspberries
- [ ] 1 lemon

Directions:

1. Peel the lemon skin into wide strips.
2. Add milk, cream, and zests in a saucepan.
3. Stir until it starts to bubble.
4. Remove from heat and cool for about a half hour.
5. Pour the minimum amount of water for the PPCXL into it.
6. In a bowl, whisk sugar with egg yolks so the sugar dissolves.
7. Pour the saucepan cream mixture slowly into the egg yolks.
8. Whisk, but don't whip, and pour through a strainer into a bowl.
9. Pour this bowl into your ramekins.
10. Wrap in foil and put in your steamer basket. If they don't all fit, you'll do a second batch.
11. Seal the lid.
12. Hit "chicken/meat" and adjust time to 12 minutes.
13. When time is up, hit "cancel" and wait for a natural pressure release.
14. Remove the ramekins and make sure the custard is almost solid and set.
15. Cool for 30-45 minutes before wrapping in plastic and storing in the fridge another 10 minutes or so to chill completely.

16. Serve with raspberries.

Nutritional Info (⅙ recipe per serving):
Total calories: 380
Protein: 8
Carbs: 46
Fat: 20
Fiber: 2

Sugar Pumpkin Pie

Serves: 8
Time: 14 minutes (4 minutes cook time, 10 minutes cool time)

Have you ever made pumpkin pie from scratch? Like with a real pumpkin? This recipe makes it easy, because the pressure cooker is able to soften up a sugar pumpkin in record time. Find a 2-3 pound sugar pumpkin, remove the seeds, chop it up, and cook for just 4 minutes! The seasoning part of the filling is made from real maple syrup and classic pumpkin-pie spices like cinnamon, cloves, and ginger. Once the filling is done, you're ready to make your pie.

Ingredients:

- [ ] 2-3 pound seeded and cut sugar pumpkin
- [ ] 2 eggs
- [ ] 1 cup water
- [ ] 1 cup whole milk
- [ ] ¾ cup maple syrup
- [ ] 1 tablespoon cornstarch
- [ ] 1 teaspoon cinnamon
- [ ] ½ teaspoon ginger
- [ ] ¼ teaspoon cloves
- [ ] 2 pinches salt

Directions:

1. Pour water into your PPCXL.
2. Put pumpkin in the steamer basket and lower into cooker.
3. Seal the lid.
4. Hit "chicken/meat" and adjust time to 4 minutes.
5. In the meantime, mix maple syrup and milk.
6. Add cinnamon, ginger, salt, cornstarch, and egg.
7. Mix until blended.
8. Hit "cancel" on your PPCXL and quick-release the pressure.
9. Strain pumpkin chunks and peel.
10. When 10 minutes has passed, and the pumpkin is cooler, push down on them to remove as much liquid as you can.
11. Put chunks into a 2-cup measuring container, pressing down, and mixing with the egg mixture.

12. The filling is ready to go!

Nutritional Info (⅛ pie-filling recipe):
Total calories: 143.9
Protein: 3.3
Carbs: 29.1
Fat: 2.3
Fiber: 2.1

Two-Ingredient Chocolate Fondue

Serves: 2-4
Time: 2 minutes

Chocolate fondue is a really easy, delicious dessert that you can easily customize. Unless you have a fondue fountain, you would have to melt chocolate over the stove or in the microwave, and that's a bit of a pain. In this recipe, you just pour cream over chocolate, and stick in the pressure cooker for 2 minutes. When it comes out, stir quickly, and the chocolate becomes smooth, sweet liquid gold.

Note: If you want to make your fondue unique, add 1 teaspoon of Amaretto liquor before closing up the pressure. Other flavor options include chili powder, peppermint extract, orange extract, or Bailey's.

Ingredients:

☐   2 cups water
☐   3.5-ounces of cream
☐   3.5-ounces of dark chocolate (minimum 70% cocoa)

Directions:

1.   Pour water into the pressure cooker and add trivet.
2.   Put the chocolate chunks into a heatproof, ceramic bowl and pour in cream.
3.   Put bowl into the cooker and seal the lid.
4.   Hit "chicken/meat" and adjust cook time to 2 minutes.
5.   When the timer beeps, hit "cancel" and quick-release.
6.   Take out the container and whisk until smooth.
7.   Serve with fruits, cookies, and so on!

Nutritional Info (¼ recipe):
Total calories: 216
Protein: 1.8
Carbs: 11.7
Fiber: 2.6
Fat: 20.3

Chocolate Custard

Serves: 6-8

Time: 56 minutes (10 minutes prep time, 36 minutes cook time, 10 minutes natural pressure release)

This chocolate custard is basically chocolate pudding for grown-ups. You begin by simmering the base (milk, cream, vanilla, sugar) in a saucepan to dissolve the sugar, and then add dark chocolate. When that's mixed, add in 6 egg yolks and pour into your baking dish. After 36 minutes in the pressure cooker, wait 10 minutes before quick-releasing. If you like your pudding warm, eat it right away, though it's also delicious when it's been chilled.

Ingredients:

- ☐ 13-ounces chopped dark chocolate
- ☐ 4 cups water
- ☐ Just over 1 cup cream (1.2 cups)
- ☐ 1 cup whole milk
- ☐ 6 whisked egg yolks
- ☐ ½ cup sugar
- ☐ 1 teaspoon vanilla extract

Directions:

1. Mix milk, vanilla, cream, and sugar in a saucepan and simmer until the sugar dissolves.
2. Remove saucepan from heat and add chocolate.
3. Once the chocolate has melted, add the egg yolks in carefully, so they don't cook.
4. Pour into a baking dish that fits in the pressure cooker.
5. Add water into your pressure cooker and lower in trivet.
6. Put baking dish on the trivet and seal the lid.
7. Hit "chicken/meat" and adjust time to 36 minutes.
8. When the timer beeps, hit "cancel" and wait 10 minutes before quick-releasing the pressure.
9. You know the custard is done when it's set, but jiggly like jello.
10. Serve hot or cold.

Nutritional Info (⅙ recipe per serving):
Total calories: 549
Protein: 9
Carbs: 55
Fat: 38
Fiber: 0

Raspberry Pudding Cake

Serves: 4

Time: 1 hour, 7 minutes (5 minutes prep time, 15 minutes steam time, 42 minutes cook time, 5 minutes cool time)

Packed with fresh raspberries, you'll want to eat this cake for breakfast. You'll notice the preparation is a little unique - you're actually steaming the cake first for 15 minutes, which means you pour hot water in the cooker and close the lid, but you aren't actually bringing it to pressure. That helps get a really moist, pudding-like texture. When that's done, you're bringing the cooker to pressure for 42 minutes to finish it off.

Ingredients:

- ☐ ½ pound raspberries
- ☐ 5-ounces whole milk
- ☐ 1 cup flour
- ☐ ½ cup cubed butter
- ☐ 1 beaten egg
- ☐ ½ cup white sugar
- ☐ 2 ½ tablespoons breadcrumbs
- ☐ 1 ½ teaspoons baking powder
- ☐ ½ teaspoon salt

Directions:

1. Grease a baking dish that will fit 4-6 cups of batter.
2. In a bowl, sift in flour, salt, and baking powder.
3. Cut the butter into the dry ingredients, so you get a crumbly texture.
4. Mix in sugar and breadcrumbs.
5. Blend the milk and egg into the dry, and fold in the blueberries.
6. Fill the baking dish ¾ of the way full with batter.
7. Butter a piece of parchment paper, and lay on top of the dish. Tie it down with a piece of kitchen string, but leave a little space over the dish so the pudding can rise.
8. Pour 2-inches of hot water into the cooker and insert the trivet.
9. Put the dish inside and close, but do not seal the lid or select a pressure setting.
10. Let the cake just sit in the cooker and steam for 15 minutes.
11. When time is up, seal the lid.
12. Hit "chicken/meat" and adjust cook time to 42 minutes.

13. When the timer beeps, turn off the cooker and quick-release the pressure.
14. Remove the baking dish and let the pudding cool for 5 minutes or so before turning the dish over on a serving plate.

Nutritional Info (¼ recipe per serving):
Total calories: 493
Protein: 8
Carbs: 60
Fat: 2
Fiber: 3.7

Brown-Butter Banana Nut Bread with Chocolate Chips

Serves: 8

Time: Overnight + 1 hour, 26 minutes (1o minutes prep time, 66 minutes cook time, 10 minutes natural pressure release)

There are a lot of memorable flavors in this recipe - the sweet bananas, earthy walnuts, chocolate, and of course, the brown butter. I recommend making the brown butter the night before, so it gets time to really set. When everything is mixed and ready to bake, it takes about 66 minutes in the pressure cooker, followed by a 10-minute natural pressure release and then quick-release.

Ingredients:

- ☐ 3 very ripe mashed bananas
- ☐ 2 cups flour
- ☐ 1 cup white sugar
- ☐ 1 cup walnuts
- ☐ ½ cup room temperature butter
- ☐ 2 room temperature eggs
- ☐ 4-ounces chocolate chips
- ☐ 1 ½ teaspoons baking soda
- ☐ ½ teaspoon sea salt

Directions:

1. Get the butter ready the night before you plan on making the bread.
2. Brown the butter by melting it in a saucepan, and letting it cook until it becomes a deep golden.
3. Pour into a bowl to cool.
4. When the butter is room-temperature, store in the fridge.
5. The next day, begin the bread by mixing eggs and sugar.
6. Add butter and mix.
7. Stir in mashed bananas.
8. Add all the dry ingredients until just mixed.
9. Fold in chocolate chips and nuts.
10. Cut out a round piece of parchment butter.

11. Grease a 6-cup bundt pan and put the paper round on the bottom.
12. Pour batter into your bundt pan.
13. Pour 1 ½ cups of water into the PPCXL.
14. Before putting the pan in the cooker, put on a paper towel, and then a piece of foil, but don't seal it on the edges, just let it sit there.
15. When the pan is in the cooker, seal the lid.
16. Hit "manual" and adjust cook time to 66 minutes.
17. When the timer beeps, hit "cancel" and wait 10 minutes before quick-releasing.
18. Cool for a few minutes and then turn over on a serving plate.

Nutritional Info (⅛ recipe per serving):
Total calories: 500
Protein: 7
Carbs: 64
Fat: 25
Fiber: 1

Conclusion

There are a lot of cookbooks out there, so I thank you for choosing my humble offering. Pressure cooking has made a huge difference in my life, and I want to share it with anyone who has felt like they are a bad chef, or just run down by how much time and effort it takes to cook healthy meals. With the Power Pressure Cooker XL, you don't have to know a bunch of fancy techniques, and you don't have to buy the most expensive ingredients at the store. With just a little knowledge that this book contains, like what pressure cooking is and how to operate an electric cooker, and easy-to-follow instructions, you can make food so good you'll wonder why it took so long to take the plunge.

There are enough recipes in this book to keep you busy for a long time, so take your time exploring. Whether you're focusing on making healthier breakfasts and are interested in all the varieties of hot cereals, or you want to start cooking impressive holiday meals without sacrificing time with your family, they were in this book. I've done my best to choose ingredients you can find just about anywhere, and included substitutions where they make sense.

Good food means a good life, and I hope pressure cooking can open new doors for you on your life's journey.

RECIPE INDEX

BEEF + LAMB

Book 1

Book 2

CHICKEN

Book 1

POULTRY

Book 2

PALEO

PORK

SEAFOOD

Book 1

Book 2

SOUPS + STEWS

Book 1

Book 2

RICE AND PASTA

Book 1

Book 2

VEGAN

Book 1

Book 2

SIDES + SNACKS

Book 1

Book 2

DESSERTS

Book 1

Book 2

I would love to give you a gift. Please visit happyhealthycookingonline.com to get these 4 amazing eBooks for free!